The New CEO Corporate Leadership Manual

The New CEO Corporate Leadership Manual

Strategic and Analytical Tools for Growth

STEVEN M. BRAGG

WILEY

John Wiley & Sons, Inc.

For general information on our other products and services or for technical support, please contact our Customer Care Department within the United States at (800) 762-2974, outside the United States at (317) 572-3993 or fax (317) 572-4002.

Wiley also publishes its books in a variety of electronic formats. Some content that appears in print may not be available in electronic books. For more information about Wiley products, visit our web site at www.wiley.com.

Library of Congress Cataloging-in-Publication Data:
Bragg, Steven M.
 The new CEO corporate leadership manual: strategic and analytical tools for growth/
Steven M. Bragg.
    p. cm.
 Includes index.
  ISBN 978-0-470-91287-4(book); ISBN 978-1-118-09306-1 (ebk); ISBN 978-1-118-09307-8 (ebk); ISBN 978-1-118-09309-2 (ebk)
 1. Leadership. 2. Chief executive officers. 3. Management. 4. Success in business. I. Title.
 HD57.7.B73 2011
 658.4'092–dc22

                                                                                      2011007208

Printed in the United States of America

10 9 8 7 6 5 4 3 2 1

Contents

Preface

The New CEO Corporate Leadership Manual is designed to give the chief executive officer (CEO) a thorough understanding of his or her primary responsibilities and what path to take to succeed as a CEO.

The first part of this book addresses the activities of the new CEO and answers such questions as:

- What should I do during my first days on the job?
- How do I measure the business?
- What is the process for developing a corporate strategy?

A major part of the CEO's job is to develop a corporate strategy. Chapters 2 through 6 are concerned with the development of high-level strategy as well as more specific considerations in such areas as finance, taxation, information technology, and outsourcing. These chapters provide answers to such questions as:

- How do I evaluate the competitive environment?
- What are the three major types of corporate strategy?
- How do I test a strategy to see if it will work?
- What should my strategy be for handling debt and equity?
- How do I develop an information technology strategy?
- When should I use outsourcing?

The corporate strategy is much more likely to be implemented if it is fully integrated into the annual budget. Accordingly, Chapters 7 and 8 provide a detailed view of how the system of budgets is constructed and the criteria for accepting a capital budget proposal. These chapters yield answers to the following questions and more:

- How does the system of budgets work?
- How can a flexible budget enhance the comparability of a budget to actual results?
- How can a budget be used as a control mechanism?
- How can I integrate throughput analysis into capital budgeting?
- How do discounted cash flows improve capital budgeting analysis?

The CEO needs to be concerned about the potential impact of a variety of risks on the company and so should be aware of them and should develop a risk mitigation plan to deal with them. Chapters 9 and 10 discuss risk management concepts and, more specifically, the risk caused by foreign exchange transactions. Examples of the questions answered by these chapters are:

- What risk management policies and procedures should I have?
- How do I develop a risk matrix?
- What types of business insurance are available?
- What types of foreign exchange hedging strategies are available?

There are three types of financial analysis that a CEO should be engaged in or at least aware of: performance metrics for the company, various types of cost reduction analysis, and the evaluation of potential acquirees. These topics are covered in Chapters 11 through 13, and answer such questions as:

- What asset utilization measurements should I track?
- Which operating performance metrics are the most useful?
- Which cash flow measurements should I monitor?
- Which reports should I use for cost reduction analysis?
- What is involved in a spend analysis system?
- What issues should I consider for a workforce reduction?
- How do I evaluate acquisition targets?
- How do I arrive at a price for an acquisition target?

The goal of many larger companies is to go public, which gives their shareholders a convenient way to sell their ownership interests and which also gives a company a potential source of new capital. The CEO should know the mechanics of conducting an initial public offering as well as how to interact with the investment community and, if the burdens of being publicly held are too great, of how to take the company private again. These topics are covered in Chapters 14 through 17, which answer these questions and more:

- What steps do I follow to complete an initial public offering?
- What are the requirements for trading on a stock exchange?
- How do I deal with analysts, brokers, investment bankers, institutional investors, and private investors?
- What is my role in an investor conference call?
- How do I take a company private?

The book concludes with an appendix that contains a handy checklist of the most important short-term steps that you should address as a new CEO.

In total, this book is a comprehensive guidebook for the CEO who needs to know about strategies, budgets, risk management, financial analysis tools, and tips on how to run a publicly held company. It should assist you in focusing on the most critical aspects of running a business and hopefully will result in a more profitable company that is better positioned to succeed in the future.

Steven M. Bragg
Centennial, Colorado
June 2011

CHAPTER 1

New CEO Activities

You have just been hired or promoted into the chief executive officer (CEO) position. How do you succeed in this role? You are in charge, so you can set any priorities you want. What activities should you pursue first, not only to succeed but also to avoid any risks to which the company is subject? This chapter addresses your immediate priorities, measurement systems, strategy and budget formulation, and other activities that you should address during your first few months on the job. If you follow these steps, you will have a good knowledge of the company's strengths and weaknesses and of the proper strategic path to follow to improve your chances of success over the long term.

Immediate Priorities

What should you do during your first few days as CEO? You are likely to be overwhelmed by a variety of immediate crises that threaten to consume all of your time. Nonetheless, you need to make room for the investigation of several key items, to see if the company is in any financial or legal difficulty. If it is, these issues override any others confronting you, since they potentially can put the company out of business in the near future.

Without question, your first step is to go over the company's cash position and short-term cash forecast with the chief financial officer (CFO). During the review, look for the next items.

- *Customers.* Unusually large overdue payments from customers, which may indicate a variety of customer selection, customer service, or product-related problems.
- *Suppliers.* Unusually rapid payments to suppliers, which may indicate cash-on-delivery payment terms, or short-payment situations caused by a history of slow payments in the past that suppliers no longer tolerate.
- *Payroll.* Large bonuses and commissions that indicate unusually high compensation plans.
- *Capital expenditures.* Imminent planned payments for expensive fixed assets, which may indicate that existing assets are worn out and need replacement.

- *Debt.* Large impending debt payments indicate the need to refinance as soon as possible.
- *Cash balance.* The most obvious item! Is the cash balance very low in relation to the size of operations? Is the company continually relying on a line of credit to meet its cash requirements?

If there appears to be a problem, either set up a periodic meeting to continually review cash or ask to be notified when the cash position reaches a certain trigger point. You do not want to have your time consumed by a series of status meetings, so the latter option is usually the better one. If cash appears to be a problem, it becomes the focus of your activities until the problem is resolved.

Another concern is any existing tax liabilities. If a company has been in financial straits, it is possible that the previous CEO authorized a delay in income tax or payroll tax payments to the government. If so, the government will impose large fines and penalties; a few states even make the CEO personally liable for unpaid payroll taxes. Given the downside consequences, it is worth your time to investigate whether these payments have been made.

The situation will be easier for you if the company already uses a third party to process payroll, since the third party will ensure that payroll taxes have been paid. To verify that income taxes have been paid, you may want to bring in auditors to review the company's books.

A company of any size is likely to be subject to the threat of lawsuits at any time, many of which have no great probability of every reaching an unfavorable settlement. Rather than wading through the details of all possible or actual lawsuits, have corporate counsel summarize just those having both a reasonable probability of success against the company and a large settlement amount. Your main concern is that a lawsuit may exist whose settlement will seriously affect the finances of the company.

In addition, look for any legal situations in which the company could potentially lose its rights to major competitive advantages, such as patents. Further, investigate whether there are any scenarios under which company officers could be charged with crimes for the company's prior actions.

If the company has a history of violating government regulations, it is possible that it may be subject to impending fines of considerable size. Further, if it has violated environmental laws, the government may be authorized to shut it down entirely or to bring such crushing fines to bear that it will have to be liquidated. The company's legal counsel should be able to inform you about the status of these matters. You may need to delve into the specific notices received to satisfy yourself regarding the severity of any violations.

If there is a large amount of outstanding debt, meet with the CFO and discuss when the principal amount of the debt is due for repayment. The CFO should have a plan for how to refinance the debt, either with replacement debt or the sale of stock. Further, discuss whether the company is exceeding any covenants imposed under the debt agreement or whether there is a reasonable chance that it will do so in the near future. Lenders often are willing to negotiate around covenant violations, but an impending debt repayment that the lender is not willing to renew is a much more serious matter.

A final issue is to meet with the audit partner and see if the company's audit firm believes that it may issue a "going concern" opinion as part of its audit of the company's financial statements. This opinion means that the auditors do not believe the company has the financial results or resources to stay in business. Lenders do not like to see a going concern opinion and may not renew outstanding debt if the company receives such an opinion. It is possible to avoid a going concern opinion by obtaining additional financial resources, so this is not necessarily a death knell for a company.

Once you have reviewed all of the immediate priorities, set aside some time to think about the company's position: Were you brought in to supervise a sinking ship? Can it be rescued? Is the job so impossible that it would be better to leave now? These are uncomfortable questions, since any new CEO wants to be successful in his or her first job. However, if the task is simply impossible, it may be better to discuss the issue immediately with the board of directors and focus on either selling or dismantling the company.

If, however, the review of immediate priorities reveals no glaring problems, you can proceed to the next task, which is measuring the basic operations of the business.

Measure the Business

The next step is to gain an overview of the company's financial results. You should schedule time with the CFO to go over the company's financial statements for the past year and the current year to date. If possible, have the CFO provide the current-year information as a trend line by month, so that you can see any changes in results. For example, if ten months have been completed in the current year, the financial report should contain ten columns of results, one for each month. When reviewing this information, you should look for these items:

- *Compare cash to profits.* If the company is reporting profits, is it also reporting a similar amount of increases in cash? There are many reasons why this may not be the case, such as capital expenditures and working capital needs. Be sure that you understand the differences between these two numbers. If you do not, there is a chance that financial shenanigans are creating profits that are not translating into real cash flow.
- *Review the revenue trend by component.* Usually multiple products and services comprise revenue. Are certain components of revenue changing dramatically? How much of it is caused by seasonality and how much by new product introductions or changes in demand?
- *Review the cost of goods sold trend.* Separate the cost of goods sold into its fixed and variable components. Review the trend of the fixed costs; they should stay relatively flat, unless the company has changed its operations recently. Also review the trend of variable costs as a percentage of sales. If this percentage is increasing, you may have a problem with increasing component costs that are not reflected in increased product prices.

- *Review the selling, general, and administrative trend lines.* These costs are mostly fixed, and so they should not change much over the short term. If there are significant trend changes, delve into the details of the specific expenses causing the issues.
- *Review the debt trend line.* An ongoing and unremitting increase in debt over time is a cause for great concern. If this is the case, and irrespective of what the stated profitability may be, the company is bleeding cash. Conversely, if the debt level is seasonal, the increase in debt is a standard outcome of the business and is not an issue.

In addition to this trend line review, have the CFO create a basic set of performance metrics and present them to you on the same trend line. Some of the key metrics to review presented next.

- *Accounts receivable turnover.* This is the net annual credit sales divided by average receivables. If the rate of receivables turnover is slowing, you have a collection problem that is impacting your cash balance. The problem may not be inadequate collections activity; it is entirely possible that the company has a variety of product or service issues that customers are unhappy with and for which they are not paying. You may need to find out exactly which customers are not paying and why, which may require further action.
- *Inventory turnover.* This is the cost of goods sold divided by inventory. Inventory turnover can be a serious problem, especially if a company does not have strong inventory controls, obsolescence reviews, and inventory disposition processes. A low inventory turnover number likely represents a quagmire of problems that may take a long time to repair and are consuming an inordinate amount of cash.
- *Accounts payable turnover.* This is total supplier purchases divided by average accounts payable outstanding. If turnover is clearly lower than supplier payment terms would normally indicate, it is likely that the CFO is prolonging payment intervals in order to avoid additional debt. This is not a good idea over the long term, since abused suppliers can drop the company or insist on very restrictive payment terms.
- *Gross margin ratio.* This is the gross margin divided by revenues, and is best viewed on a trend line. Any decline in this ratio is cause for serious concern, since it means the company is unable to pass changes in its production and purchasing costs through to its customers via price increases.
- *Debt service coverage ratio.* This is net annual operating income divided by total debt service payments. It measures the ability of a company to meet its debt obligations. If the ratio is anywhere near 1:1, even a slight decline in profits could lead to a loan default.
- *Quick ratio.* This is current assets (less inventory) divided by current liabilities. The ratio should be above 1:1, and gives an indication of a company's ability to meet its immediate accounts payable obligations. It is not a perfect indicator of liquidity, since the remaining balance on a company's line of credit can also be used to pay accounts payable, but it does give a general indication of liquidity.

Note that the ratios listed here are few in number and oriented toward short-term results. The intent of reviewing them is not to delve into the efficiency and effectiveness of specific aspects of the business but rather to determine at a gross level whether the company can generate a profit, whether it can pay its bills, and whether it has enough cash to maintain its operations. If you want to add other measurements that give an expanded view of a company's operations, refer to the more extensive set of measurements in Chapter 11, Performance Measurements.

You now have a rough idea of the company's general performance in the recent past. The next step is to predict how it will perform in the near future. There are three key parts of this prediction:

1. *Sales forecast.* This should be a weekly update from the sales manager, at whatever level of detail you want. It is best to not settle for a simple grand total, since you gain no visibility into where the sales are coming from. A better alternative is to obtain sales by product line, region, distribution channel, or store—whatever makes the most sense given the structure of the company and how it sells products or services.
2. *Backlog report.* You want to know if there are any significant changes (especially downward) in the sales backlog. You may be comfortable with a monthly update to the backlog, but consider starting with a weekly update, just to see how much the numbers vary in the short term. If a few customer orders comprise a large part of the backlog, you should know when these orders ship as well as what the backlog numbers look like without these orders included.
3. *Flash report.* The flash report is a weekly update of what the income statement will look like at the end of the month. This report contains the revenue information from the sales forecast and the accounting staff's best estimates of expenses.

It should not take long to at least initiate the steps noted here to measure the business—you can delegate all of the required tasks in a day, and have the results back a few days later. You may want to dig into certain details of the business, so multiple iterations are perfectly acceptable, as you learn more from the measurements about the operating characteristics of the company. The result will likely be a somewhat modified set of reports, with varying delivery intervals.

Now that you have a rough feel for the company's financial numbers, let us spend some time with an even more critical item: people.

Get to Know the Company

There are a number of groups of people with whom you should build relations, some more than others. The unique characteristics of each company will dictate which group is most important. For example, the CEO of an airline should spend considerable time with the pilots; the CEO of a technology company wants to have regular discussions with the engineering staff. Also, the form of interaction depends on your comfort level; some like one-on-one interaction, others prefer formal group visits, and a few even work alongside their employees. How you choose to interact is up to you. What we present here are the specific groups of people to meet; you choose the method.

- *Administrative assistant.* A good administrative assistant is incredibly valuable for delegating a broad array of tasks as well as a gatekeeper who keeps lesser issues from ever coming to your attention. You should block out a large amount of time during your first few days to sit with your administrative assistant and discuss exactly which issues can be delegated and how they should be settled. This can include going through every event in your day (and every e-mail) to determine whether your assistant could have handled it for you. It may take time to become comfortable with such a high degree of delegation, but it is very worthwhile and will save you an immense amount of time.
- *Senior managers.* As the CEO, your effectiveness ultimately is determined by the effectiveness of your management staff, so you should build close relations with all of your direct reports. There may not be a need for a formal managers' meeting as long as you can replace it with continual informal ones that keep you apprised of all key activities. Part of your initial goal in meeting with these managers is to build trust: You can rely on them to get the job done, and they can rely on you for support and the resources they need.
- *Staff.* In a larger company, you have no hope of meeting everyone, but you should block out time to at least gradually cycle through the company, meeting with selected groups of employees. This is partly so that they have an opportunity to meet with you and partly so that you can convey whatever message you may have at a level that is more personal than an e-mail or corporate memo. Meeting with the staff is more important for knowledge services companies, such as consulting, where nearly every employee is highly trained and is closely involved with customers—these people are essentially subject matter experts, who are described in the next point.
- *Subject matter experts.* Every company has a core group that is responsible for its key profit-making activity. Examples of these people are the sales staff, engineers, and consulting staff. You should make a special effort to build relations with this group, for they likely know more about the company's detailed operations and prospects than you and so can provide both good advice and warnings of impending problems.
- *Customers.* Customers are the first to know if the company is having product or service issues and can also provide valuable counsel regarding possible new products or services. In companies that have only a few large customers, CEOs may feel that this is the most important group to deal with, and so they are continually on the road, meeting with key customers.
- *Suppliers.* If the company is dependent on a few suppliers for a few key supplies that are difficult to obtain, or if some suppliers build large product components for the company, you need to build relations with them. There may not be very many suppliers who fall into this category, but if you have any, you should accord them the same level of attention that you would to a key customer.

Of the people noted here, the only one who exists specifically to improve your job performance is the administrative assistant, so block out a considerable amount of your initial time to develop a strong working relationship with this person. Of the remaining categories of people, you should not meet with them once and assume that you are through for the foreseeable future. The CEO position can be considered a gregarious one, so you need to see people and be seen by them. Work out the best method for meetings—the concept of management by wandering around works for many CEOs, or perhaps you are more comfortable with ongoing status meetings. You will likely fall into a routine fairly soon. However, do not forget that customers and suppliers are just as important as employees, so include them in your discussions.

Develop a Strategy

The development of a strategy that has a chance of working is a lengthy process, since a number of issues must be factored into it. The details of strategy development are addressed in Chapter 2, General Corporate Strategy. In this section, we cover the primary activities that you should check off while creating an initial strategy for the company.

The CEO has a central role in strategy development, but you cannot participate effectively in the process until you know what the company does—not just an overview of its activities but rather a nuts-and-bolts level of familiarity. If you were promoted to CEO from within the company, you may already have this knowledge. However, if you were hired from outside the industry, you face a steep learning curve. The only way to gain this level of understanding is total immersion in every aspect of the business. The best approach is to meet individually with those people who have been with the company a long time and who have expert-level knowledge of their subject areas. Ask every question you can think of, and expect to come back with more questions as you learn more about the company. It is extremely helpful to not just sit in an office and ask questions but to see processes in action. Expect this learning task to take up a large part of your time during your first few months as CEO.

Strategy development is not something that the CEO should engage in alone. The management team as a group has a much better understanding of the company's abilities and the industry in which it operates than any one person. Consequently, you should schedule a series of group planning sessions. During these sessions, the group needs to summarize the key competitive aspects of the industry, and the company's place within that industry. Arising out of these discussions will be a determination of what general type of strategy the company should follow: low cost, product differentiation, or niche (see Chapter 2, General Corporate Strategy, for details).

The management team's first pass at a corporate strategy will require considerable tweaking, for the team must begin a multi-iteration process of reviewing how well the company is capable of following it and adjusting the strategy (or the company) to meet the realities of how the company operates.

Example

The strategy of ABC Company calls for a much higher level of focus on customers, but the company has only the most minimal customer service function. To make the strategy work, ABC can either back away from the strategy or provide staffing and more funds to the customer service function. If it chooses the latter path, it must block out enough time to upgrade the department properly before it can implement the strategy.

Another key issue in strategy development, and one that many companies completely ignore, is how company bottlenecks impact a strategy. Bottlenecks can take many forms and be located anywhere in a company. Examples of bottlenecks are restricted supplies, expensive machinery that limits production, and sales personnel who are not able to sell more product. The management team needs to know where the company's bottlenecks are located, how to work around them to achieve greater output, and how bottleneck management impacts the strategy.

Another concern is the amount of available resources. The management team needs to evaluate the capabilities of the employees to meet the strategy as well as any growth entailed by it. Resources also may be required for facilities and equipment. If new resources are needed, there may be an ordering, delivery, and installation interval that must be factored into the timing of when the strategy is to be implemented.

Example

ABC International's management team develops a strategy to reorient the company's direction and focus solely on customers in the Iowa and Nebraska areas, where the market for its custom-designed farm implement products appear to be the highest.

However, ABC needs to establish 11 distributorships in the two states in order to have proper coverage of the customer base, and it estimates that a full year will be required before the distributorships have been assigned and all necessary training has been conducted. Accordingly, the management team adjusts its strategy to use an on-site sales force, to be supplemented by a group of distributorships.

Another concern with strategy development is accounting for any risks that have arisen or threatened the company in the past as well as any possible new risks that may arise from changes in the strategy. If a proposed change introduces a major new risk, the management team needs to consciously accept the risk, alter the strategy to avoid the risk, or build acceptable risk mitigations into the strategy.

Example

Hubie Construction is considering entering the market for constructing build-ings for local and state governments, which varies from its traditional strategy of building homes on speculation for homeowners. An examination of the pro-spective market reveals that Hubie must post a performance bond with any gov-ernment accepting its construction bids. Hubie finds that it does not have the financial resources to post a performance bond and would be at risk of bank-ruptcy if even a single government triggered such a bond.

Hubie now faces the strategic choice of avoiding the government construc-tion market or of accepting equity contributions from new shareholders in order to have the resources to post performance bonds.

There are many factors involved in strategy development, and these are enumer-ated in greater detail in the next chapter. The key point for the CEO is that a well-developed strategy cannot be created in a one-day off-site planning session. The general strategy concept may appear during such a session, but it requires a great deal more thought to arrive at a strategy that will stand up to the realities of the mar-ket and a company's specific circumstances.

Create a Budget and Related Systems

Once a strategy is in place, the management team needs to incorporate it into a workable budget, so that the company has a clear direction that enables it to ad-here to the strategy. The CEO is not responsible for the day-to-day formulation of and follow-through on the budget—that task falls on the CFO or controller. How-ever, as the CEO, you should examine the budgeting instructions being sent out to the company managers, to ensure that the instructions align with the strategy. You also should monitor the various iterations of the budget to see if they sup-port the strategy. It is very likely that you will give feedback to the CFO regarding changes to the budget in areas where the managers submitting their budgets need further instruction.

A part of the budget that you *should* become involved with is the capital budget, primarily because it may involve a large amount of the company's financial re-sources. If a company is in a capital-intensive industry, it may place large bets on new factories or large equipment installations that soak up most of the company's available cash reserves or debt, so these investment decisions call for a great deal of analysis. In particular, you should know if a particular investment increases the ca-pacity of a bottleneck operation or whether the bottleneck still exists elsewhere in the company; if the latter is the case, the investment may not improve the company's situation, so the investment should not take place.

In a great many organizations, the budgeting process takes up several weeks near the end of each fiscal year, after which the completed budget is placed in a drawer and ignored until it is time to create a new budget in the next year. You can avoid this by making adherence to the budget a primary responsibility of the CFO.

The CFO is responsible for ensuring that the company adheres to the budget, and there are a variety of controls for enforcing that this happens. For example, the accounting staff can establish responsibility for every revenue and expense line item and issue a budget versus actual report to the responsible parties at the end of each reporting period. Another control is to match compensation plans to the budget. As the CEO, you should talk to the CFO to ensure that these controls are in place and that they are operating effectively. If the controls were used in the past year and the company still ignored the budget, either the controls are not sufficient or they are not being enforced.

Once there is a budget that both you and the management team believe is workable and which dovetails with the strategy, the CFO should create a complete package of a summary-level strategy, detailed budget, compensation plans, and controls. The management team then presents it to their staffs. In a larger company, there are simply too many people for you to be deeply involved in these presentations. However, you can be involved in a supporting role. Your more important role is after the initial presentation of the package, when you need to continually reinforce the strategic message everywhere within the company, so that employees know that the CEO is backing up what their managers are telling them. It would not be too far-fetched to keep a copy of the plan and budget on your desk throughout the year, as a reminder that you must incorporate it into everything that you do.

Chapters 7 and 8, Budgeting Process and Capital Budgeting, respectively, show how the budget is formulated and how to evaluate a capital budgeting proposal.

Review the Management Team

You must work through the management team, so your success is tied directly to their competence. If the team is incompetent, the areas for which it is responsible will not meet expectations, and you therefore will be held accountable by the board of directors for that failure too. Thus, you need a method for judging the management team.

An excellent tool for evaluating managers is the strategic plan and associated budget. It presents hard, factual targets that managers are expected to achieve, so it makes sense to wait until these items are in place before actively pursuing a management review process. Now that they are in place, consider the next steps to evaluate managers.

Step 1. *Create a review system.* The human resources manager is responsible for creating a system upon which you can evaluate the management team. This should be a detailed system that lays out specific expectations for each manager and for which the managers have complete ownership (i.e., they cannot blame other factors for not meeting their assigned goals). You should have a great deal of input into the review system, especially in regard to the weighting given to each review factor.

Step 2. *Review managers.* Reviews of managers should not be an annual event, with no review activity during the intervening 364 days. You should issue feedback much more frequently, so that managers have an opportunity to improve their performance all year long. These meetings will be largely informal, involving a specific opportunity for improvement that you have noticed, with recommended actions to pursue. These frequent review intervals call for a large time commitment by you.

Step 3. *Identify prospective managers.* As a company expands and evolves, it always needs more managers. An excellent source of new managers is the existing staff, since they already have a considerable familiarity with company operations and have built their own networks within the company. Have the human resources manager develop a system to identify and groom these prospective managers; in addition, you should spend time with the human resources manager, reviewing the current circumstances of each candidate, and developing an action plan for each one. Only a large time investment in this area will yield a high-quality pool of managers in the future.

Step 4. *Replace managers.* Some managers will not work out, and you must replace them. The human resources manager should have a network of recruiters and other recruiting tools in place for identifying both internal and external candidates. You should know how this system operates and recommend adjustments to ensure that the company has the best possible pool of candidates from which to make selections.

Simply judging managers based on their ability to meet or exceed their budgeted goals is not sufficient, since it ignores a number of other measures of manager performance, such as training their employees, employee retention, and idea generation. For example, a manager who meets his expense budget by grinding down his staff about expenditure and who is the core reason for high employee turnover is hardly one you want to keep for the long term. Consequently, you should use the budget as only one of several evaluation tools. The human resources manager can assist with the development of a more comprehensive evaluation system.

Strategy development, execution on that strategy, and manager development are likely to be the three areas for which a CEO is primarily responsible. Accordingly, you should block out a large part of your time to see to it that you have the right managers in place and that you fully support them in their jobs. Only by doing so can you succeed, since they are implementing your strategy-related directives.

Review Risks

Many CEOs are held to account when a risk becomes a reality and their companies are not prepared to handle the problem. In a larger company, there may be a risk manager who considers these general types of risk as part of his job. In a smaller company, there is no such person, so either the CEO or a consultant must engage in risk review.

A good starting point for risk analysis is reviewing the industry news to see what sorts of risks have impacted other companies within the industry. Some of these issues may never have impacted the company, so you can profit from the misfortune of others by examining what happened to them and judging the probability that it also may happen to your company. In some cases, a new risk will appear that will be the harbinger of a new set of problems for the entire industry; in other cases, the problem really may impact only one competitor for a very specific reason and so is not a concern to anyone else in the industry.

Example

A competitor of ABC International builds a facility directly over a fault line and later sees the entire structure destroyed when an earthquake splits apart its foundations. This is not a risk concern that ABC's CEO needs to concern himself with, unless any ABC facilities also sit on earthquake fault lines.

Another competitor is subject to an audit by the Environmental Protection Agency (EPA) and eventually is fined a substantial amount for a variety of infractions. This is a greater concern for ABC's CEO, since the EPA may be targeting the entire industry.

You also can internalize this analysis by examining the company's own history with various risks. This analysis should go back a number of years, since the more serious risks may arise only occasionally. This analysis should include a review of the cost to the company as well as how the company dealt with them in the past in terms of a mitigation strategy.

Example

An analysis of ABC International's insurance records reveals that one facility was partially flooded 15 years ago, because it is positioned on the edge of a flood-plain. No risk mitigation strategy was adopted after the flood, because consultants concluded that such flooding would occur only once every 100 years.

A capital proposal in front of the CEO now contains a request to double the size of that facility. He needs to consider whether the risk of flooding requires relocating the expansion to a different site or whether flood prevention planning may mitigate the risk.

There may be risks in a company's contracts, such as requirements to pay large minimum fees to certain suppliers or to grant an extended product warranty period to a customer. Corporate counsel should conduct a review of all unexpired contracts to see if such risks exist.

Example

A small database and software service company (Alpha Company) was in nego-tiations with a larger firm regarding a new services contract when a lawyer for the larger firm decided to review an old contract that already existed between the two companies. He found that Alpha Company had previously licensed a database from it and guaranteed a very large minimum payment amount. Alpha had been unable to resell the database, and neither party had noticed the mini-mum payment requirement. Thus, Alpha never made the payment, and the larger firm never noticed the shortfall.

The larger company elected to enforce the contract. Alpha Company did not have the financial resources to pay the minimum amount required by the contract and threatened to enter bankruptcy if the larger firm enforced its rights. The parties eventually settled for a minor sum.

Once this review has been completed, work with corporate counsel and the risk manager to create a formal plan for risk mitigation. You should review this plan with the entire senior management team, to see if it is missing any risks and that the miti-gation steps are sound. Then bring the plan to the attention of the board of directors and solicit additional input. These steps likely will require multiple iterations as well as a periodic review to see if the company's circumstances warrant the addition or deletion of any risks.

After the risk mitigation plan is in place, it will be apparent that the company cannot completely mitigate some risks and will need to obtain insurance to address these risks. Have the risk manager summarize the coverage and limits of all existing insurance, match it against the risk mitigation plan, and see if there are any shortfalls in the insurance coverage. If so, alter the existing insurance coverage to align more precisely it with the plan.

It is difficult to conduct a risk review as a discrete analysis with a specific begin-ning and ending date, because possible risks can arise at any time and must be con-sidered at once, before they have the potential to become larger problems. Thus, the CEO needs to be prepared to review and revise the risk mitigation plan throughout the year. The steps noted here were only for an initial review, which likely will be the start of an ongoing analysis that never really ends.

Chapter 9, Risk Management: General Concepts, and Chapter 10, Risk Manage-ment: Foreign Exchange, go into considerably greater detail on a number of risk management topics.

Review Costs

Even the finest strategy and the best risk mitigation will not result in a profitable company if the CEO cannot maintain control over company costs. Consequently, the CEO should develop a system for setting cost expectations and ensuring that actual costs remain at or below the designated levels.

The first step in creating a cost control system is to have a financial analyst develop operating metrics for every department that are based on industry or functional best practice benchmarks. By doing so, you can compare actual costs incurred to what other companies have experienced. This does not always mean that you should drive down costs everywhere in a company to meet these benchmarks. If the company strategy is to excel in certain areas, you may have to spend *more* in those areas, not less. Thus, a more intelligent cost review that is tailored to a specific company should follow these steps:

Step 1. *Obtain benchmark information and match to company results.* Perform this assessment as described.

Step 2. *Review largest variances.* There will be many variances between a company's expenditures and benchmark levels, but only a small number will be so large that there are significant potential savings from engaging in a cost reduction program. Itemize these large variances.

Step 3. *Compare large variances to strategy.* Of the large variances, which ones should remain or even increase, because the company strategy involves large expenditures in those areas? Itemize the remaining large variances.

Step 4. *Compare remaining variances to reduction capabilities.* Of any remaining large variances, how many require a significant amount of management attention? Is there enough management time available to enact the necessary changes?

This four-step program likely will result in only a few types of expenditures that can be safely reduced and for which the company has the resources to enact changes. If you follow this path, there may be only a few areas of cost reduction that really warrant extensive attention each year.

Irrespective of the targeted cost reduction program just noted, you also should have the CFO install a reporting system that assigns responsibility for every expenditure to a specific person within the company and reports costs to those people. With such a system, everyone knows how their assigned costs are positioned in comparison to the budget, and they know that the CFO will be making inquiries if expenditures exceed expectations.

It is also useful to have either a formal monthly meeting to go over expenditures with the entire management team or to work through the same topic on a one-on-one basis with each manager. Either approach yields the same result: Managers know that the CEO is concerned about expenses and will be making regular inquiries to see what is being done to keep costs down.

The basic rule of company costs is that, if they are not going down, they are going up. In other words, if you are not paying attention to cost suppression, costs always are expanding for any number of reasons. Thus, you must maintain an ongoing cost review to keep management focused on this key item, with a more targeted program for specific costs where there appear to be good prospects for substantial reductions. Chapter 12, Cost Reduction Analysis, contains an array of specific tips for how to reduce costs in a number of areas.

Summary

The circumstances in which a CEO will find himself at a new company can vary substantially; you may find that the situation requires you to take steps in directions quite different from the recommendations noted in this chapter. Nonetheless, the issues described here are fundamental ones that may cause trouble for you eventually if you do not tackle them. Consequently, even if you cannot deal with these recommendations at once, at least return to them when you have time. By doing so, you will have completed the baseline tasks that most CEOs find are not only useful to their own careers but also to the prosperity of their companies.

The issues outlined in this chapter are summarized in a checklist in the Appendix, New CEO Checklist, of activities that a new CEO should pursue.

In Chapter 2, General Corporate Strategy, we turn to a discussion of the general concepts of strategy, including the competitive environment, building defenses, choosing a strategy, and testing it for validity.

PART I

Strategy Development

General Corporate Strategy

The key responsibility of the chief executive officer (CEO) is to formulate an effective strategy and to implement it over the long term. This chapter addresses the competitive environment in which companies operate, how to build defenses against competitors, the three principal types of strategies, and how to test a strategy to see if a company can achieve it.

Overview of General Corporate Strategy

The development of a general corporate strategy calls for a considerable amount of thought regarding the unique capabilities of your company and how the company best fits into its competitive environment. The best possible strategy is one that is highly defensible and allows the company to maintain above-average profitability. In particular, you should delve into the exact capabilities of your company to obtain a detailed understanding of its strengths and weaknesses. In many cases, your ideal strategy is one that builds even further on existing strengths rather than one that attempts to improve existing weaknesses. Finally, you should attempt to forecast competitive conditions within the industry to see what changes are most likely to occur in the near and medium term; your strategy should be tailored to these forecasted conditions rather than to conditions as they exist today. In this section, we address the competitive environment, building defenses against competitors, and the profit opportunities caused by product differentiation.

Competitive Environment

An industry is constantly in a state of flux, because it is being impacted from multiple directions. These changes may cause gradual change or sudden changes that may be useful or catastrophic. The CEO's job is to develop an excellent understanding of the industry, use it to forecast the structure of the industry in the near future, and accordingly develop a strategy that fits this future vision of the industry. The key factors impacting the competitive environment within an industry are listed next.

- *New competition.* If there are minimal barriers to entry in an industry, a company is constantly forced to deal with new product offerings by companies that they may not even have heard of until recently. This factor introduces a great deal of pricing pressure, since some new entrants likely will focus on low prices in order to gain market share. Also, the sheer volume of new entrants makes it difficult to predict how the competition will react to any planned strategy changes by companies that are already established in the industry. A variation on new competition is when a large outside entity acquires a company that is already positioned within the industry; when this happens, the buyer sometimes imposes a new strategy on its acquiree (along with plenty of resources), which can cause quite a disturbance within the industry.

- *Substitute products.* There may be substitute products available that customers can switch to easily. If so, the price of the substitute products may limit the ability of anyone in the industry to increase prices, which in turn limits profitability.
- *Upstream and downstream pressure.* Suppliers may have the ability to influence the prices they charge, either through the use of patents or restricted sources of supply. Conversely, customers may be able to drive down prices, usually because they command a dominant position in their industries that is difficult to avoid. Customers are in an especially good position to drive down prices if just a few of them comprise the bulk of a company's business. Both suppliers and customers can restrict the ability of an industry to garner outsize profits by shifting these profits to themselves.
- *Competitors.* In any given industry, there may be substantial differences in the level of competition between companies. In more staid, long-term industries, the level of market share held by each competitor may have been relatively fixed for some time, and no one is willing to upset the situation. Alternatively, other industries may contain a few aggressive firms that are willing to engage in a variety of practices to increase their market share. This competitive situation is by no means fixed, since a simple change in leadership at a large competitor may bring about a significant strategy change at that company which upsets the competitive situation in the entire industry. Similarly, if a key competitor goes public, thereby raising a great deal of cash, it now has the funding capability to drive change within the industry.

Example

The airline industry is a difficult one in which to compete, because it is negatively impacted by almost every competitive factor. It is easy for new competitors to enter the industry, because they can lease airplanes rather than paying for their full purchase price. Substitute products include car and train travel, while business travelers can opt to use videoconferencing instead of flying. There is upstream pressure from the suppliers of aviation fuel; if airlines pass through the cost of fuel to customers, they will lose those passengers who are price sensitive. Finally, there is intense competition between airlines, to such an extent that multiple price wars break out every year.

(continued)

In this environment, airlines must search for highly targeted niches that allow them to compete more effectively. For example, they can lock down gate assignments at airports, which allows them to block competitors from operating flights into specific airports. They also can run direct point-to-point flights into smaller airports, where there is not enough traffic to entice other airlines to offer competing flights.

In summary, the competitive environment is strongly influenced not only by the interaction of existing firms within an industry but also by the suppliers and customers of that industry, products originating in adjacent industries, and entirely new entrants. To defend itself within this environment, a CEO should consider some of the defenses that are described next.

Building Defenses

A key consideration in developing a corporate strategy is to build defenses that not only assure high profits but that are also difficult for existing competitors to overcome, and the mere existence of which may keep potential competitors from entering the industry. A number of possible strategic defenses are listed next.

- *Access to distribution channels.* A company would be well advised to lock up access to the distribution channels in its industry, through sole-distributor agreements, long-term relationship building, or the use of rich promotions. By doing so, other companies will have an extremely difficult time finding ways to distribute their offerings or at least must incur massive expenditures to do so. They even may have to create their own distribution channels to achieve any degree of success.
- *Economies of scale.* If a company builds massive facilities that are capable of creating products at a very low unit cost, competitors will be forced either to commit large capital expenditures in order to create similar facilities or to compete with higher-priced niche products. Also, potential entrants to the market will think twice before committing the amount of capital needed to compete.

Example

The beer industry is a classic case of economies of scale. A few international firms have constructed large regional breweries that can create vast amounts of beer at the lowest possible cost. These economies of scale have forced a large number of competitors into producing an array of premium niche beers, which they can brew in small local facilities with high-grade ingredients and which they sell at price points much higher than those charged by the massive international brewers.

- *Government blocking.* A company can prevail on the government within whose territory it operates to use such methods as tariffs and import controls to limit competition from companies located elsewhere in the world. This is a less reliable form of defense, since a company does not have direct control over its continuance.
- *Legal protection.* A strongly defended patent on key technology can block competitors from making any meaningful product offerings for the term of the patent. This approach also can be achieved through secrecy rather than a patent, but the company runs the risk that the product will be invented again elsewhere and patented by a competitor.
- *Product differentiation.* As described more thoroughly in the "Product Differentiation as a Defense" subsection later in this chapter, a company can use a variety of techniques to make its products and services appear sufficiently different from competing products that its customers are willing to pay a premium.
- *Raw material lock out.* Raw materials that are difficult to obtain are known as *strategic materials.* If a company can either obtain preferential access to strategic materials or buy the suppliers of the materials outright, this can be an excellent defensive move.
- *Retaliation history.* If a company has a history of responding promptly and ferociously to any attempts to impinge on its market, this may ward off any potential new entrants to the market, who can only assume that the company will treat them in a similar fashion. This defense is particularly effective when a company maintains a large cash reserve with which to fend off other companies and makes public the extent of its financial resources and willingness to use them.
- *Switching costs.* A company should make it extremely difficult for customers to switch to the offerings of competitors. The cost of switching can include replacing equipment, retraining employees, or manually transferring data. By creating switching costs, competitors must present an overwhelming value proposition to lure away customers.

Example

Square Space is a Web site hosting service that offers its customers the convenience of creating Web site pages online rather than the more traditional approach of creating pages with software on customers' computers and uploading the files to a hosting service.

By doing so, Square Space is creating enormous switching costs for its customers, who cannot realistically switch their web pages to a different hosting service. If they were to use a different hosting company, they would have to re-create every page on their Web sites from scratch. If a customer has a large number of web pages, the cost of doing so would be overwhelming.

Product Differentiation as a Defense

One of the key drivers of exceptional profitability is the ability of a company to differentiate its products or services from those of its competitors in a meaningful way. Doing this requires a large, long-term investment in such items as advertising, quality enhancement, product research, and customer service. This investment is targeted at creating a strong sense of brand loyalty with customers, to such an extent that they are willing to pay a premium (sometimes quite a large one) for the company's offerings.

Product differentiation can keep potential entrants into a market from doing so, because they recognize that it will require a considerable investment over a long period of time to create a similar level of differentiation for their offerings. The key point here is less the amount of investment involved and more the time required for a new entrant to succeed. A new player in an industry must be willing to commit to the industry for a number of years and likely will incur large losses during that time, before it can build up the brand loyalty that an existing product differentiator already has. Further, if it then chooses to pull out of the industry, it will likely incur a total loss on its investment, since most of the investment is in intangible items that are not easily sold off. Thus, product differentiation is a powerful inhibitor for new entrants to an industry.

Example

The Big Four audit firms have built up a strong level of product differentiation in an area where the key product—audit and tax services—would not appear to form a foundation for production differentiation. They have done so by investing heavily in staff training, advertising for brand awareness, and accumulating a massive number of locations. All three elements give them a considerable pricing advantage, since larger firms need their high level of expertise as well as their availability in virtually all parts of the world.

A smaller audit firm attempting to break into the niche occupied by the Big Four would have to increase its fees substantially in order to fund the additional levels of training and advertising as well as the rollout of new offices. Given the partnership structure of audit firms, which prevents the accumulation of a significant amount of capital to fund such activities, it is unlikely that any smaller audit firm can seriously threaten the competitive position of the Big Four.

Building a Strategy: General Concepts

The last section included a list of strategic defenses that companies can employ to protect their market positions. In the face of such resolute defenses, how can a CEO develop an effective strategy? There are a number of possibilities. At a high level, next we present the key concepts for properly positioning a company.

- *Sidestep a defense.* It rarely makes sense to compete in precisely the same manner as a competitor. Instead, examine the defenses that it has constructed, and determine the best way to completely sidestep them, so that the defenses no longer matter. Doing this usually requires concentrating on an entirely different strategy. For example, if a competitor always sells at the lowest price, compete by offering the best service at a higher price.

Example

Large home-project stores, such as Home Depot, have built up a seemingly irresistible defense based on their lower prices, which they obtain through vast purchasing volumes. And yet a multitude of small local hardware stores continue to exist. How? They do not compete on price at all. In fact, their prices may be twice as high as those of the larger stores.

These local stores sidestep the low-cost defense and instead compete by maintaining stores as close to homeowners as possible and by having knowledgeable staff on hand to assist them. They impose much higher prices in exchange for these conveniences.

- *Leapfrog technology.* Many industries are built on a specific type of technology. If the technology changes, market shares can become reshuffled overnight. Such technology shifts are not frequent, but if you can foresee the arrival of one, leapfrogging the existing industry technology with new technology can be a very effective way to gain market share quickly.

Example

A classic case of leapfrogging technology is cellular telephone systems. A relatively small number of cell phone towers can be used to provide phone coverage to a large area, thereby completely sidestepping the need to string wire to individual homes. This has allowed upstart companies in many third-world countries to develop phone systems in short order and give them large blocks of market share.

Existing traditional providers of land-line phone services thought that the large capital investment needed to run phone lines would have prevented any new competitors from entering their markets. They were proved wrong by technology that leapfrogged the systems on which they based their assumptions.

- *Avoid the experience curve.* A key tenet of large-scale manufacturing is the experience curve, which states that costs decline by some percentage for every doubling of production volume. If a company makes use of the experience curve, it is intentionally pursuing a low-cost strategy that new entrants presumably cannot match, since they too must build their volume in order to achieve low costs. Proper strategic positioning dictates that competing directly against such a defense likely will result in massive losses, so do not try; instead, avoid the experience curve entirely by creating a product sufficiently different that competitors must retool their facilities entirely to make competitive products, thereby eliminating their experience curve advantage.

- *Avoid declining markets.* If a market is declining, price competition will be rapacious, and likely even the last company standing will be on a shaky financial footing. Strategy in this area calls for excellent forecasting of long-term trends and selling out as soon as possible, before increased competition reduces the value of the sale.
- *Avoid price competition.* The worst way to position a company is to compete strictly on price. Only one company will win that war, and probably only after a debilitating conflict that lays waste to the industry. Further, competitors can easily drop their prices, too, so any advantage from a simple price decline may evaporate in days.
- *Focus on long-term ramp-up advantages.* One of the best ways to establish a strong competitive position is to focus on improvements that will require a long time for competitors to match. For example, creating a clearly higher-quality product will require an entire product cycle for competitors to match, by which time a company can create an even higher level of quality, and so on.

Example

Toyota spent years improving the quality of its automobiles, until it became readily apparent that its products were clearly superior to American cars. Toyota maintained this quality differential for several decades, until competitors finally caught up and Toyota's quality declined through an ill-advised cost reduction campaign. Nonetheless, Toyota earned a clear and sustainable advantage through its focus on product quality.

- *Avoid industries with excess capacity.* If an industry has too much capacity, competitors will accept low prices in order to fill their capacity. This is an ongoing problem in such industries as airlines and automobile manufacturing. In these cases, it may take years for capacity to be eliminated gradually, as competitors shift out of the industry or go bankrupt.
- *Select customers carefully.* It is not always a good idea to pursue large customers who have the potential to place very large orders; such customers have the power to exert considerable downward pricing pressure. Where possible, it is better to be selective and pursue a larger number of smaller customers who will not be in a position to impose lower prices.
- *Design products to avoid suppliers.* Some suppliers exert unusually large amounts of control over the sources of supply of certain key raw materials or own patents that allow them to raise prices. These suppliers can squeeze the profits out of an industry. To avoid this situation, make it a high priority for the engineering staff to design products that either completely eliminate or at least minimize the use of the products of certain suppliers.

Many of the general concepts noted in this section pertain to avoidance—recognizing when an industry is structured so that *no one* can earn a consistent or reasonable profit. In these cases, you need to recognize the situation and simply avoid the industry entirely. The remaining concepts pertain to a process of industry infiltration—of spotting key defenses and inserting your own strategy in such a way as to completely sidestep existing defenses. By doing so, you should rarely go head-to-head against the defenses of competitors, thereby avoiding a large amount of unnecessary expenditures.

Building a Strategy: Product Differentiation

Product differentiation involves creating a product or service (or a combination of the two) that customers consider unique. Product differentiation can follow a number of paths, such as excellent customer service, an unusually liberal product replacement policy, excellent product styling, or very high quality. The goal of this strategy is to favorably bring a company's offerings to the attention of customers, who will be more inclined because of the differentiation to buy them. A high degree of differentiation creates brand loyalty, which in turn allows a company to impose higher prices. This strategy does not focus on being a low-cost provider, although a company must keep its costs under a reasonable degree of control. Depending on the speed with which a company can churn out new product iterations, it may take a considerable amount of time—over a year in most cases—before the benefits of this strategy become apparent.

The product differentiation strategy normally does not allow for a high market share, since many customers will be unwilling to pay the company's higher prices, irrespective of the perceived benefits of its products and services.

Product differentiation is the best strategy available to most companies, since it offers endless opportunities for many companies to operate profitably within the same industry. Thus, it is much less destructive to the industry as a whole than the low-cost strategy (discussed next), where essentially one profitable company is left standing.

If a company is differentiating its products (rather than services), a key aspect of differentiation is bringing products to market at very high speed. This means that early adopters are more likely to buy the products, which gives the company a large block of market share that later market entrants will have difficulty overcoming. Thus, speed to market is itself a form of product differentiation.

Developing a high speed to market requires a number of supporting systems, including:

- *Bottleneck knowledge.* There should be excellent knowledge of exactly where any bottlenecks are located within the company, of how they may impede the introduction of new products, and of how to circumvent them or maximize their use.
- *Inventory dispositions.* A company needs excellent materials management, so that it can use up or disposition any remaining inventory that is included in or related to products that are being eliminated as new products are introduced.

- *Marketing.* There should be an extremely active marketing department that is constantly educating customers about the features of new products and that also manages an ongoing series of product introduction events. Marketing is even more important when products are complex, since it may take time to educate customers properly about their functionality.
- *Production capacity.* The company should have a large amount of dedicated production equipment available (or have suppliers with such capabilities), so that it can retool and launch new products rapidly.
- *Rapid prototyping.* There should be computer-aided design software that is linked to rapid prototype modeling equipment, which gives the capability to create prototypes of new products in a few hours.
- *Supplier capacity.* A company should have a large amount of overcapacity in its supply chain, so that it can ramp up in a very short time to meet a product release date.

Another aspect of the product differentiation strategy is to upgrade *existing* products constantly. Doing this may involve a continual series of minor improvements, a scheduled string of annual releases, or new accessories—whatever customers want to see that will create the greatest sense of customer expectation and willingness to continue purchasing from the company.

The product differentiation strategy calls for a considerable investment in personnel and the systems needed to support them. To be effective in creating innovative products in a timely manner, a company must be fully staffed in all key skill areas, have a management structure that fosters innovation and have support engineers with the latest design software and modeling equipment and must impose project tracking controls to ensure that development work remains on track.

In order to pursue the product differentiation strategy, a company must be willing to create the following environment and actions:

- Commitment to product research and development
- Excellent product design capabilities
- Building a reputation with customers for innovation
- Excellent marketing skills to reinforce the differentiation strategy
- Excellent operational coordination among the engineering, production, and sales functions to build and launch new products properly
- A supportive environment for the type of skilled labor needed to pursue this strategy

There are several risks to be aware of with the product differentiation strategy. They are listed next.

- If there is an excessive pricing difference between the prices charged by the low-cost provider and the company following a differentiation strategy, customers may not perceive that the value provided by differentiation is sufficient to justify the higher price and instead will buy from the low-cost provider. Thus, a company following the product differentiation path must ensure that it maintains a reasonable amount of control over its costs.

- Competitors copy key features of a company's differentiated products, so there is less perceived difference between what the company and its competitors offer.

An interesting side effect of product differentiation is that a sufficient level of differentiation makes it difficult for a customer to compare alternatives, which in turn tends to reduce the amount of switching between the offerings of competitors. This is a particularly powerful effect when a product is coupled with a variety of accessories, warranties, and other service features. The resulting wide array of features that are bundled under one price makes comparison shopping exceptionally difficult.

When a company engages in product differentiation, it has the opportunity to engage in several varieties of pricing, which should be tied to its overall strategy. These pricing options are listed next.

- *Skim pricing.* If the product is exceptionally differentiated from its competitors, a company can set an extremely high price. A small proportion of the potential customer base will be willing to pay this price, which gives the company exceptional profits but only a relatively small market share. If the price stays high for too long, it will attract the attention of competitors, who will enter the market and lower prices in order to grab market share. Thus, skim pricing is more of a short-term strategy, unless a company can upgrade its products continually to new offerings for which it can keep charging high prices.
- *Market pricing.* Most companies do not attempt to depart too far from the current market price of their products, as adjusted for any perceived differences in product features. This strategy works well when customers are price-sensitive. In such cases, a company keeps its prices within in a narrow band that is dictated by the market and instead differentiates itself based on such items as fast delivery, high quality, or responsive customer service. A company frequently starts with skim pricing (as noted above) to earn large profits and gradually drops its prices to meet market rates as competition intensifies.
- *Penetration pricing.* The most aggressive pricing approach is to drop prices below the standard market rate or below the value of a company's offerings (which may vary from the market rate). Since profits will decline with this strategy, the only reason for using it is to increase market share, which may provoke a similar pricing response from competitors. This approach is commonly used by new entrants, who need to expand from zero market share in order to gain a toehold in the market.
- *Experience pricing.* If a company is primarily selling employee services, it can adjust its pricing to match the experience level of its employees. Typically, a CEO wants to avoid commodity-level services, because she cannot adequately match the experience level of her staff to the prices allowed by the market.
- *Value pricing.* It is generally better to focus service offerings in high-value areas (especially ones very highly valued by customers, such as merger and acquisition assistance), where pricing can be stratospheric. As long as customers perceive an unusually large benefit from the service provided, they are less likely to shop elsewhere for a lower price.

When building a corporate infrastructure to align a company with a product differentiation strategy, consider the next structural and measurement issues.

- *Hierarchy.* Product differentiation calls for fast product development cycle times, which can be enhanced by a flat organizational structure that pushes responsibility down into the organization.
- *Employee training.* Training programs should center on product development and customer service.
- *Departmental orientation.* The engineering, marketing, and customer service departments are at the center of the product differentiation strategy and so require strong support from all other departments.
- *Measurements.* Consider tracking the cycle time required to produce new products, the number of patents, the number of products delivered by their due dates, warranty claims, customer complaints, employee turnover in key functional areas, actual versus budgeted spending on product development, and the ability of the company to meet target costs as part of the product design process.

In summary, the keys to succeeding with a product differentiation strategy are to have robust product creation processes in place that can churn out uniquely positioned products on a recurring basis, a flexible production process that can manufacture sufficient quantities to meet demand, intensive product branding activities, higher pricing to support the cost of these activities, and a cost structure that is sufficiently low to allow the company to earn a profit.

Building a Strategy: Low Cost

The intent of a low-cost strategy is to achieve such low costs that your company can price its products below those of all competitors while still achieving an adequate profit. In essence, a company must focus solely on the reduction of every conceivable cost throughout the company while also expanding rapidly in order to benefit from reduced costs as production volumes increase. As costs continually decline, the company reduces its prices, which presumably should result in more sales to customers, which builds volume even more, drives down costs more, and so on.

This strategy calls for the construction of the most efficient production facilities, the design of products that are easy to manufacture, servicing all possible customers in order to build production volumes, and the ongoing pursuit of cost reductions throughout the organization. This strategy does *not* call for excessive cost reductions in such areas as product quality and customer service; the emphasis in these areas is only to meet the average customer expectations in the industry, so that customers are not turned away by substandard performance. Cost reductions have a rapid impact on profitability, so this strategy can begin to pay off almost immediately.

A company that achieves the low-cost position within an industry occupies a highly defensible position, since any other company attempting to attack its position will have higher costs and so can offer similar prices only in exchange for very low profits or losses. Also, if the cost of materials increases, it will impact all firms in the industry equally, so the low-cost company still can maintain its competitive position.

A company pursuing a really effective low-cost strategy also will focus on shrinking the amount of processing time involved in every aspect of the business, which increases the speed with which orders arrive, are processed, and paid for. This means that a low-cost strategy should encompass reductions in the time needed for customers to place orders, the purchasing department to procure materials, the manufacturing process to produce goods, and so on. Not only does this increase the flow of cash into a company, but it also increases the speed with which customers obtain products, which increases their propensity to purchase from the company again.

Another factor in the low-cost strategy is that it must represent the lowest *total* cost from the perspective of the customer. This means that not only must the initial price paid be the lowest one but that all subsequent costs should be minimized, as well. Thus, products must be of a sufficient quality level to avoid having customers waste time returning them for repairs or replacement.

Yet another consideration for companies engaging in the low-cost strategy is concentrating on a limited product line that meets the needs of the majority of potential customers. By doing so, companies can concentrate their attention on just a few products, which makes it easier to reduce costs. Conversely, having a broad product line requires a larger support structure and more complex operations, which makes it more difficult to reduce costs. This is a key point; many CEOs who are transitioning their companies into a low-cost strategy have a hard time pruning their existing product lines and so handicap their companies in the pursuit of the lowest possible cost structure.

In order to pursue the low-cost strategy, a company must be willing to engage in these activities:

- Continual investment in whatever production facilities are required to improve efficiencies
- Just-in-time deliveries and processes that are designed to reduce the overall investment in inventory
- Investment in the industrial engineering staff required to optimize production efficiencies
- Investment in a supplier quality assurance system, to improve the quality of incoming components
- Investment in the design engineers needed to optimize product designs that are easy to manufacture
- Partnerships with key suppliers to enhance the generation of cost-reduction ideas
- The willingness to eliminate low-quality customers who pay late and use an inordinate amount of the company's resources in such areas as warranty claims, product returns, and customer service
- The willingness to outsource those functions that can be handled by a supplier at a lower cost (see Chapter 6, Outsourcing Strategy)
- A strong control environment where all costs are examined carefully and actions taken to reduce them wherever possible
- A tightly organized hierarchical organization structure that is focused on cost reduction throughout the organization

There are also several risks to be aware of with the low-cost strategy. They are listed next.

- There must be a continual commitment to reinvest in the latest and most efficient production facilities. If a company ever declines to do so, it soon will find that a more aggressive competitor willing to make greater investments has taken over the low-cost lead in the market.
- Competitors can watch the mistakes made by the low-cost leader and ramp up more quickly by avoiding those mistakes.
- There is a risk that the company will be so focused on cost reduction that it will not perceive changes in the market related to noncost items, such as customer service, which it must match in order to remain competitive in the eyes of its customers.
- A company will lose its production volume advantage if it creates too many differentiated products, since each product will require a smaller production volume, which in turn leads to increased costs.
- A company with an intense low-cost focus tends to be a rigid organization that has a hard time changing to meet new market needs, since it is oriented toward adherence to existing policies and procedures.
- This strategy can result in the bankruptcy of any firm that does not succeed. If several companies are pursuing the low-cost strategy, price wars will be continual, as each one attempts to garner more sales in order to drive down its costs. The usual result is similar to a battlefield, with many dying competitors and one severely wounded victor.

When building a corporate infrastructure to align the company with a low-cost strategy, consider the next structural and measurement issues.

- *Hierarchy.* Achieving low costs requires a strong control system and capacity management, which in turn usually involves the construction of a multilayered corporate hierarchy that closely monitors costs throughout the organization.
- *Employee training.* Training programs should center on cost reductions, so such concepts at six sigma, production process improvement, and total quality management are likely training topics.
- *Departmental orientation.* The concerns of the engineering and production departments are paramount, with all other departments supporting their focus on the high-volume production of easily manufactured goods.
- *Measurements.* Consider tracking the variable cost of each product on a trend line. This includes tracking throughput of the production operation, capacity of the bottleneck operation, defect rates, production yields, percentage of product scrap and rework, equipment breakdowns, cost of inspections and testing, supplier quality ratings, inventory turnover, inventory obsolescence, accounts receivable turnover, bad debt percentage, number of innovations originating with suppliers, and overhead costs.

In summary, the low-cost strategy requires an extremely tight focus on pruning costs everywhere in an organization while building the sales of a limited number of products. The result can be a highly defensible position with the largest market share in an industry, but it also tends to burden the successful company with a rigid hierarchy and a vast array of policies and procedures.

Building a Strategy: Focus on a Niche

A possible strategic alternative is to focus a company's attention solely on a specific group of customers, geographic region, specific product, or some similar form of segmentation. By doing so, you are electing service not to an entire industry but rather a small, carefully defined portion of it. This strategy is built on the premise that customers in your target niche will be willing to pay a premium for highly targeted offerings. This approach works only if the niche focus results in a product or service that customers perceive to be substantially unique in comparison to the offerings of the rest of the industry. Also, it takes a considerable amount of time to build up a strong niche position, so expect several years to pass before the benefits of the strategy become clear. Examples of the niche strategy are listed next.

- *Custom-designed products.* Requires a strong knowledge of customer design requirements and rapid product iterations.
- *Complete solutions.* Companies buying complex products want to have a supplier not only install them but also train the staff in how to use them, and they are willing to pay a premium price for this complete package. Examples are complex computer hardware and software solutions or production machinery.
- *Specialty materials.* Requires the use of high-grade or special-use materials, such as fireproof materials or materials having a high tensile strength.
- *Fail-safe products.* Requires the use of redundant systems, tight tolerances, and high-quality materials to create products that rarely fail. Usually requires a strong customer service function, on-site repair capability, and long-term warranty to present a complete solution to customers.
- *Rapid delivery.* Requires a localized distribution system in areas where there is a high concentration of potential customers willing to pay for fast delivery (likely limited to large metropolitan areas).
- *Professional users.* Professional users of many products demand high reliability, fast product replacement, or on-site repairs that more casual users are less concerned about.
- *Selection.* Requires an investment in product sizes that are not normally stocked and that may require long inventory turnover periods. For example, a shoe retailer could stock unusually small or large shoe sizes or a clothier could stock suits for large men.

There are several risks to be aware of with the niche strategy. They are listed next.

- If there is an excessive pricing difference between the prices charged by the low-cost provider and the company following a niche strategy, customers may not perceive that the value provided by the niche focus is sufficient to justify the

higher price and instead will buy from the low-cost provider. Thus, a company following the niche path must ensure that it maintains a reasonable amount of control over its costs.
- Competitors may provide an even tighter focus on a particular niche, thereby outcompeting a company in its chosen location in the market. Without a prompt reaction to this threat, a company may find itself with a *very* small share of the market.

In order to pursue the niche strategy, a company must be willing to engage in many of the activities already noted for the product differentiation and low-cost strategies, but targeted more tightly at a specific niche. In addition, it must spend a (seemingly) inordinate amount of time selecting which customers it wants to deal with and then servicing their needs. Since the right customers can be incredibly profitable, a niche-oriented company wants to service them for many years and is willing to invest a great deal in these relationships.

When building a corporate infrastructure to align the company with a niche strategy, consider the next structural and measurement issues.

- *Customer loyalty program.* A customer loyalty program, such as giving points on purchases to encourage repeat business, is ideal for a company pursuing a niche strategy, since it wants to build long-term relationships with its customers.
- *Hierarchy.* The niche strategy calls for an intense customer focus, which can be enhanced by a flat organizational structure that pushes responsibility down into the organization, allowing employees to make spot decisions to improve a company's relationship with customers.
- *Employee training.* Training programs should center on product development, customer service, and customer retention.
- *Departmental orientation.* The engineering and customer service departments are at the center of the niche strategy.
- *Marketing.* The niche strategy requires considerable attention to marketing. Since business with the correct customer can generate outsize profits for many years, marketing efforts must be targeted unusually carefully toward a specific niche and, more particularly, toward certain customers within that niche. This may require the use of highly granular marketing that may reach only a few dozen recipients rather than a broad-based national campaign that would be more appropriate for one of the other strategies.
- *Measurements.* Consider tracking customer retention, customer satisfaction, the number of testimonials from customers, the number of products sold per customer, on-time delivery percentage, stockout percentage, proposal success rate, the estimated lifetime value of customers acquired, profit per customer, and the percentage of customers below a certain profit threshold.

In summary, the niche orientation requires capabilities that are drawn from both of the other strategies, with a primary focus on product differentiation. This strategy does not necessarily focus on unique products. Instead, it represents a focus on the particular needs of a precisely defined set of customers. The result is typically a mix of both products and services, with an enormous emphasis on customer service.

Building a Strategy: Impact of the Internet

The Internet makes it more difficult for a company to establish a secure and defensible strategic position, for these reasons:

- *New competitors.* The Internet broadens the pool of suppliers from which a customer is willing to buy, expanding its geographical reach from local suppliers to ones located anywhere in the country (though international shipping costs still tend to impose restrictions beyond the national level). With this much larger pool of competitors, there is inevitably a greater degree of price competition.
- *More potential product choices.* The Internet makes it easier for a customer to research a broader array of products, including products that are in adjacent markets and that they normally would not be aware of. This makes it easier to switch to competing products.
- *Supplier competition.* Suppliers no longer need a distributor network in order to sell their goods to customers. Instead, they can set up storefronts on the Internet and sell directly to the end customer. This takes sales away from distributors and retailers and tends to boost the sales of suppliers.
- *Focus on price.* The use of the Internet by so many potential customers tends to concentrate attention on price as the main competitive factor, which gives those companies pursuing a low-cost strategy a significant advantage. Those companies pursuing a niche strategy may find that their niches evaporate in the face of the increased focus on price.
- *Reduce traditional sales channels.* The Internet may create a somewhat larger overall market for products, but realistically most of the sales made through it are coming at the expense of traditional sales channels. Thus, those companies depending on, or part of, the traditional sales channels may see their sales decline. Also, because of the ability to research prices easily through the Internet, customers have more bargaining power when purchasing through a more traditional sales channel.

These factors certainly increase the level of competition, but they do not weaken competitive strategy to such an extent that a CEO should abandon all hope of making a strategy succeed. Instead, the Internet is really just one of many factors to be considered and to be incorporated into the formulation of strategy.

Building a Strategy: Additional Comments

The preceding sections have outlined the three types of strategy: product differentiation, low cost, and focusing on a niche. Several additional comments regarding the strategies are presented next.

- *Critical processes.* When you create a strategy, you need also to identify those processes that will support the specific strategy and ensure that those processes support the strategy to the fullest extent possible. It is not necessary to upgrade unrelated processes if they do not directly support the specific strategy adopted. This is a critical point: A company cannot afford to waste the time or resources to upgrade processes that do not need to be upgraded, so be very precise about exactly which processes are integral parts of a strategy, and focus solely on them.

Example

The CEO of ABC Company decides to implement a product differentiation strategy. To alter ABC to fully match this strategic vision, she doubles the size of the customer service function and installs an online customer complaint system; both of these changes create a feedback loop regarding product problems that the engineering staff can use to design better products.

- *Process reinforcement.* Certain processes within a company must reinforce the overall strategy. For example, a highly customized product may call for a large design team in the sales department to configure customer orders properly as well as on-site follow-up by the sales staff later on to ensure that the products met customer requirements. If a company does not engage in proper process reinforcement, a weakness in one process may greatly weaken the entire value proposition that it is presenting to its customers.

Example

Google launched an innovative cell phone that it sold directly to customers. The phone was well designed and had features that exceeded the offerings of most other competitors, but it did not sell very well when prospective customers learned that Google had not adequately staffed its customer support function to receive customer calls, resulting in long waits.

- *Distinctiveness.* The ultimate goal of a strategy (other than profits!) is to make the company distinct from its competitors in the eyes of its customers. This means that a company must differentiate itself from its competitors by performing its services in different ways or by performing entirely different services. The same concepts apply to products. This distinctiveness concept can apply to nearly all aspects of a company that are visible to the outside world: product design, manufacturing, delivery, marketing, and so on.
- *Strategic continuity.* It may take several years to roll out a strategy properly, and it takes many more years to reinforce the company's commitment to that strategy internally. For example, a product differentiation strategy may call for the hiring, training, and integration of a group of top-notch product designers, which may require several years to achieve. Consequently, it is extremely important not to

bounce between strategies. Commit to a single strategy and see it through until such time as it becomes apparent that the company cannot sustain a competitive advantage with that strategy.

Example

When Jolly Rancher Candies was an independent company, its owners decided to give its hard candy products an "Old West" marketing angle, which strongly differentiated it from its competitors. One aspect of this decision was to hire an artist to paint western panorama scenes on the sides of its delivery trucks, which roamed the country, delivering the "Old West" message.

Thus far, we have offered clarification of how to improve a foray into a particular strategy. In addition, we have these comments about strategy-related failings:

- *Using multiple strategies.* It may seem tempting to pursue multiple strategies at once, on the grounds that you can build up a ferocious competitive position by presenting a posture that competitors have no way of circumventing. This is flawed logic, because pursuing multiple strategies does not allow a company to fully realize the gains to be garnered from a single strategy and does allow a more fully committed competitor to achieve better results with a single strategy. For example, a company that wants to pursue both the low-cost and product differentiation strategies will find that its low-cost orientation does not allow it to invest enough funds in product development. Similarly, pursuing both the low-cost and niche strategies means that you cannot generate enough sales volume in any niche to drive down costs sufficiently to become the low-cost provider.
- *Stuck in the middle.* What happens when there is no clear strategy, so that a company is, figuratively speaking, stuck in the middle of all the strategies? In this case, a company does not have the production volume or organizational structure to achieve the low-cost position nor the talent pool to produce differentiated products reliably. The result of this lack of corporate direction is a complete inability to impose above-market pricing, so that profits are likely to be anemic.
- *Unprofitable industries.* There is a saying that a bad industry always beats a good management team. This is true, because structural problems in an industry may make it impossible for *any* strategy, no matter how well formulated or implemented, to succeed.
- *Profitable industries.* The reverse of the preceding point is also true—an industry that is gifted with strong defenses, such as massive barriers to entry and favorable government regulations, may allow all market participants to earn outsize profits, no matter how poorly executed their strategies (if any) may be.
- *Market fragmentation factors.* A CEO may find that, despite considerable attention to strategy, her company simply cannot gain market share. If so, it is possible that natural factors are keeping the industry in a highly fragmented state that any company would have trouble counteracting. For example, if success in an industry is based on personal service, a large amount of creative input, or local

contacts, or is subject to a high degree of local government regulation, these factors support large numbers of small local or regional competitors, none of which has a reasonable chance of achieving any significant growth in market share.

In short, the harsh reality is that not having a strategy of some kind likely will lead to subpar profits, if not eventual bankruptcy. In addition, even having a well-defined strategy may not be sufficient if a company is located in an unprofitable or highly fragmented market. Thus, not only does the CEO need to attend to strategy formulation, but she also must question whether her company should be competing in certain industries.

Strategy Testing

Once you have formulated an initial corporate strategy, you should examine it to see if the company is capable of achieving it. In many cases, the management team tries to impose variations on the same strategy on a company through multiple years; if the company has not succeeded in achieving it in the past, you need to find out precisely why this keeps happening. Several thoughts regarding areas that may make a strategy unachievable are presented next.

- *Bottlenecks.* Are there any bottleneck operations or personnel who restrict the ability of the company to achieve its goals? For example, a manufacturing company has a multimillion-dollar machine through which all production flows; any increase in sales requires either an investment in a new machine or the outsourcing of work to potential competitors.
- *Compensation structure.* Does the current system of compensation support the strategy? For example, if the strategy requires that employees work as teams to better service customers, this may not work if the bonus system is designed to reward individual performance.
- *Competitor reaction.* How will competitors react, once the company's strategy becomes clear to them? For example, if the strategy is to be the low-cost leader, will the current low-cost leader simply drop its prices even lower in order to maintain its position?
- *Conflicting culture.* If the strategy represents a significant change from the prior strategy, can the established corporate culture change itself enough to support the new strategy? For example, if a company currently is designed to support a strong product research function in order to create new products constantly, it may be quite difficult to reorient employees toward a high-volume, low-cost strategy where the culture must refocus itself on paring costs throughout the organization.
- *Conflicting goals.* Do some goals conflict with each other? For example, if a strategy is to expand sales dramatically through the hiring of more sales staff, a goal to reduce the proportion of educational expenditures might prevent new sales personnel from being trained adequately.
- *Conflicting resources.* Are there enough resources to achieve goals? For example, a company cannot expand into new geographic markets easily unless it also

creates an adequate infrastructure in advance to service the new markets, which may require a sales staff, distribution network, and retail locations.

- *Fiefdoms.* Are there managers who fiercely protect their turf and will attempt to block the strategy if it impinges on their proclaimed areas of control? For example, an engineering manager who runs all product development may not take kindly to attempts to outsource the product development function.
- *Management expertise.* Does the management team have a sufficiently high level of expertise to implement the strategy? For example, if key managers recently have been promoted and still are uncertain of themselves in their new roles, can they realistically engage in a significant structural change in the company?
- *Pacing.* Can the pace of change called for by the strategy be adequately supported by the company? For example, if a bank plans to open a new branch office once a week, does the company must have sufficient corporate staff to lease space, construct locations, staff them, and train new employees on that rollout schedule?

Many of the issues noted here revolve around employees, since their management styles, work capacity, and accustomed work habits play a major role in the ability of a company to implement its strategy. Thus, your first consideration is whether the staff is capable of implementing the strategy. The second most important consideration is the presence of a bottleneck, which in some situations also centers on the staff. If there is a cast-iron bottleneck that impedes the growth of the business, you must resolve that issue before attempting to implement the strategy.

Summary

This chapter has given an overview of general strategic concepts as well as more detail regarding the three basic types of strategic direction, which are based on product differentiation, low cost, and market niches. The CEO should certainly settle on one of these strategies. However, this is by no means the end of the corporate planning process. The CEO also needs to consider strategic issues in many other areas that tie back into the general corporate strategy. These issues encompass finance, taxation, information technology, and outsourcing. The next chapters address strategic concerns in these areas, which the CEO must weave into the general strategy in order to create a comprehensive strategy package that will work together to advance the company's fortunes most effectively.

CHAPTER 3

Financial Strategy

The chief executive officer (CEO) is responsible for overall corporate strategy, and a significant part of that strategy includes the strategic financial decisions that the chief financial officer (CFO) makes.

In this chapter, we review a number of common decision areas that a CFO is likely to face and that the CEO should be aware of. They generally are grouped in the order in which the topics can be found on the balance sheet and the income statement.

Cash

Corporate management should pay particular attention to the amount of risk associated with a firm's exposure to its foreign currency transactions as well as its overall relations with those banks handling its financial transactions. These issues are discussed in this section.

Reducing Foreign Currency Exposure

A CEO whose company engages in international trade must be concerned about potential changes in the value of its trading partners' currencies. For example, if a company sells products to a French company and receives payment after the euro loses value, the company absorbs the reduction in value of the euro, creating a loss.

If foreign currency transaction volumes are small, the potential risk of loss will be correspondingly small, and so is not worth much review by the CEO. However, it may be worth reviewing if large foreign contracts are contemplated. If a company engages in substantial foreign trade, reducing foreign currency exposure is so large an issue that the CEO should consider creating a hedging department that does nothing but track and mitigate this issue. This topic is dealt with in considerable detail in Chapter 10, Risk Management: Foreign Exchange.

Deciding to Change a Banking Relationship

A good banking relationship is extremely important to the CEO. It should involve excellent responsiveness by all departments of the bank, minimal transaction-processing errors, moderate fees, reasonable levels of asset collateralization on loans, online access to transactional data, and the ability to process more advanced transactions, such as letters of credit. Larger companies with massive transaction volumes and lending needs are the most likely to find all of these needs fulfilled. However, smaller entities will not represent enough business to a bank to warrant this level of service and so most likely will suffer in the areas of customer service and advantageous loan terms.

Of particular concern to the CEO of an expanding business is growing beyond the capabilities of a small local bank that it may have begun doing business with when it first started. Smaller banks may offer reasonable attentiveness but are unlikely to offer online transaction processing, letters of credit, or any form of international transaction support.

Given these issues, there are several key factors in deciding when to change a banking relationship. The first is a simple lack of responsiveness by the bank, which seems most common with large banks that service thousands of business customers—one gets lost in the shuffle. This is primarily a problem when special transactions are needed that require a bank officer, such as letters of credit or wire transfers. A second reason is outgrowing the capabilities of the bank, as already noted. Be certain that additional capabilities truly are needed before switching banks for this reason, given the difficulty of severing a banking relationship. The third and least justifiable reason for changing banks is the cost of the relationship. When compared to the cost of other business expenses, banking fees are comparatively inexpensive and so should be a reason to sever a banking relationship only when combined with some other factor, such as poor service.

Changing a banking relationship is extremely difficult for the accounting and treasury departments, because they must shift a large array of banking transactions from one bank to another. The next list highlights the number of changes required to switch banks.

- Adopt a corporate resolution to switch banks.
- Open up accounts at the new bank.
- Order check stock for the new accounts.
- Contact suppliers who are paid with Automated Clearing House (ACH) debits from the old accounts, and have them switch to the new accounts.
- Continue with bank reconciliations for the old accounts until all checks have cleared.
- Wire all remaining funds from the old accounts to the new accounts.
- Close the old accounts.
- Shred all remaining check stock.
- Have auditors review both the old and new bank accounts at year-end.
- Arrange for new loan agreements with the new bank.
- Pay off old loans with funds from new loans.
- Cancel old loans.

The volume and intricacy of the number of steps required to shift banks should make management think twice before proceeding with a banking change. It is much easier to leave well enough alone unless there are significant factors favoring a change.

Investments

The CEO is interested in maximizing the return on company investments, but only to the extent that risk is not substantially increased. It is also useful to monitor the rates paid on outstanding bonds and refund them if there are lower-cost alternatives available. This section addresses both issues.

Maximizing Return on Assets

A CEO can gain an excellent understanding of a company's efficiency through close attention to the return on assets (ROA) measurement. Since this measure also is tracked by analysts and investors, it is wise to understand its components, how they can be manipulated to enhance the ROA, and how these changes should be made in light of overall company strategy.

As shown in Exhibit 3.1, the ROA measure is composed of margins (on the left side of the exhibit) and asset turnover (on the right side). Multiplying the earnings percentage by asset turnover yields the return on assets. Many companies have a long tradition of squeezing every possible cost out of their operations, which

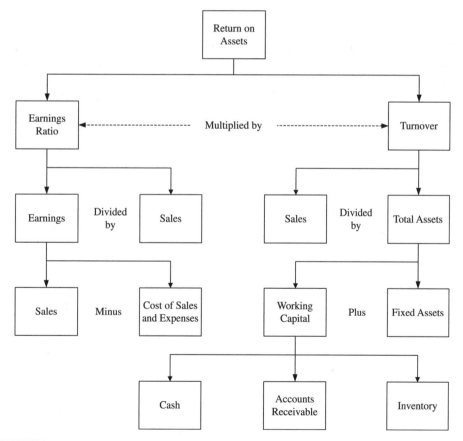

EXHIBIT 3.1 Components of the Return on Assets

certainly addresses the first half of the ROA equation. However, asset turnover is either ignored or given a much lower priority. The CEO should investigate this latter portion of the calculation to see what asset reductions, both in the areas of working capital and fixed assets, can be achieved on order to arrive at a higher ROA.

Working capital reduction techniques are addressed in the "Working Capital" section later in this chapter. Fixed asset reductions can be achieved through a well-managed capital budgeting process (see Chapter 8, Capital Budgeting) as well as through constant investigation and disposal of potentially unused assets and the use of outsourcing in order to shift expensive facility and equipment costs to suppliers.

When investigating ROA improvement opportunities, be aware that an excessive amount of cost and asset reduction can harm a company by such means as reducing the quality of its products, giving it minimal excess production capacity to use during high-volume periods, and reducing the size of its research and development activities. Thus, improving ROA should not be taken to extremes, although the CEO should certainly be mindful of it.

Bond Refunding Decision

A company can buy back bonds from investors prior to their due dates, but only if there is a call provision on the bond or if it was issued originally as a serial bond. The call provision gives the company the right to buy the bond back on a specific series of dates over the life of the bond while the serial bond approach sets different maturity dates on sets of bonds within a total bond offering. Thus, the call provision gives a company the option to refund bonds whereas the serialization feature requires the company to refund them. In either instance, the presence of these refunding features on a bond will decrease its value, resulting in a higher effective interest rate that the company must pay.

In this case, the CEO and CFO must make a decision in advance of a bond offering to add refunding features to the bonds. If there is no reasonable prospect of having funds available to pay off the bonds early, and if the interest rate being paid appears reasonable, there is no particular need for the refunding features. However, if this is not the case, it would be prudent to add a call provision, since this option gives the firm the ability to refund the bonds without necessarily being required to do so. A serialization feature is less useful, since it incorporates a direct requirement to make cash payments at regular intervals to refund specific bonds, whereas there may be better uses for these funds.

If there is a concern that the presence of either type of call feature will result in a more expensive interest rate, consider adding other features to the bonds, such as convertibility or warrants, that will increase the value of the bonds to investors, thereby keeping the effective interest rate from being increased.

Working Capital

The CEO periodically reviews the company's investment in working capital in order to keep it from ballooning and thereby endangering the company's cash position.

Working capital is also an excellent source of cash, when properly managed. This section covers the details of working capital management.

Working Capital Reduction Methodology

The CEO is constantly in search of a ready source of inexpensive funding for the company. One of the best sources is working capital, which is accounts receivable plus inventory, minus accounts payable. These are the "float" funds required to keep the business operating from day to day. By reducing the amount of accounts receivable and inventory or extending the payment terms on accounts payable, you can achieve a ready source of zero-cost cash. Some of the actions you can take to access these funds discussed next.

Accounts Receivable

- *Automate collection record keeping.* Tracking of collection calls, including who was reached, when the call occurred, and what was promised, is a time-consuming chore that is highly subject to error. By obtaining a computerized database that is linked to a company's accounts receivable records, the collections staff can increase its collection efficiency greatly.
- *Bill recurring invoices early.* If a customer subscribes to a long-term service or maintenance contract, it can be billed slightly earlier in hopes of receiving payment sooner.
- *Change the terms of commission payments.* The sales staff should be paid commissions based on cash received from customers rather than on sales made to them. By doing so, the sales staff has a vested interest in finding creditworthy customers and in collecting from them.
- *Encourage ACH payments.* If a customer has a long-term relationship with the company, request that it set up ACH payments so that payments are wired directly into the company's bank account, thereby avoiding any mail float.
- *Encourage credit card payments.* If billings are relatively small, note on the invoices that the company accepts a variety of credit card payments so that customers will be encouraged to use this approach to accelerate cash flow.
- *Factor account receivable.* Arrange with a lender to pay the company at the time of billing, using accounts receivable as collateral.
- *Grant early payment discounts.* Offer discounts to customers if they pay within a few days of receiving the invoice.
- *Install lockboxes.* Set up bank lockboxes near customer sites, and have them mail their payments to the lockboxes. By doing so, you can greatly reduce the mail float associated with the payments.
- *Stratify collections.* Stratify accounts receivable by size, and assign the bulk of the collection staff's time to the largest items so that the full force of the collections department is brought to bear on those items yielding the largest amount of cash.
- *Tighten credit.* Closely review the payment histories of existing customers, and run more intensive checks on new customers, thereby cutting back on the amount of bad debt.

Inventory

- *Consolidate storage locations.* If there are many warehouses, the company probably is storing the same inventory items in multiple locations. By consolidating storage locations, some of this duplication can be eliminated.
- *Install a materials planning system.* A material requirements planning (MRP) system will allow a company to determine exactly what material it needs and by what date. These systems typically result in massive drops in inventory levels and the elimination of overpurchases.
- *Install just-in-time (JIT) manufacturing techniques.* Many manufacturing practices are included in the general JIT concept, such as rapid setup times, cell-based manufacturing, and minimal production runs. These techniques require minimal work-in-process (WIP) inventory and also generate far less scrap.
- *Maintain accurate bills of material.* It is impossible to create a working MRP or JIT system without knowing exactly what parts are required to manufacture a product. Consequently, a bill of material accuracy rate of at least 98% is the foundation for other initiatives that will greatly reduce inventory levels.
- *Return parts to suppliers.* If parts are not needed, return them to suppliers for cash or credit.
- *Stock fewer finished goods.* The distribution of product sales follows a bell curve. Where the bulk of all sales are concentrated into only a few inventory items, someone should review periodically the inventory items that rarely sell to see if they should be stocked at all.
- *Store subassemblies rather than finished goods.* Inventory subassemblies potentially can be configured into a multitude of finished goods whereas a finished good must be sold "as is." Consequently, a strategy to keep inventory at the sub-assembly level until the last possible moment will result in fewer stock-keeping units (SKUs) and therefore a smaller inventory investment.

Accounts Payable

- *Avoid prepayments.* If a supplier insists that the company make prepayments on various goods or services, try to reduce the amount of the prepayments or spread out the payment intervals, thereby reducing the up-front cash commitment.
- *Extend payments a reasonable amount.* Suppliers typically do not start collection efforts on an overdue invoice until a number of days have passed beyond the invoice due date. A company can take advantage of this grace period by judiciously extending payment dates for a few additional days. However, this strategy can result in lower reported credit levels by credit reporting agencies and certainly will not endear the company to its suppliers.
- *Negotiate longer payment terms.* It might be possible to negotiate longer payment terms with suppliers, although this might involve offsetting terms, such as larger order commitments or higher product prices.
- *Use a charge card to extend payments.* Many suppliers allow their invoices to be paid with credit cards. By doing so on the payment due date and then waiting to pay the credit card bill until the cycle closing date for the credit card, payment terms can be extended substantially.

Although you can implement this entire checklist to break free a large amount of cash, there are a number of issues to be considered before doing so. For example, tightening credit might run counter to an overall corporate strategy to accept higher bad debt losses in exchange for greater sales to high-risk customers. Similarly, unilaterally extending payment terms to a key supplier can damage the operating relationship between the business partners, perhaps resulting in higher prices charged by the supplier or a lower shipment priority. As another example, the decision to stock fewer finished goods can damage customer service, especially when a company has built its reputation on having a wide range of inventory items available for customers at all times. Further, a company in a low-margin business may be unable to factor its receivables or accept credit card payments, because the resulting credit fees will eat into its margins too much. Thus, the management team can implement the preceding suggestions only after due consideration of their impact on overall company strategy.

The inventory reduction decision is covered in more detail in the next section.

Inventory Reduction Decision

A truly cost-conscious CEO who wants also to increase cash flow will pursue continual reductions in inventory aggressively, by any means possible, since this potentially can free up a considerable quantity of cash and eliminate the expenses associated with inventory carrying costs. However, there are other issues to consider before running rampant with ongoing inventory reductions.

First, consider the classes of inventory involved, and target only those inventory types that will not have an adverse affect on other company operations. For example, a reduction in finished goods inventory can severely impact sales, since customers may purchase from stock only, not wanting to wait for something to be ordered or produced. This is particularly important for service-intensive retail businesses, such as those that claim to have *all* parts on hand, *all* the time. Costs also may go up in this situation if lower stocks are kept on hand, because the company may be forced to pay overnight shipping fees to obtain needed stock for customer orders. However, finished goods inventory levels still can be reduced by tracking usage trends by product and reducing safety stock levels for those items that show declining sales trends.

WIP inventory can be an enormous working capital burden for companies with inefficient manufacturing processes, but large inventory reductions can wreak havoc in this area unless managed properly. It may be necessary to maintain large WIP balances in front of bottleneck production operations, since the cost of losing bottleneck production may be higher than the cost of the buffering inventory. Also, in the absence of a proper shop floor production system, large quantities of WIP may be the only way to run the manufacturing process with any semblance of order. Consequently, it is better first to review the manufacturing operations in detail to see where there are legitimately excessive WIP quantities and then install manufacturing systems, such as manufacturing resources planning (MRP II) or JIT systems that can be used to reduce WIP levels gradually as the manufacturing process becomes more highly structured and easier to manage. Also, be aware that old piles of WIP frequently disguise large proportions of obsolete or out-of-specification parts that no one wants to discard. Consequently, an inventory write-down is a common result of reductions in the WIP inventory area.

Raw materials is one of the best areas in which to implement an inventory reduction. This is where the full force of an MRP II or JIT implementation is felt, clearly exposing any inventory items that are not currently required for planned production needs. However, this analysis may reveal a number of raw material items that are obsolete and therefore have minimal or reduced value, resulting in a significant write-down in the inventory valuation. Alternatively, it may be necessary to accept significant restocking fees to convince a supplier to take back unwanted goods. It might be useful to have the purchasing staff create a list of which unused products can be returned to suppliers as well as the restocking fees that will be charged, so you can have a general idea of the costs involved with this form of inventory reduction.

There are several issues to be aware of when attempting to reduce inventories. First, as just noted, attempts to reduce inventory without proper consideration of the net impact on other parts of the business, such as in reduced customer service, actually may *increase* costs. Second, there is a limit to how much inventory can be squeezed out of a company without an offsetting investment in manufacturing planning systems whose efficiencies will help drive the inventory reduction. Thus, inventory reduction is not an easy decision; cutbacks require careful consideration of offsetting costs as well as their impact on other parts of the business.

Fixed Asset Lease versus Buy Decisions

In a leasing situation, the company pays a lessor for the use of equipment that is owned by the lessor. Under the terms of this arrangement, the company pays a monthly fee; the lessor records the asset on its books and takes the associated depreciation expense while also undertaking to pay all property taxes and maintenance fees. The lessor typically takes back the asset at the end of the lease term, unless the company wishes to pay a fee at the end of the agreement period to buy the residual value of the asset and record it on the company's books as an asset.

A leasing arrangement tends to be rather expensive for the lessee, since it is paying for the interest cost, profit, taxes, maintenance, and decline in value of the asset. However, it would have had to pay for all these costs except the lessor's profit and the interest cost if it had bought the asset, so this can be an appealing option, especially for the use of those assets that tend to degrade quickly in value or usability and that therefore would need to be replaced at the end of the leasing period anyway.

The cost of a lease tends to be high, since the number of variables included in the lease calculation (e.g., down payment, interest rate, asset residual value, and trade-in value) makes it very difficult for the lessee to determine the true cost of what it is obtaining. Consequently, when using leasing as the financing option of choice, be careful to review the individual costs that roll up into the total lease cost, probably using a net present value analysis to ensure that the overall expenditure is reasonable (see Chapter 8, Capital Budgeting).

Payables

You should be aware of the early payment discount decisions being made by the controller, since these can impact the timing of cash flows. Of more importance in terms of their overall impact are the decisions to centralize payments with a payment factory and whether to install spend management practices. These topics are covered in this section.

Early Payment Discount Decisions

Some suppliers note on their invoices that a discount will be granted to the customer if it pays the invoice early. An example of such an offer is "2/10 N/30," which stands for "take 2% off the price if you pay within 10 days, or pay the full amount in 30 days." The basic calculation for calculating the savings from these offers is:

$$\frac{\text{Discount lost}}{\text{Dollar proceeds usable by not taking discount}}$$

$$\times \frac{360}{\text{Number of days can use money by not taking discount}}$$

Example

The Columbia Rafting Company has an opportunity to take a 1% discount on an invoice for a new raft if it makes the payment in 10 days. The invoice is for $12,000 and normally is payable in 30 days. The calculation is:

$$\frac{\$120}{\$11,880} \times \frac{360}{20}$$

$$1.01\% \times 18 = 18.2\% \text{ Interest rate on the discount}$$

The 18.02% interest rate on the early payment discount in the example probably makes it an attractive deal. However, also consider the availability of cash before taking such an offer. For example, what if there are no funds available, or if the corporate line of credit cannot be extended to make the early payment? Even if the cash is available, but there is a risk of cash shortfall in the near term, you may not be able to take such an offer. In short, no matter how attractive an early payment discount may be, near-term cash shortages can interfere with taking an early payment discount.

Payment Factory Decisions

In a typical accounts payable environment, a company allows its subsidiaries to manage their own payables processes, payments, and banking relationships. The results are higher transaction costs and banking fees, since each location uses its own staff and has little transaction volume with which to negotiate reduced banking fees.

An improvement on this situation is the *payment factory*, which is a centralized payables and payment processing center. It is essentially a subset of an enterprise resources planning (ERP) system that is targeted at payables. It features complex software with many interfaces, since it must handle incoming payment information in many data formats, workflow management of payment approvals, a rules engine to determine the lowest-cost method of payment, and links to multiple banking systems.

Key payment factory benefits include a stronger negotiating position with the company's fewer remaining banks, better visibility into funding needs and liquidity management, and improved control over payment timing.

The payment factory is especially effective when the payables systems of multinational subsidiaries are centralized, since cross-border banking fees can be reduced significantly. For example, a payment factory can offset automatically payments due between company subsidiaries, which results in smaller cash transfers and similarly reduced foreign exchange charges, wiring costs, and lifting fees (a fee charged by the bank receiving a payment) while also routing payments through in-country accounts to avoid these international fees.

There are several problems with payment factories, such as the million-dollar cost of the software and gaining the cooperation of the various subsidiaries that no longer will have control over their payments.

Spend Management Decisions

Spend management systems allow a company to monitor its expenditures and potentially save a great deal of money through improved purchasing. Using these systems, companies can analyze their expenditures in a number of ways: by commodity, supplier, business unit, and so on. They then summarize this information for centralized procurement negotiations with suppliers, thereby reducing costs. Spend management suppliers usually add contract management capabilities and even set up electronic supplier catalogs so that users can conduct online ordering with a predefined set of suppliers. They also impose better controls over spending, since their systems require access passwords, approval cycles, contract compliance alerts, and supplier performance measurements.

However, these systems are extremely expensive to install and maintain. Some suggestions for creating a low-budget spend management system are listed next.

■ *Identify unauthorized purchases with exception reports.* The reason for centralizing procurement contracts is to negotiate lower prices in exchange for higher purchasing volumes, so anyone purchasing from an unauthorized supplier is reducing a company's ability to rein in its costs. To identify these people, create a table of approved suppliers and match it against the vendor ledger for each period, yielding a report that lists how much was spent with various unauthorized suppliers. It is also useful to record in an empty purchasing or payables field the name of the requisitioning person, who can be tracked down and admonished for incorrect purchasing practices.

- *Impose a penalty system.* People resist centralization, especially when it involves eliminating their favorite suppliers. Although penalties may be considered a coercive approach to resolving the problem, the imposition of a graduated penalty scale will eliminate unauthorized spending rapidly. For example, a department might incur a $100 penalty for one unauthorized expenditure, $1,000 for the next, and $10,000 for the next.
- *Restrict procurement cards to specific suppliers.* If there is a procurement card system in place, it might be possible to restrict purchases to specific suppliers, thereby achieving centralized purchasing without any central oversight of the process. If there is no procurement card system, consider obtaining a credit card from each designated supplier and restricting purchases to those cards.
- *Require officer-level approval of all contracts.* Department and division managers love to retain control over supplier relationships by negotiating their own deals with local suppliers. By enforcing a corporate-wide policy that all purchasing contracts be countersigned by a corporate officer, contract copies can be collected in one place for easier examination by a central purchasing staff.
- *Add granularity to the chart of accounts.* To gain a better knowledge of costs, consider altering the chart of accounts to subdivide expenses by individual department and go a step further by adding subcodes that track costs at an additional level of detail. For example, if the existing account code is 5020 for the travel expense account and the revised code is 5020-01 to track travel costs for just the engineering department, consider adding a set of subcodes, such as 5020-01-XX, to track more detailed expenditures within the travel category, such as airfare (code 5020-01-01), hotels (code 5020-01-02), and rental cards (code 5020-01-03). This approach requires careful definition of spending categories and can result in data entry errors if there are too many subcategories of expenses. Also, it will not be of much use if reports cannot be created to interpret and present this extra level of expense information properly.

These suggestions will not result in a seamless in-house spend management system. However, they will yield somewhat greater control over expenses and more visibility into the nature of a company's expenditures.

Debt

Acquiring Debt Decisions

The CEO should regularly review the need to acquire more debt as part of an overall funding strategy that can include other forms of financing, such as reducing working capital requirements or conducting an equity offering. Consider the next factors as part of the debt decision.

- *Existing loan covenants.* A legal agreement for an existing loan may allow no further debt until the current debt is either paid off or reduced to a specific level. Covenants also may limit the debt/equity ratio (see next item), making it impossible to obtain more debt without first adding equity.
- *Current debt level in relation to equity.* Lenders will look askance at additional requests for debt if there is not a counterbalancing amount of equity. A company with a high debt/equity ratio is likely to be told to find more equity before being granted additional debt.
- *Debt due dates.* Try not to obtain new debt having a due date identical to that of existing debt, so there will be less risk of having to refinance large amounts of debt at the same time.
- *Business cycles.* Some businesses have natural revenue peaks and valleys that greatly reduce their ability to pay loans during slow periods. This type of business needs a higher proportion of equity in order to avoid the risk of loan defaults.
- *Product cycles.* If a company's product lines are aging and facing cancellation, it might have little ability to pay off loans that come due after the projected termination date of the products.
- *Net operating loss (NOL) carryforwards.* If a business has large NOLs that it can use to offset its income, it will have no immediate use for the tax deductibility of interest, although using debt still can delay the use of NOLs into later years.
- *Need for a borrowing reserve.* Always plan to have more debt available through a line of credit than is actually needed, so unforeseen cash requirements can be handled easily.

Realistically, a company will be stymied more by the first two bullet points than the remaining ones. If there is too much debt already on the balance sheet, or if legal provisions of existing loans are too restrictive, there will be no way to obtain more debt in the short term. The remaining bullet points are more advisory in nature; you should take them into account, but in reality you may have to take any deal offered if obtaining debt in the short term is a critical priority.

Refinancing Decisions

You should review the cost of all types of company debt regularly to see if it is too expensive and therefore worthy of refinancing. Although this may seem like a simple matter, there are several issues to take into consideration. First, the company may have a very tight relationship with a single lender who has extended all of the company's debt to it; if so, paying off the most expensive loan in the debt portfolio will not endear this critical lender to the company. Under this scenario, it may not even be possible to refinance a single loan within the portfolio, because the lender has cross-collateralized all of the company's assets on the various loan documents. Because no collateral is available to secure a loan with a different lender, the company can refinance the debt only by shifting the entire loan package to a new lender.

Another consideration is when the debt you want to replace has a fixed interest rate, but the least expensive replacement debt carries a variable interest rate. The decision to switch from the security of a fixed rate to a situation where the rate could increase substantially should be subject to considerable debate. You can reduce the risk of a rapid rate increase by negotiating an annual cap on any rate increases during the term of the new loan or by entering into an interest rate swap to convert the variable interest rate into a fixed interest rate.

The decision to adopt a variable rate loan frequently is driven by the expected loan payoff date, such that maximum interest rate increases still would not exceed the current fixed loan rate by the time the loan should be paid off.

Example

The International Pickle Company has a long-term loan that carries a 10% fixed interest rate. The company expects to pay off this loan in five years. In the meantime, the company has been offered a 6% variable-rate loan with an annual interest rate cap increase of 1.5% that would not take effect until the end of each year. This means that, even if interest rates skyrocket over the next five years, the new loan still would be less expensive than the existing loan until the end of the fourth year of the loan. Based on this analysis, the CEO decides to accept the new variable-rate loan agreement and uses the proceeds to pay off the company's fixed-rate loan.

Convertible Security Issuance Decisions

A convertible security is a bond that can be converted into common stock. The common stock price at which the bond can be converted is based on the conversion ratio, which is the ratio of the number of shares that can be purchased with each bond. For example, if a $1,000 bond has a conversion ratio of 10, it can be converted into ten shares, which translates into a share price of $100. This does not mean that the holder of a bond will immediately convert the shares, however; that will happen only when the market price of the stock equals or exceeds the amount indicated by the conversion ratio. If the market price of the common stock exceeds the price indicated by the conversion ratio, the price of the bond also will rise, since its value, based on its convertibility, is now greater than its price based on the stream of future interest payments from the company in payment for the bond.

A convertible security is worthy of much attention by the CEO if a company does not want to pay back the underlying principal on its bonds. This is most common in a high-growth situation where all cash will be needed for the foreseeable future. Also, by converting debt to equity, a company can improve its debt/equity ratio, which will improve relations with lenders while also eliminating the need to pay interest on the bonds that no longer exist. Further, you can make a debt offering look more attractive to investors by giving them some upside potential if the common stock subsequently increases in value, which should result in a reduction in the interest rate on the debt. This is particularly important if market conditions otherwise would necessitate a high interest rate. Finally, a company can convert a group of existing debt holders into a group of shareholders, which means that it has a (presumably) friendly and long-term group of investors now holding its stock. The only downsides of this approach are that the increased number of shares will reduce the earnings per share and that control will be spread over a larger group of investors, which might weaken the stake of a majority owner.

Disclosure Reporting Decisions

An established company with a mature business model discloses a different set of performance metrics to investors and analysts than does a newer company that is on a more rapid growth path. The CEO must decide at what point the types of disclosures change to match the current or expected business model. For example, a mature company should emphasize the disclosure of such basic financial performance information as gross and net margins and cash flow as well as such basic operational issues as customer retention, capacity utilization, and revenue per employee. Conversely, a company on a rapid growth path should place more emphasis in its disclosures on the level of expenditures for research and development and marketing as well as sales from new products, patents granted, and share of market.

Equity

One of the most important and far-reaching of all CEO decisions is whether to obtain debt or equity financing, since high debt levels can imperil a firm's existence, and additional equity may reduce the return to existing shareholders. This topic and others are covered in this section.

Debt versus Equity Funding Decisions

Debt is almost always a less expensive source of funding than equity, because investors expect significant returns on their investments while the interest cost of debt is tax-deductible, rendering debt less expensive. Furthermore, during the usual periods of inflation, a company pays back its debt with less expensive dollars, making it an even less expensive source of funding. However, there are several other issues to consider when determining whether to pursue debt or equity as the next source of funding.

The first issue is that the senior management team or the company owners may be uncomfortable with the prospect of obtaining more debt, no matter how available or inexpensive it may be. This happens most frequently in privately owned firms with later-generation owners who are most concerned with maintaining their long-term source of income. It is less common with entrepreneurs who are willing to take more risks or with public companies where you are allowed to balance the risk of debt default with the reduced cost of using more debt than equity.

Even if the owners and managers are willing to obtain more debt, the lenders might not be willing to provide it. This problem arises when a company has poor or highly variable cash flows, is already highly leveraged, or has a history either of not paying off its debts in a timely manner or of violating its loan covenants. If so, the company probably will have to turn to an equity offering with incentive clauses (see the next section).

Even if lenders are ready and willing to issue more debt, there might be no collateral left on the balance sheet to assuage their levels of anxiety about repayment risk. If so, the company might be forced to accept a high interest rate, an early payoff date, or highly restrictive covenants, or might allow the lender to take a junior position on any corporate assets. If these options do not work for the lender, once again the company will be forced to shift to an equity offering.

It is evident from this discussion that debt is generally the preferred source of funding, with the CEO only seriously considering the procurement of equity when it is either impractical to obtain more debt or if doing so would put the company at serious risk of defaulting on its loans.

Type of Equity Offering Decisions

You can issue two types of equity: common or preferred stock. The terms of common stock typically are laid down in the articles of incorporation and include specific terms required by the state in which the company is incorporated. You normally would consider a common stock offering only when several circumstances exist. First, the existing shareholders must not be concerned about a dilution in their ownership interests through this new issuance (unless the new shares are being sold to them, in which case ownership percentages will change only among the existing shareholders). This is a major concern in cases where the bulk of a company's stock is owned by a small number of individuals.

The second circumstance is that the company's lenders are becoming uncomfortable with a high level of debt and wish to balance it with more equity. This pressure also could come from the board of directors, which may not want to run the risk of default if there are large loans outstanding.

The CEO generally decides to sell common stock only when all other sources of less expensive funds have been exhausted, because shareholders typically have a much higher expectation of return on investment than is the case for other fund providers.

A variation on a common stock offering is *preferred stock*. This equity instrument can come in a variety of flavors, including a fixed or variable interest rate that may or may not be cumulative, allow conversion to common stock, have the ability to be called by the company at any time or at fixed intervals—the range of possible features is endless. The exact terms of a preferred stock issuance should be tailored to the perceived needs of the pool of potential investors. For example, if a company's stock has a history of being highly variable, investors may want the option to convert it to common stock in order to take advantage of a possible increase in the stock price at a later date.

Onerous terms also can be added to a preferred stock issuance in order to ensure that investors will accept the offering at an acceptable price. For example, its terms can state that, in the event of a company sale, the preferred shareholders will receive 100% of their investment back before common shareholders receive anything. In order to protect their rights in this regard, the preferred shareholders also may have an override vote on any contemplated mergers, acquisitions, or significant asset sales. These additional terms might seem oner-ous, but they can ensure a high price for the stock.

Example

The Xtreme Running Shoe Company is attempting to obtain additional debt financing, but the company's lenders are concerned about the debt/equity ratio and insist on an additional equity infusion prior to granting any additional loans. Unfortunately, it is a bear market, and the company's valuation has been driven lower than usual, so any sale of common stock would result in an excessive degree of dilution for the existing shareholders in relation to the amount of equity obtained. Accordingly, the company issues a special class of preferred stock, containing an above-market interest rate on annual dividend payments as well as a guaranteed conversion at the investors' option to common stock at a favorable rate in five years' time. Thus, potential investors are willing to pay more for the stock, which gives them short-term dividend income plus a poten-tial equity kicker in the medium term.

Dividend Issuance Decisions

The decision to issue dividends requires consideration of many issues. Consider that investors prefer to see a *steady and reliable* stream of dividends. Thus, a well-mean-ing initial dividend issuance could spark calls from investors who expect to keep seeing it. If so, the board of directors might feel obligated to continue the payments, even if the company needs the money for other purposes.

Another issue is the impact of loan restrictions on dividends. Many lenders allow no dividends at all as part of their loan requirements or at least no increase in the preexisting level of dividends. Their reasoning is obvious, since otherwise a com-pany might take out a loan to pay its shareholders, thereby leaving fewer assets for the lender to attach in the event of a bankruptcy. Thus, the lending institution has a major impact on the decision to issue dividends and typically precludes an issuance when a company's debt load is so heavy that lenders would begin to restrict divi-dends in any event.

Another issue is that dividend payments represent a reduction of retained earn-ings. When dividends are paid, equity is reduced, which will create a higher debt/equity ratio. If a lender has imposed a maximum debt/equity ratio as part of a loan agreement, it is possible that a dividend issuance will place the company in a state of noncompliance with its loan covenants.

Another concern with the initial declaration of dividends is that it may cause cur-rent investors to sell their shares. Some investors prefer to buy the shares of compa-nies that pour all of their excess funds into growth while others look for a steady source of income from dividends. When a company initially starts paying dividends, it might experience the sudden departure of its growth-oriented investor base in fa-vor of a new group of income-oriented investors, which may cause the stock price to fluctuate more than normal until the new group of investors is in place.

Another consideration regarding the dividend issuance decision is a company's ability to obtain debt. If it has ready access to credit markets, corporate management will be more likely to issue dividends, since the company is reasonably assured of obtaining replacement funding. Conversely, if credit sources are scarce, a company will be more inclined to hoard its cash in order to provide a buffer for any future financial problems; this leaves less cash available for a dividend.

A key concern is cash flow. If a company has an extremely unstable cash flow, perhaps shifting from cash drains in some months to major inflows during others, a potentially long-term obligation such as creating an expectation to issue dividends is a bad idea. Even if there is enough cash on hand to make the payment, the company might need the cash in the short term and thus cannot afford to obligate it.

From a taxation perspective, dividends are not deductible as an expense, as opposed to interest payments on debt. This makes equity a more expensive form of funding than debt by the amount of a corporation's incremental tax rate.

A reason in favor of issuing dividends is that the Internal Revenue Service (IRS) will penalize a company for accumulating an excessive amount of earnings. The IRS considers accumulated earnings of less than $150,000 to be sufficient for the working capital needs of service businesses, such as accounting, engineering, architecture, and consulting firms. It considers accumulations of anything under $250,000 to be sufficient for most other types of businesses. A company can argue that it needs a substantially larger amount of accumulated earnings if it can prove that it has specific, definite, and feasible plans that will require the use of the funds within the business. Another valid argument is that a company needs a sufficient amount of accumulated earnings to buy back the company's stock that is held by a deceased shareholder's estate. If these conditions are not apparent, the IRS will declare the accumulated earnings to be taxable.

Perhaps the chief reason for avoiding a dividend is a high-growth situation where a company must pour all available funds into its working capital in order to sustain its rate of growth in new customer orders. In such cases, the rapidly increasing value of the firm will be reflected in an increased stock price that should more than compensate investors for any lost dividends. Alternatively, if a company has minimal growth prospects, a better use of the funds might be to return them to investors in the form of dividends.

An alternative to a dividend issuance is to buy back shares from investors. By accepting this buyout, investors probably will (depending on their circumstances) claim a long-term capital gain on the transaction, which is taxed at a lower rate than dividend income. This approach is especially good for situations where a company has obtained a temporary increase in its cash flows but does not necessarily have prospects for future cash flows of a similar size and so does not want to set investor expectations for a long series of dividend payments.

Example

The Breakout Software Company, a maker of prison databases, has two components to its business, which are long-term database subscriptions and software

(continued)

(*continued*)

consulting. The database portion of the business generates a steady stream of cash flows that can be predicted with great reliability for the next few years. The consulting business, however, is tied to short-term contracts and so results in highly variable cash flows. Based on this information, the CEO recommends to the board of directors a dividend that is based on a percentage of the subscription cash flows while recommending a stock buyback that is based on the short-term cash flows from the consulting business. This dual approach links the appropriate dividend policy to the nature of the firm's underlying cash flows.

Product Elimination Decisions

Pareto analysis holds that 80% of the activity in a given situation is caused by 20% of the population. This rule is strongly applicable to the profitability of a company's products, where 80% of the total profit is generated by 20% of the products. Of the remaining 80% of the product population, it is reasonable to assume that some make no profit at all. Consequently, the CEO should mandate periodically a review of all company product offerings to determine which products should be withdrawn from the marketplace. This is a valuable analysis for a number of reasons:

- *Complexity.* In general, too many products lead to an excessive degree of system complexity within a company in order to support those products.
- *Excessive inventory.* Each inventory item usually contains some unique parts, which require additional storage space in the warehouse as well as a working capital investment in those parts, and the risk of eventual obsolescence. Further, the presence of unique parts in a product may be the sole reason why the purchasing department continues to deal with the supplier; canceling the product allows the company to reduce the number of suppliers it uses, thereby gaining greater volume discounts with the remaining suppliers.
- *Engineering time.* If there are changes to products, the engineering staff must update the bill of material and labor routing records, all of which take time.
- *Marketing literature.* The marketing department usually maintains a unique set of literature for each product, which requires periodic updating and reprinting.
- *Servicing cost.* The customer support staff must be trained in the unique features of each product, so they can adequately answer customer questions.
- *Warranty cost.* Some products have a considerable warranty cost, possibly due to design flaws or inadequate materials that require sizeable warranty reserves.

When conducting a product withdrawal analysis, do not assume that some expenses will be eliminated along with a product. Instead, an expense may have been allocated to a product but still will remain once the product is gone. For example, the canceling of a single product is unlikely to result in the actual elimination of a customer support position. Instead, customer support overhead now must be paid for by the smaller remaining pool of products. Thus, it is extremely important to include only direct costs in a product withdrawal analysis and to exclude any overhead allocations. To be certain that a product cancellation is not merely shifting overhead costs elsewhere, it is useful to develop before-and-after pro forma financial statements to see if there is really an improvement in profitability resulting from the cancellation.

As noted, only direct costs should be used in calculating the profitability of a product for purposes of the cancellation decision. This results in the next formula:

Standard list price (1)
− Commission (2)
− Buyer discounts (3)
− Material cost (4)
− Scrap cost (5)
− Outsourced processing (6)
− Inventory carrying cost (7)
− Packaging cost (8)
− Unreimbursed shipping cost (9)
− Warranty cost (10)
= Profit (loss)

Comments regarding this formula are presented next, and match the numbers next to each line item in the formula.

1. *Standard list price.* If a product has a number of prices based on volume discounts or other criteria, it may be necessary to create a model using the costs itemized in the model to determine the breakeven price below which no profit is earned. The result could be a decision not necessarily to cancel the product but to not sell it at less than a certain discounted price, below which it makes no profit.
2. *Commission.* Salespeople may earn a commission on product sales. If these commissions are clearly identifiable with a specific product and will not be earned if the product is not sold, include the commission in the product cost.
3. *Buyer discount.* The inclusion of buyer discounts in the calculation calls for some judgment. It should not be included if discounts are rare events and make up only a small dollar amount. If discounts are common, calculate an average discount amount and deduct it from the standard list price.
4. *Material cost.* This is the cost of any materials included in the manufacture of a product.
5. *Scrap cost.* If a standard amount of scrap can be expected as part of the production process that is specifically identifiable with a product, include this cost in the profitability calculation.
6. *Outsourced processing.* If any production work related to the product is completed by an outside entity, the cost of this work should be included in the calculation on the grounds that the entire cost of the outsourced processing will be eliminated along with the product.
7. *Inventory carrying cost.* This should be only the incremental inventory carrying cost, which is usually only the interest cost of the company's investment in inventory specifically related to the product. It should not include the cost of warehouse storage space or insurance, since both of these costs are fixed in the short term and are very unlikely to change as a result of the elimination of a single

product. For example, if a company leases a warehouse, it is obligated to make monthly lease payments irrespective of the amount of storage space being used by inventory used for a specific product.

8. *Packaging cost.* Include the cost of any packaging materials used to contain and ship the product, but only if those materials cannot be used for other products.

9. *Unreimbursed shipping cost.* If the company is absorbing the cost of shipments to customers, include this cost, net of volume discounts from the shipper.

10. *Warranty cost.* Although normally a small expense on a per-unit basis, an improperly designed product or one that includes low-quality parts may have an extremely high average warranty cost. If significant, this cost should be included in the profitability analysis.

In addition, note that production labor costs are *not* included in the calculation. The reason is that production labor rarely varies directly with the level of production; instead, a fixed number of workers will be in the production area every day, irrespective of the level of work performed. Thus, the cancellation of a product will not impact the number of workers employed. However, if a product cancellation will result in the verifiable and immediate elimination of labor positions, the incremental cost of the eliminated labor should be included in the calculation.

A product that is clearly unprofitable still might be needed by a key customer who orders other, more profitable products from the company. If so, combine the profits of all sales made to that customer to ensure that the net combined profit is sufficiently high to warrant the retention of the unprofitable product. If this is not the case, consider canceling the unprofitable product and negotiating with the customer for a price reduction on other products in order to retain the customer.

Another cancellation issue is the presence of dependent products. *Ancillary products* are supplements to the main product that provide additional profits to the overall product line. For example, the profit margin on a cell phone may be negative, but there may be a sufficiently high profit level on extra cell phone batteries, car chargers, headsets, and phone covers to more than offset the loss on the initial product sale. In these cases, the margins on all ancillary products should be included in the profitability analysis.

Finally, the frequency of product profitability reviews will depend greatly on product life cycles. If products have very short life cycles, sales levels will drop rapidly once products enter the decline phase of their life cycles, potentially leaving the company with large stocks of excess inventory. In these situations, it is critical to conduct frequent reviews in order to keep a company's investment in working capital from becoming excessive.

There are also two nonfinancial reasons for retaining unprofitable products that must be considered before canceling a product. First, a company may want to offer to customers a full range of product offerings so they can purchase anything they need from the company without having to go to a competitor. Doing this may require the retention of a product whose absence would otherwise create a hole in the corporate product line. Second, it may be necessary to offer a product in a specific market niche in order to keep competitors from entering a market that the company considers to be crucial to its ongoing viability.

Step Cost Reductions

A key decision is whether to incur a step cost. This is an incremental fixed cost, such as the creation of a new overhead position, that will permanently increase a company's cost base. Adding such costs may be required if the current staff is simply unable to address the needs of existing sales and production levels, and needs the help. Nonetheless, you should review this decision in light of its impact on profitability. It is entirely possible that profits are maximized *just prior to* the incurrence of a step cost, since it may require significant additional sales to offset the step cost.

There are several factors to consider when mulling over this decision. One is the sales point at which profits will match the level just before the incurrence of the step cost.

Example

A printing plant is experiencing a ramp-up in sales, and its CEO decides to invest in a new press to meet the demand. The press is leased, and costs increase by $250,000 per year. Gross margins are 30%, so the plant must generate $833,333 per year in additional sales just to cover the step cost represented by the new press.

The printing plant's other departments can support incremental new sales of only an additional $500,000 without the incurrence of even more step costs, so it is impossible to achieve the $833,333 sales level required to pay for the printing press.

Yet another factor to consider is the stability of incremental new sales required to pay for a step cost. To continue with the preceding example, the CEO should not lease the press if the incremental sales driving the decision are for a short-term deal with a firm expiration date or with an uncertain future that is not supported by a long-term purchase order. Consequently, you should take into consideration the market served by the company, the level of competition, potential price wars, and related factors before deciding to incur a step cost.

The printing press example is a major step costing decision. However, most step costs are much more minor, with small jumps in cost that have a minimal incremental impact on the bottom line. Nonetheless, these additions gradually eat away at profits over time. To gain control over them, set up elaborate approval mechanisms for any step costs incurred outside of the normal budgeting process. For these costs included in the budget, the financial analysis team will have more time to conduct an analysis of why each step cost is needed, how improved efficiencies might avoid the cost, whether to outsource rather than incur the cost, and so on. The step costing decision is one of the most crucial to a company on an ongoing basis and therefore deserves a substantial amount of management attention.

Temporary Labor Decisions

In many organizations, particularly those in the service industry, the largest expense by far is for payroll. Consequently, the CEO should be deeply involved in decisions to alter the size of the workforce. This is a particular concern in areas where the business is highly seasonal, requires experienced personnel, operates under a union agreement, or is subject to burdensome state unemployment taxes. Consider these key decision points:

- *Seasonality.* If a business has a highly variable sales season, this is a key indicator in favor of using temporary labor during the peak season, leaving only a small core of seasoned employees for the remainder of the year. A classic example is the amusement park, where temporary staffers know in advance that they will be employed only for a few months. However, this is not such a simple decision when the experience level required of the staff is relatively high, since it may be difficult to obtain new help with the requisite knowledge base when sales ramp up again. In such situations, consider level-loading the production facility, so that it produces the same amount of products every month, irrespective of short-term sales needs; this presents separate inventory management issues that also must be evaluated. If this is not an option, a corporate investment in a significant training program to ramp up new employees quickly may be a reasonable alternative.
- *Technical skill requirements.* Temporary labor agencies have available pools of very experienced, technically capable people who can step into almost any position. Nonetheless, a strategically critical position should be brought in house and provided with a proper benefits package, on the grounds that the company wants to retain the person in that position for as long as possible. In this case, cost issues are secondary to retention.
- *Turnover rate of existing in-house staff.* There may be no decision to make between the use of temporary versus in-house full-time staff if the full-time staff turns over with great regularity. This is a common problem in low-skilled, highly repetitive environments, such as base-level positions on the factory floor.
- *Unemployment taxes.* If a company constantly hires and fires staff as it experiences rapid changes in its required staffing levels, it will experience increasing state unemployment rates. State unemployment agencies annually review the amount of unemployment benefits made to a company's former employees and alter the company's prospective tax rate for the next year to make the company foot the bill for these payments. If a company creates a large pool of former employees who are drawing unemployment benefits, it is setting itself up for an increase of potentially several percent in its payroll taxes.
- *Union agreements.* A labor force represented by a union can greatly restrict a company's ability to lay off the regular workforce. This may lead to the extensive use of temporary employees for short-term requirements rather than running the risk of hiring more staff into the union who will be difficult to let go. The union may suggest giving its members high-cost overtime rather than bringing in temporary employees, thereby increasing their total pay. However, quality problems can arise after employees work too many hours, making this a choice of diminishing returns.

Example

The CEO of SecureTech Consulting must decide whether to bring in temporary labor for a government system security consulting project or to hire the personnel directly. The company has a long tradition of not laying off personnel, so the CEO wants to be sure that these people will be needed after the current government contract has been completed. Accordingly, she talks to the business development vice president to see if the government contract may be extended past its current one-year term. The response is that the government will make a firm commitment for extended funding after it has reviewed the quality of SecureTech's work for the first three months of the contract. Based on this information, the CEO elects to hire personnel through an information technology temporary services agency for the first three months of the contract and pay a small recruiting fee to hire them full time if the contract is extended. If the contract is not extended, she will keep them on temporary status and let them go at the end of the contract.

Example

The CEO of the Stereo Devices Company must make a recommendation about hiring stereo system installers for the crucial holiday season. A good stereo installer with above-average customer skills is considered a key employee worth retaining, but the company can afford to keep only half the installer staff during slower parts of the year. A major consideration is the quality of work provided to customers by the installers, which in the past has proven to be of a lower standard when short-term staff were used. Accordingly, the CEO authorizes a considerable jump in overtime hours allowed during the holiday season by the more experienced staff while hiring only a minimum number of short-term personnel who act as assistants to the more experienced staff.

In both examples, monetary concerns were not the only reasons for the decisions being made. On the contrary, the consulting firm wanted to avoid breaking a company tradition of avoiding layoffs and the installation company wanted the best possible customer service. Less expensive alternatives were available, but both CEOs decided that key company values came first.

Divestiture Decisions

A CEO occasionally considers the divestiture of some portion of the business, for a variety of reasons. For example, the CEO may feel that the company will be worth more to investors if it is broken into pieces, although this reasoning is difficult to prove. Another reason is that the management team is having difficulty allocating capital between various portions of the entity or one business segment is using most of the capital, essentially starving other business segments of funds. The same reasoning can apply to the time of the management team, which may be unreasonably allocated to fix the problems of one business unit; in this case, the management team may be of the opinion that managing a smaller firm will be easier on them and better for the company as a whole. A divestiture may also seem attractive if the management team decides to steer the company in a different strategic direction, which may call for the divestiture of all business segments that are considered to be unrelated to the new direction. In a few cases, a company may even be forced by the government to divest because of antitrust issues. Whatever the initial reason given, you should explore the issue by focusing on the inherent value of the subject business segment to the company, what kind of effort or funding it would take to more fully achieve the benefits of that segment within the company, and what would happen to the company's competitive position if the segment were divested. By reviewing these issues, you should be able to arrive at a defensible conclusion regarding the best action to be taken.

When looking into the size and structure of a divestiture, there are several issues to consider. First, is there a clearly identifiable entity that can be broken away from the company? For example, separate facilities and staff should be clearly identifiable as belonging to the business segment to be divested. Second, the business segment must be one that can operate profitably on its own, which means that it must address a clearly identifiable market, have an appropriate infrastructure for that market, and therefore be able to compete successfully in it.

If these conditions apply, consider the type of structure that the divestiture should follow. For example, the business segment can be spun off to existing shareholders. This is an excellent approach from the perspective of the shareholders, who will avoid an income tax liability by receiving qualified shares in the new entity. A spin-off also allows the management team to avoid the hassle of dealing with a buyer, setting its own terms for the divestiture instead. A variation on the spin-off is a carve-out, where the company makes shares in the new entity available through an initial public offering rather than as a stock distribution to shareholders. Yet another variation is a sale to the management team of the business segment, which typically structures the deal as a leveraged buyout, involving little capital and large amounts of debt. Finally, a divestiture can be accomplished through a sale to another company, although this approach can involve a painful amount of negotiation, legal fees, contingent fees, and a lower price than might be achieved by other means.

Summary

This chapter presented a multitude of financial strategy decisions that a CEO is likely to encounter. It may at first appear that some of these decisions need to be addressed only at long intervals, when there is an immediate need. For example, the decision to offer a particular type of equity is needed only when a new offering is anticipated—right? Not at all. On the contrary, a forward-thinking CEO should review this chapter at regular intervals as part of his ongoing strategic planning process, perhaps as often as on a quarterly basis. By doing so, you can review the background information used to make earlier decisions, test them in light of new information, and incrementally (or substantially) revise the decisions. To use the previous example, you can continually evaluate the types of equity being offered, even if there is no immediate need for new equity, in order to see if the firm's capital structure requires revision. Similarly, a regular review of the inventory liquidation decision is needed to test inventory levels in light of any new manufacturing systems or customer service goals; the early payment discount decision must be reviewed in light of any changes in the corporate cost of capital or short-term cash flow requirements. Similar reasons apply to the review of all other decisions noted in this chapter. In short, the CEO must test all assumptions used to make key financial decisions continually and must revise those decisions accordingly.

CHAPTER 4

Tax Strategy

T he obvious objective of tax strategy is to minimize the amount of cash paid out for taxes. However, this strategy directly conflicts with the general desire to report as much income as possible to shareholders, since more reported income results in more taxes. Only in the case of privately owned firms do these conflicting problems go away, since the owners have no need to impress anyone with their reported level of earnings and would prefer simply to retain as much cash in the company as possible by avoiding the payment of taxes.

For those chief executive officers (CEOs) who are intent on reducing their corporation's tax burdens, there are six primary goals to include in their tax strategies, most of which involve increasing the number of differences between the book and tax records, so that reportable income for tax purposes is reduced or at least delayed. The six items are listed next.

1. *Accelerate deductions.* By recognizing expenses sooner, you can force expenses into the current reporting year that would otherwise be deferred. The primary deduction acceleration involves depreciation, for which a company typically uses the modified accelerated cost recovery system, an accelerated depreciation methodology acceptable for tax reporting purposes, or straight-line depreciation, which results in a higher level of reported earnings.
2. *Take all available tax credits.* A credit results in a permanent reduction in taxes and so is highly desirable. Credits may be available from local, state, and federal governments and may be allowed for a variety of items, such as investments in green technology or research activities or for operating in an economic development zone.
3. *Avoid nonallowable expenses.* A few expenses, notably meals and entertainment, are completely or at least partially not allowed for purposes of computing taxable income. A key company strategy is to reduce these types of expenses to the bare minimum, thereby avoiding any lost benefits from nonallowable expenses.
4. *Increase tax deferrals.* There are a number of situations in which taxes can be deferred, such as when payments for acquisitions are made in stock or when revenue is deferred until all related services have been performed. This can shift a large part of the tax liability into the future, when the time value of money results in a smaller present value of the tax liability than would otherwise be the case.

5. *Obtain tax-exempt income.* Consider investing excess funds in municipal bonds, which are exempt from both federal income taxes and the income taxes of the state in which they were issued. The downside of this investment is that the return on municipal bonds is less than the return on other forms of investment, due to their inherent tax savings.

6. *Recognize income in low-tax jurisdictions.* If a company has a number of subsidiaries that are located in tax jurisdictions that have significant differences in income tax rates, use transfer pricing to increase the amount of reportable income in those tax jurisdictions having the lowest tax rates and reduce the amount of reportable income in those jurisdictions having the highest tax rates. For example, shift all intellectual property into a subsidiary located in a low-tax region and have it charge royalties to the other subsidiaries for use of the intellectual property. This strategy calls for expert legal advice.

No single tax strategy will be applicable to every company, since the tax laws are so complex that the CEO must construct a strategy that is tailored to the specific circumstances in which a company finds itself. Nonetheless, there are a number of taxation areas that you should be aware of when creating a tax strategy using the preceding goals. These areas are listed in alphabetical order through the remainder of this chapter, ranging from the accumulated earnings tax to unemployment taxes. Peruse these topics to see if they should be incorporated into your company's overall tax strategy.

Accumulated Earnings Tax

There is a double tax associated with a company's payments of dividends to investors, because it first must pay an income tax from which dividends *cannot* be deducted as an expense, and investors must pay income tax on the dividends received. Understandably, closely held companies prefer not to issue dividends in order to avoid the double taxation issue. However, this can result in a large amount of capital accumulating within a company. The Internal Revenue Service (IRS) addresses this issue by imposing an accumulated earnings tax on what it considers to be an excessive amount of earnings that have not been distributed to shareholders.

The IRS considers accumulated earnings of less than $150,000 to be sufficient for the working needs of service businesses, such as accounting, engineering, architecture, and consulting firms. It considers accumulations of anything under $250,000 to be sufficient for most other types of businesses. A company can argue that it needs a substantially larger amount of accumulated earnings if it can prove that it has specific, definite, and feasible plans that will require the use of the funds within the business. Another valid argument is that a company needs a sufficient amount of accumulated earnings to buy back a company's stock that is held by a deceased shareholder's estate.

If these conditions are not apparent, the IRS will declare the accumulated earnings to be taxable at a rate of 15%. Also, interest payments to the IRS will be due from the date when the corporation's annual return was originally due. This tax is designed to encourage organizations to issue dividends on a regular basis to their shareholders, so that the IRS can tax the shareholders for this form of income.

There are a number of ways to avoid this tax, such as incurring additional expenses to drive down reported earnings or by switching the form of incorporation to an S corporation.

Cash Method of Accounting

The normal method for reporting a company's financial results is the accrual basis of accounting, under which expenses are matched to revenues within a reporting period. However, for tax purposes, it is sometimes possible to report income under the cash method of accounting. Under this approach, revenue is not recognized until payment for invoices is received, while expenses are not recognized until paid.

The cash basis of accounting can result in a great deal of manipulation from the perspective of the IRS, which discourages but does not prohibit its use. As an example of income manipulation, a company might realize that it will have a large amount of income to report in the current year and probably will have less in the following year. Accordingly, it prepays a number of supplier invoices at the end of the year, so that it recognizes them at once under the cash method of accounting as expenses in the current year. The IRS prohibits this type of behavior under the rule that cash payments recognized in the current period can relate only to current-year expenses. Nonetheless, it is a difficult issue for the IRS to police. The same degree of manipulation can be applied to the recognition of revenue, simply by delaying billings to customers near the end of the tax year. Also, in situations where there is a sudden surge of business at the end of the tax year, possibly due to seasonality, the cash method of accounting will not reveal the sales until the following year, since payment on the invoices from customers will not arrive until the following year. Consequently, the cash method tends to underreport taxable income.

In order to limit the use of this method, the IRS prohibits it if a company has any inventories on hand at the end of the year. The reason for this is that expenditures for inventory can be so large and subject to manipulation at year-end that a company theoretically could alter its reported level of taxable income to an enormous extent. The cash basis is also not allowable for any C corporation, a partnership that has a C corporation for a partner, or a tax shelter. However, within these restrictions, it is allowable for an entity with average annual gross receipts of $5 million or less for the three years ending with the prior tax year as well as for any personal services corporation that provides at least 95% of its activities in the services arena.

The IRS imposes some accrual accounting concepts on a cash-basis organization in order to avoid some of the more blatant forms of income avoidance. For example, if a cash-basis company receives a check payment at the end of its tax year, it might be tempted not to cash the check until the beginning of the next tax year, since doing so would push the revenue associated with the check into the next year. To avoid this problem, the IRS uses the concept of *constructive receipt*, which requires you to record the receipt when it is made available to you without restriction (whether it is actually recorded on the company's books at that time or not).

Inventory Valuation

It is allowable to value a company's inventory using one method for book purposes and another for tax purposes, except in the case of the last-in, first-out (LIFO) inventory valuation method. In this case, the tax advantages to be gained from the use of LIFO are so significant that the IRS requires a user to employ it for both book and tax purposes. Furthermore, if LIFO is used in any one of a group of financially related companies, the entire group is assumed to be a single entity for tax reporting purposes, which means that they all must use the LIFO valuation approach for both book and tax reporting. This rule was engendered in order to stop the practice of having LIFO-valuation companies roll their results into a parent company that used some other method of reporting, thereby giving astute companies high levels of reportable income and lower levels of taxable income at the same time.

Mergers and Acquisitions

A key factor to consider in corporate acquisitions is the determination of what size taxable gain will be incurred by the seller as well as how the buyer can reduce the tax impact of the transaction in the current and future years. In this section, we briefly discuss the various types of transactions involved in an acquisition, the tax implications of each transaction, and whose interests are best served by the use of each one.

There are two ways in which an acquisition can be made, each with different tax implications. First, the acquirer can purchase the acquiree's stock, which might trigger a taxable gain to the seller. Second, the acquirer can purchase the acquiree's assets, which triggers a gain on sale of the assets as well as another tax to the shareholders of the selling company, who must recognize a gain when the proceeds from liquidation of the business are distributed to them. Because of the additional taxation, a seller generally will want to sell a corporation's stock rather than its assets.

When stock is sold to the buyer in exchange for cash or property, the buyer establishes a tax basis in the stock that equals the amount of the cash paid or fair market value of the property transferred to the seller. Meanwhile, the seller recognizes a gain or loss on the eventual sale of the stock that is based on its original tax basis in the stock, which is subtracted from the ultimate sale price of the stock.

It is also possible for the seller to recognize no taxable gain on the sale of a business if it takes some of the acquiring company's stock as full compensation for the sale. However, there will be no tax only if *continuity of interest* in the business can be proven by giving the sellers a sufficient amount of the buyer's stock to prove that they have a continuing financial interest in the buying company. A variation on this approach is to make an acquisition over a period of months, using nothing but voting stock as compensation to the seller's shareholders, but for which a clear path of ultimate control over the acquiree can be proven. Another variation is to purchase at least 80% of the fair market value of the acquiree's assets solely in exchange for stock.

When only the assets are sold to the buyer, the buyer can apportion the total price among the assets purchased, up to their fair market value (with any excess portion of the price being apportioned to goodwill). This method is highly favorable from a taxation perspective, since now the buyer has adjusted its basis in the assets substantially higher; it can claim a much larger accelerated deprecation expense in the upcoming years, thereby reducing both its reported level of taxable income and its tax burden. From the seller's perspective, the sale price is allocated to each asset sold for the purposes of determining a gain or loss; as much of this as possible should be characterized as a capital gain (since the related tax is lower) or as an ordinary loss (since it can offset ordinary income, which has a higher tax rate).

The structuring of an acquisition transaction so that no income taxes are paid must have a reasonable business purpose besides the avoidance of taxes. Otherwise, the IRS has been known to require tax payments on the grounds that the structure of the transaction has no reasonable business purpose other than tax avoidance.

Net Operating Loss Carryforwards

Since income taxes can be the single largest expense on the income statement, you should be aware of any net operating loss (NOL) carryforwards that a company may have and how they can be used. An NOL can be carried back and applied against profits recorded in the two preceding years, with any remaining amount being carried forward for the next 20 years, when it can be offset against any reported income. If there still is an NOL left after the 20 years have expired, the remaining amount can no longer be used. You can also choose to ignore the carryback option and only use an NOL for carryforward purposes. The standard procedure is to apply all of an NOL against the income reported in the earliest year, with the remainder carrying forward to each subsequent year in succession until the remaining NOL has been exhausted. If an NOL has been incurred in each of multiple years, you should apply them against reported income (in either prior or later years) in order of the first NOL incurred. This rule is used because of the 20-year limitation on an NOL, so that an NOL incurred in an earlier year can be used before it expires.

The NOL is a valuable asset, since it can be used for many years to offset future earnings. A company buying another entity that has an NOL certainly will place a high value on the NOL and may even buy the entity strictly in order to use its NOL. To curtail this type of behavior, the IRS has created the Section 382 limitation, under which there is a limitation on the use of an NOL if there is at least a 50% change in the ownership of an entity that has an unused NOL. The limitation is derived through a complex formula that essentially multiplies the acquired corporation's stock times the long-term tax-exempt bond rate. To avoid this problem, a company with an unused NOL that is seeking to expand its equity should consider issuing straight preferred stock (no voting rights, no conversion privileges, and no participation in future earnings) in order to avoid any chance that the extra equity will be construed as a change in ownership.

Nexus

A company might have to complete many more tax forms than it would like and remit taxes to more government entities, if it can be established that it has nexus within a government's area of jurisdiction. Consequently, it is very important to understand how nexus is established.

The rules vary by state, but nexus generally is considered to have occurred if a company maintains a facility of any kind within a state or if it pays the wages of someone within that state. In some locales, the definition is expanded to include the transport of goods to customers within the state on company-owned vehicles (although nexus is not considered to have occurred if the shipment is made by a third-party freight carrier). A more liberal interpretation of the nexus rule is that a company has nexus if it sends sales personnel into the state on sales calls or training personnel there to educate customers, even though they are not based there permanently. To gain a precise understanding of how the nexus rules are interpreted by each state, it is best to contact the department of revenue at each state government or review the nexus rules listed on their Web sites.

If nexus has been established, a company must file to do business within the state, which requires a small fee and a refiling once every few years. In addition, it must withhold sales taxes on all sales within the state. This is the most laborious issue related to nexus, since sales taxes may be different for every city and county within each state, necessitating a company to keep track of potentially thousands of different sales tax rates. Also, some states may require the remittance of sales taxes every month, although this can be reduced to as little as once a year if the company predicts that it will have minimal sales taxes to remit, as noted on its initial application for a sales tax license.

Some states and local governments also will subject a company to property or personal property taxes on all assets based within their jurisdictions, which necessitates even more paperwork.

Although the amount of additional taxes paid may not be that great, the key issue related to the nexus concept is that the additional time required to track tax liabilities and file forms with the various governments may very well require additional personnel in the accounting department. This can be a major problem for those organizations in multiple states and should be a planning issue when determining the capacity of the accounting department to process tax-related transactions. Some organizations with a number of subsidiaries will avoid a portion of the tax filing work by accepting the nexus concept for only those subsidiaries that are clearly established within each governmental jurisdiction, thereby avoiding the tax filing problems for all other legal entities controlled by the parent corporation.

S Corporation

The S corporation is of considerable interest, because it generally does not pay taxes. Instead, it passes reported earnings through to its shareholders, who report the income on their tax returns. This avoids the double taxation that arises in a C corporation, where a company's income is taxed and the dividends it issues to its shareholders are taxed as income to them a second time. The amount of income is allocated to each shareholder on a simple per-share basis. If a shareholder has held stock in the corporation for less than a full year, the allocation is on a per-share, per-day basis. The per-day part of this calculation assumes that a shareholder still holds the stock through and including the day when the stock is disposed of; a deceased shareholder will be assumed to retain ownership through and including the day that he or she dies.

An S corporation has unique taxation and legal protection aspects that make it an ideal way to structure a business if there are a small number of shareholders. Specifically, it can be created only if there are no more than 75 shareholders, if only one class of stock is issued, and if all shareholders agree to the S corporation status. All of its shareholders must be either citizens or residents of the United States. Shareholders also are limited to individuals, estates, and some types of trusts and charities. Conversely, this means that C corporations and partnerships cannot be shareholders in an S corporation. Because S corporations are required to issue only a single class of stock, some organizations will choose not to organize in this manner, for it does not allow for preferential returns or special voting rights by some shareholders.

There are a few cases where an S corporation can owe taxes. For example, it can be taxed if it has accumulated earnings and profits from an earlier existence as a C corporation and its passive income is more than 25% of total gross receipts. It also can be liable for taxes on a few types of capital gains, recapture of the old investment tax credit, and LIFO recapture. If any of these taxes apply, the S corporation must make quarterly estimated income tax payments. By contrast, an S corporation is not subject to the alternative minimum tax.

If you want to terminate the status of an S corporation and revert to a different form of organization, you must obtain the written consent of more than 50% of the shareholders. If the decision is made to become an S corporation again, there is a five-year waiting period from the last time before you can do so again, unless you obtain special permission from the IRS.

Sales and Use Taxes

Sales taxes are imposed at the state, county, and city levels—often by all three at once. It is also possible for a special tax to be added to the sales tax and applied to a unique region, such as the construction of a baseball stadium or to support a regional mass transit system. The sales tax is multiplied by the price paid on goods and services on transactions occurring within the taxing area. However, the definition of goods and services that are required to be taxed will vary by state (not usually at the county or city level) and so must be researched at the state level to determine the precise basis of calculation. For example, some states do not tax food sales, on the grounds that this is a necessity whose cost should be reduced as much as possible, while other states include it in their required list of items to be taxed.

A company is required to charge sales taxes to its customers and remit the resulting receipts to the local state government, which will split out the portions due to the local county and city governments and remit these taxes on the company's behalf to those entities. If the company does not charge its customers for these taxes, it is still liable for them and must pay the unbilled amounts to the state government, although it has the right to bill its customers after the fact for the missing sales taxes. Doing this can be a difficult collection chore, especially if sales are primarily over the counter, where there are few transaction records that identify the customer. Also, a company is obligated to keep abreast of all changes in sales tax rates, so that it charges its customers for the correct amount; if it does not do so, it is liable to the government for the difference between what it actually charged and the statutory rate. If a company overcharges its customers, the excess also must be remitted to the government.

The state in which a company is collecting sales taxes can decide how frequently it wants the company to remit taxes. If there are only modest sales, the state may decide that the cost of paperwork exceeds the value of the remittances and will require only an annual remittance. It is more common to have quarterly or monthly remittances. The state will review the dollar amount of remittances from time to time and adjust the required remittance frequency based on this information.

All government entities have the right to audit a company's books to see if the proper sales taxes are being charged, so a company theoretically can be subject to three sales tax audits per year—one each from the city, county, and state revenue departments. Also, since these audits can come from any taxing jurisdiction in which a company does business, there could be literally thousands of potential audits.

The obligation to collect sales taxes is based on the concept of nexus, which was covered earlier in this chapter. If nexus exists, sales taxes must be collected by the seller. If not, the recipient of purchased goods instead has an obligation to compile a list of items purchased and remit a use tax to the appropriate authority. The use tax is in the same amount as the sales tax. The only difference is that the remitting party is the buyer instead of the seller. Use taxes also are subject to audits by all taxing jurisdictions.

If the buyer of a company's products is including them in its own products for resale to another entity, the buyer does not have to pay a sales tax to the seller. Instead, the buyer will charge a sales tax to the buyer of its final product. This approach is used under the theory that a sales tax should be charged only one time on the sale of a product. However, it can be a difficult chore to explain the lack of sales tax billings during a sales tax audit, so you should halt sales taxation only if the buyer sends a sales tax exemption form. Instead the sales tax exemption certification may be named a resale certificate, depending on the issuing authority. It also can be issued to government entities, which are generally exempt from sales and use taxes. As a general rule, you always should charge sales taxes unless there is a sales tax exemption certificate on file; otherwise, the company is liable for the remittance of sales taxes in the event of an audit.

Transfer Pricing

Transfer pricing is a key tax consideration, because it can result in the permanent reduction of an organization's tax liability. The permanent reduction is caused by the recognition of income in different taxing jurisdictions that may have different tax rates.

The basic concept behind the use of transfer pricing to reduce a company's overall taxes is that a company transfers its products to a division in another country at the lowest possible price if the income tax rate is lower in the other country, or at the highest possible price if the tax rate is higher. By selling to the division at a low price, the company will report a very high profit on the final sale of products in the other country, which is where that income will be taxed at a presumably lower income tax rate.

For example, Exhibit 4.1 shows a situation in which a company with a location in Countries Alpha and Beta has the choice of selling goods either in Alpha or transferring them to Beta and selling them there. The company is faced with a corporate income tax rate of 40% in Country Alpha. To avoid some of this income tax permanently, the company sells its products to another subsidiary in Country Beta, where the corporate income tax rate is only 25%. By doing so, the company still earns a profit ($60,000) in Country Alpha, but the bulk of the profit ($125,000) now appears in Country Beta. The net result is a consolidated income tax rate of just 28%.

The IRS is well aware of this tax avoidance strategy and has developed tax rules that do not eliminate it, but which will reduce the leeway that you have in altering reportable income. Under Section 482 of the IRS Code, the IRS's preferred approach for developing transfer prices is to use the market rate as its basis. However, very few products can be compared reliably and consistently to the market rate, with the exception of commodities, because there are costing differences between them. Also, in many cases, products are so specialized (especially components that are custom-designed to fit into a larger product) that there is no market rate against which they can be compared. Even if there is some basis of comparison between a product and the average market prices for similar products, you still have some leeway in which to alter transfer prices, because the IRS will allow you to add special charges based on the cost of transferring the products, or extra fees,

	Country Alpha Location	Country Beta Location
Sales to subsidiary:		
Revenue	$1,000,000	
Cost of goods sold	850,000	
Profit	$150,000	
Profit percentage	15%	
Sales outside of company:		
Revenue		$1,500,000
Cost of goods sold		1,000,000
Profit		$500,000
Profit percentage		33%
Income tax percentage	40%	25%
Income tax	$60,000	$125,000
Consolidated income tax	$185,000	
Consolidated income tax percentage	28%	

EXHIBIT 4.1 Income Tax Savings from Transfer Pricing

such as royalty or licensing fees that are imposed for the subsidiary's use of the parent company's patents or trademarks, or for administrative charges related to the preparation of any documentation required to move products between countries. It is also possible to alter slightly the interest rates charged to subsidiaries (although not too far from market rates) for the use of funds sent to them from the parent organization.

If there is no basis on which to create prices based on market rates, the IRS's next most favored approach is to calculate the prices based on the *work-back method*. Under this approach, you begin at the end of the sales cycle by determining the price at which a product is sold to an outside customer and then subtract the subsidiary's standard markup percentage and its added cost of materials, labor, and overhead, which results in the theoretical transfer price. The work-back method can result in a wide array of transfer prices, since a number of different costs can be subtracted from the final sale price, such as standard costs, actual costs, overhead costs based on different allocation measures, and overhead costs based on cost pools that contain different types of costs.

If that approach does not work, the IRS's third most favored approach is the *cost plus method*. As the name implies, this approach begins at the other end of the production process and compiles costs from a product's initiation point. After all costs are added before the point of transfer, you add a profit margin to the product, thereby arriving at a transfer cost that is acceptable by the IRS. However, once again, the costs that are included in a product are subject to the same points of variation that were noted for the work-back method. In addition, the profit margin added should be the standard margin added for any other company customer, but it can be quite difficult to determine if there are a multitude of volume discounts, seasonal discounts, and so on. Consequently, the profit margin added to a product's initial costs can be subject to a great deal of negotiation.

An overriding issue to consider, no matter what approach is used to derive transfer prices, is that taxing authorities can become highly irritated if a company continually pushes the outer limits of acceptable transfer pricing rules in order to maximize its tax savings. When this happens, a company can expect continual audits and penalties on disputed items as well as less favorable judgments related to any taxation issues. Consequently, it makes a great deal of sense to consistently adopt pricing policies that result in reasonable tax savings, are fully justifiable to the taxing authorities of all involved countries, and do not push the boundaries of acceptable pricing behavior.

Another transfer pricing issue that can modify a company's pricing strategy is the presence of any restrictions on cash flows out of a country in which it has a subsidiary. In these instances, it may be necessary to report the minimum possible amount of taxable income at the subsidiary, irrespective of the local tax rate. The reason is that the only way for a company to retrieve funds from the country is through the medium of an account receivable, which must be maximized by billing the subsidiary the highest possible amount for transferred goods. In this case, tax planning takes a backseat to cash flow planning.

Yet another issue that may drive a company to set pricing levels that do not result in reduced income taxes is that a subsidiary may have to report high levels of income in order to qualify for a loan from a local credit institution. This is especially important if the country in which the subsidiary is located has restrictions on the movement of cash, so that the parent company would be unable to withdraw loans that it makes to the subsidiary. As was the case for the last item, cash flow planning is likely to be more important than income tax reduction.

A final transfer pricing issue to be aware of is that the method for calculating taxable income may vary in other countries. This situation may lead you to believe—erroneously—that another country has a lower tax rate. A closer examination of how taxable income is calculated might reveal that some expenses are restricted or not allowed at all, resulting in an actual tax rate that is much higher than originally expected. Consultation with a tax expert for the country in question prior to setting up any transfer pricing arrangements is the best way to avoid this problem.

Unemployment Taxes

Both state and federal governments will charge a company a fixed percentage of its payroll each year for the expense of unemployment funds that are used to pay former employees who have been released from employment. State governments administer the distribution of these funds and compile an experience rating on each company, based on the number of employees it has laid off in the recent past. Based on this experience rating, it can require a company to submit larger or smaller amounts to the state unemployment fund in future years. Increased unemployment payments can become a considerable burden if a company has a long history of lay-offs. Consequently, you should consider the use of temporary employees or out-sourcing if this will give a firm the ability to retain a small number of key employees and avoid layoffs while still handling seasonal changes in workloads. Also, if a company is planning to acquire another entity but plans to lay off a large number of the acquiree's staff once the acquisition is completed, it may make more sense to acquire the acquiree's assets only and to selectively hire a few of its employees, thereby re-taining a pristine unemployment experience rating with the local state government.

The federal unemployment tax is imposed on a company if it has paid employees at least $1,500 in any calendar quarter or had at least one employee for some portion of a day within at least 20 weeks of the year. In short, nearly all companies will be required to remit federal unemployment taxes. For the 2011 calendar year, the tax rate is 6.2% of the first $7,000 paid to each employee; this tends to concentrate most federal unemployment tax remittances into the first quarter of the calendar year. In many states, you can take a credit against the federal unemployment tax for up to 5.4% of taxable wages, which results in a net federal unemployment tax of only .8%.

If a company is shifting to a new legal entity, perhaps because of a shift from a partnership to a corporation, or from an S corporation to a C corporation, it will have to apply for a new unemployment tax identification number with the local state authorities. This is a problem if the organization being closed down had an unusually good experience rating, since the company will be assigned a poorer one until a new experience rating can be built up over time, which will result in higher un-employment taxes in the short term. To avoid this problem, you should contact the local unemployment taxation office to request that the old company's experience rating be shifted to the new one.

Summary

This chapter presented a set of general tax planning goals and proceeded directly into a series of specific tax topics that should be considered when creating and updating a tax strategy. For example, the presence of an accumulated earnings tax may force a CEO to recommend the issuance of enough dividends to avoid the tax, while the mergers and acquisitions section shows how you must structure an acquisition in order to minimize the incurrence of income taxes for all parties. From a tax processing perspective, a firm understanding of the "Nexus" and "Sales and Use Tax" sections is crucial for maximizing the efficiency with which tax forms are filed. Also, you should thoroughly understand the transfer pricing topic in order to realize permanent reductions in federal income taxes. Thus, the CEO must have a broad-based knowledge of a variety of taxation topics, which in turn allows for a tax strategy that considers all aspects of company operations, financing methods, locations, and corporate structure.

CHAPTER 5

Information Technology Strategy

The chief executive officer (CEO) should have a strong interest in the information technology (IT) area, since it can require a great deal of capital investment. Companies tend to invest too much money in IT or spend it on the wrong projects, because they do not invest the time up front to determine how IT can dovetail most effectively into the overall business strategy. In this chapter, we look at why IT strategy is important to the CEO, how to develop an IT strategy properly, and what specific IT projects are likely to be of value, depending on the general type of business strategy that a company intends to follow.

Reasons for Devising an Information Technology Strategy

The standard corporate approach to the development of an IT strategy is to continue the funding of existing projects and to approve funding for additional projects as presented by the IT manager until a predetermined cap on expenditures is reached. This approach completely avoids any linkage of IT investments to a company's overall business strategy, likely resulting in lost opportunities to improve the business. However, there are several IT decision points at which a CEO could insert the need for a complete evaluation of the IT strategy, thereby creating a closer fit between IT projects and the general business direction. These decision points are:

- *When merging entities.* When a company acquires another company, there will be questions about whose systems will be used for various functions or whether systems should be kept separate. This is an excellent time to conduct a thorough review of the reasons why either company's systems should be used, allowing for the best of breed to be retained.
- *When major cost reductions are needed.* When a company finds itself losing so much money that it must conduct a detailed review of all costs company-wide, this is a good excuse for an IT strategy review. Note, however, that this review will be skewed heavily in the direction of cost reductions rather than toward how strategy can be used to enhance the business.
- *When have an IT project request overload.* This is one of the most common reasons for creating an IT strategy. The IT manager is completely overwhelmed by

the number of requests being dropped on his department and complains to senior management for assistance in sorting through the requests; this results in an IT strategy that is used primarily as a sorting device for picking the most necessary projects.

■ *When current IT systems are failing.* When in-house legacy systems are beginning to fail for any number of reasons—loss of key programmers, excessive transaction volume, and so on—the CEO can push for the development of an IT strategy to use as a framework for the creation of replacement systems. The only problem is that the systems may be failing so rapidly that the strategy development process is rushed.

■ *When the company's organizational structure is being changed.* From time to time, senior management may decide to reorganize a company based on geographical locations, new managers running different functions, and so on. The existing IT systems may be overburdened by the information requirements of the new structure, which is an ideal time for an IT strategy review.

■ *When existing systems interfere with functional efficiency.* This problem arises most frequently in companies whose main target is to reduce costs continually in order to be the low-cost producer. Eventually they will reduce costs to the point where the procedures surrounding the existing IT systems are interfering with further cost improvements, resulting in a strategy review just to see how the systems can be altered from a cost-reduction standpoint.

■ *When new management is hired.* When a new CEO is installed and brings in his own staff to run a company, they may conduct a complete spring cleaning of the company, which may include existing IT systems. This is an excellent opportunity for an IT strategy review, since new directions can be determined without any interference from the old management team.

No matter which of these circumstances is used as an excuse to create an IT strategy, you should incorporate it into an ongoing schedule of IT strategy reviews, so that incremental adjustments can be made to the plan over time as the overall business strategy changes.

Developing the Information Technology Strategy

The first step in the development of an IT strategy is the formation of an IT steering committee that is given responsibility for creating the strategy. It is essential that this group be comprised of people from all key functional areas of the company, so that its decisions have a better chance of being accepted by the entire company. The CEO should attend these meetings, as should the manager of the IT function. However, there should be no additional IT representatives, unless required for special information, since a heavy IT weighting will tend to skew decisions in the direction of what is needed technically rather than what the entire business needs.

The committee is responsible for creating IT strategies and prioritizing IT projects based on those strategies, but it must forward this work to the executive committee for final approval. It is also responsible for the review and approval of new IT projects that are submitted from around the company. In order to avoid having the committee be bogged down by the review of *all* requested IT projects, it should limit its scope to reviews of only the largest and most expensive projects, letting the IT manager handle all smaller issues.

Once assembled, the steering committee first should spend considerable time learning about the overall corporate strategies, which it will use to formulate the IT strategy. This initial learning stage can take as little as one day if a formal strategy document has already been created. However, it is more likely that the company operates without one, in which case the committee must interview members of senior management to gather information that they can assemble into a strategy.

The process of learning about the business strategy likely will require a considerable amount of education about the general operating framework of the company. For example, the committee members should know whether the company: uses make-to-order or make-to-stock production; uses single or multiple warehouses; back-flushes its production records; processes transactions in multiple currencies; has special government reporting requirements; outsources various functions; swaps product designs with its suppliers; and others. This level of detailed knowledge about operations is crucial for later determining the types of IT projects that can be implemented to assist the company's overall strategy most effectively.

With a general business strategy in hand, the committee can create an IT strategy that supports the business strategy by shoring up weak areas that are considered important to the business and by increasing the capabilities of areas where the company wishes to maintain a strong competitive posture. To this end, the strategy should include a detailed list of corporate strengths and weaknesses and a discussion of how the IT strategy will impact them. In addition, it should anticipate the need to compete with the IT projects currently under development at competing firms, to the extent that this information can be ascertained. Another approach for developing possible strategies is to conduct a benchmarking review of IT projects at other companies, possibly of organizations located completely outside the company's industry. For ideas about what types of strategies can be implemented, see the "Specific Applications" section later in the chapter. This step is an ongoing process that is updated constantly in light of changes to the general strategy and so tends to require incremental adjustments to the priorities assigned to various projects.

With an IT strategy in place, the steering committee must next determine what specific IT projects to complete in order to implement the strategy. Doing this requires a detailed knowledge of precisely what IT functionality is already present as well as the types of projects required to bridge the gap between current and desired capabilities. The analysis also should consider the technical ability of the in-house IT department in order to understand how much outside assistance may be required for certain projects. This review of in-house talent breaks down the capabilities of personnel into such categories as subject matter experts, process experts, application development experts, and systems maintenance personnel. By doing so, the committee can spot those areas in which a lack of personnel skills could make it exceedingly difficult to implement a new project. The committee also should determine the proportion of IT staff time currently being used to maintain existing IT systems, since this tends to absorb most staff time, leaving little for new development efforts of any kind. This problem sometimes can be overcome by the judicious replacement of custom-developed software with packaged software that is supported by an outside party, thereby reducing the maintenance efforts of the IT department.

Further, the committee should include a detailed examination of the projects currently under development and the amount of resources and time required to complete them. In many cases, it may make sense to complete projects that are already under development, even if they fall well outside the requirements of the IT strategy, simply because they require minimal effort to finish.

This detailed level of review can be a massive effort, especially if the company has many product lines, locations, or divisions. In order to complete at least some portion of the work as soon as possible, the committee can limit its scope by focusing only on specific areas. The limitation criterion can be whether the resulting information will be critical to business operations, if it will be used by more than one functional area, or if it results in information sharing with other business partners. Of course, the overriding criterion will be if the business strategy states that a specific target area is considered the primary opportunity for the business as a whole. If the IT plan's scope is limited in this manner, the committee should prioritize the value of the remaining parts of the business and add them to the IT strategy as time allows.

Even with an IT strategy in place that clearly defines what types of projects should be approved, it still will be difficult for the committee to assign exact priorities to different IT projects, due to the wide variety of possible projects. Any or all of the next techniques can be used to accomplish this prioritization:

- *Building block approach.* Assign high priorities to those projects needed as building blocks for later projects that cannot be completed until the first projects are implemented. For example, a company-wide network must be completed before an enterprise resources planning (ERP) system can be installed throughout a company.

- *Portfolio approach.* When cash resources are reduced, a company tends to cancel all high-risk IT projects and focus its efforts on those with a clear and likely payoff. However, this approach runs the risk of never achieving a breakthrough technical advantage. A better approach is to identify those projects with potentially high payoffs and assign a small proportion of the IT budget to them, even if there is a strong risk of failure.

- *Competing standards approach.* If a project requires the use of one of a set of competing industry standards, it may be worthwhile to delay the implementation until it becomes more clear as to which of the standards will emerge as the dominant one. Otherwise, a company may find itself having invested funds in a technology for which there is a shrinking base of support expertise.

- *Forced ranking.* Sequentially compare the value of each project to every other proposed project in order to create a ranking. For example, Project A is compared to all other proposed projects. If the committee considers it to be the top priority, it is assigned that ranking. Then the committee individually compares all remaining projects against each other to determine the next most critical project. Once priorities have been assigned using this approach, the committee takes another pass at the list and compares each project to the one immediately below, and reiterates this process until it is satisfied with the ranking.

- *Payoff approach.* Every project proposal should be accompanied by a cost-benefit proposal. Although the committee can choose to ignore this information in the interests of long-term strategy, the ability of an IT project to generate a profit, especially when prioritizing among short-term projects, should not be ignored.

Of the prioritization methods just described, strong consideration should be given to the forced ranking approach, but within the larger framework of specific business strategies. For example, if a massive jump in sales through the use of a more efficient, wireless-enabled sales force is considered the primary business strategy, all key projects related to this strategy can be ranked higher than those of the next most important strategy. Then the building block prioritization approach can be used to determine the initial prioritization of projects within each group of projects, while a forced ranking can be conducted on the remaining projects.

Throughout the process of defining the IT strategy, conducting a gap analysis, and assigning priorities to specific projects, the steering committee must be mindful of the need for in-depth communication of its activities with the CEO, the IT department, and the company as a whole. This is necessary to ensure the highest level of support and cooperation by all parties when it comes time to implement the set of projects that the steering committee recommends to the CEO.

Technical Strategies

The primary point of this chapter is the development of a list of IT projects that will support a company's overall business strategy. Nonetheless, the IT department itself is likely to have a few thoughts about the underlying structure of IT systems to be used. These are technical issues that a CEO is not likely to be conversant with, but you should keep in mind the next few points when discussing technical strategies with the IT staff.

- *Use scalable components.* If a company has any prospects of expanding, eventually it will run the risk of outgrowing its existing computer infrastructure. Therefore, ask about the scalability of any new systems that the IT staff wants to install. A truly scalable system should handle substantially more transaction volume easily or at least do so through a logical upgrade path.
- *Use open standards.* Avoid the use of proprietary systems whenever possible, since these systems are linked to the fortunes of their suppliers. They also tend to be more expensive than open systems and attract fewer independent developers who provide add-on applications. This goal tends to be long term and sometimes expensive, and so must be reviewed in light of other targets and how this goal will impact them.

- *Use the same architecture for as long as possible.* Despite the preceding recommendation to switch to open standards, you also face the problem of keeping the IT investment as low as is prudent. One approach for doing so is to force the IT department to prolong the use of existing standards for as long as possible. Once the architecture changes, a slew of related expenses will arise, such as training, software, and hardware. It is wise to force the IT staff to consider carefully the likely longevity of any IT architecture it wants to adopt.
- *Use packaged software.* Many companies suffer from the not-invented-here syndrome and prefer to sink large amounts of cash into the development of IT systems that could have been purchased from a supplier. The advantage of using a packaged system is its lower cost, support by the supplier, and relative absence of bugs (since many customers are testing it and feeding back their comments to the supplier). Packaged software should be avoided only when a prospective application is so company-specific that no packaged solutions are available.
- *Use few suppliers.* IT suppliers love to pin the blame for a system failure on other suppliers. The obvious solution is to concentrate IT purchases with the smallest possible number of suppliers. Another reason for using few suppliers is that volume purchases can result in purchase discounts. If there is no way to avoid hiring many suppliers, at least designate a lead supplier, to whom other suppliers act as subcontractors and who is responsible for fixing system problems.
- *Centralize only the most important information.* Data warehouses are touted as a wonderful way to centralize and organize all of a company's key information, but they are also expensive and labor-intensive to create and maintain. Consequently, you should examine carefully the need to store various types of information in this repository as well as the incremental cost of doing so, and include only those data items for which a clear value can be seen.

There are many more considerations in the development of a technical strategy that supports the overall IT strategy, but they are well beyond the scope of this book. The bullet points noted here are most useful to the CEO as general guidelines to consider when discussing technical strategy issues with the IT department.

Specific Applications

Thus far, we have looked at the general structure that a CEO should pursue when developing an IT strategy. However, the question remains: What specific IT activities are most worthwhile for a company that is pursuing a specific type of strategy? Circumstances will vary wildly by individual company, but the next list of activities generally will be most useful when conducted under the indicated strategies.

- *Explosive sales growth strategy.* In this strategy, a company has chosen to increase sales at the highest possible rate, ignoring cost efficiencies, product improvements, or other internal efficiencies in the short term. It should consider installing computer systems for its dealers and sales representatives that give them direct access to the company's quote and order status database. It may wish to provide wireless access to its sales representatives, so they can access information more easily from the field. It also can create a quoting system for the sales staff that tracks which quotes are under development, which have been submitted, and which have been won as well as the reasons for lost quotes. Senior management will want daily access to sales information, especially for new sales regions. Also, the strategy could include a complete standardization of systems installed at all new company locations, in order to reduce the maintenance workload of the IT staff. In general, the company should consider installing packaged customer relationship management (CRM) software for use by its sales staff in order to have a centralized database of customer information.

- *Great customer service strategy.* In this strategy, a company chooses to expend extra effort to ensure top-level service to its customers, probably combined with higher product costs that customers are willing to pay in exchange for the service. It should consider giving its customers electronic access to information about their orders, perhaps through an Internet connection. It also should allow them to place electronic orders. In addition, there should be in-house databases to track the status of customer complaints as well as product or service quality issues and the status of all field service orders. These systems also can be integrated with global positioning systems, so that customers can see exactly where their shipments are located around the world. Company management should have immediate access to these databases to see where problems are arising; this approach could be advanced to "push" technology, where customers are notified automatically by the system when a problem arises. The company also should have a product recall system in place, perhaps including tracking by production lots, so that product problems can be dealt with rapidly and efficiently. In addition, the system should have a linkage between the order entry and part ordering or manufacturing systems, so that delivery commitments can be made automatically and online, with customer access to this information.

- *Product improvement strategy.* In this strategy, a company elects to upgrade its products and develop new ones constantly, on the assumption that customers will pay a premium for them. It should consider installing systems that allow it to swap drawings and other product documents electronically with its business partners. It also can implement project management systems that allow for concurrent product development by multiple departments. Further, systems should allow the management team to track time to market on all product development projects as well as development problems. There also should be a database of product component costs that stores cost information for a variety of product configurations and purchasing or production volumes, which is useful for meeting target costing goals. In addition, there should be advanced cost accounting systems for accumulating product costs at any stage of the development process. Also, a prototyping system should allow for rapid product designs and modeling applications. Finally, systems may be needed for tracking all stages of product patent applications and for product licensing agreements with other companies.

■ *Low-cost strategy.* In this strategy, a company chooses to limit its service level and range of product offerings, concentrating instead on selling products at the absolute lowest attainable cost. One possible application under this strategy is the acquisition of a manufacturing resources planning (MRP II) package, which creates an orderly flow of resources through a manufacturing facility, resulting in much better use of materials, equipment, and personnel. Another option is the installation of a just-in-time (JIT) manufacturing system, although this involves fewer computer systems, with a greater emphasis on the reconfiguration of the shop floor, reducing the size of production runs, and altering the size and timing of supplier deliveries. Another possibility is the use of supply chain management (SCM) software, which gives suppliers a transparent view of what customer orders have reached the company and when they must send in parts in order for the company to meet its product schedule. A mandatory system to have in place is a comprehensive bill of materials database that is maintained with the highest degree of accuracy, since this information is needed to drive a variety of parts-ordering systems. Also, if IT is considered a less strategic capability, some portions of it can be outsourced overseas to take advantages of lower labor costs.

In addition to the basic strategies just noted, there are general types of operations or situations in which certain types of IT projects are more likely to be found. For example, a publicly held company may want to achieve a rapid closing of its financial transactions at the end of each quarter and so may be more interested in advanced software systems that will allow it to do so. A public company also may want fast access to key metrics so that it can pass this information along to its investors; for this reason, it may be more inclined to invest in an executive information system. Other projects high on its list may be a data warehouse, a CRM system containing up-to-date forecasting capabilities, and an accurate backlog tracking system.

Another type of company operation is the international corporation. This entity requires accounting software with multicurrency capabilities as well as world-wide electronic meeting capabilities that can be provided through instant messaging, a wide area network, and video conferencing. Also, if company management wishes to centralize selected worldwide transactions, it can invest in an ERP system or, at a lower level, just the customer service and purchasing functions.

A company type requiring significantly different IT systems is the service business. In this case, taking care of key employees and tracking who has key knowledge are critical to corporate success. Consequently, IT systems should track employee training, benefits, hiring, rewards, performance reviews, and turnover as well as applicants for specific positions. If the people in this business are knowledge-intensive, such as consultants, they also should be supplied with wireless communications to other employees, so they can quickly obtain information relevant to their clients.

Finally, the classic manufacturing operation requires many of the systems previously noted under the low-cost strategy. The previously noted MRP or JIT systems can be integrated into a company-wide ERP system in order to share information across all departments that may be of the most use to the manufacturing function.

Further, IT systems should allow the manufacturing operation to create products in a make-to-order mode, which is the least inventory-intensive form of production. There also can be supplier certification systems that allow the receiving department to cancel incoming inspections for prequalified goods; a cost estimation system is critical for the design of new products. There should be an engineering changes– tracking database that notes the times when product modifications will be swapped into the existing production process.

Clearly, the types of systems installed will vary widely, depending on the type of business strategy that the management team chooses to pursue. Even when the range of choices is narrowed down into any of the preceding strategic directions, there still may be too many possible projects from which to pick. If so, the selection criteria noted earlier in the "Developing the Information Technology Strategy" section in this chapter should be used to locate those few projects with the greatest potential to give the company's strategy a boost.

Summary

As may have become evident in this chapter, a company with a proper IT strategy is well on its way to devising an extremely successful overall business strategy. The selection of the proper set of IT project priorities requires considerable time and the involvement of all parts of the company but results in excellent use of limited capital to support the most important business activities. When these strategies are created in light of what is being done at competing firms, a company has a good chance of establishing a strong competitive position from which it can be dislodged only with great difficulty.

CHAPTER **6**

Outsourcing Strategy

A general strategy that the chief executive officer (CEO) should consider is the selective use of outsourcing for some parts of her company. The use of outsourcing has exploded, with many companies using it primarily to drive down their costs. As noted in this chapter, there are other reasons besides cost for using outsourcing. The chapter includes a discussion of the many risks that go along with moving a function to a supplier. Also, it discusses who makes the outsourcing decision and how this may vary by the function to be outsourced. Finally, there is a brief description of the suppliers who provide outsourcing services—how they operate and why they can provide services of higher quality than a company's in-house functions.

Overview of Outsourcing

There are many reasons why a CEO should consider outsourcing a function. These reasons include anticipated cost savings, the need for better skills and management, and handling overflow situations. A company will be more likely to outsource a function if there are multiple reasons for doing so, such as the need for reducing costs as well as selling off assets to the supplier (two reasons that go hand in hand for a financially troubled company). Some of the primary reasons to outsource are listed next.

- *Acquire new skills.* A company may find that its in-house skill set is inadequate for a given function, which may result in minimal, if any, improvements to the function in the future. A company can overcome this problem by handing over the function to a supplier that specializes in that function and that therefore is highly competent in its administration, using well-trained and experienced staff as well as the most current procedures and technological advances. This reason is most commonly used for outsourcing functions that require high skill levels, such as engineering and computer services.
- *Acquire better management.* A company may find that an in-house function is not performing as expected, not because of any problems with the staff but because of poor management. Symptoms are high turnover, absenteeism, poor work products, and missed deadlines. It can be very hard to obtain quality management, so outsourcing the function to a supplier just to gain access to the

supplier's better management can be a viable option. It also may be possible to "rent" management from the supplier. This can be a good option in all functional areas, although it is more common in areas requiring high levels of expertise, such as engineering.

■ *Enhance controls.* In the era of Sarbanes-Oxley, company management is increasingly concerned about its ability to provide sufficient control over its operations. By shifting some functions to a quality supplier whose operations can be certified readily, a considerable proportion of the pressure to maintain adequate controls can be alleviated. This is a particularly important issue when the accounting function is outsourced, since many key control points are located in that area.

■ *Focus on strategy.* A company's managers typically spend the bulk of each day handling the routine operations of their functional areas—the tactical aspects of the job. By outsourcing a function while retaining the core management team, a company can give the tactical part of each manager's job to a supplier, which allows the management team to spend far more time on such strategy-related issues as market positioning, new product development, acquisitions, and long-term financing issues.

■ *Focus on core functions.* A company has a very small number of functions that are key to its survival. It may want to focus all of its energies on those functions and distribute all other functions among a group of suppliers who are capable of performing them well enough that company management will not have to be bothered with the details. A company even may want to outsource core functions that are expected to become less important in the near future due to changes in the nature of the business. A company even can outsource a function that is considered key to company survival if it can find a supplier that can perform the function better—in short, the company should keep only the core functions that *the company can do better than any supplier.* For example, a company may be the low-cost manufacturer in its industry, which allows it to maintain a large enough pricing advantage over its competitors to be guaranteed a large share of the market. Management then can focus solely on the manufacturing function and outsource everything else.

■ *Avoid major investments.* A company may find it has a function that is not as efficient as it could be due to a lack of investment in it. If the company keeps the function in-house, eventually it will have to make a major investment in order to modernize the function. By outsourcing the function, the company can avoid having to make this investment permanently. Furthermore, it can use outsourcing to keep up with the latest technology. The most advanced suppliers realize that their ongoing use of and investment in the latest technology allows them to drive down costs and attract more customers, so companies and suppliers have mutually beneficial goals in this area. For example, a company outsourcing its entire accounting function frequently can take advantage of the most advanced enterprise resources planning software—such as Oracle or SAP—being used by the supplier.

■ *Assist a fast-growing situation.* If a company is acquiring market share rapidly, the management team will be stretched to its limits building the company up so that it can handle the vastly increased volume of business. In such situations, the management team will desperately need additional help in running the company. A supplier can step in and take over a function so that the management team can focus its attention on a smaller number of core activities. This is especially useful when the supplier has a sufficient preexisting capacity to handle massive increases in transactional volume by the company; rapid scalability becomes a crucial outsourcing advantage.

- *Handle overflow situations.* A company may find that there are times of the day or year when a function is overloaded for reasons that are beyond its control. In these situations, it may be cost effective to retain a supplier to which the excess work will be shunted when the in-house staff is unable to keep up with demand. This is a reasonable alternative to the less palatable option of overstaffing the in-house function in order to deal with overflow situations that may occur only a small percentage of the time. This is a popular option for help desk services as well as customer support, where excess incoming calls are sent to the supplier rather than having customers wait online for an excessively long time.
- *Improve flexibility.* This is similar to using outsourcing to handle overflow situations, except that the supplier gets the entire function, not just the overflow business. When a function experiences extremely large swings in work volume, it may be easier to eliminate the fixed cost of an internal staff and move the function to a supplier that will be paid only for the actual work done. This converts a fixed cost into a variable cost—the price of the supplier's services will fluctuate directly with the transaction volume it handles.
- *Improve ratios.* Some companies are so driven by their performance ratios that they will outsource functions solely to improve the ratios. For example, outsourcing a function that involves transferring assets to the supplier will increase the company's return on assets. The functions most likely to improve this ratio are those heavy in assets, such as maintenance, manufacturing, and computer services. Another ratio that can be improved is profitability per person. To enhance this, a company could outsource all functions involving large numbers of employees, such as manufacturing or sales.
- *Jump on the bandwagon.* A company may decide to outsource a function simply because everyone else is doing it. If a major company suddenly dives into outsourcing, other companies will give the activity more credence and will be more likely to outsource, too. Also, a large amount of coverage of outsourcing in various national or industry-specific publications will give company management the impression that outsourcing is the coming trend, and they must use it or fail. For example, due to the large amount of publicity surrounding some of the very large computer services outsourcing deals, the bandwagon effect probably has led to additional outsourcing deals for the computer services function.
- *Enhance credibility.* A small company can use outsourcing as a marketing tool. It can tell potential customers the names of its suppliers, implying that since its functions are being maintained by such well-known suppliers, the company's customers can be assured of a high degree of quality service. In these instances, the company will want to hire the best-known suppliers, since it wants to draw from their prestige. Also, for key functions, the company even may want to team up with a supplier to make joint presentations to company customers, since having the supplier's staff present gives the company additional credibility.
- *Maintain old functions.* A company may find that its in-house staff is unable to maintain its existing functions while also shifting to new technology or a new

location. Outsourcing is a good solution here, for it allows the company to focus its efforts on implementing new initiatives while the supplier maintains existing day-to-day functions. This reason is most common in computer services, where suppliers are hired to maintain old legacy systems while the in-house staff works on a transition to an entirely new computer system.

■ *Reduce costs.* A company may emphasize cost savings for a variety of reasons, such as being in a poor financial position or because of a goal to increase profits. Reducing costs by using a supplier is possible but not in all situations. A supplier clearly has lower costs if it can centralize the work of several companies at one location, such as a central truck maintenance facility or a data processing center. It can lower costs if it can buy materials or supplies at lower costs by using volume purchasing. It also can purchase assets from a company and lease the assets back as part of an outsourcing deal, thereby giving the company an up-front cash infusion. Finally, suppliers' costs are lower than a company's because suppliers typically exercise very tight control over fringe benefits, have lean overhead structures, and use advanced telecommunications to employ staff in low-wage areas around the world. Further, they can achieve greater capacity utilization if they have multiple clients, since they can reallocate staff to match fluctuations in each client's transaction volume. Yet another cost-reduction technique is for suppliers to base their operations in countries that offer extensive tax holidays or tax breaks in exchange for employing their citizens.

■ *Improve performance.* A company may find that it has a function that has bloated costs or inadequate performance. To shake up the function, company management can put it out to bid and include the internal function's staff in the bidding process. The internal staff then can submit a bid alongside outside suppliers that commits it to specific service levels and costs. If the bid proves to be competitive, management can keep the function in-house but hold the function's staff to the specific costs and performance levels noted in its bid. As long as suppliers are told up front that the internal staff will be bidding and that the selection will be a fair process, they should not have a problem with this type of competition.

■ *Begin a strategic initiative.* The CEO may declare a complete company reorganization, and outsourcing can be used to put an exclamation point on her determination to really change the current situation. By making such a significant move at the start of the reorganization, employees will know that management is serious about the changes and will be more likely to assist in making the transition to the new company structure.

Before deciding to outsource based on one of the preceding reasons, the CEO should consider the underlying reasons why outsourcing is being considered in the first place. It may be due to one of the listed reasons, but a deeper problem may be that the function in question is not doing a good job of advertising its accomplishments or of showing that the cost of keeping the function in-house is offset adequately by the resulting benefits. In these cases, it may do no good to outsource the function; management may be replacing a perfectly adequate in-house staff that is not good at publicizing itself with a supplier that performs no better but is quick to point out how much it is doing for the company. If you think this may be an issue, bring in a consultant to review the performance of the in-house function and see if it is, in fact, doing a reasonable job.

You also should understand that it is not necessary to outsource an entire function; instead, you can cherry-pick tasks within the function that are clearly worthy of being outsourced and keep all other tasks in-house. This method reduces the risk of having the chosen supplier do a bad job of handling its assigned tasks, since fewer tasks are at risk, and it allows the company to hand over the remaining functional tasks to the supplier as it becomes more comfortable with the supplier's performance. For example, a company can outsource just the help desk part of its computer services function, or it may add network services, telephone services, application development, or data center operations tasks to one or more suppliers. These options are all available to the manager who is edging into a decision to outsource.

The typical outsourcing path that a company follows starts with a function that has minimal strategic value and will not present a problem even if the supplier does a poor job of providing the service. If the company's experience with these low-end functions proves successful, company management will be more likely to advance to outsourcing those functions with more strategic value or with more company-threatening consequences if the provided service is inadequate. These functions include accounting, human resources, and logistics. Finally, if the company continues to perform well with all or part of those functions outsourced, it will consider moving to outsourcing the most important functions; typically, these are manufacturing, computer services, and engineering (although this may vary considerably by industry). This progression is shown in Exhibit 6.1. Thus, many companies experiment with outsourcing functions of low importance and later include functions with more strategic importance, depending on their earlier experience with the other functions.

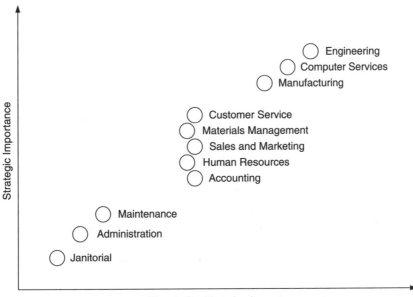

EXHIBIT 6.1 Typical Outsourcing Path

The list of reasons to outsource appears to contain an overpowering number of reasons why you should outsource every corporate function. However, the next section contains a number of cautionary thoughts to consider before calling in a supplier.

Outsourcing Risks

Although there are many good reasons to outsource a function, there are also a number of risks associated with doing so. These can range from minor pricing issues to nonperformance by the supplier of a key function. The CEO must be aware of these risks before making the decision to hand over a function to a supplier. This section lists several of those risks as well as how to mitigate them. The risks are listed next.

- *Future change in supplier circumstances.* One risk is that the supplier's situation may change in the future, causing problems in the outsourcing relationship. For example, the supplier may have financial difficulties, be bought out by a company that does not want to be in the outsourcing business, or undergo a shift in strategy that forces it to provide different services. Also, the technology needed to service the company's needs may change over time, and the supplier may no longer be able to service that new technology. These risks can be lowered by having an independent consultant perform a thorough analysis of the capabilities, financial performance, and competitive positioning of a prospective supplier as well as by ensuring that there is a termination clause in the outsourcing contract that allows the company to back out of the contract if any of the listed circumstances occur. Also, these risks are less important if there are a large number of competing suppliers to which the company's business can be shifted. Alternatively, the risk is greater if there are few competing suppliers.
- *Perceived risk lower than actual.* Another risk is that available information about the success of outsourcing usually is skewed in favor of success stories. An excess of this type of information may lead company management to the conclusion that it must outsource a function (the bandwagon effect) when in reality the number of outsourcing successes is fewer than reported. This skewing problem is caused by the timing of stories about outsourcing—they are almost always published for outsourcing deals that have just been signed, when no problems between companies and their suppliers have yet surfaced. These stories find their way into various publications because they are being pushed by the public relations departments of the suppliers as a form of free advertising. These same suppliers are not going to go out of their way to advertise the failure of any outsourcing deals, nor will the companies for which they are working, since neither party wants to acquire a reputation for not being able to manage an outsourcing deal.
- *Political fallout.* A very serious risk, especially for a large company that dominates a local economy, is that there can be significant fallout within the community if the company lays off a large number of workers as a result of an outsourcing arrangement. There are many outsourcing deals where employees are not rehired by the supplier, so this throws many employees

out of work. If the local economy is highly dependent on the company, this loss of work can generate a very large outpouring of bad feelings, quite possibly resulting in local boycotts, strikes, and bad publicity that may spill over into the national press. This is less of a risk for companies located in large metropolitan areas, where laid-off workers can find new jobs with less difficulty within the region. One way to mitigate this risk is to pick only those suppliers that guarantee that they will hire a large proportion of the company's employees and retain them for a fairly long time, such as a minimum of one year. The person deciding to outsource should consider the impact on the local community before doing so.

- *Supplier failure.* It is possible that a company can outsource a function that is critical to its existence, watch the supplier fail at providing the service, and have this bring about the failure of the entire company. This risk is heaviest for the major corporate functions, such as computer services, engineering, or manufacturing. Only by carefully selecting the appropriate supplier, tightly controlling the transition to the supplier, and continually monitoring the supplier's subsequent activities can this risk be mitigated.

- *Loss of confidential information.* There are a number of outsourcing scenarios where a company must send confidential information to its supplier, such as human resources, accounting, computer services, and engineering. There is a serious risk that this information may be stolen or lost at the supplier location. This is a particular concern where low-wage workers have access to sensitive information and have a monetary incentive to sell it.

- *Local responsibility.* When a company outsources work that it is performing for its own clients, the company is ultimately responsible for the quality of that work. For example, an accounting firm that does the tax returns for its clients can be sued by those clients if the tax returns are outsourced to a third party that completes them improperly.

- *Job loss.* Finally, there is the risk that the person sponsoring the switch to outsourcing may lose his or her job if the outsourcing does not work. Outsourcing is a major change, in some cases involving the transfer of large parts of a company to a supplier and possibly having the supplier run a strategically major function for the company. If these changes do not work as planned, the outsourcing drive could backfire on the project sponsor and lead to a dismissal. In short, sponsoring such a major change and seeing it fail can lead to termination of one or more of a company's management staff.

Generally speaking, some functions can be outsourced at considerably less risk to a company than others. For example, benefits administration, maintenance, and telemarketing are considered to be low risk, because they are not core areas and usually can be switched to a new supplier fairly rapidly. In contrast, customer service, accounting transactions, and computer services require considerably more effort to switch to a new supplier and can impact company operations severely if they are improperly handled. Thus, these areas are of at least medium risk. Finally, such areas as investment analysis, cash flow forecasting, and product pricing could have rapid catastrophic results if improperly handled and so are considered to be high-risk functions for outsourcing.

Thus, there are a number of serious risks to be factored into the decision to outsource a function. These risks can, in some cases, bring down the company or significantly worsen its competitive or financial position, so they must be weighed carefully alongside the many reasons why it is a good idea to outsource a function.

Initiating Outsourcing

The person within a company who makes the decision to outsource will vary depending on the function. For example, a low-level manager can easily outsource the janitorial function and may even be safe in not notifying senior management of the decision to do so. The same goes for most administrative functions and some aspects of maintenance. However, it is inappropriate for most other functions to be outsourced without the input of the most senior company executives. Most functions are not only more strategically important than janitorial services, but they also involve laying off large numbers of people or significantly changing the cost structure of the company. Therefore, it is most appropriate for the CEO to make the final decision to outsource. For major outsourcing decisions involving very large layoffs or cost savings, the board of directors may vote on the issue. If a lower-level manager tries to make the decision for any function but the few exceptions already noted, the decision should be moved up to the CEO instead; the decision is just too important for anyone else to make.

Companies that Take Over Outsourced Functions

Moving a company function to a supplier is an important decision that may have a major negative impact on the company if the arrangement does not go well. The CEO should be aware of how suppliers operate and what their objectives are before making the decision to hand them a key company function, since this knowledge may impact the CEO's decision. This section explores how suppliers make money in the outsourcing arena, how they compete against each other, the areas in which a supplier can truly provide a cost savings to the company, and how the company should treat a top-notch supplier. Only by understanding the supplier's operating situation can a CEO make an informed decision on whether to outsource a function.

A supplier makes money by standardizing a portion of the work involved with a function. The supplier has become so good at one activity that it can regularly beat the performance of any company with which it does business. The supplier may achieve this cost advantage by paying particular attention to streamlining the function, by using only the most experienced and knowledgeable management, by using only the latest technology, or by having such a large-volume operation that it can obtain very low costs per transaction. For example, a computer services provider has lower processing costs because it can run all of the program processing for many companies through one large data processing center that combines the overhead for all of those companies into one facility—this is a permanent cost advantage that a company cannot match.

The key point to note in the preceding paragraph is that a supplier has a cost advantage in only a *portion* of a function. It usually does not have an advantage for any customized work that is, by definition, incapable of being standardized. For this part of the work related to a function, it is likely that the company and not the supplier is the low-cost provider because the company does not have to earn a profit when it performs the function, nor does it incur any overhead costs to market the function. What this means for someone making the decision to outsource is that the supplier will focus on its ability to provide low-cost services during its presentation to company management, but there are many activities within a function area that a supplier *cannot* provide at a lower cost; if anything, it will cost the company *more* money to outsource! Of course, a function still may be worth outsourcing for many reasons that are not related to cost, as were discussed earlier in this chapter.

How do suppliers compete against each other? The CEO must know this in order to differentiate among the bids received from various suppliers. First, nearly all suppliers try to lock in a company for as long a contract period as possible. Not only does this give the supplier an assured flow of revenues, but it also locks out its competitors from dealing with the company. Second, suppliers try to keep the initial cost of a contract as low as possible in order to obtain a company's business and build various clauses into the contract that allow it to increase its prices later. This gives the supplier the lowest initial bid in order to obtain the company's business but still allows it to earn a profit on a deferred basis. Third, suppliers like to offer free consulting services not only in advance but also during the term of their relationship with a company. These services are targeted toward recommending the services of the supplier to the company and sometimes focus on the FUD principle: *f*ear, *u*ncertainty, and *d*oubt—for example, if you do not outsource immediately with us, and not to the competition, all kinds of terrible things will happen. The CEO can counteract these supplier techniques by reducing the length of contract terms, examining the total cost of a supplier proposal over the full term of the contract, and taking the results of free supplier consulting work with a liberal degree of skepticism.

There are a small number of truly top-notch suppliers in every functional area. These suppliers usually have all of the business they can handle, for they have acquired a reputation for exceptional service that keeps companies coming back to them. In these cases, the company must be extremely careful to treat the supplier as well as possible. If the company does not know how to treat a supplier, or abuses it as a matter of course (as some old-style purchasing managers are still prone to do), the top-quality supplier will shut down the relationship immediately, and nothing the company can do will bring it back. This can be a major problem for a functional area where the remaining suppliers are of a clearly lower quality, and it may result in a company having to take a function back in-house because there are no other reliable suppliers left that can provide the service. The CEO should review the company's ability to handle suppliers prior to making the decision to outsource—if the company has a habit of chewing up suppliers, it may be best to forget about any outsourcing until the company's supplier relations problems are fixed.

When considering the services of a top-of-the-line supplier, the person making the outsourcing decision must realize that the supplier will want access to more information than the company has been used to revealing. This information may include the company's long-range plan, since the supplier may need to change its production capacity to meet the expanding needs of the company. In addition, and for the same reason, the supplier may need continuing access to the company's production schedules. Company management even may have to include key suppliers in the annual budgeting and long-range planning process—not as sources of information but as active participants. If management is not comfortable with this prospect, it may not want to outsource a function.

If a company is willing to engage in a tight relationship with a top supplier, it should envision further stages in the relationship with the supplier, which may include equity investments in each other, cross-licensing, joint ventures, or even an acquisition by one party of the other. The relationship may become so close that the company and its supplier have major stakes in the survival of each other; this may lead to financial support by one entity if the other is in danger of failing. This type of close relationship is very uncommon with the more inexpensive functions or with those that have a minimal strategic value, such as maintenance or office administration functions, but is becoming more common with suppliers of the more important functions, such as engineering, manufacturing, or computer services. Once again, if this level of commitment to a supplier is not something that a company is comfortable with, it may not want to outsource any functions, or it may restrict its outsourcing activities to the lowest-level functional areas.

There is an important caveat to consider when envisioning a close relationship with a supplier: It may be more interested in earning a profit at the expense of the company than in forming a closer relationship with the company. For many lower-quality suppliers or for those in the lesser functional areas (e.g., office administration or janitorial services), suppliers are not interested in a cozy relationship with a company unless it leads to more profits. They will not want access to company records or be involved in its budgeting or long-range planning activities. Instead, these suppliers just want to make a higher-than-average profit. In these cases, which are by far the most common of all outsourcing relationships, the CEO must realize that there is no point in inviting a supplier to company meetings, involving it in budgeting or other planning processes, or creating strategic partnerships; the supplier will not have the company's best interests at heart, only its own. This might result in failed joint ventures, lowered expectations, and costs that are higher than anticipated. It is difficult for a CEO to determine which kind of supplier—profit oriented or relationship oriented—is bidding to provide outsourcing services to the company, but it is important to find out, since this issue has an enormous impact on the long-term relations between the company and the supplier. For the CEO, the best sources of information on this issue are the supplier's references, the supplier's reputation in the industry, and face-to-face meetings with the supplier's management.

When the CEO decides to give an important company function to a supplier, the situation is similar to a father giving his daughter away in marriage: He wants to know as much as possible about the person who is on the receiving end. The CEO must know the supplier's expectations for making money from the outsourcing deal, whether the supplier really can offer a cost savings, and how those savings are generated. The manager must know how a supplier will behave when competing with fellow suppliers and how this impacts relations with the company. In addition, the CEO must know how to treat top-notch suppliers (if they can be attracted at all) as well as the level of integration needed to retain this kind of supplier. Finally, the

CEO must be able to differentiate between the supplier that wants a long-term partnership and the supplier that is focused solely on short-term profits.

Summary

This chapter concerned the key decisions surrounding outsourcing: when to outsource a function and who makes the decision. A large number of reasons were given that could form the basis for a decision to outsource a function, either individually or in combination. The CEO can use the risks itemized in this chapter to offset the reasons favoring outsourcing. A short discussion of who should make the decision to outsource concluded that for all but the most minor functions, this decision should be confined to senior management. Finally, there was a brief discussion of the suppliers to which functions would be given. Although this did not directly fit into the overall theme of the chapter, which was the decision-making process surrounding the key outsourcing decisions, it is important for CEOs to understand the nature of the suppliers to which they are giving control over large parts of their companies.

PART II

The Budget

CHAPTER 7

Budgeting Process

The budget is an important planning tool, for it provides the basis for the orderly management of activities within a company. A properly created budget will funnel funding into those activities that a company has determined to be most essential, as defined in its strategic plan. Furthermore, it provides a bridge between strategy and tactics by itemizing the precise tactical events that will be funded, such as the hiring of personnel or acquisition of equipment in a key department. Once the budget has been approved, it also acts as the primary control point over expenditures, since it should be compared to purchase requisitions prior to purchases being made, so that the level of allowed funding can be ascertained. In addition, the results of specific departments can be compared to their budgets, which is an excellent device for determining the performance of department managers. For all of these reasons, a comprehensive knowledge of the budgeting process is crucial for the chief executive officer (CEO).

In this chapter, we look at the system of budgets and how they are linked together, review a sample budget, cover the key elements of flex budgeting, and finish with coverage of the control systems that can be used if a budget is available.

System of Interlocking Budgets

A properly designed budget is a complex web of spreadsheets that account for the activities of virtually all areas within a company. As noted in Exhibit 7.1, the budget begins in two places, with both the revenue budget and research and development (R&D) budget. The revenue budget contains the revenue figures that the company believes it can achieve for each upcoming reporting period. These estimates come partially from the sales staff, which is responsible for estimates of sales levels for existing products within their current territories. Estimates for the sales of new products that have not yet been released and for existing products in new markets will come from a combination of the sales and marketing staffs, who will use their experience with related product sales to derive estimates. The greatest fallacy in any budget is to impose a revenue budget from the top management level without any input from the sales staff; this can result in a company-wide budget that is geared toward a sales level that is most unlikely to be reached.

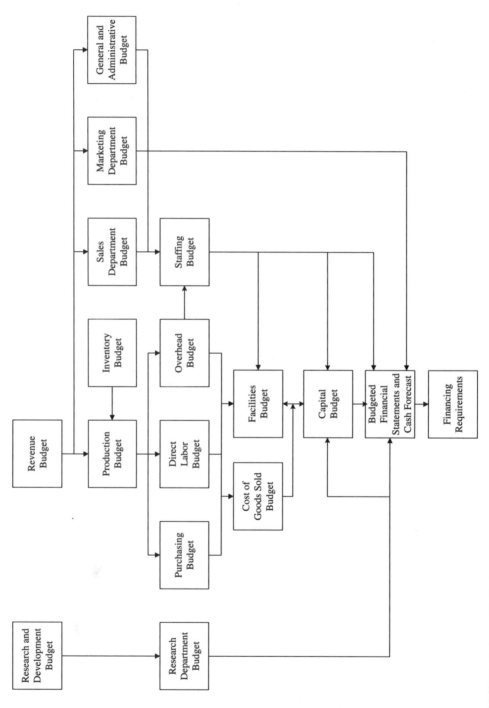

EXHIBIT 7.1 System of Budgets

A revenue budget requires prior consideration of a number of issues. For example, a general market share target will drive several other items within the budget, since greater market share may come at the cost of lower unit prices or higher credit costs. Another issue is the compensation strategy for the sales staff, since a shift to higher or lower commissions for specific products or regions will be a strong incentive for the sales staff to alter their selling behavior, resulting in some changes in estimated sales levels. Yet another consideration is which sales territories are to be entered during the budget period—those with high target populations may yield very high sales per hour of sales effort while the reverse will be true if the remaining untapped regions have smaller target populations. It is also necessary to review the price points that will be offered during the budget period, especially in relation to the pricing strategies that are anticipated from competitors. If there is a strategy to increase market share as well as to raise unit prices, the budget may fail due to conflicting activities. Another major factor is the terms of sale, which can be extended, along with easy credit, to attract more marginal customers; conversely, they can be retracted in order to reduce credit costs and focus company resources on a few key customers. A final point is that the budget should address any changes in the type of customer to whom sales will be made. If an entirely new type of customer will be added to the range of sales targets during the budget period, the revenue budget should reflect a gradual ramp-up that will be required for the sales staff to work through the sales cycle of the new customers.

Once all of these factors have been ruminated on and combined to create a preliminary budget, the sales staff also should compare the budgeted sales level per person to the actual sales level that has been experienced in the recent past to see if the company has the existing capability to make the budgeted sales. If not, the revenue budget should be ramped up to reflect the time it will take to hire and train additional sales staff. The same cross-check can be conducted for the amount of sales budgeted per customer, to see if historical experience validates the sales levels noted in the new budget.

Another budget that initiates other activities within the system of budgets is the R&D budget. This is not related to the sales level at all (as opposed to most other budgets) but instead is a discretionary budget that is based on the company's strategy to derive new or improved products. The decision to fund a certain amount of project-related activity in this area will drive a departmental staffing and capital budget that is, for the most part, completely unrelated to the activity conducted by the rest of the company. However, there can be a feedback loop between this budget and the cash budget, since financing limitations may require management to prune some projects from this area. If so, the management team must work with the R&D manager to determine the correct mix of projects with both short-range and long-range payoffs that still will be funded.

The production budget is driven largely by the sales estimates contained within the revenue budget. However, it also is driven by the inventory-level assumptions in the inventory budget. The inventory budget contains estimates by the materials management supervisor regarding the inventory levels that will be required for the upcoming budget period. For example, a new goal may be to reduce the level of finished goods inventory from 10 turns per year to 15. If so, some of the products required by the revenue budget can be bled off from the existing finished goods inventory stock, requiring smaller production requirements during the budget period. Alternatively, if there is a strong focus on improving the level of customer service, it may be necessary to keep more finished goods in stock, which will require more production than is strictly called for by the revenue budget. This concept also can be extended to work-in-process (WIP) inventory, where the installation of advanced production planning systems, such as manufacturing resources planning or just in time (JIT), can be used to reduce the level of required inventory. Also, JIT purchasing techniques can be used to reduce the amount of raw materials inventory that is kept on hand. All of these assumptions should be delineated clearly in the inventory budget, so that the management team is clear about what systemic changes will be required in order to effect altered inventory turnover levels. Also, one should be aware that any advanced production planning system takes a considerable amount of time to install and tune, so it is best if the inventory budget contains a gradual ramp-up to different planned levels of inventory.

Given this input from the inventory budget, the production budget is used to derive the unit quantity of required products that must be manufactured in order to meet revenue targets for each budget period. Doing this involves a number of interrelated factors, such as the availability of sufficient capacity for production needs. Of particular concern should be the amount of capacity at the bottleneck operation. Since this tends to be the most expensive capital item, it is important to budget a sufficient quantity of funding to ensure that this operation includes enough equipment to meet the targeted production goals. If the bottleneck operation involves skilled labor rather than equipment, the human resources staff should be consulted regarding its ability to bring in the necessary personnel in time to improve the bottleneck capacity in a timely manner.

Step costing is also an important consideration when creating the production budget. Costs will increase in large increments when certain capacity levels are reached. The management team should be fully aware of when these capacity levels will be reached so that it can plan appropriately for the incurrence of added costs. For example, the addition of a second shift to the production area will call for added costs in the areas of supervisory staff, an increased pay rate, and higher maintenance costs. The inverse of this condition also can occur, where step costs can decline suddenly if capacity levels fall below a specific point.

The expense items included in the production budget should be driven by a set of subsidiary budgets: the purchasing, direct labor, and overhead budgets. These budgets can simply be included in the production budget, but they typically involve such a large proportion of company costs that it is best to lay them out separately in greater detail in separate budgets. Comments on these budgets are presented next.

■ *Purchasing budget.* The purchasing budget is driven by several factors, the first of which is the bill of materials that comprises the products that are planned for production during the budget period. These bills must be accurate, or else the purchasing budget can include seriously incorrect information. In addition, there should be a plan for controlling material costs, perhaps through the use of concentrated buying through few suppliers or through the use of long-term contracts. If materials are highly subject to market pressures, comprise a large proportion of total product costs, and have a history of sharp price swings, a best-case and worst-case costing scenario should be added to the budget so that managers can review the impact of costing issues in this area. If a JIT delivery system from suppliers is contemplated, the purchasing budget should reflect a possible increase in material costs caused by the increased number of deliveries from suppliers. It is also worthwhile to budget for a raw material scrap and obsolescence expense; there should be a history of costs in these areas that can be extrapolated based on projected purchasing volumes.

■ *Direct labor budget.* Do not make the mistake of budgeting for direct labor as a fully variable cost. The production volume from day to day tends to be relatively fixed and requires a set number of direct labor personnel on a continuing basis to operate production equipment and manually assemble products. Further, the production manager will realize much greater production efficiencies by holding onto an experienced production staff rather than letting them go as soon as production volumes make small incremental drops. Accordingly, it is better to budget based on reality, which is that direct labor personnel usually are retained, even if there are ongoing fluctuations in the level of production. Thus, direct labor should be shown in the budget as a fixed cost of production, within certain production volume parameters.

Also, this budget should describe staffing levels by type of direct labor position; the amount of direct labor is driven by labor routings, which are documents that describe the exact type and quantity of staffing needed to produce a product. When multiplied by the unit volumes located in the production budget, the result is an expected level of staffing by direct labor position. This information is most useful for the human resources staff, which is responsible for staffing the positions.

The direct labor budget also should account for any contractually mandated changes in hourly rates, which may be itemized in a union agreement. Such an agreement also may have restrictions on layoffs, which should be accounted for in the budget if this will keep labor levels from dropping in proportion with budgeted reductions in production levels. Such an agreement may require that layoffs be conducted in order of seniority, which may force higher-paid employees into positions that normally would be budgeted for less expensive laborers. Thus, the presence of a union contract can result in a much more complex direct labor budget than would normally be the case.

The direct labor budget also may contain features related to changes in the efficiency of employees and any resulting changes in pay. For example, one possible pay arrangement is to pay employees based on a piece rate, which directly ties their performance to the level of production achieved. This method probably will apply only to portions of the workforce, so the direct labor budget may involve pay rates based on both piece rates and hourly pay. Another issue is that any drastic increases in the budgeted level of direct labor personnel likely will result in some initial declines in labor efficiency, since it takes time for new employees to learn their tasks. If this is the case, the budget should reflect a low level of initial efficiency with a ramp-up over time to higher levels that will result in greater initial direct labor costs. Finally, efficiency improvements may be rewarded with staff bonuses from time to time; if so, these bonuses should be included in the budget.

■ *Overhead budget.* The overhead budget can be simple to create if there are no significant changes in production volume from the preceding year, because this budget involves a large quantity of static costs that will not vary much over time. Included in this category are machine maintenance; utilities; supervisory salaries, wages for the materials management, production scheduling, and quality assurance personnel; facilities maintenance; and depreciation expenses. Under the no-change scenario, the most likely budgetary alterations will be to machinery or facilities maintenance, which are dependent on the condition and level of usage of company property.

If there is a significant change in the expected level of production volume, or if new production lines are to be added, you should examine this budget in great detail. The underlying production volumes may cause a ripple effect that results in wholesale changes to many areas of the overhead budget. Of particular concern is the number of overhead-related personnel who must be either laid off or added when capacity levels reach certain critical points, such as the addition or subtraction of extra work shifts. Costs also tend to rise substantially when a facility is operating at very close to 100% capacity, since a high usage level tends to call for an inordinate amount of effort to maintain on an ongoing basis.

The purchasing, direct labor, and overhead budgets can be summarized into a cost of goods sold budget. This budget should incorporate, as a single line item, the total amount of revenue, so that all manufacturing costs can be deducted from it to yield a gross profit margin on the same document. This budget is referred to constantly during the budget creation process, since it tells management if its budgeting assumptions are yielding an acceptable gross margin result. Because it is a summary-level budget for the production side of the budgeting process, this is also a good place to itemize any production-related statistics, such as the average hourly cost of direct labor, inventory turnover rates, and the amount of revenue dollars per production person.

Thus far, we have reviewed the series of budgets that descend in turn from the revenue budget and through the production budget. However, there are other expenses that are unrelated to production. These are categories in a separate set of budgets. The first is the sales department budget, which includes the expenses that the sales staff must incur in order to achieve the revenue budget, such as travel and entertainment as well as sales training. Of particular concern in this budget is the amount of budgeted headcount that is required to meet the sales target. It is essential that the actual sales per salesperson from the most recent completed year of operations be compared to the same calculation in the budget to ensure that there is a sufficiently large budget available for an adequate number of sales personnel. Inadequate sales staffing is a common problem, for companies often make the false assumption that the existing sales staff can make heroic efforts to exceed its previous-year sales efforts by a great deal. Furthermore, the budget must account for a sufficient time period in which new sales personnel can be trained and form an adequate base of customer contacts to create a meaningful stream of revenue for the company. In some industries, this learning curve may be only a few days, but it can be the better part of a year if considerable technical knowledge is required to make a sale. In the latter case, it is likely that the procurement and retention of qualified sales staff is the key element of success for a company; for this reason, the sales department budget is one of the most important elements of the entire budget.

The marketing budget also is closely tied to the revenue budget, for it contains all of the funding required to roll out new products, merchandise them properly, advertise for them, test new products, and so on. A key issue here is to ensure that the marketing budget is fully funded to support any increases in sales noted in the revenue budget. It may be necessary to increase this budget by a disproportionate amount if you are trying to create a new brand, issue a new product, or distribute an existing product in a new market. These costs can easily exceed any associated revenues for some time. A common budgeting problem is not to provide sufficient funding in these instances, leading to a significant drop in expected revenues.

Another nonproduction budget that is integral to the success of the corporation is the general and administrative budget. This budget contains the cost of the corporate management staff, plus all accounting, finance, and human resources personnel. Since this is a cost center, the general inclination is to reduce these costs to the bare minimum. However, in order to do so, there must be a significant investment in technology to achieve reductions in the manual labor usually required to process transactions; thus, there must be some provision in the capital budget for this area.

There is a feedback loop between the staffing and direct labor budgets and the general and administrative budget, because the human resources department must staff itself based on the amount of hiring or layoffs that are anticipated elsewhere in the company. Similarly, a major change in the revenue volume will alter the budget for the accounting department, because many of the activities in this area are driven by the volume of sales transactions. Thus, the general and administrative budget generally requires a number of iterations in response to changes in many other parts of the budget.

Although salaries and wages should be listed in each of the departmental budgets, it is useful to list the total headcount for each position through all budget periods in a separate staffing budget. By doing so, the human resources staff can tell when specific positions must be filled, so that recruiting efforts can be timed most appropriately. This budget also provides good information for the person responsible for the facilities budget, since he or she can use it to determine the timing and amount of square footage requirements for office space. Rather than being a stand-alone budget, the staffing budget tends to be one whose formulas are closely intertwined with those of all other departmental budgets; for this reason, a change in headcount information on this budget automatically translates into a change in the salaries expense on other budgets. It is also a good place to store the average pay rates, overtime percentages, and average benefit costs for all positions. By centralizing this cost information, the human resources staff can more easily update budget information. Since salary-related costs tend to comprise the highest proportion of costs in a company (excluding materials costs), this budget tends to be a heavily used one.

The facilities budget is based on the level of activity that is estimated in many of the budgets just described. For this reason, it is one of the last budgets to be completed. This budget is closely linked to the capital budget, since expenditures for additional facilities will require more maintenance expenses in the facilities budget. This budget typically contains expense line items for building insurance, maintenance, repairs, janitorial services, utilities, and the salaries of the maintenance personnel employed in this function. It is crucial to estimate the need for any upcoming major repairs to facilities when constructing this budget, because these can greatly amplify the total budgeted expense.

Another budget that includes input from virtually all areas of a company is the capital budget. This budget should comprise either a summary listing of all main fixed asset categories for which purchases are anticipated or else a detailed listing of the same information; the latter case is recommended only if there are comparatively few items to be purchased. The capital budget is of great importance to the calculation of corporate financing requirements, since it can involve the expenditure of sums far beyond those that are encountered normally through daily cash flows. The capital budget should be examined carefully to determine if it has an impact on a company's bottleneck operation. All too often, expenditures are made that make other operations more efficient but that do not increase a company's ability to produce more product by increasing the capacity of the bottleneck operation. For more information about this topic, see Chapter 8, Capital Budgeting. It also is necessary to ensure that capital items are scheduled for procurement sufficiently far in advance of related projects that they will be fully installed and operational before the scheduled first activity date of the project. For example, a budget should not itemize revenue from a printing press for the same month in which the press is scheduled to be purchased; it may take months to set up the press. A final item is that capital purchases may be tied to the pet projects of senior managers rather than to the strategic or tactical goals of the company. Consequently, it may be useful to review all capital items in the budget to ensure that they are needed in order to meet these goals.

The end result of all budgets just described is a set of financial statements that reflect the impact on the company of the upcoming budget. At a minimum, these statements should include the income statement and cash flow statement, since these are the best evidence of fiscal health during the budget period. The balance sheet is less necessary, because the key factors on which it reports are related to cash, and that information is contained already within the cash flow statement. These reports should be linked directly to all the other budgets, so that any changes to the budgets will appear immediately in the financial statements. The management team will examine these statements closely and make numerous adjustments to the budgets in order to arrive at a satisfactory financial result.

The budget-linked financial statements are also good places to store related operational and financial ratios, so that the management team can review this information and revise the budgets in order to alter the ratios to match benchmarking or industry standards that may have been set as goals. Typical measurements in this area can include revenue and income per person, inventory turnover ratios, and gross margin percentages. This type of information is also useful for lenders, who may have required minimum financial performance results as part of loan agreements, such as a minimum current ratio or debt/equity ratio.

The cash forecast is of exceptional importance, for it tells company managers if the proposed budget model is feasible. If cash projects result in major cash needs that cannot be met by any possible financing, the model must be changed. The assumptions that go into the cash forecast should be based on strictly historical fact rather than the wishes of managers. This stricture is particularly important in the case of cash receipts from accounts receivable. If the assumptions are changed in the model to reflect an advanced rate of cash receipts that exceeds anything that the company has heretofore experienced, it is very unlikely that it will be achieved during the budget period. Instead, it is better to use proven collection periods as assumptions and alter other parts of the budget to ensure that cash flows remain positive.

The cash forecast is a particularly good area in which to spot the impact of changes in credit policy. For example, if a company wishes to expand its share of the market by allowing easy credit to marginal customers, it should lengthen the assumed collection period in the cash forecast to see if there is a significant downgrading of the resulting cash flows.

The last document in the system of budgets is the discussion of financing alternatives. This is not strictly a budget, although it will contain a single line item, derived from the cash forecast, that itemizes funding needs during each period itemized in the budget. In all other respects, it is simply a discussion of financing alternatives, which can be quite varied. It may involve a mix of debt, supplier financing, preferred stock, common stock, or some other more innovative approach. The document should contain a discussion of the cost of each form of financing, the ability of the company to obtain it, and when it can be obtained. Managers may find that there are so few financing alternatives available, or the cost of financing is so high, that the entire budget must be restructured in order to avoid the negative cash flow that calls for the financing. There also may be a need for feedback from this document back into the budgeted financial statements in order to account for the cost of obtaining the funding as well as any related interest costs.

In the next section, we review an example of the budgets that have just been described, to see how they are formatted and link together to result in a cohesive set of budgets that can be used to conduct future operations of a business.

Sample Budget

In this section, we review several variations on how a budget can be constructed, using a number of examples. The first budget covered is the revenue budget, which is shown in Exhibit 7.2. The exhibit uses quarterly revenue figures for a budget year rather than monthly, in order to conserve space. It contains revenue estimates for three different product lines that are designated as Alpha, Beta, and Charlie.

The Alpha product line uses a budgeting format that identifies the specific quantities that are expected to be sold in each quarter as well as the average price per unit sold. This format is most useful when there are not so many products that such a detailed delineation would create an excessively lengthy budget. It is a very useful format, for the sales staff can go into the budget model and alter unit volumes and

EXHIBIT 7.2 Revenue Budget for the Fiscal Year Ended xx/xx/02

	Quarter 1	Quarter 2	Quarter 3	Quarter 4	Totals
Product Line Alpha:					
Unit price	$ 15.00	$ 14.85	$ 14.80	$ 14.75	—
Unit volume	14,000	21,000	25,000	31,000	91,000
Revenue subtotal	$ 210,000	$ 311,850	$ 370,000	$ 457,250	$1,349,100
Product Line Beta:					
Revenue subtotal	$1,048,000	$1,057,000	$1,061,000	$1,053,000	$4,219,000
Product Line Charlie:					
Region 1	$ 123,000	$ 95,000	$ 82,000	$ 70,000	$ 370,000
Region 2	$ 80,000	$ 89,000	$ 95,000	$ 101,000	$ 365,000
Region 3	$ 95,000	$ 95,000	$ 65,000	$ 16,000	$ 271,000
Region 4	$ 265,000	$ 265,000	$ 320,000	$ 375,000	$1,225,000
Revenue subtotal	$ 563,000	$ 544,000	$ 562,000	$ 562,000	$2,231,000
Revenue grand total	$1,821,000	$1,912,850	$1,993,000	$2,072,250	$7,799,100
Quarterly revenue proportion	23.3%	24.5%	25.6%	26.6%	100.0%
Statistics:					
Product line proportion:					
Alpha	11.5%	16.3%	18.6%	22.1%	17.3%
Beta	57.6%	55.3%	53.2%	50.8%	54.1%
Charlie	30.9%	28.4%	28.2%	27.1%	28.6%
Product line total	100.0%	100.0%	100.0%	100.0%	100.0%

prices quite easily. An alternative format is to reveal this level of detail only for the most important products and to lump the revenue from other products into a single line item, as is the case for the Beta product line.

The most common budgeting format is used for the Beta product line, where we avoid the use of detailed unit volumes and prices in favor of a single lump-sum revenue total for each reporting period. This format is used when there are multiple products within each product line, making it cumbersome to create a detailed list of individual products. However, this format is the least informative and gives no easy way to update the supporting information.

Yet another budgeting format is shown for the Charlie product line, where projected sales are grouped by region. This format is most useful when there are many sales personnel, each of whom has been assigned a specific territory in which to operate. This budget can be used to judge the ongoing performance of each salesperson.

These revenue reporting formats also can be combined, so that the product line detail for the Alpha product can be used as underlying detail for the sales regions used for the Charlie product line—although this method will result in a very lengthy budget document.

A statistics section at the bottom of the revenue budget itemizes the proportion of total sales that occurs in each quarter, plus the proportion of product line sales within each quarter. Although it is not necessary to use these exact measurements, it is useful to include some type of measure that informs the reader of any variations in sales from period to period.

Both the production and inventory budgets are shown in Exhibit 7.3. The inventory budget is itemized at the top of the exhibit, where we itemize the amount of planned inventory turnover in all three inventory categories. There is a considerable ramp-up in WIP inventory turnover, indicating the planned installation of a manufacturing planning system of some kind that will control the flow of materials through the facility.

EXHIBIT 7.3 Production and Inventory Budgets for the Fiscal Year Ended xx/xx/02

	Quarter 1	Quarter 2	Quarter 3	Quarter 4	Totals
Inventory Turnover Goals:					
Raw Materials Turnover	4.0	4.5	5.0	5.5	4.8
W-I-P Turnover	12.0	15.0	18.0	21.0	16.5
Finished Goods Turnover	6.0	6.0	9.0	9.0	7.5
Product Line Alpha Production:					
Beginning Inventory Units	15,000	21,000	20,000	15,000	—
Unit Sales Budget	14,000	21,000	25,000	31,000	91,000
Planned Production	20,000	20,000	20,000	27,375	87,375
Ending Inventory Units	21,000	20,000	15,000	11,375	
Bottleneck Unit Capacity	20,000	20,000	20,000	40,000	
Bottleneck Utilization	100%	100%	100%	68%	
Planned Finished Goods Turnover	15,167	15,167	11,375	11,375	

The production budget for just the Alpha Product Line is shown directly below the inventory goals. This budget is not concerned with the cost of production but rather with the number of units that will be produced. In this instance, we begin with an on-hand inventory of 15,000 units, and try to keep enough units on hand through the remainder of the budget year to meet both the finished goods inventory goal at the top of the exhibit and the number of required units to be sold, which is referenced from the revenue budget. The main problem is that the maximum capacity of the bottleneck operation is 20,000 units per quarter. In order to meet the revenue target, we must run that operation at full bore through the first three quarters, irrespective of the inventory turnover target. This capacity constraint is especially important because the budget indicates a jump in bottleneck capacity in the fourth quarter from 20,000 to 40,000 units; this will occur when the bottleneck operation is stopped for a short time while additional equipment is added to it. During this stoppage, there must be enough excess inventory on hand to cover any sales that occur. Consequently, production is planned for 20,000 units per quarter for the first three quarters, followed by a more precisely derived figure in the fourth quarter that will result in inventory turns of 9.0 at the end of the year, exactly as planned.

The production budget can be enhanced with the incorporation of planned machine downtime for maintenance as well as for the planned loss of production units to scrap. It is also useful to plan for the capacity needs of nonbottleneck work centers, since these areas will require varying levels of staffing, depending on the number of production shifts needed.

The purchasing budget is shown in Exhibit 7.4. It contains several different formats for planning budgeted purchases for the Alpha Product Line. The first option summarizes the planned production for each quarter; this information is brought forward from the production budget. We then multiply this by the standard unit cost of materials to arrive at the total amount of purchases that must be made in order to support sales adequately. The second option identifies the specific cost of each component of the product so that management can see where cost increases are expected to occur. Although this version provides more information, it occupies a great deal of space on the budget if there are many components in each product or many products. A third option, shown at the bottom of the exhibit, summarizes all purchases by commodity type. This format is most useful for the company's buyers, who usually specialize in certain commodity types.

The purchasing budget can be enhanced by adding a scrap factor for budgeted production, which will result in slightly higher quantities to buy, thereby leaving less chance of running out of raw materials. Another upgrade to the exhibit would be to schedule purchases for planned production some time in advance of the actual manufacturing date, so that the purchasing staff will be assured of having the parts on hand when manufacturing begins. A third enhancement is to round off the purchasing volumes for each item into the actual buying volumes that can be obtained on the open market. For example, it may be possible to buy the required labels only in volumes of 100,000 at a time, which would result in a planned purchase at the beginning of the year that would be large enough to cover all production needs through the end of the year.

EXHIBIT 7.4 Purchasing Budget for the Fiscal Year Ended xx/xx/02

	Quarter 1	Quarter 2	Quarter 3	Quarter 4	Totals
Inventory Turnover Goals:					
Raw Materials Turnover	4.0	4.5	5.0	5.5	4.8
Product Line Alpha Purchasing (Option 1):					
Planned Production	20,000	20,000	20,000	27,375	
Standard Material Cost/Unit	$ 5.42	$ 5.42	$ 5.67	$ 5.67	
Total Material Cost	$108,400	$108,400	$113,400	$155,216	$485,416
Product Line Alpha Purchasing (Option 2):					
Planned Production	20,000	20,000	20,000	27,375	
Molded Part	$ 4.62	$ 4.62	$ 4.85	$ 4.85	
Labels	$ 0.42	$ 0.42	$ 0.42	$ 0.42	
Fittings and Fasteners	$ 0.38	$ 0.38	$ 0.40	$ 0.40	
Total Cost of Components	$ 5.42	$ 5.42	$ 5.67	$ 5.67	
Product Line Alpha Purchasing (Option 3):					
Plastic Commodities					
Molded Parts Units	20,000	20,000	20,000	27,375	
Molded Parts Cost	$ 4.62	$ 4.62	$ 4.85	$ 4.85	
Adhesives Commodity					
Labels Units	20,000	20,000	20,000	27,375	
Labels Cost	$ 0.42	$ 0.42	$ 0.42	$ 0.42	
Fasteners Commodity					
Fasteners Units	20,000	20,000	20,000	27,375	
Fasteners Cost	$ 0.38	$ 0.38	$ 0.40	$ 0.40	
Statistics:					
Materials as Percent of Revenue	36%	36%	38%	38%	

EXHIBIT 7.5 Direct Labor Budget for the Fiscal Year Ended xx/xx/02

	Quarter 1	Quarter 2	Quarter 3	Quarter 4	Totals	Notes
Machining Department:						
Sr. Machine Operator	$ 15,120	$ 15,372	$ 23,058	$ 23,058	$ 76,608	
Machining Apprentice	$ 4,914	$ 4,964	$ 9,929	$ 9,929	$ 29,736	
Expense subtotal	$ 20,034	$ 20,336	$ 32,987	$ 32,987	$106,344	
Paint Department:						
Sr. Paint Shop Staff	$ 15,876	$ 16,128	$ 16,128	$ 16,128	$ 64,260	
Painter Apprentice	$ 5,065	$ 5,216	$ 5,216	$ 5,216	$ 20,714	
Expense subtotal	$ 20,941	$ 21,344	$ 21,344	$ 21,344	$ 84,974	
Polishing Department:						
Sr. Polishing Staff	$ 16,632	$ 11,844	$ 11,844	$ 11,844	$ 52,164	
Polishing Apprentice	$ 4,360	$ 4,511	$ 4,511	$ 4,511	$ 17,892	
Expense subtotal	$ 20,992	$ 16,355	$ 16,355	$ 16,355	$ 70,056	
Final Assembly Department:						
General Laborer	$ 63,735	$ 66,950	$ 69,755	$ 72,529	$272,969	3.5%
Expense subtotal	$ 63,735	$ 66,950	$ 69,755	$ 72,529	$272,969	
Expense grand total	$125,702	$124,985	$140,441	$143,215	$534,343	
Statistics:						
Union Hourly Rates:						
Sr. Machine Operator	$15.00	$15.25	$15.25	$15.25		
Machining Apprentice	$ 9.75	$ 9.85	$ 9.85	$ 9.85		
Sr. Paint Shop Staff	$15.75	$16.00	$16.00	$16.00		
Painter Apprentice	$10.05	$10.35	$10.35	$10.35		
Sr. Polishing Staff	$11.00	$11.75	$11.75	$11.75		
Polishing Apprentice	$ 8.65	$ 8.95	$ 8.95	$ 8.95		
Headcount by Position:						
Sr. Machine Operator	2	2	3	3		
Machining Apprentice	1	1	2	2		
Sr. Paint Shop Staff	2	2	2	2		
Painter Apprentice	1	1	1	1		
Sr. Polishing Staff	3	2	2	2		
Polishing Apprentice	1	1	1	1		

The direct labor budget is shown in Exhibit 7.5. This budget assumes that only one labor category will vary directly with revenue volume—that category is the final assembly department, where a percentage in the far right column indicates that the cost in this area will be budgeted at a fixed 3.5% of total revenues. In all other cases, there are assumptions for a fixed number of personnel in each position within each production department. All of the wage figures for each department (except for final assembly) are derived from the planned hourly rates and headcount figures noted at the bottom of the page. This budget can be enhanced with the addition of separate line items for payroll tax percentages, benefits, shift differential payments, and overtime expenses. The cost of the final assembly department also can be adjusted to account for worker efficiency, which will be lower during production ramp-up periods when new, untrained employees are added to the workforce.

A sample of the overhead budget is shown in Exhibit 7.6. In this exhibit, we see that the overhead budget really is made up of a number of subsidiary departments, such as maintenance, materials management, and quality assurance. If the budget of any of these departments is large enough, it makes sense to split it off into a separate budget, so that the managers of those departments can see their budgeted expectations more clearly. Of particular interest in this exhibit is the valid capacity range noted on the far right side of the exhibit. This range signifies the production activity level within which the budgeted overhead costs are accurate. If the actual capacity utilization were to fall outside of this range, either high or low, a separate overhead budget should be constructed with costs that are expected to be incurred within those ranges.

A sample cost of goods sold budget is shown in Exhibit 7.7. This format splits out each of the product lines noted in the revenue budget for reporting purposes and subtracts from each one the materials costs that are noted in the purchases budget. This method results in a contribution margin for each product line that is the clearest representation of the impact of direct costs (i.e., material costs) on each one. We summarize these individual contribution margins into a summary-level contribution margin and then subtract the total direct labor and overhead costs (as referenced from the direct labor and overhead budgets) to arrive at a total gross margin. The statistics section also notes the number of production personnel budgeted for each quarterly reporting period plus the average annual revenue per production employee; these statistics can be replaced with any operational information that management wants to see at a summary level for the production function, such as efficiency levels, capacity utilization, or inventory turnover.

The sales department budget is shown in Exhibit 7.8. This budget shows several different ways in which to organize budget information. At the top of the budget is a block of line items that lists the expenses for those overhead costs within the department that cannot be linked specifically to a salesperson or region. In cases where the number of sales staff is quite small, *all* of the department's costs may be listed in this area.

Another alternative is shown in the second block of expense line items in the middle of the sales department budget, where all of the sales costs for an entire product line are lumped together into a single line item. If each person on the sales staff is assigned exclusively to a single product line, it may make sense to break down the budget into separate budget pages for each product line and to list all of the expenses associated with each product line on a separate page.

A third alternative is shown in Exhibit 7.8, where we list a summary of expenses for each salesperson. This format works well when combined with the departmental overhead expenses at the top of the budget, since this accounts for all of the departmental costs. However, this format brings up a confidentiality issue, since the compensation of each salesperson can be inferred from the report. Also, this format would include the commission expense paid to each salesperson. Because commissions are a variable cost that is directly associated with each incremental dollar of sales, they should be itemized as a separate line item within the cost of goods sold.

EXHIBIT 7.6 Overhead Budget for the Fiscal Year Ended xx/xx/02

	Quarter 1	Quarter 2	Quarter 3	Quarter 4	Totals	Valid Capacity Range
Supervision:						
Production Manager Salary	$ 16,250	$ 16,250	$ 16,250	$ 16,250	$ 65,000	—
Shift Manager Salaries	$ 22,000	$ 22,000	$ 23,500	$ 23,500	$ 91,000	40%–70%
Expense subtotal	$ 38,250	$ 38,250	$ 39,750	$ 39,750	$ 156,000	
Maintenance Department:						
Equipment Maint. Staff	$ 54,000	$ 56,500	$ 58,000	$ 60,250	$ 228,750	40%–70%
Facilities Maint. Staff	$ 8,250	$ 8,250	$ 8,500	$ 8,500	$ 33,500	40%–70%
Equipment Repairs	$ 225,000	$ 225,000	$ 275,000	$ 225,000	$ 950,000	40%–70%
Facility Repairs	$ 78,000	$ 29,000	$ 12,000	$ 54,000	$ 173,000	40%–70%
Expense subtotal	$ 365,250	$ 318,750	$ 353,500	$ 347,750	$1,385,250	
Materials Management Department:						
Manager Salary	$ 18,750	$ 18,750	$ 18,750	$ 18,750	$ 75,000	—
Purchasing Staff	$ 28,125	$ 18,750	$ 18,750	$ 18,750	$ 84,375	40%–70%
Materials Mgmt. Staff	$ 28,000	$ 35,000	$ 35,000	$ 35,000	$ 133,000	40%–70%
Production Control Staff	$ 11,250	$ 11,250	$ 11,250	$ 11,250	$ 45,000	40%–70%
Expense subtotal	$ 86,125	$ 83,750	$ 83,750	$ 83,750	$ 337,375	
Quality Department:						
Manager Salary	$ 13,750	$ 13,750	$ 13,750	$ 13,750	$ 55,000	—
Quality Staff	$ 16,250	$ 16,250	$ 16,250	$ 24,375	$ 73,125	40%–70%
Lab Testing Supplies	$ 5,000	$ 4,500	$ 4,500	$ 4,500	$ 18,500	40%–70%
Expense subtotal	$ 35,000	$ 34,500	$ 34,500	$ 42,625	$ 146,625	
Other Expenses:						
Depreciation	$ 14,000	$ 15,750	$ 15,750	$ 15,750	$ 61,250	—
Utilities	$ 60,000	$ 55,000	$ 55,000	$ 60,000	$ 230,000	40%–70%
Boiler Insurance	$ 3,200	$ 3,200	$ 3,200	$ 3,200	$ 12,800	—
Expense Subtotal	$ 77,200	$ 73,950	$ 73,950	$ 78,950	$ 304,050	
Expense Grand Total	$ 601,825	$ 549,200	$ 585,450	$ 592,825	$2,329,300	

EXHIBIT 7.7 Cost of Goods Sold Budget for the Fiscal Year Ended xx/xx/02

	Quarter 1	Quarter 2	Quarter 3	Quarter 4	Totals
Product Line Alpha:					
Revenue	$ 210,000	$ 311,850	$ 370,000	$ 457,250	$1,349,100
Materials Expense	$ 108,400	$ 108,400	$ 113,400	$ 155,216	$ 485,416
Contribution Margin $$	$ 101,600	$ 203,450	$ 256,600	$ 302,034	$ 863,684
Contribution Margin %	48%	65%	69%	66%	64%
Product Line Beta:					
Revenue	$1,048,000	$1,057,000	$1,061,000	$1,053,000	$4,219,000
Materials Expense	$ 12,000	$ 14,000	$ 15,000	$ 13,250	$ 54,250
Contribution Margin $$	$1,036,000	$1,043,000	$1,046,000	$1,039,750	$4,164,750
Contribution Margin %	99%	99%	99%	99%	99%
Product Line Charlie:					
Revenue	$ 563,000	$ 544,000	$ 562,000	$ 562,000	$2,231,000
Materials Expense	$ 268,000	$ 200,000	$ 220,000	$ 230,000	$ 918,000
Contribution Margin $$	$ 295,000	$ 344,000	$ 342,000	$ 332,000	$1,313,000
Contribution Margin %	52%	63%	61%	59%	59%
Total Contribution Margin $$	$1,432,600	$1,590,450	$1,644,600	$1,673,784	$6,341,434
Total Contribution Margin %	79%	83%	83%	81%	81%
Direct Labor Expense:	$ 125,702	$ 124,985	$ 140,441	$ 143,215	$ 534,343
Overhead Expense:	$ 601,825	$ 549,200	$ 585,450	$ 592,825	$2,329,300
Total Gross Margin $$	$ 705,073	$ 916,265	$ 918,709	$ 937,744	$3,477,791
Total Gross Margin %	39%	48%	46%	45%	44%
Statistics:					
No. of Production Staff*	23	22	22	23	
Ave. Annual Revenue per Production Employee	$ 316,696	$ 347,791	$ 362,364	$ 360,391	

*Not including general assembly staff.

117

EXHIBIT 7.8 Sales Department Budget for the Fiscal Year Ended xx/xx/02

	Quarter 1	Quarter 2	Quarter 3	Quarter 4	Totals
Departmental Overhead:					
Depreciation	$ 500	$ 500	$ 500	$ 500	$ 2,000
Office supplies	$ 750	$ 600	$ 650	$ 600	$ 2,600
Payroll taxes	$ 2,945	$ 5,240	$ 5,240	$ 8,186	$ 21,611
Salaries	$ 38,500	$ 68,500	$ 68,500	$107,000	$ 282,500
Travel and entertainment (T&E)	$ 1,500	$ 1,500	$ 1,500	$ 2,000	$ 6,500
Expense subtotal	$ 44,195	$ 76,340	$ 76,390	$118,286	$ 315,211
Product Line Alpha:	$ 32,000	$ 18,000	$ 0	$ 21,000	$ 71,000
Expenses by Salesperson:					
Jones, Milbert	$ 14,000	$ 16,500	$ 17,000	$ 12,000	$ 59,500
Smidley, Jefferson	$ 1,000	$ 9,000	$ 8,000	$ 12,000	$ 30,000
Verity, Jonas	$ 7,000	$ 9,000	$ 14,000	$ 12,000	$ 42,000
Expense subtotal	$ 22,000	$ 34,500	$ 39,000	$ 36,000	$ 131,500
Expenses by Region:					
East Coast	$ 52,000	$ 71,000	$ 15,000	$ 0	$ 138,000
Midwest Coast	$ 8,000	$ 14,000	$ 6,000	$ 12,000	$ 40,000
West Coast	$ 11,000	$ 10,000	$ 12,000	$ 24,000	$ 57,000
Expense subtotal	$ 71,000	$ 95,000	$ 33,000	$ 36,000	$ 235,000
Expense grand total	$137,195	$205,840	$148,390	$190,286	$ 681,711
Statistics:					
Revenue per salesperson	$607,000	$637,617	$664,333	$690,750	$2,599,700
T&E per salesperson	$ 500	$ 500	$ 500	$ 667	$ 2,167

A final option listed at the bottom of the example is to itemize expenses by sales region. This format works best when there are a number of sales personnel within the department who are clustered into a number of clearly identifiable regions. If there are no obvious regions or if there is only one salesperson per region, the better format would be to list expenses by salesperson.

At the bottom of the budget is the usual statistics section. The sales department budget is concerned only with making sales, so it should be no surprise that revenue per salesperson is the first item listed. Also, since the primary sales cost associated with this department is usually travel costs, the other statistical item is the travel and entertainment cost per person.

Exhibit 7.9 shows a sample marketing budget. As was the case for the sales department, this one also itemizes departmental overhead costs at the top, which leaves space in the middle for the itemization of campaign-specific costs in the middle. The campaign-specific costs can be lumped together for individual product lines, as is the case for product lines Alpha and Beta in the exhibit, or with subsidiary line items, as

EXHIBIT 7.9 Marketing Department Budget for the Fiscal Year Ended xx/xx/02

	Quarter 1	Quarter 2	Quarter 3	Quarter 4	Totals
Departmental Overhead:					
Depreciation	650	750	850	1,000	3,250
Office supplies	200	200	200	200	800
Payroll taxes	4,265	4,265	4,265	4,265	17,060
Salaries	$55,750	$55,750	$55,750	$55,750	223,000
Travel and entertainment	5,000	6,500	7,250	7,250	26,000
Expense subtotal	65,865	67,465	68,315	68,465	270,110
Campaign-Specific Expenses:					
Product Line Alpha	14,000	26,000	30,000	0	70,000
Product Line Beta	18,000	0	0	24,000	42,000
Product Line Charlie					0
Advertising	10,000	0	20,000	0	30,000
Promotional Tour	5,000	25,000	2,000	0	32,000
Coupon Redemption	2,000	4,000	4,500	1,200	11,700
Product Samples	2,750	5,250	1,250	0	9,250
Expense subtotal	51,750	60,250	57,750	25,200	194,950
Expense grand total	117,615	127,715	126,065	93,665	465,060
Statistics:					
Expense as percent of total sales	6.5%	6.7%	6.3%	4.5%	6.0%
Expense proportion by quarter	25.3%	27.5%	27.1%	20.1%	100.0%

is shown for product line Charlie. A third possible format, which is to itemize marketing costs by marketing tool (e.g., advertising, promotional tour, coupon redemption, etc.), generally is not recommended if there is more than one product line, since there is no way for an analyst to determine the impact of individual marketing costs on specific product lines. The statistics at the bottom of the page attempt to compare marketing costs to sales; however, the results should be treated only as approximations, since marketing efforts usually will not result in immediate sales but rather will result in sales that build over time. Thus, the time lag after incurring a marketing cost makes it difficult to determine the efficacy of marketing activities.

A sample general and administrative budget is shown in Exhibit 7.10. This budget can be quite lengthy, including such additional line items as postage, copier leases, and office repair. Many of these extra expenses have been pruned from the exhibit in order to provide a compressed view of the general format to be used. The exhibit does not lump together the costs of the various departments that typically are included in this budget but rather identifies each one in separate blocks; this format is most useful when there are separate managers for the accounting and human resources functions, so that they will have a better understanding of their budgets. The statistics section at the bottom of the page itemizes a benchmark target of the total

EXHIBIT 7.10 General and Administrative Budget for the Fiscal Year Ended xx/xx/02

	Quarter 1	Quarter 2	Quarter 3	Quarter 4	Totals	Notes
Accounting Department:						
Depreciation	4,000	4,000	4,250	4,250	16,500	
Office supplies	650	650	750	750	2,800	
Payroll taxes	4,973	4,973	4,973	4,973	19,890	
Salaries	$65,000	$65,000	$65,000	$65,000	260,000	
Training	500	2,500	7,500	0	10,500	
Travel and entertainment	0	750	4,500	500	5,750	
Expense subtotal	75,123	77,873	86,973	75,473	315,440	
Corporate Expenses:						
Depreciation	450	500	550	600	2,100	
Office supplies	1,000	850	750	1,250	3,850	
Payroll taxes	6,598	6,598	6,598	6,598	26,393	
Salaries	$86,250	$86,250	$86,250	$86,250	345,000	
Insurance, business	4,500	4,500	4,500	4,500	18,000	
Training	5,000	0	0	0	5,000	
Travel and entertainment	2,000	500	500	0	3,000	
Expense subtotal	105,798	99,198	99,148	99,198	403,343	
Human Resources Department:						
Benefits programs	7,284	7,651	7,972	8,289	31,196	0.4%
Depreciation	500	500	500	500	2,000	
Office supplies	450	8,000	450	450	9,350	
Payroll taxes	2,869	2,869	2,869	2,869	11,475	
Salaries	$37,500	$37,500	$37,500	$37,500	150,000	
Training	5,000	0	7,500	0	12,500	
Travel and entertainment	2,000	1,000	3,500	1,000	7,500	
Expense subtotal	55,603	57,520	60,291	50,608	224,021	
Expense grand total	236,523	234,591	246,411	225,278	942,804	
Statistics:						
Expense as proportion of revenue	13.0%	12.3%	12.4%	10.9%	12.1%	
Benchmark comparison	11.5%	11.5%	11.5%	11.5%	11.5%	

general and administrative cost as a proportion of revenue. This is a particularly useful statistic to track, since the general and administrative function is a cost center and requires such a comparison in order to inform management that these costs are being held in check.

A staffing budget is shown in Exhibit 7.11. It itemizes the expected headcount in every department by major job category. It does not attempt to identify individual positions, as doing so can lead to an excessively lengthy list. Also, because there may be multiple positions identified within each job category, the *average* salary for each cluster of jobs is identified. If a position is subject to overtime pay, its expected

EXHIBIT 7.11 Staffing Budget for the Fiscal Year Ended xx/xx/02

	Quarter 1	Quarter 2	Quarter 3	Quarter 4	Average Salary	Overtime Percent
Sales Department:						
Regional Sales Manager	1	2	2	3	$120,000	0%
Salesperson	2	4	4	6	$ 65,000	0%
Sales Support Staff	1	1	1	2	$ 34,000	6%
Marketing Department:						
Marketing Manager	1	1	1	1	$ 85,000	0%
Marketing Researcher	2	2	2	2	$ 52,000	0%
Secretary	1	1	1	1	$ 34,000	6%
General and Administrative:						
President	1	1	1	1	$175,000	0%
Chief Operating Officer	1	1	1	1	$125,000	0%
Chief Financial Officer	1	1	1	1	$100,000	0%
Human Resources Mgr.	1	1	1	1	$ 80,000	0%
Accounting Staff	4	4	4	4	$ 40,000	10%
Human Resources Staff	2	2	2	2	$ 35,000	8%
Executive Secretary	1	1	1	1	$ 45,000	6%
Research Department:						
Chief Scientist	1	1	1	1	$100,000	0%
Senior Engineer Staff	3	3	3	4	$ 80,000	0%
Junior Engineer Staff	3	3	3	3	$ 60,000	0%
Overhead Budget:						
Production Manager	1	1	1	1	$ 65,000	0%
Quality Manager	1	1	1	1	$ 55,000	0%
Materials Manager	1	1	1	1	$ 75,000	0%
Production Scheduler	1	1	1	1	$ 45,000	0%
Quality Assurance Staff	2	2	2	3	$ 32,500	8%
Purchasing Staff	3	2	2	2	$ 37,500	8%
Materials Mgmt. Staff	4	5	5	5	$ 28,000	8%
Total Headcount	39	42	42	48		

overtime percentage is identified on the right side of the budget. Many sections of the budget should have linkages to this page, so that any changes in headcount here will be reflected automatically in the other sections. This budget may have to be restricted from general access, since it contains salary information that may be considered confidential information.

The facilities budget tends to have the largest number of expense line items. A sample of this format is shown in Exhibit 7.12. These expenses may be offset by some rental or sublease revenues if a portion of the company facilities is rented out to other organizations. However, this revenue is shown in this budget only if the revenue amount is small; otherwise, it is more commonly found as an "other

EXHIBIT 7.12 Facilities Budget for the Fiscal Year Ended xx/xx/02

	Quarter 1	Quarter 2	Quarter 3	Quarter 4	Totals
Facility Expenses:					
Contracted Services	$ 5,500	$ 5,400	$ 5,000	$ 4,500	$ 20,400
Depreciation	$29,000	$29,000	$28,000	$28,000	$114,000
Electricity Charges	$ 4,500	$ 3,500	$ 3,500	$ 4,500	$ 16,000
Inspection Fees	$ 500	$ 0	$ 0	$ 500	$ 1,000
Insurance	$ 8,000	$ 0	$ 0	$ 0	$ 8,000
Maintenance Supplies	$ 3,000	$ 3,000	$ 3,000	$ 3,000	$ 12,000
Payroll Taxes	$ 1,148	$ 1,148	$ 1,148	$ 1,186	$ 4,628
Property Taxes	$ 0	$ 5,000	$ 0	$ 0	$ 5,000
Repairs	$15,000	$ 0	$29,000	$ 0	$ 44,000
Sewage Charges	$ 250	$ 250	$ 250	$ 250	$ 1,000
Trash Disposal	$ 3,000	$ 3,000	$ 3,000	$ 3,000	$ 12,000
Wages—Janitorial	$ 5,000	$ 5,000	$ 5,000	$ 5,500	$ 20,500
Wages—Maintenance	$10,000	$10,000	$10,000	$10,000	$ 40,000
Water Charges	$ 1,000	$ 1,000	$ 1,000	$ 1,000	$ 4,000
Expense grand total	$85,898	$66,298	$88,898	$61,436	$302,528
Statistics:					
Total Square Feet	52,000	52,000	78,000	78,000	
Square Feet/Employee	839	813	1,219	1,099	
Unused Square Footage	1,200	1,200	12,500	12,500	

revenue" line item on the revenue budget. A statistics section at the bottom of this budget refers to the total amount of square feet occupied by the facility. A very effective statistic is the amount of unused square footage, which can be used to conduct an ongoing program of selling off, renting, or consolidating company facilities.

The research department's budget is shown in Exhibit 7.13. It is most common to segregate the department-specific overhead that cannot be attributed to a specific project at the top of the budget and cluster costs by project below that. By doing so, the management team can see precisely how much money is being allocated to each project. This number may be of use in determining which projects must be canceled or delayed as part of the budget review process. The statistics section at the bottom of the budget notes the proportion of planned expenses in the categories of overhead, research, and development. These proportions can be examined to see if the company is allocating funds to the right balance of projects that most effectively meets its product development goals.

The capital budget is shown in Exhibit 7.14. This format clusters capital expenditures by a number of categories. For example, the first category, entitled "budget-related expenditures," clearly focuses attention on those outgoing payments that will increase the company's key productive capacity. The payments in the third quarter under this heading are related directly to the increase in bottleneck capacity that was shown in the production budget (Exhibit 7.3) for the fourth quarter. The budget also contains an automatic assumption of $7,000 in capital expenditures for any net increase in nondirect labor headcount, which encompasses the cost of computer

EXHIBIT 7.13 Research Department Budget for the Fiscal Year Ended xx/xx/02

	Quarter 1	Quarter 2	Quarter 3	Quarter 4	Totals
Departmental Overhead:					
Depreciation	500	500	400	400	1,800
Office supplies	750	2,000	1,500	1,250	5,500
Payroll taxes	9,945	9,945	9,945	11,475	41,310
Salaries	$130,000	$130,000	$130,000	$150,000	540,000
Travel and entertainment	0	0	0	0	0
Expense subtotal	141,195	142,445	141,845	163,125	588,610
Research-Specific Expenses:					
Gamma Project	20,000	43,500	35,000	12,500	111,000
Omega Project	5,000	6,000	7,500	9,000	27,500
Pi Project	14,000	7,000	7,500	4,500	33,000
Upsilon Project	500	2,500	5,000	0	8,000
Expense subtotal	39,500	59,000	55,000	26,000	179,500
Development-Specific Expenses:					
Latin Project	28,000	29,000	30,000	15,000	102,000
Greek Project	14,000	14,500	15,000	7,500	51,000
Mabinogian Project	20,000	25,000	15,000	10,000	70,000
Old English Project	6,250	12,500	25,000	50,000	93,750
Expense subtotal	68,250	81,000	85,000	82,500	316,750
Expense grand total	248,945	282,445	281,845	271,625	1,084,860
Statistics:					
Budgeted number of patent applications filed	2	0	1	1	4
Proportion of expenses:					
Overhead	56.7%	50.4%	50.3%	60.1%	217.5%
Research	15.9%	20.9%	19.5%	9.6%	65.8%
Development	27.4%	28.7%	30.2%	30.4%	116.6%
Total Expenses	100.0%	100.0%	100.0%	100.0%	400.0%

equipment and office furniture for each person. If the company's capitalization limit is set too high to list these expenditures on the capital budget, a similar line item should be inserted into the general and administrative budget, so that the expense can be recognized under the office supplies or some similar account.

The capital budget also includes a category for profit-related expenditures. Any projects listed in this category should be subject to an intensive expenditure review, using cash flow discounting techniques to ensure that they return a sufficient cash flow to make their acquisition profitable to the company. Other categories in the budget cover expenditures for safety or required items, which tend to be purchased with no cash flow discounting review. An alternative to this grouping system is to list only the sum total of all capital expenditures in each category; this method is used most frequently when there are far too many separate purchases to list on the

EXHIBIT 7.14 Capital Budget for the Fiscal Year Ended xx/xx/02

	Quarter 1	Quarter 2	Quarter 3	Quarter 4	Totals
Bottleneck-Related Expenditures:					
Stamping Machine			$150,000		$150,000
Facility for Machine			$ 72,000		$ 72,000
Headcount-Related Expenditures:					
Headcount Change ×					
$7,000 Added Staff	$ 0	$ 21,000	$ 0	$42,000	$ 63,000
Profit-Related Expenditures:					
Blending Machine		$ 50,000			$ 50,000
Polishing Machine		$ 27,000			$ 27,000
Safety-Related Expenditures:					
Machine Shielding		$ 3,000	$ 3,000		$ 6,000
Handicap Walkways	$8,000	$ 5,000			$ 13,000
Required Expenditures:					
Clean Air Scrubber			$ 42,000		$ 42,000
Other Expenditures:					
Tool Crib Expansion				$18,500	$ 18,500
Total expenditures	$8,000	$106,000	$267,000	$60,500	$441,500

budget. Another variation is to list only the largest expenditures on separate budget lines and cluster together all smaller ones. The level of capital purchasing activity will determine the type of format used.

All of the preceding budgets roll up into the budgeted income and cash flow statement, shown in Exhibit 7.15. This format lists the grand totals from each preceding page of the budget in order to arrive at a profit or loss for each budget quarter. In the example, we see that a large initial loss in the first quarter is offset gradually by smaller gains in later quarters to arrive at a small profit for the year. However, the presentation continues with a cash flow statement that has less positive results. It begins with the net profit figure for each quarter, adds back the depreciation expense for all departments, and subtracts out all planned capital expenditures from the capital budget to arrive at cash flow needs for the year. This figure tells us that the company will experience a maximum cash shortfall in the third quarter. This format can be made more precise by adding in time lag factors for the payment of accounts payable and the collection of accounts receivable.

The final document in the budget is an itemization of the finances needed to ensure that the rest of the budget can be achieved. An example is shown in Exhibit 7.16, which carries forward the final cash position at the end of each quarter that was the product of the preceding cash flow statement. This line shows that there will be a maximum shortfall of $223,727 by the end of the third quarter. The next section of

EXHIBIT 7.15 Budgeted Income and Cash Flow Statement for the Fiscal Year Ended xx/xx/02

	Quarter 1	Quarter 2	Quarter 3	Quarter 4	Totals
Revenue:	$1,821,000	$1,912,850	$1,993,000	$2,072,250	$7,799,100
Cost of Goods Sold:					
Materials	$ 388,400	$ 322,400	$ 348,400	$ 398,466	$1,457,666
Direct Labor	$ 125,702	$ 124,985	$ 140,441	$ 143,215	$ 534,343
Overhead					
Supervision	$ 38,250	$ 38,250	$ 39,750	$ 39,750	$ 156,000
Maintenance Department	$ 365,250	$ 318,750	$ 353,500	$ 347,750	$1,385,250
Materials Management	$ 86,125	$ 83,750	$ 83,750	$ 83,750	$ 337,375
Quality Department	$ 35,000	$ 34,500	$ 34,500	$ 42,625	$ 146,625
Other Expenses	$ 77,200	$ 73,950	$ 73,950	$ 78,950	$ 304,050
Total Cost of Goods Sold	$1,115,927	$ 996,585	$1,074,291	$1,134,506	$4,321,309
Gross Margin	$ 705,073	$ 916,265	$ 918,709	$ 937,744	$3,477,791
Operating Expenses					
Sales Department	$ 137,195	$ 205,840	$ 148,390	$ 190,286	$ 681,711
General and Admin. Dept.					
Accounting	$ 75,123	$ 77,873	$ 86,973	$ 75,473	$ 315,440
Corporate	$ 105,798	$ 99,198	$ 99,148	$ 99,198	$ 403,343
Human Resources	$ 55,603	$ 57,520	$ 60,291	$ 50,608	$ 224,021
Marketing Department	$ 117,615	$ 127,715	$ 126,065	$ 93,665	$ 465,060
Facilities Department	$ 85,898	$ 66,298	$ 88,898	$ 61,436	$ 302,528
Research Department	$ 248,945	$ 282,445	$ 281,845	$ 271,625	$1,084,860
Total Operating Expenses	$ 826,176	$ 916,888	$ 891,609	$ 842,290	$3,476,963
Net Profit (Loss)	–$ 121,103	–$ 624	$ 27,100	$ 95,455	$ 828

	Quarter 1	Quarter 2	Quarter 3	Quarter 4	Totals
Cash Flow:					
Beginning Cash	$ 100,000	$ 20,497	–$ 34,627	–$ 223,727	
Net Profit (Loss)	–$ 121,103	–$ 624	$ 27,100	$ 95,455	$ 828
Add Depreciation	$ 49,600	$ 51,500	$ 50,800	$ 51,000	$ 202,900
Minus Capital Purchases	–$ 8,000	–$ 106,000	–$ 267,000	–$ 60,500	–$ 441,500
Ending Cash	$ 20,497	–$ 34,627	–$ 223,727	–$ 137,772	

the budget outlines several possible options for obtaining the required funds (which are rounded up to $225,000): debt, preferred stock, or common stock. The financing cost of each one is noted in the far right column, where we see that the interest cost on debt is 9.5%, the dividend on preferred stock is 8%, and the expected return by common stockholders is 18%.

The third section on the page lists the existing capital structure, its cost, and the net cost of capital. This section is quite important, for anyone reviewing this document can see what impact the selection of any of the financing options will have on the capital structure. For example, the management team may prefer the low cost of debt but also can use the existing capital structure presentation to see that this will result in a very high proportion of debt to equity, which increases the risk that the company cannot afford to repay the debt to the lender.

EXHIBIT 7.16 Financing Budget for the Fiscal Year Ended xx/xx/02

	Quarter 1	Quarter 2	Quarter 3	Quarter 4	Financing Cost
Cash Position:	$20,497	–$34,627	–$223,727	–$137,772	
Financing Option One:					
Additional Debt		$225,000			9.5%
Financing Option Two:					
Additional Preferred Stock	$225,000				8.0%
Financing Option Three:					
Additional Common Stock	$225,000				18.0%
Existing Capital Structure:					
Debt	$400,000				9.0%
Preferred Stock	$150,000				7.5%
Common Stock	$500,000				18.0%
Existing Cost of Capital	11.8%				
Revised Cost of Capital:					
Financing Option One	10.7%				
Financing Option Two	11.2%				
Financing Option Three	12.9%				

Note: Tax rate equals 38%.

The fourth and final part of the budget calculates any changes in the cost of capital that will arise if any of the three financing options are selected. A footnote points out the incremental corporate tax rate—this is of importance to the calculation of the cost of capital, because the interest cost of debt can be deducted as an expense, thereby reducing its net cost. In Exhibit 7.16, selecting additional debt as the preferred form of financing will result in a reduction in the cost of capital to 10.7% whereas a selection of high-cost common stock will result in an increase in the cost of capital, to 12.9%. These changes can have an impact on what types of capital projects are accepted in the future, for the cash flows associated with them must be discounted by the cost of capital in order to see if they result in positive cash flows. Accordingly, a reduction in the cost of capital will mean that projects with marginal cash flows will become more acceptable; the reverse will be true for a higher cost of capital.

The budgeting examples shown here can be used as the format for a real-life corporate budget. However, it must be adjusted to include a company's chart of accounts and departmental structure, so that it reflects actual operations more accurately. Also, it should include a detailed benefits and payroll tax calculation page, which will itemize the cost of Social Security taxes, Medicare, unemployment insurance, worker's compensation insurance, medical insurance, and so on. These costs are a substantial part of a company's budget and yet often are lumped together into a simplistic budget model that does not accurately reflect their true cost.

Although the budget model presented here may seem excessively large, it is necessary to provide detailed coverage of all aspects of the corporation, so that prospective changes to it can be modeled accurately through the budget. Thus, a detailed format is strongly recommended over a simple, summarized model.

Flex Budget

One problem with the budget model shown in the last section is that many of the expenses listed in it are directly tied to the revenue level. If the actual revenue incurred is significantly different from the budgeted figure, so many expenses also will shift in association with the revenue that the comparison of budgeted to actual expenses will not be valid. For example, if budgeted revenues are $1 million and budgeted material costs are $450,000, you would expect a corresponding drop in the actual cost of materials incurred if actual revenues drop to $800,000. A budget-to-actual comparison would show a significant difference in the cost of materials, which in turn would cause a difference in the gross margin and net profit. This issue also arises for a number of other variable or semivariable expenses, such as salesperson commissions, production supplies, and maintenance costs. Also, if there are very large differences between actual and budgeted revenue levels, other costs that are more fixed in nature also will change, such as the salaries, office supplies, and even facilities maintenance (since facilities may be sold off or added to, depending on which direction actual revenues have gone). These represent large step cost changes that will skew actual expenses so far away from the budget that it is difficult to conduct any meaningful comparison between the two.

A good way to resolve this problem is to create a flexible, or flex, budget that itemizes different expense levels depending on changes in the amount of actual revenue. In its simplest form, the flex budget uses percentages of revenue for certain expenses rather than the usual fixed numbers. This method allows for an infinite series of changes in budgeted expenses that are tied directly to revenue volume. However, this approach ignores changes to other costs that do not change in accordance with small revenue variations. Consequently, a more sophisticated format also incorporates changes to many additional expenses when certain larger revenue changes occur, thereby accounting for step costs. By making these changes to the budget, a company will have a tool for comparing actual to budgeted performance at many levels of activity.

Although the flex budget is a good tool, it can be difficult to formulate and administer. One problem with its formulation is that many costs are not fully variable; instead, they have a fixed cost component that must be included in the flex budget formula. Another issue is that a great deal of time can be spent developing step costs. Consequently, the flex budget tends to include only a small number of step costs as well as variable costs whose fixed cost components are not fully recognized.

Budgetary Control Systems

There are several ways in which a budget can be used to enhance a company's control systems so that objectives are met more easily and it is more difficult for costs to stray from approved levels.

One of the best methods for controlling costs is to link the budget for each expense within each department to the purchasing system. By doing so, the computer system will automatically accumulate the total amount of purchase orders that have been issued thus far against a specific account and will refuse any further purchase orders when the budgeted expense total has been reached. This approach can involve the comparison of the monthly budget to monthly costs or of costs to annual budgeted totals. The latter approach can cause difficulty for the inattentive manager, since actual expenses may be running well ahead of the budget for most of the year, but the system will not flag the problem automatically until the entire year's budget has been depleted. Alternatively, a comparison to monthly budgeted figures may result in so many warning flags on so many accounts that the purchasing staff is unable to purchase many items. One workaround for this problem is to use a fixed overage percentage by which purchases are allowed to exceed the budget; another possibility is to compare only cumulative expenses to quarterly budget totals, which reduces the total number of system warning flags.

Another budgetary control system is to compare actual to budgeted results for the specific purpose of evaluating the performance of employees. For example, the warehouse manager may be judged based on actual inventory turnover of 12x, which compares unfavorably to a budgeted turnover rate of 15x. Similarly, the manager of a cost center may receive a favorable review if the total monthly cost of her cost center averages no more than $152,000. This also works for the sales staff, who can be assigned sales quotas that match the budgeted sales levels for their sales territories. In this manner, a large number of employees can have their compensation levels directly tied to the achievement of budgeted goals. This is a highly effective way to ensure that the budget becomes a fixture in the lives of employees.

Yet another budgetary control system is to use it as a feedback loop to employees. This can be done by issuing a series of reports at the end of each reporting period that are designed specifically to match the responsibilities of each employee. For example, Exhibit 7.17 shows a single revenue line item that is reported to a salesperson for a single territory. The salesperson does not need to see any other detailed comparison to the budget, because he is not responsible for anything besides the specific line item that is reported to him. This reporting approach focuses the attention of many employees on just those segments of the budget that they have control over. This approach can result in the creation of dozens or even hundreds of reports by the accounting department, but the reports can be automated on most packaged accounting software systems, so that only the initial report creation takes up much accounting time.

An additional control use for the budget is to detect fraud. The budget usually is based on several years of actual operating results, so unless there are major changes in activity levels, actual expense results should be fairly close to budgeted expectations. If not, often variance analysis is used to find out what happened. This process

EXHIBIT 7.17 Line Item Budget Reporting for Specific Employees

Account No.	Description	Actual Results	Budgeted Results	Variance
4500-010	Arizona Revenue	$43,529	$51,000	–$7,471

is an excellent means for discovering fraud, since fraudulent activities usually result in a sudden surge in expense levels, which the resulting variance analysis will detect. The two instances in which this control will not work is when the fraud has been in existence for a long time (and so is incorporated into the budgeted expense numbers already) or the amount of fraud is so low that it will not create a variance large enough to warrant investigation.

Summary

This chapter primarily addressed the mechanics of constructing a budget and various formats in which it can be presented. The CEO needs to know these details in order to see if the existing corporate budget is adequate for the purpose of planning and controlling company operations. It is entirely possible that some aspects of the existing budget are not adequate, so use the model presented in this chapter to spot weaknesses in the current company budget and to update it. By doing so, you create a better, more detailed tool for managers to use in matching the expectations outlined in the strategic plan to their day-to-day activities.

Many of the expenses included in a typical budget are not especially adjustable, since they relate to a fixed payroll, programs, and facilities. However, there is usually considerably more leeway in the purchase of fixed assets, which are addressed in Chapter 8.

CHAPTER 8

Capital Budgeting

O ne of the most common financial analysis tasks that a chief executive officer (CEO) confronts is evaluating capital investments. In some industries, the amount of money poured into capital improvements is a very substantial proportion of sales, so it is worthy of a great deal of analysis to ensure that a company is investing its cash wisely in internal improvements. In this section, we review the concept of the hurdle rate as well as multiple approaches for evaluating capital investments. We also discuss problems with the capital investment approval process and cash flow modeling issues and finish with a discussion of the postcompletion project analysis, which brings to a close the complete cycle of evaluating a capital project over the entire course of its acquisition, installation, and operation.

Hurdle Rate

How do you form a basis on which to conduct an evaluation of a fixed asset purchase proposal? What makes a good capital investment? Is it the project with the largest net cash flow, or the one that uses the least capital, or some other standard of measure?

The standard criterion for investment is the *hurdle rate*. This is the discounting rate at which all of a company's investments must exhibit a positive cash flow. It is called a hurdle rate because the summary of all cash flows must exceed, or hurdle, this rate, or else the underlying investments will not be approved. The use of a discount rate is extremely important, for it reduces the value of cash inflows and outflows scheduled for some time in the future, so that they are comparable to the value of cash flows in the present. Without the use of a discount rate, we would judge the value of a cash flow ten years in the future to be the same as one that occurs right now. However, the difference between the two is that the funds received now also can earn interest for the next ten years, whereas there is no such opportunity to invest the funds that will arrive in ten years. Consequently, a discount rate is the great equalizer that allows us to make one-to-one comparisons between cash flows in different periods.

The hurdle rate is derived from the *cost of capital*. This is the average cost of funds that a company uses and is based on the average cost of its debt, equity, and various other funding sources that are combinations of these two basic forms of funds. For example, if a company has determined its cost of capital to be 16%, the discounted cash flows (DCFs) from all of its new capital investments, using that discount rate, must yield a positive return. If they do not, the funds flow resulting from the company's capital investments will not be sufficient for it to pay for the funds it invested. Thus, the hurdle rate is the primary basis on which to review potential capital investments.

A company may choose to use several hurdle rates, depending on the nature of the investment. For example, if the company must install equipment to make its production emissions compliant with federal air quality standards, there is no hurdle rate at all—the company *must* complete the work or be fined by the government. At the opposite extreme, a company may assign a high hurdle rate to all projects that are considered unusually risky. For example, if capital projects are for the extension of a current production line, there is very little perceived risk, and a hurdle rate that matches the cost of capital is deemed sufficient. However, if the capital expenditure is for a production line that creates equipment in a new market, where the company is the first entrant, and no one knows what kind of sales will result, the hurdle rate may be set a number of percentage points higher than the cost of capital. Thus, different hurdle rates can apply to different situations.

Having now given the reasons why the hurdle rate is the fundamental measuring stick against which all capital investments are evaluated, we deal with the one exception to the rule: the payback period.

Payback Period

We have just seen how the primary criterion for evaluating a capital investment is its ability to return a profit that exceeds a hurdle rate. However, this method misses one important element, which is that it does not fully explain investment risk in a manner that is fully understandable to managers. Investment risk can be defined as the chance that the initial investment will not be earned back or that the rate of return target will not be met. Discounting can be used to identify or weed out such projects, simply by increasing the hurdle rate. For example, if a project is perceived to be risky, an increase in the hurdle rate will reduce its net present value, which makes the investment less likely to be approved by management. However, management may not be comfortable dealing with DCF methods when looking at a risky investment—it just wants to know how long it will take until invested funds are returned. Although this is a decidedly unscientific way to review cash flows, the author has yet to find a management team that did not insist on seeing a payback calculation alongside other, more sophisticated analysis methods.

There are two ways to calculate the payback period. The first method is the easiest to use but can yield a skewed result. That calculation is to divide the capital investment by the average annual cash flow from operations. For example, in Exhibit 8.1, we have a stream of cash flows over five years that is heavily weighted toward the time periods that are farthest in the future. The sum of those cash flows is $8,750,000, which is an average of $1,750,000 per year. We also assume that the initial capital investment was $6,000,000. Based on this information, the payback period is $6,000,000 divided by $1,750,000, which is 3.4 years. However, if we review the

EXHIBIT 8.1 Stream of Cash Flows for
a Payback Calculation

Year	Cash Flow
1	$1,000,000
2	1,250,000
3	1,500,000
4	2,000,000
5	3,000,000

stream of cash flows in the exhibit, it is evident that the cash inflow did not cover the investment at the 3.4-year mark. In fact, the actual cash inflow did not exceed $6,000,000 until shortly after the end of the fourth year. What happened? The stream of cash flows in the example was so skewed toward future periods that the annual *average* cash flow was not representative of the annual actual cash flow. Thus, we can use the averaging method only if the stream of future cash flows is relatively even from year to year.

The most accurate way to calculate the payback period is to do so manually. This means that we deduct the total expected cash inflow from the invested balance, year by year, until we arrive at the correct period. For example, we have re-created the stream of cash flows from Exhibit 8.1 in Exhibit 8.2, but with an extra column that shows the net capital investment remaining at the end of each year. We can use this format to reach the end of year 4; we know that the cash flows will pay back the investment sometime during year 5, but we do not have a month-by-month cash flow that tells us precisely when. Instead, we can assume an average stream of cash flows during that period, which works out to $250,000 per month ($3,000,000 cash inflow for the year, divided by 12 months). Since there was only $250,000 of net investment remaining at the end of the fourth year, and this is the same monthly amount of cash flow in the fifth year, we can assume that the payback period is 4.1 years.

As already stated, the payback period is not a highly scientific method, because it completely ignores the time value of money. Nonetheless, it tells management how much time will pass before it recovers its invested funds, which can be useful information, especially in environments, such as high technology, where investments must attain a nearly immediate payback before they become obsolete. Accordingly, it is customary to include the payback calculation in a capital investment analysis,

EXHIBIT 8.2 Stream of Cash Flows for a Manual Payback Calculation

Year	Cash Flow	Net Investment Remaining
0	$ 0	$6,000,000
1	1,000,000	5,000,000
2	1,250,000	3,750,000
3	1,500,000	2,250,000
4	2,000,000	250,000
5	3,000,000	—

although it must be strongly supplemented by DCF analyses, which are described in the next two sections.

Net Present Value

The typical capital investment is composed of a string of cash flows, both in and out, that will continue until the investment eventually is liquidated at some point in the future. These cash flows are comprised of many things: the initial payment for equipment, continuing maintenance costs, salvage value of the equipment when it is eventually sold, tax payments, receipts from product sold, and so on. The trouble is, since the cash flows are coming in and going out over a period of many years, how do we make them comparable for an analysis that is done in the present? As noted earlier in the section on hurdle rates, we can use a discount rate to reduce the value of a future cash flow into what it would be worth right now. By applying the discount rate to each anticipated cash flow, we can reduce and add them together, which yields a single combined figure that represents the current value of the entire capital investment. This is known as its net present value (NPV).

For an example of how NPV works, we have listed in Exhibit 8.3 the cash flows, both in and out, for a capital investment that is expected to last for five years. The year is listed in the first column, the amount of the cash flow in the second column, and the discount rate in the third column. The final column multiplies the cash flow from the second column by the discount rate in the third column to yield the present value of each cash flow. The grand total cash flow is listed in the lower right corner of the table.

Notice that the discount factor in Exhibit 8.3 becomes progressively smaller in later years, because cash flows farther in the future are worth less than those that will be received sooner. The discount factor is published in present value tables, which are listed in many accounting and finance textbooks. They are also a standard feature in midrange hand-held calculators. Another variation is to use the next formula to compute a present value manually.

$$\frac{\text{Present value of}}{\text{a future cash flow}} = \frac{(\text{Future cash flow})}{(1 + \text{Discount rate})^{(\text{squared by number of discounting periods})}}$$

EXHIBIT 8.3 Simplified Net Present Value Example

Year	Cash Flow	Discount Factor[*]	Present Value
0	−$100,000	1.000	−$100,000
1	+25,000	.9259	+23,148
2	+25,000	.8573	+21,433
3	+25,000	.7938	+19,845
4	+30,000	.7350	+22,050
5	+30,000	.6806	+20,418
		Net Present Value	+$6,894

[*] Discount factor is 8%.

Using this formula, if we expect to receive $75,000 in one year, and the discount rate is 15%, the calculation is:

$$\text{Present value} = \frac{\$75,000}{(1+.15)^1}$$

$$\text{Present value} = \$65,217.39$$

The example shown in Exhibit 8.3 was of the simplest possible kind. In reality, there are several additional factors to take into consideration. First, there may be multiple cash inflows and outflows in each period rather than the single lump sum that was shown in the example. If you want to know precisely what the cause of each cash flow is, it is best to add a line to the NPV calculation that clearly identifies the nature of each item and discounts it separately from the other line items. Another issue is which items to include in the analysis and which to exclude. The basic rule of thumb is that an item that impacts cash flow must be included; anything that does not impact cash flow is not included. The most common cash flow line items to include in an NPV analysis are listed next.

- *Cash inflows from sales.* If a capital investment results in added sales, all gross margins attributable to that investment must be included in the analysis.
- *Cash inflows and outflows for equipment purchases and sales.* There should be a cash outflow when a product is purchased as well as a cash inflow when the equipment is no longer needed and is sold off.
- *Cash inflows and outflows for working capital.* When a capital investment occurs, it normally involves the use of some additional inventory. If there are added sales, there probably will be additional accounts receivable. In either case, these are additional investments that must be included in the analysis as cash outflows. Also, if the investment is ever terminated, the inventory presumably will be sold off and the accounts receivable collected, so there should be line items in the analysis, located at the end of the project time line, showing the cash inflows from the liquidation of working capital.
- *Cash outflows for maintenance.* If there is production equipment involved, periodic maintenance will be needed to ensure that it runs properly. If there is a maintenance contract with a supplier that provides the servicing, this, too, should be included in the analysis.
- *Cash outflows for taxes.* If there is a profit from new sales that are attributable to the capital investment, the incremental income tax that can be traced to those incremental sales must be included in the analysis. Also, if there is a significant quantity of production equipment involved, the annual personal property taxes that can be traced to that equipment should be included.
- *Cash inflows for the tax effect of depreciation.* Depreciation is an allowable tax deduction. Accordingly, the depreciation created by the purchase of capital equipment should be offset against the cash outflow caused by income taxes. Although depreciation is really just an accrual, it does have a net cash flow impact caused by a reduction in taxes and so should be included in the NPV calculation.

The NPV approach is the best way to see if a proposed capital investment has a sufficient rate of return to justify the use of any required funds. Also, because it reveals the amount of cash created in excess of the corporate hurdle rate, it allows management to rank projects by the amount of cash they potentially can spin off, which is a good way to determine which projects to fund if there is not enough cash available to pay for an entire set of proposed investments.

In the next section, we look at an alternative discounting method that focuses on the rate of return of a capital investment's cash flows rather than the amount of cash left over after being discounted at a standard hurdle rate, as was the case with the NPV methodology.

Internal Rate of Return

The end result of an NPV calculation is the amount of money that is earned or lost after all related cash flows are discounted at a preset hurdle rate. This is a good evaluation method, but what if management wants to know the overall return on investment (ROI) of the same stream of cash flows? Also, what if the NPV was negative, but only by a small amount, so that management wants to know how far a project's rate of return varies from the hurdle rate? Also, what if management wants to rank projects by their overall rates of return rather than by their NPVs? All of these questions can be answered by using the internal rate of return (IRR) method.

The IRR method is very similar to the NPV method, because we use the same cash flow layout, itemizing the net inflows and outflows by year. The difference is that, using the IRR method, we alter use a high-low approach to find the discount rate at which the cash flows equal zero. At that point, the discount rate equals the rate of ROI for the entire stream of cash flows associated with the capital investment. To illustrate how the method works, we begin with the standard NPV format that was listed in the last section. This time we have a new set of annual cash flows, as shown in Exhibit 8.4. The difference between this calculation and the one used for NPV is that we are going to guess at the correct rate of return and enter this amount in the "Internal Rate of Return" column. We enter the discount rates for each year, using a low-end assumption of a 7% rate of return.

The end result of the calculation is that we have a positive net present value of $13,740. Since we are shooting for the IRR percentage at which the net present value is zero, we must increase the IRR. If the net present value had been negative, we would have reduced the IRR percentage instead. We will make a higher guess at an IRR of 9%, and run the calculation again, which is shown in Exhibit 8.5.

EXHIBIT 8.4 Internal Rate of Return Calculation, Low Estimate

Year	Cash Flow	Internal Rate of Return = 7%	Present Value
0	−$250,000	1.000	−$250,000
1	+55,000	.9345	+51,398
2	+60,000	.8734	+52,404
3	+65,000	.8163	+53,060
4	+70,000	.7629	+53,403
5	+75,000	.7130	+53,475
		Net Present Value	+$13,740

EXHIBIT 8.5 Internal Rate of Return Calculation, High Estimate

Year	Cash Flow	Internal Rate of Return = 9%	Present Value
0	–$250,000	1.000	–$250,000
1	+55,000	.9174	+50,457
2	+60,000	.8417	+50,502
3	+65,000	.7722	+50,193
4	+70,000	.7084	+49,588
5	+75,000	.6499	+48,743
		Net Present Value	–$517

The result of the calculation in Exhibit 8.5 is very close to an NPV of 9%. If we want to try a few more high-low calculations, we can zero in on the IRR more precisely. In the example, the actual IRR is 8.9%.

The IRR is best used in conjunction with the NPV calculation, because it can be misleading when used by itself. One problem is that the IRR favors those capital investments with very high rates of return, even if the total dollar return is rather small. An example is when a potential investment of $10,000 has a return of $3,000, which equates to a 30% rate of return, and is ranked higher than a $100,000 investment with a return of $25,000 (which has a 25% rate of return). In this case, the smaller project certainly has a greater rate of return, but the larger project will return more cash in total than the smaller one. If there were enough capital available for only one of the two projects, perhaps $100,000, and the smaller project were selected because of its higher rate of return, the total return would be less than optimal, because much of the funds are not being invested at all. In this situation, only $3,000 is being earned, even though $100,000 can be invested, which yields only a 3% return on the total pool of funds. Thus, if there are too many capital investments chasing too few funds, selecting investments based on nothing but their IRR may lead to suboptimal decisions.

Another issue is that the IRR calculation assumes that all cash flows thrown off by a project over the course of its life can be reinvested at the same rate of return. This is not always a valid assumption, since the earnings from a special investment that yields a uniquely high rate of return may not be investable at anywhere close to the same rate of return.

Despite its shortcomings, the IRR method is a scientifically valid way to determine the rate of return on a capital investment's full stream of cash flows. However, because it does not recognize the total amount of cash spun off by an investment, it is best used in conjunction with the NPV calculation in order to yield the most complete analysis of a capital investment.

Throughput-Based Capital Budgeting

The traditional capital budgeting approach involves having the management team review a series of unrelated requests from throughout the company, each one asking for funding for various projects. Management decides whether to fund each request based on the DCFs projected for each one. If there are not sufficient funds available for all requests having positive DCFs, those with the largest cash flows or highest percentage returns are usually accepted first, until the funds run out.

There are several problems with this type of capital budgeting. First and most important, there is no consideration of how each requested project fits into the entire *system* of production—instead, most requests involve the local optimization of specific work centers that may not contribute to the total throughput of the company. Second, there is no consideration of the bottleneck operation, so managers cannot tell which funding requests will result in an improvement to the efficiency of that operation. Third, managers tend to engage in a great deal of speculation regarding the budgeted cash flows resulting from their requests, resulting in inaccurate DCF projections. Since many requests involve unverifiable cash flow estimates, it is impossible to discern which projects are better than others.

A greater reliance on throughput accounting concepts eliminates most of these problems. The priority for funding should be placed squarely on any projects that can improve the capacity of the bottleneck operation, based on a comparison of the incremental additional throughput (revenue minus totally variable expenses) created to the incremental operating expenses and investment incurred.

Any investment requests not involving the bottleneck operation should be subject to an intensive critical review, which likely will result in their rejection. Since they do not impact the bottleneck operation, these investments cannot impact system throughput in any way, so their sole remaining justification must be the reduction of operating expenses or the mitigation of some type of risk.

The one exception to investing in nonbottleneck operations is when there is so little excess capacity in a work center that it has difficulty recovering from downtime. This can be a major problem if the lack of capacity constantly causes the bottleneck operation to run out of work. In this case, a good investment alternative is to invest in a sufficient amount of additional capacity to ensure that the system can recover rapidly from a reasonable level of downtime. If a manager is applying for a capital investment based on this reasoning, he should attach to the proposal a chart showing the capacity level at which the targeted resource has been operating over the past few months as well as the severity of work shortages at the bottleneck that are caused by that operation.

At what point should a company invest in more of the bottleneck operation? In many cases, the company has specifically designated a resource to be its bottleneck, because it is so expensive to add additional capacity, so this decision is not to be taken lightly. The decision process is to review the impact on the incremental change in throughput caused by the added investment, less any changes in operating expenses. Because this type of investment represents a considerable *step cost* (where costs and/or the investment will jump considerably as a result of the decision), management usually must make its decision based on the perceived level of long-term throughput changes rather than on smaller expected short-term throughput increases.

The issues just noted have been addressed in the summary-level capital budgeting form shown in Exhibit 8.6. This form splits capital budgeting requests into three categories: (1) constraint related, (2) risk related, (3) non–constraint related. The risk-related category covers all capital purchases for which the company must meet a

Capital Request Form

Project name: _____

Name of project sponsor: _____

Submission date: _____   Project number: _____

Constraint-Related Project	Approvals

Initial expenditure: $ _____

Additional annual expenditure: $ _____

Impact on throughput: $ _____

Impact on operating expenses: $ _____

Impact on ROI: $ _____

(Attach calculations)

All   _____
    Process Analyst

$100,000   _____
    Supervisor

$100,001–
$1,000,000   _____
    President

$1,000,000+   _____
    Board of Directors

Risk-Related Project	Approvals

Initial expenditure: $ _____

Additional annual expenditure: $ _____

Description of legal requirement fulfilled or
risk issue mitigated (attach description as needed):

_____

_____

< $50,000   { Corporate Attorney _____

    Chief Risk Officer _____

$50,001+   _____
    President

$1,000,000+   _____
    Board of Directors

Non-Constraint-Related Project	Approvals

Initial expenditure: $ _____

Additional annual expenditure: $ _____

☐ Improves sprint capacity?
  Attach justification of sprint capacity increase

☐ Other request
  Attach justification for other request type

All   _____
    Process Analyst

<$10,000   _____
    Supervisor

$10,001–
$100,000   _____
    President

$100,000+   _____
    Board of Directors

EXHIBIT 8.6 Throughput-Based Capital Request Form

legal requirement or for which there is a perception that the company is subject to an undue amount of risk if it does *not* invest in an asset. All remaining requests that do not clearly call into the constraint-related or risk-related categories drop into a catch-all category at the bottom of the form. The intent of this format is to differentiate clearly among different types of approval requests, with each one requiring different types of analysis and management approval.

The approval levels vary significantly in the throughput-based capital request form. Approvals for constraint-related investments include a process analyst (who verifies that the request actually will impact the constraint) as well as generally higher-dollar approval levels for lower-level managers—the intent is to make it easier to approve capital requests that will improve the bottleneck operation. Approvals for risk-related projects first require the joint approval of the corporate attorney and chief risk officer, with added approvals for large expenditures. Finally, the approvals for non–constraint-related purchases involve lower-dollar levels, so the approval process is intentionally made more difficult.

Problems with the Capital Budget Approval Process

A significant problem with the capital budget approval process is that the senior-level managers who are chiefly responsible for approving new capital expenditures are also responsible for generating an adequate ROI from the company's existing capital base. This means that they will be less likely to approve the construction of any radical new systems that will render the older infrastructure obsolete. Consequently, new projects probably will be approved only if they involve the enhancement of existing systems, which likely will involve only modest improvements in productivity.

One way to resolve this problem is to set aside a large amount of cash to be handed out by a lower-level group of employees. This group should not be responsible for the existing infrastructure and should preferably be younger and of an entrepreneurial mind-set. This group should be oriented toward the funding of project start-ups, with funds being allocated to prototype development, market trials, or expansions of a business case.

Another solution is to offer significant cash payouts if new ideas succeed in the marketplace. The prospect of large personal rewards may push managers to take greater risks than normally would be the case. Also, this method tends to create a feedback loop where evidence of actual cash payouts breeds even more ideas, which generates more payouts, and so on.

Yet another approach is to fund an in-house venture capital firm. The company can give this group general strategic directions and let it search for funding opportunities both inside and outside the company. By shifting investment authority away from the management team and onto a group of trained venture capitalists, it is likely that funding decisions will be different.

Finally, another approach is to alter the capital budgeting guidelines so that riskier projects will be approved more easily at lower funding levels. This method allows potentially high-return projects to at least receive initial funding to see if the concept works.

All of these variations on project funding are designed to keep a company from reinvesting in minor efficiency improvements to its existing infrastructure, instead allowing the company an opportunity to create major improvements in its ROI.

Cash Flow Modeling Issues

The cash flow concepts used for most NPV or IRR projects assume a simplified decision process where funding occurs once at the beginning of the project, after which a steady and predictable series of cash flows occur over a multiyear period. In reality, several additional decisions might occur during the investment period that can alter the value of a project dramatically. They are described next.

- *Deferred start date.* There may be a sufficient level of uncertainty regarding a project that it makes sense to hold off on its initiation until additional research can be conducted. However, delaying the project also may result in a reduction in the level of market share attained, since competitors will have a better opportunity to position their products in the market first. Thus, additional variables in the cash flow scenario are a combination of a delay in cash outflow and reduced long-term revenues.
- *Early cancellation.* If the expenditure of funds occurs over a lengthy period of time or requires additional investments at discrete intervals, management has the option to cancel the project early in order to minimize potential losses. If there appears to be a significant probability of early cancellation, consider creating an additional cash flow model that includes this scenario.
- *Add more capital later in project.* If there is a possibility that a project may yield additional profits through additional investments at various points in the future, another scenario may include the amount of any additional investments and the cash flows to be gained from them. Conversely, more cash may be needed when the project being created is of the experimental variety, and there is a risk that construction and implementation problems will require an additional investment. If considered significant, these options should be included in the cash flow model.
- *Alter project cost structure.* It may be possible to pay less cash up front in exchange for higher variable costs over the remainder of the project, as would be the case when more staffing is used instead of automated equipment (or vice versa). Depending on the changes in the timing and amounts of cash flows resulting from such decisions, it may be necessary to construct a separate cash flow forecast for each option.

The scenarios just noted bring up the prospect of having multiple possible variations on the cash flows from a prospective new project. Which one should be included in the formal cash flow analysis that is presented to management for approval? All of them. To do so, create a decision tree that outlines all cash flow options, with each option assigned a probability of occurrence. For each node on the decision tree, calculate its probability times its value outcome and sum all the nodes. This approach gives management valuable insight into the probability of different cash flow alternatives. The only problem with the decision tree model is that the calculation becomes cumbersome after more than a few cash flow options are added to it.

Funding Decisions for Research and Development Projects

The traditional approach to research and development (R&D) funding is to require all R&D proposals to pass a minimum ROI hurdle rate. However, when there is limited funding available and too many investments passing the hurdle rate to all be funded, managers tend to pick the most likely projects to succeed. This selection process usually results in the least risky projects being funded; such projects typically are extensions of existing product lines or other variations on existing products that will not achieve breakthrough profitability. An alternative that is more likely to achieve a higher return on R&D investment is to apportion investable funds into multiple categories—a large percentage that is to be used only for highly risky projects with associated high returns, and a separate pool of funds specifically designated for lower-risk projects with correspondingly lower levels of return. The exact proportions of funding allocated to each category will depend on management's capacity for risk as well as the size and number of available projects in each category. This approach allows a company the opportunity to achieve a breakthrough product introduction that it probably would not have funded if a single hurdle rate had been used to evaluate new product proposals.

If this higher-risk approach to allocating funds is used, it is likely that a number of new product projects will be abandoned prior to their release into the market, on the grounds that they will not yield a sufficient ROI or will not be technologically or commercially feasible. This is not a bad situation, since some projects are bound to fail if a sufficiently high level of project risk is acceptable to management. Conversely, if no projects fail, this is a clear sign that management is not investing in sufficiently risky investments. To measure the level of project failure, calculate *R&D waste*, which is the amount of unrealized product development spending (e.g., the total expenditure on canceled projects during the measurement period). Even better, divide the amount of R&D waste by the total R&D expenditure during the period to determine the proportion of expenses incurred on failed projects. Unfortunately, this measure can be manipulated easily by accelerating or withholding the declaration of project termination. Nonetheless, it does give a fair indication of project risk when aggregated over the long term.

Although funding may be allocated into broad investment categories, management still must use a reliable method for determining which projects will receive funding and which will not. The standard approach is to apply a discount rate to all possible projects and to select those having the highest NPV. However, the NPV calculation does not include several key variables found in the expected commercial value (ECV) formula, making the ECV the preferred method. The ECV formula requires you to multiply a prospective project's NPV by the probability of its commercial success, minus the commercialization cost, and multiply the result by the probability of technical success, minus the development cost. Thus, the intent of using ECV is to include all major success factors into the decision to accept or reject a new product proposal. The formula is:

$$(((\text{Project net present value} \times \text{probability of commercial success})$$
$$- \text{commercialization cost}) \times (\text{probability of technical success}))$$
$$- \text{product development cost}$$

Example

The Moravia Corporation collects the following information about a new project for a battery-powered lawn trimmer, where there is some technical risk that a sufficiently powerful battery cannot be developed for the product:

Project net present value	$4,000,000
Probability of commercial success	90%
Commercialization cost	$ 750,000
Probability of technical success	65%
Product development cost	$1,750,000

Based on this information, Moravia computes this ECV for the lawn trimmer project:

$$((($4,000,000 \text{ project net present value}$$
$$\times 90\% \text{ probability of commercial success})$$
$$- $750,000 \text{ commercialization cost})$$
$$\times (65\% \text{ probability of technical success}))$$
$$- $1,750,000 \text{ product development cost}$$

$$\text{Expected commercial value} = $102,500$$

Even if some projects are dropped after being run through the preceding valuation analysis, this does not mean that they should be canceled for good. On the contrary, these projects may become commercially viable over time, depending on changes in price points, costs, market conditions, and technical viability. Consequently, the R&D manager should conduct a periodic review of previously shelved projects to see if any of the factors just noted have changed sufficiently to allow the company to reintroduce a project proposal for development.

Postcompletion Project Analysis

The greatest failing in most capital review systems is not in the initial analysis phase but in the postcompletion phase, because there is not one. If there is no methodology for verifying that managers enter accurate information into the approval forms, which is done by comparing actual results to them, managers eventually will figure out that they can alter the numbers in the approval forms in order to beat the corporate hurdle rates, even if this information is incorrect. However, if managers know that their original estimates will be reviewed carefully and critiqued for some time into the future, they will be much more careful in completing their initial capital requests. Thus, analysis at the back end of a capital project will lead to great accuracy at the front end.

Analysis of actual expenditures can begin before a capital investment is fully paid for or installed. An analyst should subtotal the payments made by the end of each month and compare them to the total projected by the project manager. A total that significantly exceeds the approved expenditure would be grounds for an immediate review by top management. This approach works best for the largest capital expenditures, where reviewing payment data in detail is worth the extra effort by the accounting staff if it can prevent large overpayments. It is also worthwhile when capital expenditures cover long periods of time, so that a series of monthly reviews can be made. However, it is not a worthwhile approach if the expenditure in question is for a single item that is made with one payment; this type of purchase still can be reviewed by comparing the company's purchase order total to the amount noted on the capital investment proposal form.

Once a project is completed, cash inflows may result from it. If so, a quarterly comparison of actual to projected cash inflows is the most frequent comparison to be made, with an annual review being sufficient in many cases. Such a review keeps management apprised of the performance of all capital projects and lets project sponsors know that their estimates will be the subject of considerable scrutiny for as far into the future as they had projected originally. For those companies that survive based on the efficiency of capital usage, it may even be reasonable to tie manager pay reviews to the accuracy of their capital investment request forms.

An example of a postcompletion project analysis is shown in Exhibit 8.7. In this example, the top of the report compares actual to budgeted cash outflows while the middle compares all actual cash outflows to the budget. Note that the cash outflows section is complete, since these were all incurred at the beginning of the project, whereas the inflows section is not yet complete, because the project has completed only the third year of a five-year plan. To cover the remaining two years of activity, there is a column for estimated cash inflows, which projects them for the remaining years of the investment, using the last year in which actual data are available. This projected information can be used to determine the NPV. We compare the actual

EXHIBIT 8.7 Comparison of Actual to Projected Capital Investment Cash Flows

Description	Actual	Projected Actual	Budget	Actual Present Value[*]	Budget Present Value[*]
Cash Outflows					
Capital Items	$1,250,000	—	$1,100,000	$1,250,000	$1,100,000
Working Capital	750,000	—	500,000	750,000	500,000
Total Outflows	$2,000,000	—	$1,600,000	$2,000,000	$1,600,000
Cash Inflows					
Year 1	250,000		$ 250,000	$ 229,350	$ 229,350
Year 2	375,000		400,000	315,638	336,680
Year 3	450,000		500,000	347,490	386,100
Year 4		450,000	500,000	318,780	354,200
Year 5		450,000	500,000	292,455	324,950
Total Inflows	$1,075,000	$900,000	$2,150,000	$1,503,713	$1,631,280
Net Present Value	—	—	—	–$ 496,287	+$ 31,280

[*] Uses discount rate of 9%.

and projected NPVs at the bottom of the report, so that management can see if there are any problems worthy of correction. In this case, the initial costs of the project, both in terms of capital items and working capital, were so far over budget that the actual NPV is solidly in the red. In this case, management should take a hard look at reducing the working capital, since this is the single largest cash drain in excess of the budget, while also seeing if cash inflow can be increased to match the budgeted annual amounts for the last two years of the investment.

Summary

In this chapter, we have gone over some of the most fundamental analyses that a CEO will see: the use of the payback period, net present value, internal rate of return, and throughput concepts to determine whether to investment in a capital project. Just as important to this analysis, although unfortunately overlooked by all too many companies, is the postimplementation review of partially or fully completed capital investments. This information is important because it tells a company which investments have succeeded and which have failed. Only by mastering all the techniques discussed in this chapter can you become an efficient analyzer of capital investment issues, with the ability to invest funds in the correct projects.

PART III

Risk Management

CHAPTER 9

Risk Management: General Concepts

S ome well-managed companies have fallen because they did not pay attention to risk. For example, it is difficult to recover from a fire that destroys a data center or production facility, or from the theft of all one's securities and cash. Although rare, these occurrences can be so catastrophic that it is not possible to recover. An otherwise healthy organization is destroyed, throwing many people out of work and eliminating the equity stake of the owners.

On a lesser scale and much more common are the lawsuits that nearly every company must face from time to time. These may relate to employee injuries, customer or supplier claims regarding contracts, or perhaps sexual harassment or some form of discrimination. These lawsuits do not normally end a company's existence, but they can cripple it if awards are excessive or the company is not in a solid financial position to begin with.

This chapter covers the risk management policies and procedures that keep a company from being seriously injured by these and other types of risk-related problems. In addition, it notes the role of the risk manager in mitigating a company's risk by modifying internal systems as well as by purchasing insurance. The types of insurance that a company can buy are also discussed as well as how to select a broker or underwriter to help service a company's needs. The chapter concludes with coverage of a risk management report that clearly identifies a company's risks and how they are being addressed.

The more specialized area of foreign exchange risk management is addressed separately in Chapter 10, Risk Management: Foreign Exchange.

Risk Management Policies

A company must determine the amount of risk that it is willing to undertake. When the board of directors attempts to quantify this amount, it often finds that it is uncomfortable with the level of risk it currently has and mandates more action, through new policies, that reduce the level of risk. The policies can include a number of risk management issues, such as the financial limits for risk assumption or retention, self-insurance parameters, the financial condition of insurance providers, and captive insurance companies. The policies do not have to cover some issues that are already

EXHIBIT 9.1 Comprehensive Policy for Risk Management

1. ABC Company will obtain insurance only from companies with an A.M. Best rating of at least B++.
2. All self-insurance plans will be covered by an umbrella policy that covers all losses exceeding $50,000.
3. No insurance may be obtained from captive insurance companies.
4. The company must always have current insurance for the following categories, and in the stated amounts:
   - Director's and officer's insurance, $5 million
   - General liability insurance, $10 million
   - Commercial property insurance that matches the replacement cost of all structures and inventory
   - Business interruption insurance, sufficient for four months of operations

required by law, such as workers' compensation insurance. An example of a comprehensive insurance policy is noted in Exhibit 9.1.

There are several key points to consider in the exhibit. First, a company may be tempted to purchase very inexpensive insurance, which typically comes from an insurance provider that is in poor financial condition. If the company subsequently files a claim on this insurance, it may find that the provider is not in a position to pay it. Consequently, the first policy item defines the minimum financial rating that an insurance provider must attain before the company will purchase insurance from it. Another point is that a company wants to put a cap on the maximum amount of all risks that it is willing to tolerate, so that it cannot be blindsided by a large loss that is not covered by insurance. The second policy point, which requires a cap on self-insured risks, covers this problem. Finally, the board of directors may feel more comfortable defining the precise amount of insurance coverage needed in specific areas. Although the policy shows a few specific insurance amounts, it is usually better to define a formula for calculating the appropriate amount of insurance, such as commercial property insurance, that will cover the replacement cost of structures and inventory. This keeps the amount defined on the policy from becoming outdated due to changing business conditions.

Risk Management Planning

Companies have a bad habit of structuring their risk planning to deal with events that have occurred before, rather than what may appear in the future. For example, if a lawsuit previously had been brought against a company for illegal software copying, the company probably will have a comprehensive software auditing system in place, but it may have no plans to deal with the earthquake fault line running directly under corporate headquarters, because there has been no earthquake in the past century.

Risk management planning needs to encompass considerably more than systems that were installed to deal with past events. Even if it has not occurred yet, the chief executive officer (CEO) should be aware of any significant risk of a natural disaster occurring that could affect the company. This does not mean just the earthquakes, fires, hailstorms, floods, and tsunamis that can impact company facilities but also their impact on key customers and suppliers, and what the disaster would mean for the company in terms of lost sales or reduced supplies.

Another problem area is catastrophes caused by complex system failure. For example, an airline manufacturer may need to consider the stresses caused on existing airframes if it installs satellite television reception nodules on the airframes; the airframes were not designed to have additional items bolted onto them, so the level of complexity has increased, resulting in a heightened chance of system failure (airframe cracking). The same concept applies to any business engaged in highly complex systems, such as chemical processing facilities, oil pipelines, and cruise ships. This concept even can apply to the rewiring of an office building with additional cabling for a variety of purposes—power running through nearby cables may interfere with the data in a communications cable that inadvertently was run alongside it. The solution is to bring together engineers and maintenance personnel who are responsible for these systems and have them review problem scenarios as well as ongoing incident reports to see if they are a prelude to a major problem arising.

Yet another risk area is acts of internal sabotage or terrorism from outside organizations, which can involve product tampering, theft of information, computer viruses, or even employee kidnappings. In this case, it is useful to have technical specialists from both within and outside of the company devise scenarios for destroying or at least penetrating to company assets and create countermeasures to reduce the risk of actual incidents occurring.

To coordinate the analysis of such scenarios, it is useful to create a crisis management team (CMT) that determines what risks are most likely to happen. It can do this by creating a questionnaire that asks recipients, in a broad-based format, where they feel the company is most at risk. The questionnaire should be distributed to both managers and specialists in key operational areas throughout the company, so that responses represent a wide cross-section of the company. If the results are too many identified risks to address properly, the CMT should reduce the list to a more manageable size, perhaps the top one or two dozen, based on such issues as probability of occurrence and impact on the company. Given the large number of potential risks, it is useful to categorize the risks visually with a matrix such as the one shown in Exhibit 9.2, where each risk is identified by a letter (N = natural disaster, S = systemic problem, and X = external threat) and a number, which are identified below the matrix. The table also identifies graphically how each risk is addressed; a square indicates a risk transfer through insurance while a circle indicates a retained risk. For example, kidnapping is assigned the code X2 as an external threat and has been mitigated through the use of kidnap and ransom insurance, so it is situated in a square. A matrix of this type is an easy way to visualize the status of a company's principal risks.

The CMT also should create monitoring systems to spot the targeted risks as soon as they occur (or if events occur that make them more likely), and actively create systems either to prevent or to deal with the selected set of risks. This group should regularly reevaluate its chosen set of most likely risks to see if they must be modified to deal with changing circumstances, which may include a new company strategy, sales into a politically at-risk country, a major acquisition, and so on.

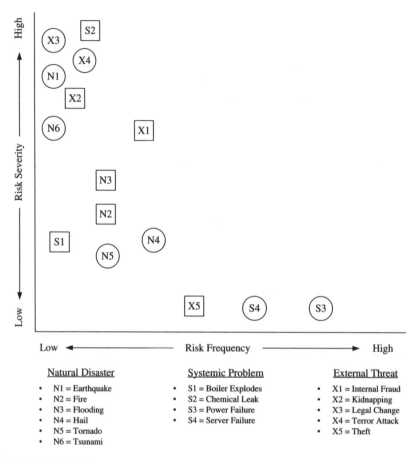

EXHIBIT 9.2 Risk Matrix

Once the basic risk management system is in place, the CMT must ensure that risk examination becomes an ongoing process, which calls for policies and procedures as well as a monitoring system to verify that all parts of the company regularly update risk information. For larger entities with additional funding, it may be possible to create computer systems that regularly extract data elements from computer databases that are key indicators of risk factors and present them in summary format to the CMT and the senior management team.

Manager of Risk Management

In most large companies, the risk management function is assigned to a manager, who reports to the chief financial officer, treasurer, or controller. This executive is charged with the responsibility of implementing procedures consistent with the corporate risk management policy (as noted in Exhibit 9.1). This person works closely with other functional areas, such as engineering, safety and health, personnel and industrial relations, production, plant security, legal, and accounting. It is important that this person have a thorough knowledge of the company's operations, products, and services as well as risk history, so that she can evaluate risks and exposure properly. Within these constraints, the job description of the typical risk manager is:

- Ascertain and appraise all corporate risks.
- Estimate the probability of loss due to these risks.
- Ensure compliance with local, state, and federal requirements regarding insurance.
- Select the optimum method for protecting against losses, such as changes to internal procedures or by acquiring insurance.
- Work with insurance agents, brokers, consultants, and insurance company representatives.
- Supervise a loss prevention program, including planning to minimize losses from anticipated crises.
- Maintain appropriate records for all aspects of insurance administration.
- Continually evaluate and keep abreast of all changes in company operations.
- Stay current on new techniques being developed in the risk management field.
- Conduct a periodic audit of the risk management program to ensure that all risks have been identified and covered.

Risk Management Procedures

Once the risk management policies have been defined, it is necessary to determine a number of underlying procedures to support them. These procedures guide the actions of the risk manager in ensuring that a company has taken sufficient steps to ensure that risks are kept at a minimum. The procedures follow a logical sequence of exploring the extent of risk issues, finding ways to mitigate those risks internally, and then using insurance to cover any risks that cannot otherwise be reduced. In more detail, the procedures can be divided into five steps.

Step 1. *Locate risk areas.* Determine all hazards to which the company is subject by performing a complete review of all properties and operations. This should include a review not only of the physical plant but also of contractual obligations, leasehold requirements, and government regulations. The review can be completed with insurable hazard checklists that are provided by most insurance companies, with the aid of a consultant, or by reviewing historical loss data provided by the company's current insurance firm. However, the person conducting this review must guard against the FUD principle (*f*ear, *u*ncertainty, and *d*oubt) that all insurance companies practice. That is, they tend to hone in on every conceivable risk and amplify the chance of its occurrence, so that a company will purchase a lot of unnecessary insurance. The best way to avoid this problem is to employ an extremely experienced risk manager who knows which potential risks can be ignored safely. The next areas, at a minimum, should be reviewed.:

- *Buildings and equipment.* The risk manager should list the type of construction, location, and hazards to which each item is exposed. Each structure and major piece of equipment should be listed separately. The current condition of each item should be determined and its replacement cost evaluated.

- *Business interruption.* The risk manager should determine the amount of lost profits and continuing expenses resulting from a business shutdown as the result of a specific hazard.
- *Liabilities to other parties.* The risk manager should determine the risk of loss or damage to other parties by reason of company products, services, operations, or the acts of employees. This analysis should include a review of all contracts, sales orders, purchase orders, leases, and applicable laws to determine what commitments have been undertaken and what exposures exist.
- *Other assets.* The risk manager should review cash, inventory, and accounts receivable to determine the possible exposure to losses by fire, flood, theft, or other hazards.

Step 2. *Determine the risk reduction method.* Match each risk area with a method for dealing with it. The possible options for each risk area include avoidance, reduction of the hazard, retaining the hazard (i.e., self-insurance), or transferring the risk to an insurance company. Note that only the last option in this list includes the purchase of insurance; a company can implement many procedures to reduce a risk without resorting to insurance. The selection of a best option is based on a cost-benefit analysis that offsets the cost of each hazard against the cost of avoiding it, factoring in the probability of the hazard's occurrence. The general categories of risk reduction are:

- *Duplicate.* A company can retain multiple copies of records to guard against the destruction of critical information. In addition, key systems, such as local area networks, telephone systems, and voice mail storage, can be replicated at off-site locations to avoid a shutdown caused by damage to the primary site. For example, airlines maintain elaborate backup systems for their seat reservation databases.
- *Prevent.* A company can institute programs to reduce the likelihood and severity of losses. For example, some companies invite the Occupational Safety and Health Administration (OSHA) to inspect their premises and report on unsafe conditions; the companies then correct the issues to reduce their risk of loss. If a company requires employees to wear hardhats in construction areas, a falling brick still may cause an accident, but the hardhat will reduce the incident's severity. Examples of prevention techniques include improving lighting, installing protective devices on machinery, and enforcing safety rules.
- *Segregate.* A company can split up key assets such as inventory and distribute it to multiple locations (e.g., warehouses). For example, the military maintains alternate command centers in case of war.

Step 3. *Implement internal changes to reduce risks.* Once the types of risk avoidance have been determined, it is time to implement them. Doing so usually involves new procedures or installations, such as fire suppression systems in the computer processing facility or altered cash tracking procedures that will discourage an employee from stealing money. Change to procedures can be a lengthy process, for it includes working with the staff of each functional area to create a new procedure that is acceptable to all users as well as following up with periodic audits to ensure that the procedures still are being followed.

Step 4. *Select a broker.* Every company will require some insurance, unless it takes the hazardous approach of self-insuring virtually every risk. It is necessary to select a broker who can assist the company in procuring the best possible insurance. The right broker can be of great help in this process, not just in picking the least expensive insurance but also in selecting the correct types of coverage, determining the financial strength of insurers, postloss service, and general knowledge of the company's business and of the types of risk that are most likely to occur in that environment. Unfortunately, many companies look for new brokers every few years on the principle that a long-term broker eventually will raise prices and gouge the company. In reality, a long-term relationship should be encouraged, since the broker will gain a greater knowledge of the company's risks as problems occur and claims are received, giving him a valuable insight into company operations that a new broker does not have.

Step 5. *Determine the types of insurance to be purchased.* Once the broker has been selected, the risk manager can show the preliminary results of the insurance review to the broker, and they can mutually determine the types of insurance needed to supplement the actions already taken internally to mitigate risk.

These steps allow a risk manager to determine the types and potential severity of a company's risks as well as how to reduce those risks, either through internal changes or by purchasing various types of insurance coverage.

Types of Business Insurance

The types of business insurance that can be purchased include:

- *Boiler and machinery.* Covers damage to the boilers and machinery as well as payments for injuries caused by the equipment. Providers of this insurance also review the company's equipment and issue a report recommending safety improvements.
- *Business interruption.* Allows a company to pay for its continuing expenses and in some cases will pay for all or part of its anticipated profits.
- *Commercial property.* The minimum "basic form" of this insurance covers losses from fires, explosions, wind storms, hail, vandalism, and other perils. The "broad form," which is an expanded version, covers everything in the basic form plus damage from falling objects, the weight of snow, water damage, and some causes of building collapse. Optional coverage includes an inflation escalator clause, replacement of destroyed structures at the actual replacement cost, and coverage of finished goods at their selling price (instead of at their cost).
- *Comprehensive auto liability.* This coverage is usually mandatory and requires a minimum level of coverage for bodily injury and property damage.

- *Comprehensive crime.* Covers property theft, robbery, safe and premises burglary, and employee dishonesty; in the case of employee dishonesty, the company purchases a fidelity bond, which can cover a named individual, a specific position, or all employees. Some policies also cover ransom payments.
- *Directors' and officers'.* Provides liability coverage to corporate managers for actions taken while acting as an officer or director of the corporation. Directors' and officers' (D&O) insurance includes three types of agreements: The Side A agreement provides coverage to directors and officers for which the company cannot pay while the Side B agreement reimburses the company for any payments it makes to directors and officers for the cost of claim settlements and legal defense work. The Side C agreement provides coverage to the company for claims made against the corporate entity. There are several clauses to be aware of in a D&O contract that can void or reduce coverage. Always look for the next clauses, and attempt to strike them from the contract or at least reduce their impact.
    - Claims caused by fraudulent acts are not covered. Allow this clause only if the fraudulent acts are based on criminal activity, since a claim settlement that does not include the admission of guilt will retain insurance coverage.
    - If the corporate financial statements are considered part of the company's D&O application, any restatement of the financial statements can result in voided coverage.
    - If the D&O policy includes coverage for other types of risks, the total policy limit may be exceeded by other types of claims, leaving no coverage for the directors and officers. Accordingly, always specify separate policy limits just for the D&O coverage.
    - Coverage could be terminated by the bankruptcy of the company.
    - Coverage could be denied if a claim is based on the release of pollutants.
- *General liability.* Covers claims involving accidents on company premises as well as by its products, services, agents, or contractors. An umbrella policy usually applies to liability insurance and provides extra coverage after the primary coverage is exhausted. An umbrella policy has few exclusions.
- *Group life, health, and disability.* There are several types of life insurance; *split-dollar life insurance* covers an employee, and its cost is split between the company and the employee; *key person insurance* covers the financial loss to the company in case an employee dies; and a *cross-purchase plan* allows the co-owners of a business to buy out the share of an owner who dies. *Health insurance* typically covers the areas of hospital, medical, surgical, and dental expenses. *Disability insurance* provides income to an individual who cannot work due to an injury or illness. The disability insurance category is subdivided into *short-term disability* (payments made while recovering one's health following an injury or illness) and *long-term disability* (continuing payments with no anticipation of a return to work).
- *Inland marine.* Covers company property that is being transported. Examples of covered items include trade show displays and finished goods being shipped.
- *Ocean marine and air cargo.* Covers the transporting vehicle (including loss of income due to loss of the vehicle), liability claims against the vehicle's owner or operator, and the cargo.

- *Workers' compensation.* Provides medical and disability coverage to workers who are injured while performing duties related to their jobs. The insurance is mandatory, the employer pays all costs, and no legal recourse is permitted against the employer. There are wide variations in each state's coverage of workers' compensation, including levels of compensation, types of occupations that are not considered, and the allowability of negligence lawsuits.

Types of Insurance Companies

There are several types of insurance companies. Each one may serve a company's insurance needs very well, but there are significant differences between them that a company should be aware of before purchasing an insurance contract. The types of insurance companies are listed next.

- *Captive insurance company.* This is a stock insurance company that is formed to underwrite the risks of its parent company or in some cases a sponsoring group or association.
- *Lloyd's of London.* This is an underwriter operating under the special authority of the English Parliament. It may write insurance coverage of a nature that other insurance companies will not underwrite, usually because of high risks or special needs not covered by a standard insurance form. It also provides the usual types of insurance coverage.
- *Mutual.* This is a company in which each policyholder is an owner and where earnings are distributed as dividends. If a net loss results, policyholders may be subject to extra assessments. In most cases, however, nonassessable policies are issued.
- *Reciprocal organization.* This is an association of insured companies that is independently operated by a manager. Advance deposits are made, against which are charged the proportionate costs of operations.
- *Stock company.* This is an insurance company that behaves like a normal corporation—earnings not retained in the business are distributed to shareholders as dividends and not to policyholders.

Another way to categorize insurance companies is by the type of service offered. For example, a *monoline* company provides only one type of insurance coverage while a *multiple line* company provides more than one kind of insurance. A *financial services company* provides not only insurance but also financial services to customers.

A company also can use *self-insurance* when it deliberately plans to cover losses from its own resources rather than through those of an insurer. Self-insurance can be appropriate in any of these cases:

- When the administrative loss of using an insurer exceeds the amount of the loss
- When a company has sufficient excess resources available to cover even the largest claim
- When excessive premium payments are the only alternative
- When insurance is not available at any price

A form of partial self-insurance is to use large deductibles on insurance policies, so that a company pays for all but the very largest claims. Finally, a company can create a *captive insurer* that provides insurance to the parent company. Captive insurers can provide coverage that is tailored to the parent organization and can provide less dependence on the vagaries of the commercial insurance market. A variation on the captive insurer concept is a *fronting program*, in which a parent company buys insurance from an independent insurance company, which then reinsures the exposure with a captive of the parent company. This technique is used to avoid licensing the captive insurer in every state where the parent company does business, although the captive insurer still must be authorized to accept reinsurance. Fronting also allows the parent company to obtain local service from the independent insurance company while shifting the exposure to the captive company. In whatever form the self-insurance may take, the risk manager should work with the controller to determine the amount of loss reserves to set aside to pay for claims as they arise.

In some states, a company can become a self-insurer for workers' compensation. To do this, a company must qualify under state law as a self-insurer, purchase umbrella coverage to guard against catastrophic claims, post a surety bond, and create a claims administration department to handle claims. The advantages of doing this are lower costs (by eliminating the insurer's profit) and better cash flow (because there are no up-front insurance payments). The disadvantages of this approach are extra administrative costs as well as the cost of qualifying the company in each state in which the company operates.

These are some of the variations that a company can consider when purchasing insurance, either through a third party, a controlled subsidiary, or by providing its own coverage.

Evaluating the Health of an Insurance Carrier

A company that depends on an insurance carrier to mitigate significant portions of its risk must be aware of the financial health of the carrier. Otherwise, the insurer may fail, forcing the company to assume risk itself or find coverage elsewhere on short notice—and quite possibly at a higher price. Although there are rating systems for insurance carriers (such as those issued by A. M. Best, located at www.ambest.com), you can gain an understanding of the operating characteristics of a carrier that indicate future problems, quite possibly before its official rating changes to reflect those characteristics. These characteristics are noted next.

A key warning sign is when a carrier concentrates an excessively high proportion of its insurance line in an area suffering from high payouts, such as California earthquake coverage, pollution coverage, or D&O liability insurance. This is a strong indicator that its reserves are being drained, which may lead to a ratings drop and possibly a decision by the carrier to exit certain types of insurance coverage.

When reviewing an insurer's financial statements, earnings volatility is a general indicator of trouble. This is most common with smaller carriers, which have concentrated their business in too small a geographic area or in only a few insurance lines, so they have not spread their risk sufficiently in the event of major problems in one or two areas. This level of insurance concentration leads to wild gyrations in earnings, which is a strong indicator of future bankruptcy. Also, even if there is minimal earnings volatility, watch out for low net income or minimal cash flows, which indicate poor management. Even worse, cash outflows will eat into the carrier's reserves, leaving less available for future payouts. Another issue when reviewing financials is significant charges to earnings. Although a carrier should be credited with recognizing insurance losses when it posts a large write-down, the fact remains that the carrier expects significant losses in the near term. When all of these factors are considered together—earnings volatility, low or negative income or cash flows, and write-downs—a clear picture emerges of the true financial condition of an insurer.

Insurers are having increasing difficulty recovering receivables from reinsurers, which have tightened their reviews of potential payouts considerably. Thus, an increase in reinsurance receivables over several years is an indicator of potential trouble, especially if management confirms this in its discussion of financial results in the carrier's annual 10-K report.

A final cause for concern is an excessively high rate of growth in an insurer's policyholders. This is a difficult issue to evaluate, for high growth simply may mean that an insurer has developed an entirely new type of insurance and is acquiring market share before anyone else begins to compete. However, the more common scenario is that the insurer is essentially buying market share with excessively low policy pricing, which eventually will cut into its net income, cash flow, and reserves when it begins to experience high payout levels in proportion to its income from those policies.

Unfortunately, there is no completely quantitative way to evaluate the financial health of an insurer—an examination of its business practices is also necessary to understand what its near-term financial condition is likely to be. As noted, there are a number of ways in which a watchful CEO can gain a general understanding of the short-term problems of an insurer, which may allow enough time to shift insurance coverage to a new carrier that is likely to remain in a better financial position.

Annual Risk Management Report

The risk manager should issue a risk management report to the board of directors and CEO every year. This document reviews all perceived risks to which a company is subject and describes the steps taken to mitigate those risks. It is of great value, because the board and CEO need to know the extent of potential risks and how they can impact company operations. The contents of a typical risk management report are described in this section, including an example based on an organization that provides training in high-risk outdoor activities.

The risk management report contains four sections. The first is an overview that describes the contents of the report, the timing of when it is issued, and to whom it is delivered. The second section itemizes all risks that are perceived to be significant. If every possible risk were to be listed, the document might be too voluminous for easy reading. These risks should be grouped with subheadings

EXHIBIT 9.3 Example of a Risk Management Report

Section II: Review of Risks

- *Risk related to education:*
  1. Risk of school equipment failing
  2. Risk of accidents due to improper instruction

Section III: Ways to Cover Risks

- *Risk of school equipment failing.* School equipment is reviewed and replaced by the school governing committees on a regular basis. Instructors are also authorized to remove equipment from use immediately if they spot unusual damage that may result in equipment failure.
- *Risk of accidents due to improper supervision.* School instructors must first serve as assistant instructors under the supervision of a more experienced instructor, who evaluates their skills and recommends advancement to full instructor status. The typical instructor has previously completed all prerequisite courses and has considerable outdoor experience. All instructors must have taken a mountain-oriented first aid class within the last year.

Section IV: Supplemental Insurance Coverage

- *Risk of school equipment failing.* The general liability policy covers this risk for the first $500,000 of payments to a claimant. The umbrella policy covers this risk for an additional $5 million after the coverage provided by the general liability policy is exhausted.
- *Risk of accidents due to improper instruction.* Same insurance coverage as for the risk of school equipment failing.

rather than appearing as an enormous list that is difficult for the reader to digest. The third section notes the ways to cover those risks, *excluding insurance* (which is addressed in the fourth section). These methods include operational changes, such as altered procedures or processes, or additional training. Finally, the fourth section notes the insurance that has been purchased to provide additional coverage to those risk areas that cannot be covered adequately by internal changes. These four sections give the board and CEO adequate knowledge of a company's efforts in the risk management area.

The example in Exhibit 9.3 presents an extract from the risk management report of an organization that provides outdoor training classes. The example skips the overview section and proceeds straight to the enumeration of risks, how they are covered, and what types of insurance are also needed.

Summary

Any company is subject to a broad array of risks, some of which can cause severe difficulties or even ruin the business. Given the potential for disaster, the CEO needs to be aware of the key risks to which her business is subjected and be able to structure a system for dealing with it. This system should encompass policies and procedures as well as a risk manager to oversee them, and the selective use of insurance to further mitigate risks. This chapter has provided an overview of the key elements in a risk management system, which the CEO can use to verify whether her company's risk mitigation activities are sufficient.

CHAPTER 10

Risk Management: Foreign Exchange

When a company accepts foreign currency in payment for its goods or services, it accepts some level of foreign exchange risk, since the value of that currency in comparison to the company's home currency may fluctuate enough between the beginning of the contract and receipt of funds to seriously erode the underlying profit on the sale. This is becoming more of an issue over time, because global competition is making it more likely that a company *must* accept payment in a foreign currency.

When dealing in foreign currencies, a company must determine its level of exposure, create a plan for how to mitigate that risk, engage in daily activities to implement the plan, and properly account for each transaction. Each of these steps is covered in this chapter.

Foreign Exchange Quote Terminology

Before delving into foreign exchange risk, it is useful to understand the terminology used in the foreign exchange quotation process. When comparing the price of one currency to another, the *base currency* is the unit of currency that does not fluctuate in amount, while the *quoted currency* or *price currency* does fluctuate. The U.S. dollar is used most commonly as the base currency. For example, if the dollar is the base currency and $1 is worth €0.7194, this quote is called the *indirect quote* of presenting a quote for euro. However, if the euro is used as the base currency, the same quote becomes $1.39 per €1 (and is calculated as 1/0.7194), and is referred to as a *direct quote*. The direct quote is the inverse of the indirect quote. If neither the base currency nor the quoted currency is the U.S. dollar, the exchange rate between the two currencies is called a *cross rate*.

As an example of an indirect quote, the U.S. dollar is listed first and the currency it is being paired with is listed second. Thus, a USD/EUR quote (dollars/euro) means that $1 equals €0.7194. Conversely, a EUR/USD (euro/dollars) quote is a direct quote, and means that €1 equals $1.3900. The key factor to remember with any quote pairing is that the first currency referenced always has a unit value of 1.

Most exchange rates are quoted to four decimals, since the sums involved in currency transactions are so large that the extra few decimals can have a meaningful impact on payments. A *point* is a change of one digit at the fourth decimal place of a quote.

A foreign exchange dealer will quote both *bid* and *offer* foreign exchange prices. The bid price is the price at which the dealer will purchase a currency while the ask price is the price at which the dealer will sell a currency.

The current exchange rate between any two currencies is known as the *spot rate*. When two parties to a foreign exchange transaction exchange funds, this is on the *delivery date* or *value date*. When a company requires foreign exchange immediately, it engages in a *spot settlement*, although actually there is a one- to two-day delay in final settlement of the transaction.

Example

Toledo Toolmakers learns from its bank on June 1 that it has just received €50,000. Toledo wants to convert these funds into dollars, so it calls its bank and requests the U.S. dollar exchange rate in euro. The bank quotes an exchange rate of $1.3900 per €1. The company immediately sells the euro at the rate of 1.3900. Settlement is completed two working days later, on the delivery date of June 3, when Toledo will receive $35,971.

Nature of Foreign Exchange Risk

Let us assume that a company's home currency is the U.S. dollar. If, during the interval when a customer is obligated to pay the company, the dollar appreciates against the customer's currency, the customer is paying with a reduced-value currency, which causes the company to record a foreign exchange loss once it is paid.

Example

Toledo Toolmakers sells goods to an Italian company for €100,000. At the time of sale, €1 is worth $1.39079 at the spot rate, which is a total sale price of $139,079. The customer is not obligated to pay until 90 days have passed; upon receipt of the euro payment in 90 days, the value in dollars will be based on the spot rate at the time of receipt. On the day when payment is received, the spot rate has dropped to $1.3630, which reduces the value of the payment to $136,300, resulting in a decline of $2,779, or 2%. Toledo must record this reduction as a loss.

There is also a possibility that exchange rates will move in the opposite direction, which creates a gain for the selling company. Smaller firms that do not engage in much foreign currency trade are more likely to accept the gains and losses from changes in the spot rate. However, doing this can cause wild swings in the profitability of larger firms with substantial multicountry trading activity. These firms are more likely to seek a solution that reduces their earnings volatility. Hedging is the solution, and a broad array of possible solutions are covered later in this chapter.

Before considering hedging solutions, a chief executive officer (CEO) needs to know if there is any currency risk that requires such a solution—and that is not always a simple matter to determine. The next section discusses this problem.

Data Collection for Foreign Exchange Risk Management

Determining the extent of a company's currency risk can be a frustrating exercise for the foreign exchange specialist, who is often at the receiving end of a flood of disorganized information arriving from the accounting, budgeting, tax, and treasury departments. The specialist must somehow aggregate this information, not only into a current statement of currency positions but also into a reliable forecast of where currency positions are expected to be in the near to medium term. This information is used as the foundation for a hedging strategy.

A large firm with an enterprise resources planning (ERP) system can accumulate its existing net currency exposures from the ERP system automatically, but such is not the case for a company with more distributed accounting systems; its staff likely will accumulate the information manually from each subsidiary and load it into an electronic spreadsheet in order to net out the positions of each subsidiary and determine the level of currency exposure. Obviously, those with an ERP system have a significant advantage in determining the amount of this *booked exposure.*

The currency forecast can be unusually difficult to formulate, because a company may have many subsidiaries, each of which has some level of exposure in multiple currencies that varies continually. Ideally, there should be a forecast for each currency, which can result in a multitude of forecasts. To manage the forecasting workload, the foreign exchange specialist usually constructs forecasts only for those currencies in which the company is most heavily committed and ignores currencies where the company generally has minimal currency positions. The resulting *forecasted exposure* estimates the most likely size of currency transactions that will occur in the near and medium term, so that hedging plans can be made to mitigate these exposures.

Booked exposure, especially when derived from ERP information, should be quite accurate. However, forecasted exposure is only moderately accurate in the near term, and its accuracy declines rapidly within a year. This reduced accuracy strongly impacts the amount of hedging that a company may be willing to engage in, as discussed in the next section.

Foreign Exchange Hedging Strategies

A variety of foreign exchange hedging strategies are noted in this section. The three main strategy groupings are to:

1. Not hedge the exposure
2. Hedge the exposure through business practices
3. Hedge the exposure with a derivative

Also, within the third category, you must decide on what level of exposure to hedge. One possible strategy could be to hedge 100% of booked exposures, 50% of forecasted exposures over the next rolling 12-month period, and 25% of forecasted exposures over the following 12-month period. This gradually declining *benchmark hedge ratio* for longer forecast periods is justifiable on the assumption that the level of forecast accuracy declines over time, so that one should hedge against the minimum amount of exposure that almost certainly will occur.

Example

The CEO of Toledo Toolmakers compares his trailing six-month stream of euro-denominated cash flows (in thousands) to the original forecast, which appears in Exhibit A.

EXHIBIT A Sample Forecasted and Actual Cash Flow Stream (Stable)

	Jan	Feb	Mar	Apr	May	Jun
Forecast	€3,051	€3,293	€4,011	€3,982	€3,854	€3,702
Actual	2,715	3,015	3,742	3,800	3,750	3,509
€ Variance	–336	–278	–269	–182	–104	–193
% Variance	–11%	–8%	–7%	–5%	–3%	–5%

The forecasted cash flow is consistently higher than the actual cash flow by 5% to 10%, which is a very high level of forecasting accuracy and is indicative of mature and stable cash flows. In this case, the CEO can safely adopt a 90% benchmark hedge ratio, which should hedge nearly all of the forecasted exposure. However, what if a company has more difficulty in predicting its cash flows? Exhibit B reveals a considerably more variable cash flow situation.

EXHIBIT B Sample Forecasted and Actual Cash Flow Stream (Unstable)

	Jan	Feb	Mar	Apr	May	Jun
Forecast	€3,051	€3,293	€4,011	€3,982	€3,854	€3,702
Actual	2,142	3,409	4,000	1,862	3,915	2,274
€ Variance	–909	116	–11	–2,120	61	–1,428
% Variance	–30%	4%	0%	–53%	2%	–39%

In this more difficult forecasting environment, the average variance of actual cash flows from the forecast is 21%, but it is also lower than the forecast by 41% in half of the reporting periods. In this environment, the CEO may well feel justified in adopting a benchmark hedge ratio of only 60% in order to hedge only that portion of cash flows that is most likely to occur.

The benchmark hedge ratio does not need to be consistent across the entire currency portfolio. There may be significant differences in the level of forecasting accuracy by currency, so a high-confidence currency forecast with little expected volatility can be matched with a higher benchmark hedge ratio, while a questionable forecast may justify a much lower ratio. Introducing this higher degree of granularity into the hedging strategy allows for better matching of hedging activity to foreign exchange risk.

The benchmark hedge ratio is also important from the perspective of the availability of hedge accounting. If the benchmark hedge ratio can be proven to cause a high probability of hedging effectiveness, hedge accounting (which can delay the recognition of hedging gains and losses) can be used. Consequently, an ongoing analysis of the most appropriate benchmark hedge ratio would leave open the option of using hedge accounting.

The three main foreign exchange hedging strategies are discussed in the next subheadings.

Do-Not-Hedge Strategy: Accept the Risk

Not hedging the exposure is the simplest strategy of all. A company can accept the foreign exchange risk and record any gains or losses on changes in the spot rate as they occur. The size of a company's currency exposure may dictate whether to hedge or not. For a smaller currency position, the expense associated with setting up and monitoring a hedge may be greater than any likely loss from a decline in the spot rate. Conversely, as a company's currency positions increase in size, the risk also increases and makes this strategy less acceptable.

The next seven strategies are all internal business practices that reduce currency exposure.

BUSINESS PRACTICES STRATEGY: INSIST ON HOME CURRENCY PAYMENT   It is possible to insist on being paid in the company's home currency, so that the foreign exchange risk shifts entirely to the customer. This is a likely strategy for a company that is dominant in its industry and that therefore can impose terms on its customers. However, smaller firms will find that they have a modest competitive advantage if they allow customers to pay in their own currencies.

The worst option is to offer a customer a choice of currencies in which to make a payment; it will invariably use the one having the more favorable exchange rate. The company essentially bears the downside risk in this scenario, with no upside potential.

BUSINESS PRACTICES STRATEGY: CURRENCY SURCHARGES   If a customer will not pay in a company's home currency, a related option is to bill the customer a currency surcharge if the company incurs a foreign exchange loss between the time of billing and payment. The surcharge may not be billed for minor changes in the exchange rate (to avoid paperwork) but is triggered by a significant decline in the exchange rate. Customers are rarely happy about this, since they are taking on the foreign exchange risk, and they cannot budget for the amount of the surcharge. It is also hardly a competitive advantage for a company to impose this practice on its customers.

BUSINESS PRACTICES STRATEGY: GET PAID ON TIME   When a company deals with a counterparty in another country, the payment terms may be quite long, due to longer delivery schedules, border-crossing delays, or simply longer customary payment intervals in the other country. If a payment period is unusually prolonged, the company is exposed to changes in the spot rate to a much greater extent than would be the case if the payment interval were compressed. Consequently, it behooves a company's sales staff to strive constantly toward sales agreements with shorter payment terms while the collections staff should be unusually aggressive in collecting from foreign customers.

BUSINESS PRACTICES STRATEGY: FOREIGN CURRENCY LOANS   It is possible to offset a foreign currency risk exposure by creating a counter liability, such as a loan. To do so, a company can borrow an amount of money in the foreign currency that matches the amount of the receivable. When the customer pays off the receivable, the company uses the proceeds to pay off the loan—all in the same currency. This is an especially attractive option if foreign interest rates on debt are low or if there are tax advantages peculiar to the foreign tax location of which the company can take advantage.

BUSINESS PRACTICES STRATEGY: SOURCING CHANGES   If there is a large amount of foreign currency cash flows coming from a specific country, one way to hedge this risk is to start using suppliers located in the same country. By doing so, the company can find a ready use for the incoming currency, by turning it around and sending it right back to the same country. A more permanent possibility is to either buy or build a facility in that country, which will require currency not only for the initial capital investment but also to fund continuing operations. This is a particularly favorable option if local government subsidies offer the company additional cost savings. However, local sourcing is not a good option if it will interrupt a smoothly operating supply chain.

BUSINESS PRACTICES STRATEGY: FOREIGN CURRENCY ACCOUNTS   If a company regularly receives and pays out funds in a particular foreign currency, it may make sense to open a foreign exchange account in which it maintains a sufficient currency balance to meet its operational needs. This approach can be cost effective because otherwise the company would have to buy the foreign currency in order to pay those suppliers requiring payment in that currency and separately sell the same currency upon receipt of customer payments. Although the company still is accepting the risk of loss on fluctuations in the exchange rate, it is eliminating the cost of continually buying and selling the currency.

Such a bank account does not necessarily have to be held in the country where the currency originates. It is also possible, and likely more efficient, to maintain a variety of currency accounts in a single major currency center, such as New York, London, or Amsterdam.

BUSINESS PRACTICES STRATEGY: NETTING ARRANGEMENTS   A company that regularly conducts business in multiple countries must spend a considerable amount of time settling foreign exchange transactions. It may buy and sell the same currencies many times over as it processes individual payables and receivables. There are three ways to reduce the volume of these transactions, depending on the number of parties involved.

1. *Unilateral netting*. A company can aggregate the cash flows among its various subsidiaries to determine if any foreign exchange payments between the subsidiaries can be netted, with only the (presumably) smaller residual balances being physically shifted. This method reduces the volume of foreign exchange cash flows and therefore the associated foreign exchange risk.
2. *Bilateral spreadsheet netting*. If two companies located in different countries transact a great deal of business with each other, they can track the payables owed to each other, net out the balances at the end of each month, and one party pays the other the net remaining balance.
3. *Multilateral centralized netting*. Multiple parties that wish to net transactions are much too complex to manage with a spreadsheet. Instead, the common approach is to net transactions through a centralized exchange, such as Arizona-based Euro-Netting (www.euronetting.com). Under a centralized netting system, each participant enters its payables into a centralized database through an Internet browser or some other file upload system, after which the netting service converts each participant's net cash flows to an equivalent amount in each participant's base currency and uses actual traded exchange rates to determine the final net position of each participant. The exchange operator pays or receives each participant's net position and uses the proceeds to offset the required foreign exchange trades.

Each type of netting arrangement can involve a broad array of payment types, covering such areas as products, services, royalties, dividends, interest, loans, and hedging contracts.

When bilateral or multilateral netting is used, the parties usually sign a master agreement that itemizes the types of netting to be performed as well as which contracts or purchase orders are to be included in the arrangement.

Although netting can be a highly effective way to reduce foreign exchange transaction costs, some governments do not recognize the enforceability of netting arrangements, because they can undermine the payment rights of third-party creditors. Consequently, consult a qualified attorney prior to entering into a netting arrangement.

The remaining strategies in this section involve the use of derivatives to hedge foreign exchange risk.

Hedging Strategy: Forward Exchange Contracts

Under a forward exchange contract, which is the most commonly used foreign exchange hedge, a company agrees to purchase a fixed amount of a foreign currency on a specific date and at a predetermined rate. This method allows the company to lock in the rate of exchange up front for settlement at a specified date in the future. The counterparty is typically a bank, which requires a deposit to secure the contract, with a final payment due in time to be cleared by the settlement date. If the company has a credit facility with the bank acting as its counterparty, the bank can allocate a portion of that line to any outstanding forward exchange contracts and release the allocation once the contracts have been settled. The forward exchange contract is considered to be an over-the-counter transaction, because there is no centralized trading location and customized transactions are created directly between parties.

Example

Toledo Toolmakers has a €100,000 receivable at a spot rate of 1.39079. Toledo can enter into a forward foreign exchange (FX) contract with a bank for €100,000 at a forward rate of 1.3900, so that Toledo receives a fixed amount of $139,000 on the maturity date of the receivable. When Toledo receives the €100,000 payment, it transfers the funds to the bank acting as counterparty on the forward FX contract and receives $139,000 from the bank. Thus, Toledo has achieved its original receivable amount of $139,000, even if the spot rate has declined during the interval.

The price of a currency on the maturity date (its forward price) is comprised of the spot price, plus a transaction fee, plus or minus points that represent the interest rate differential between the two currencies. The combination of the spot rate and the forward points is known as the *all-in forward rate*. The interest rate differential is calculated in accordance with these two rules:

1. The currency of the country having a higher interest rate trades at a discount.
2. The currency of the country having a lower interest rate trades at a premium.

For example, if the domestic interest rate is higher than that of the foreign currency, forward points are deducted from the spot rate, which makes the foreign currency less expensive in the forward market. The result of this pricing is that the forward price should make the buyer indifferent to taking delivery immediately or at some future date. Thus, if the spot price of euro per dollar were 0.7194 and there was a discount of 40 points for forwards having a one-year maturity, the all-in forward rate would be 0.7154.

The calculation of the discount or premium points follows this formula:

$$\text{Premium/discount} = \text{Exchange rate} \times \text{Interest rate differential} \times \frac{\text{Days of contract duration}}{360}$$

Example

The six-month U.S. dollar money market rate is 2.50%, and the six-month euro money market rate is 3.75%. The USD/EUR exchange rate is 0.7194. The number of days in the forward exchange contract is 181. Because the euro interest rate

(continued)

exceeds the dollar interest rate, the dollar is at a premium to the euro. Thus, the USD/EUR forward exchange rate exceeds the spot rate. The premium is calculated as:

0.7194 spot rate × .0125 interest differential × (181/365 days) = .0045 premium

The premium is therefore 45 points, which results in a USD/EUR forward exchange rate of 0.7194 + 0.0045, or 0.7239.

There are a few problems with forward exchange contracts to be aware of. First, because they are special transactions between two parties, it can be difficult to sell them to a third party. Also, the transaction premium offered may not be competitive.

Another problem is that the arrangement relies on the customer paying the company on or before the date when the forward FX contract matures. To continue using Toledo Toolmakers in an example, its terms to a European Union customer may require payment in 60 days, so it enters into a forward contract to expire in 63 days, which factors in an allowance of three extra days for the customer to pay. If the customer does not pay within 63 days, Toledo still has to deliver euro on that date to fulfill its side of the forward contract.

It is possible to mitigate this problem with the variability of customer payments by entering into a *forward window contract*. This arrangement has a range of settlement dates during which the company can settle the outstanding contract at the currency rate noted in the contract. This contract is slightly more expensive than a standard forward exchange contract, but it makes matching incoming customer payments to the terms of the contract much easier.

A related problem is when a company enters into a forward exchange contract to hedge an anticipated cash flow, but the cash flow never transpires, perhaps because a sale was canceled. In this case, you can enter into an offsetting forward exchange contract to negate the initial contract.

Example

Toledo Toolmakers learns on July 15 that a Belgian customer has financial difficulties and has defaulted on a payment of €250,000 that Toledo expected to receive on October 15. Unfortunately, Toledo already sold this amount through a forward exchange contract having a EUR/USD exchange rate of 1.3900, with a settlement date of October 15. Since it now has an obligation to deliver currency that will not be available on October 15, it needs to enter into an offsetting agreement to buy 250,000 euro on the same date.

Since the date of the original contract, the exchange rate has worsened, so that Toledo now enters into a three-month forward exchange contract having a EUR/USD rate of 1.3850. On the settlement date, Toledo buys €250,000 for $346,250 (€250,000 × $1.3850) and sells them for $347,500 (€250,000 × $1.3900), thereby incurring a loss of $1,250.

A variation on the forward contract is the *nondeliverable forward*. Under this arrangement, the only payment made between the parties is the difference between the spot rate and the forward rate. This net-cash solution can greatly reduce the total gross amount of funds being transferred.

Hedging Strategy: Currency Futures

A currency future is the same as a forward exchange contract, except that it trades on an exchange. Each contract has a standardized size, expiry date, and settlement rules. The primary currency futures center with substantial volume is the Chicago Mercantile Exchange (CME). The CME offers futures trading between the major currencies as well as some of the emerging market currencies; however, the volume of contracts in the emerging market currencies is quite low.

These contracts normally are handled through a broker, who charges a commission. There is also a margin requirement, so that the buyer may be called on to submit additional funds over time if the underlying futures contract declines in value. Part of this margin is an initial deposit whose size is based on the contract size and the type of position being acquired. All futures contracts are marked to market daily, with the underlying margin accounts being credited or debited with the day's gains or losses. If the balance of the margin account drops too far, the contract buyer must contribute more funds to the margin account. If the buyer does not update her margin account as required, it is possible that the position will be closed out.

Since currency futures have standard sizes and expiry dates, it is quite likely that a futures hedging strategy will not exactly match the underlying currency activity. For example, if a company needs to hedge a projected receipt of €375,000 and the related futures contract trades only in units of €100,000, the company has the choice of selling either three or four contracts, totaling €300,000 and €400,000, respectively. Further, if the projected currency receipt date varies from the standard futures contract expiry date, the company will be subject to some foreign exchange risk for a few days. Thus, the standardized nature of currency futures contracts results in an imperfect hedge for users.

Example

Toledo Toolmakers ships product to a German customer in February and expects to receive a payment of €425,000 on June 12. Toledo elects to hedge the transaction by selling a futures contract on the CME. The standard contract size for the EUR/USD pairing is €100,000, so Toledo sells four contracts to hedge its expected receipt of €425,000. This contract always expires on Fridays; the nearest Friday following the expected receipt date of the euro is on June 15, so Toledo enters into contracts having that expiry date. Because the standardized futures contracts do not exactly fit Toledo's transaction, Toledo is electing not to hedge €25,000 of the expected receipt, and it also will retain the risk of exchange rate fluctuations between its currency receipt date of June 12 and its currency sale date of June 15.

Hedging Strategy: Currency Options

A foreign currency option requires the payment of a premium in exchange for a right to use one currency to buy another currency at a specified price on or before a specified date. A *call option* permits the buyer to buy the underlying currency at the strike price while a *put option* allows the buyer to sell the underlying currency at the strike price.

An option is easier to manage than a forward exchange contract, because a company can choose not to exercise its option to sell currency if a customer does not pay it. Not exercising an option is also useful when it becomes apparent that a company can realize a gain on changes in the exchange rate that would not have been the case if it were tied into a forward exchange contract.

Options are especially useful for those companies interested in bidding on contracts that will be paid in a foreign currency. If they do not win the bid, they simply can let the option expire, without any obligation to purchase currency. If they win the bid, they have the option of taking advantage of the exchange rate that they locked in at the time they formulated the bid. Thus, options allow a company to realize the original margin that it quoted to a customer rather than potentially having the margin erode due to exchange risk.

In an option agreement, the cost to the buyer is fixed up front while the cost to the seller is potentially unlimited—which tends to increase the cost of the option to the point where the seller is willing to take on the risk associated with the contract. From the seller's perspective, the amount of an option premium is based on the strike price, time to expiration, and the volatility of the underlying currency. If the currency is highly volatile, it is more likely that the buyer will exercise the option, which increases the risk for the seller. Thus, an option for a nonvolatile currency is less expensive, since it is unlikely to be exercised.

Currency options are available both over the counter and are traded on exchanges. Those traded on exchanges are known as *listed options*. The contract value, term, and strike price of a listed option is standardized, whereas these terms are customized for an over-the-counter option.

Within an option agreement, the *strike price* states the exchange rate at which the underlying currency can be bought or sold; the *notional contract amount* is the amount of currency that can be bought or sold at the option of the buyer; and the *expiry date* is the date when the contract will expire if not previously exercised. If the option is *in the money*, the buyer can exercise it at a better price than the current exchange rate. If the option is *at the money*, the buyer can exercise it at the current market price. The option is considered to be *out of the money* if the buyer can exercise it only at an exchange rate that is worse than the market rate. A *European-style option* is exercisable only on the expiry date while an *American-style option* can be exercised at any time prior to and including the expiry date.

The problem with an option is that it requires the payment of an up-front premium to purchase it, so not exercising the option means that the fee is lost. This may be fine if a gain from currency appreciation offsets the fee, but it is an outright loss if the nonexercise was caused by the customer not paying on time.

A more complicated version of the option is the *foreign exchange collar*. Under this strategy, a company buys one option and sells another at the same time, using

Example

Toledo Toolmakers buys a 90-day option to buy €100,000 at $1.3900 for a fee of $4,000, which it plans to use as a hedge against a €100,000 payment from a customer that is due in 90 days. At the end of the option contract, the spot rate is $1.4350. Toledo elects to not exercise the option, thereby receiving €100,000 from its customer that can be exchanged at the spot price of $1.4350, for a total of $143,500. Thus, Toledo has gained $4,500 on the differential in the spot price, less $4,000 for the cost of the option, for a net profit of $500.

the same expiry date and the same currencies. Doing so establishes an exchange rate range for a company. The upper limit of the exchange rate is established by the option the company buys while the lower limit is established by the option that the company sells. If the exchange rate remains within the upper and lower price points of the collar, neither option is exercised. By accepting a moderate range of acceptable prices, a company can offset the cost of the premium paid for the purchased option with the premium from the option that is sold. The options are usually European style, so they are exercised only on the expiry date.

Example

Toledo Toolmakers is contractually obligated to pay a French supplier €500,000 in three months. The current EUR/USD exchange rate is 1.3900. Toledo does not want to pay an option premium. The three-month EUR/USD forward exchange rate is 1.3950, and the company is willing to accept a variation of 0.02 both above and below this rate, which means that the acceptable currency range is from 1.3750 to 1.4150. The option premium for selling euro at 1.4150 is 0.10, and Toledo also can earn the same premium for buying euro at 1.3750. Thus, the cost of one option is exactly offset by the earnings from the other option, resulting in a net option cost of zero.

The actual exchange rate on the settlement date is 1.4300, so the company exercises the option to sell €500,000 at 1.4150, thereby avoiding an incremental loss of $7,500, which Toledo otherwise would have incurred if it had been forced to sell euro at 1.4300.

Another issue with options is that they must be marked to market at the end of every reporting period, with the gain or loss recorded in the company's financial statements.

Hedging Strategy: Currency Swaps

A currency swap is a spot transaction on the over-the-counter market that is executed at the same time as a forward transaction, with currencies being exchanged at both the spot date and the forward date. One currency is bought at the spot rate and date, and the transaction is reversed at the forward date and rate. Thus, once the swap expires, both parties return to their original positions. The currency swap acts as an investment in one currency and a loan in another. The amount of a foreign exchange swap usually begins at $5 million, so this is not an option for smaller foreign exchange cash positions.

Because the exchange rates of both transactions are set at the time of the initial transaction, the difference between the two rates is caused by the interest differential between the two currencies over the duration of the swap.

Example

Toledo Toolmakers has excess euro that it will need in nine months to pay for a capital project in Europe. In the interim, the company wants to invest the euro in a short-term instrument while also obtaining use of the funds in U.S. dollars to cover its operating cash flow needs. To do so, Toledo engages in an FX swap with its bank, under which it buys $10 million at a 0.7194 USD/EUR exchange rate and sells €7,194,000. Simultaneously, Toledo agrees to sell back $10 million of U.S. dollars in nine months at a rate of 0.7163 and buy back €7,163,000. The difference between the spot rate and forward rate of 0.0031 represents the interest rate differential between euro and U.S. dollars over the nine months spanned by the swap agreement, or $31,000. Toledo earns the extra interest because it has chosen to invest in the currency having the higher interest rate.

The currency swap is useful when a company forecasts a short-term liquidity shortfall in a specific currency and has sufficient funds in a different currency to effect a swap into the currency where funds are needed. In addition, the company offsets what is likely to be a high interest rate on the short-term debt with the lower interest rate that it was earning on funds in a different currency.

Example

Toledo Toolmakers has a short-term negative euro account balance of €500,000, which it expects will continue for the next six months. During that time, Toledo must pay its bank London Interbank Offering Rate (LIBOR) plus 2% for the current account deficit. At the current LIBOR rate of 3.5% and EUR/USD spot rate of 1.3900, this represents an interest expense of $19,113, which is calculated as:

$$\$19,113 = €500,000 \times 1.3900 \text{ exchange rate} \times 5.5\% \text{ interest rate} \times (180/360 \text{ days})$$

(continued)

(*continued*)

Toledo has several million U.S. dollars available, so it engages in a six-month swap of dollars for euro, thereby eliminating the negative account balance. The interest rates in Europe and the United States are identical, so there is no premium or discount between the currencies. Toledo was earning the LIBOR rate on its short-term investments. The interest income that it gave up by engaging in the swap was $12,163, which is calculated as:

$$\$12,163 = €500,000 \times 1.3900 \text{ exchange rate} \times 3.5\% \text{ interest rate} \times (180/360 \text{ days})$$

Thus, by using a swap to use low-interest investments to offset higher-cost debt, Toledo saves $6,950.

The currency swap is also useful when a foreign currency cash flow is delayed, and a company normally would be obligated to sell the currency on the expected receipt date, as per the terms of a forward exchange contract. To meet this contractually obligated payment, a company can swap its other currency reserves into the currency that must be sold and reverse the transaction later, when the expected cash flow eventually arrives.

Hedging Strategy: Proxy Hedging

If a company elects to receive a currency that is not actively traded, it may have a difficult time locating a hedge in the same currency. However, changes in the value of the currencies of a large economic area, such as Southeast Asia, tend to be closely correlated with each other. If the CEO feels that this correlation will continue, it may make sense to hedge through a highly correlated currency instead. However, just because the respective values of a currency pair were highly correlated in the past does not mean that they will continue to be correlated in the future; a multitude of political and economic issues can break the correlation.

Summary

Forward exchange contracts are the most heavily used form of hedging, for two reasons. First, they are very inexpensive, having a modest transactional cost. Second, they are an over-the-counter product and so can be tailored precisely to a company's individual needs. However, they firmly lock a company into the current spot rate, giving it no opportunity to participate in any future favorable price movements. Although a company could use partial hedging to give itself some upside potential, this is also a two-way street, with increased risk of loss if exchange rates move in the wrong direction.

Currency futures are entered into and sold off more easily, because they are standardized products that trade through a formal exchange system. However, these conveniences also present a problem, since a company's hedging requirements cannot precisely fit the amount or timing of available futures contracts. Futures also suffer from the same problem as forward exchange contracts: They leave no room to participate in any future favorable price movements.

Currency options have a clear advantage over the preceding two strategies in that they allow a buyer to exercise an option or let it lapse, thereby allowing a company to take advantage of favorable price movements. Against this major benefit is ranged the biggest problem with options: the premium imposed by the option seller. In practice, companies tend to buy options that are relatively far out of the money, since these options are less expensive, but doing so means that they must retain some FX risk. Because of the premium, options appear to be the most expensive alternative; however, you also must factor in the opportunity cost of using forward exchange contracts or currency futures where you cannot take advantage of favorable price swings. When netted against the option premium, the cost of options does not appear to be so prohibitive. Options also require closer monitoring than other strategies, because you must judge exactly when to exercise them.

In summary, forward exchange contracts and currency futures are easier and less expensive to engage in than options, and thus are favored by organizations with simpler treasury operations and conservative risk profiles. Options are more expensive in the short term and require closer monitoring but can be financially rewarding to more aggressive companies.

PART IV

Financial Analysis

CHAPTER 11

Performance Measurements

This chapter contains the 27 most important performance measurement ratios for a chief executive officer (CEO) to use, covering asset utilization, operating performance, cash flow, liquidity, solvency, return on investment, and market performance. Each measurement description includes an overview, notes on how to derive the calculation, and how it is used in an example.

Asset Utilization Measurements

The ratios noted in this section primarily focus on the level of a company's sales in relation to its other key operating variables, such as working capital, headcount, and total expenses. They are designed to give you a quick overview of the sufficiency of sales being generated.

Sales/Working Capital Ratio

It is exceedingly important to keep the amount of cash used by an organization at a minimum, so that its financing needs are reduced. One of the best ways to determine changes in the overall usage of cash over time is the ratio of sales to working capital. This ratio shows the amount of cash required to maintain a certain level of sales. It is most effective when tracked on a trend line, so that management can see if there is a long-term change in the amount of cash required by the business in order to generate the same amount of sales. For instance, if a company has elected to increase its sales to less creditworthy customers, it is likely that they will pay more slowly than regular customers, thereby increasing the company's investment in accounts receivable. Similarly, if the management team decides to increase the speed of order fulfillment by increasing the amount of inventory for certain items, the inventory investment will increase. In both cases, the ratio of working capital to sales will worsen due to specific management decisions. An alternative usage for this ratio is for budgeting purposes, since budgeted working capital levels can be compared to the historical amount of this ratio to see if the budgeted working capital level is sufficient.

The formula is to compare sales to working capital, which is accounts receivable, plus inventory, minus accounts payable. Do not use annualized gross sales in the calculation, since it would include in the sales figure the amount of any sales that have already been returned and therefore are already included in the inventory figure. The formula is:

$$\frac{\text{Annualized Net Sales}}{(\text{Accounts Receivable} + \text{Inventory} - \text{Accounts Payable})}$$

For example, the Jolt Power Supply Company has elected to reduce the amount of inventory it carries for some of its least-ordered stock items, with a goal of increasing inventory turnover from twice a year to four times a year. It achieves its inventory goal quite rapidly by selling back some of its inventory to its suppliers in exchange for credits against future purchases. Portions of its operating results for the first four quarters after this decision was made are presented next.

	Quarter 1	Quarter 2	Quarter 3	Quarter 4
Revenue	$320,000	310,000	290,000	280,000
Accounts Receivable	107,000	103,000	97,000	93,000
Inventory	640,000	320,000	320,000	320,000
Accounts Payable	53,000	52,000	48,000	47,000
Total Working Capital	694,000	371,000	369,000	366,000
Sales/Working Capital Ratio	1:.54	1:.30	1:.32	1:.33

The accounts receivable turn over at a rate of once every 30 days, which does not change through the term of the analysis. Inventory dropped in the second quarter to arrive at the new inventory turnover goal while the amount of accounts payable stays at one-half of the revenue level, reflecting a typical distributor's gross margin of 50% throughout all four periods. The resulting ratio shows that the company has indeed improved its ratio of working capital to sales, but at the price of some lost sales to customers who apparently were coming to the company because of its broad inventory selection.

Days of Working Capital

A company can use a very large amount of working capital to generate a small volume of sales, which represents a poor use of assets. The inefficient asset use can lie in any part of working capital: excessive quantities of accounts receivable or inventory in relation to sales, or very small amounts of accounts payable. The days of working capital measure, when tracked on a trend line, is a good indicator of changes in the efficient use of working capital. A low number of days of working capital indicates a highly efficient use of working capital. However, working capital levels will vary through the year, depending on a company's business cycle, which will alter the days of working capital figure depending on the month of the year. For example, if a firm has a Christmas selling season, it will build inventory until its prime selling season, resulting in a gradual increase in the days of working capital measure for most of the year.

The formula is to add together the current balance of accounts receivable and inventory, and subtract accounts payable. Then divide the result by sales per day (annual sales divided by 365). The formula is:

$$\frac{(\text{Accounts receivable} + \text{Inventory} - \text{Accounts payable})}{\text{Net sales}/365}$$

For example, the Electro-Therm Company, maker of electronic thermometers, has altered its customer service policy to guarantee a 99% fulfillment rate within one day of a customer's order. To do that, it has increased inventory levels for many stock-keeping units. Electro-Therm's chief financial officer (CFO) is concerned about the company's use of capital to sustain this new policy; she has collected the information in the next table to prove her point to the company CEO.

Time Period	Accounts Receivable	Inventory	Accounts Payable	Working Capital	Net Sales	Sales Per Day	Days of Working Capital
Year before policy change	602,000	1,825,000	493,000	2,920,000	5,475,000	15,000	195
Year after policy change	723,000	2,760,000	591,000	4,074,000	6,570,000	18,000	226

The table reveals that Electro-Therm's management has acquired an additional $1,095,000 of revenue (assuming that incremental sales are driven solely by the customer service policy change) at the cost of a nearly equivalent amount of investment in inventory. Depending on the firm's cost of capital, inventory obsolescence rate, and changes in customer retention rates, the new customer service policy may or may not be considered a reasonable decision.

Sales per Person

Sales per person is one of the most closely watched of all performance measures. It is based on the assumption that employees are at the core of a company's profitability, so high degrees of efficiency in this area are bound to result in strong profitability. It is also a standard benchmark in many industries.

The formula is to divide revenue for a full year by the total number of full-time equivalents (FTEs) in the company. An FTE is the combination of staffing that equals a 40-hour week. For example, two half-time employees would be counted as one FTE. The formula is:

$$\frac{\text{Annualized Revenue}}{\text{Total Full-Time Equivalents}}$$

As an example, the operations manager of the Twirling Washing Machine Company wants to determine the sales per person for his company. The company has annual revenues of $4,200,000. Its headcount is:

Department	Headcount
Direct labor department	22
Direct labor part-time staff	6
Production supervisors	2
Material handling department	4
Sales, general and administrative	10
Administrative part-time staff	2
Engineering department	8

In total, the company has 54 employees. However, if we assume that the part-time staff all work half time, the eight part-time positions can be reduced to four FTEs, which decreases the total headcount to 50 personnel. The calculation results in overall sales per employee of $84,000, which is $4,200,000 in revenues, divided by 50 employees.

Sales Backlog Ratio

The sales backlog ratio is an extremely useful tool for determining a company's ability to maintain its current level of production. If the ratio is dropping rapidly over several consecutive months, it is likely that the company soon will experience a reduction in sales volume as well as overcapacity in its production and related overhead areas, resulting in imminent losses. Conversely, a rapid jump in the ratio indicates that a company cannot keep up with demand and soon may experience both customer relations problems from delayed orders and a need for additional capital expenditures and staff hirings to increase its productive capacity.

The formula is to divide the most current total backlog of sales orders by sales. It is generally best not to use annualized sales in the denominator, because sales may vary considerably over that period, due to the influence of seasonality. A better denominator is sales over just the preceding quarter. The formula is:

$$\frac{\text{Backlog of Orders Received}}{\text{Sales}}$$

A variation on this formula is to determine the number of days of sales contained in the backlog, which is achieved by comparing the backlog to the average daily sales volume that a company typically produces. This formula is:

$$\frac{\text{Total Backlog}}{\text{Annual Sales}/360\,\text{Days}}$$

For example, the sales and backlog data for the Jabber Phone Company are shown in the next table.

	January	February	March
Rolling 3-month sales	$4,500,000	$4,750,000	$4,800,000
Month-end backlog	2,500,000	2,000,000	1,750,000
Sales backlog ratio	.55:1	.42:1	.36:1

The table reveals that the company's sales are continuing to increase over time while its backlog is decreasing. The change was caused by an increase in the company's productive capacity for cell phones. As a result, the company gradually is clearing out its backlog and converting it into sales. However, the management team must be aware that, if the trend continues, eventually the company will clear out its entire backlog and find itself with a sudden reduction in sales, unless it greatly increases its sales and marketing efforts to build the backlog back up to a higher level.

Breakeven Point

The breakeven point determines the sales level at which a company exactly breaks even. This figure is useful for determining how much extra productive capacity is available after breakeven sales have been manufactured, which tells the management team how much profit theoretically can be generated at maximum capacity levels. It also is good for determining changes in the breakeven point resulting from decisions to add fixed costs (especially when replacing variable production costs with fixed automation costs). In addition, it can be used to determine changes in profits when the sales staff is contemplating making changes in product prices.

The formula is to divide the average gross margin percentage into total operating costs. Be sure to include all operating costs outside of the cost of goods sold in this calculation—only extraordinary items that are in no way related to ongoing operations should be excluded from the formula, which is:

$$\frac{\text{Total Operating Expenses}}{\text{Average Gross Margin Percentage}}$$

For example, the Reef Shark Acquisition Company is looking into the purchase of a sewing thread company. Its two key concerns are the breakeven point of the acquiree and the presence of any overhead costs that it can eliminate by centralizing functions at its corporate headquarters. Its due diligence team constructs this table of information:

	Before Acquisition
Maximum sales capacity	$10,000,000
Current average sales	9,500,000
Gross margin percentage	35%
Total operating expenses	3,500,000
Breakeven point	$10,000,000
Operating expense reductions	750,000
Revised breakeven level	$ 7,857,000
Maximum profits with revised breakeven point	$ 750,050

The table clearly shows that the acquiree currently has a breakeven point so high that it is essentially incapable of ever turning a profit, since the breakeven level is the same as its maximum productive capacity. However, the removal of some key overhead costs reduces the breakeven point to such an extent that the acquirer will be able to generate a significant return from the existing sales level. The revised breakeven level is determined by subtracting the operating expense reductions of $750,000 from the existing operating expenses of $3,500,000, and dividing the remaining $2,750,000 in operating expenses by the gross margin of 35% to arrive at a new breakeven point of $7,857,000. The maximum potential profit figure of $750,050 is derived by subtracting the revised breakeven point from the maximum possible sales capacity level of $10,000,000 and multiplying the result by the gross profit percentage.

Margin of Safety

The margin of safety is the amount by which sales can drop before a company's breakeven point is reached. It is particularly useful to know the margin of safety in situations where large portions of a company's sales are at risk, such as when they are tied up in a single customer contract that can be canceled. Knowing the margin of safety gives you a good idea of the probability that a company may find itself in difficult financial circumstances caused by sales fluctuations.

The formula is to subtract the breakeven point from the current sales level and divide the result by the current sales level. To calculate the breakeven point, divide the gross margin percentage into total fixed costs. This formula can be broken down into individual product lines for a better view of risk levels within business units. The formula is:

$$\frac{\text{Current Sales Level} - \text{Breakeven Point}}{\text{Current Sales Level}}$$

For example, the Fat Tire Publishing House, Inc. is contemplating the purchase of several delivery trucks to assist in the delivery of its *Fat Tire Weekly* mountain biking magazine to a new sales region. The addition of these trucks will add $200,000 to the operating costs of the company. Key information related to this decision is noted in the next table.

	Before Truck Purchase	After Truck Purchase
Sales	$2,300,000	$2,700,000
Gross margin percentage	55%	55%
Fixed expenses	$1,000,000	$1,200,000
Breakeven point	$1,818,000	$2,182,000
Profits	$ 265,000	$ 285,000
Margin of safety	21%	19%

The table shows that the margin of safety is reduced from 21% to 19% as a result of the truck acquisition. However, profits are expected to increase by $20,000, so the management team must weigh the risk of adding expenses to the benefit of increased profitability.

Operating Performance Measurements

The measurements noted in this section focus on the margins derived by at business when certain types of expenses are included. The most highly recommended measurement is the operating profit percentage, especially when tracked on a trend line, since it shows operating results before any special adjustments are added that might otherwise cloud the picture of a company's truly underlying performance.

Core Growth Rate

Companies regularly trumpet their ability to increase revenues year after year. But how much of that growth is due to acquisitions, accounting changes, or product price increases? By stripping out these forms of manufactured revenue, it is much easier to see if a company's core operations actually are growing, and by how much. However, the information used in this formula can be difficult to obtain and may involve the use of approximations, especially for the determination of changes caused by revenue recognition policies and the determination of an average annual price increase. Consequently, the results should be considered approximations of the actual core growth rate.

The formula is to subtract from the current annual revenue the annual revenue from five years ago, revenue from acquisitions at the point of acquisition, and any revenue changes arising from altered revenue recognition policies. Divide the result by the annual revenue from five years ago, divide this result by 5 to annualize it, and subtract the company's average annual price increase over the five-year measurement period. The formula is:

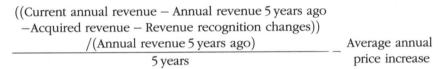

If information about the company's average annual price increase is not available, consider using the change in price of the underlying commodity or industry segment, as measured by either the Consumer Price Index or the Product Price Index.

For example, the president of the Premier Concrete Group (PCG) recently has claimed that the company has experienced average annual compounded growth of 12%. An outside analyst wants to verify this claim by calculating PCG's core growth rate. PCG's current revenue is $88 million, and its revenue five years ago was $50 million. During that period, PCG acquired companies having a total of $27 million in revenues when they were acquired. Also, PCG benefited from altered revenue recognition policies that increased its revenue by $5 million. The analyst also learns that the concrete industry's average annual price increase during the measurement period was 2%. The analyst determines PCG's core growth rate with this calculation:

$$
\frac{\begin{array}{l}((\$88\text{ million current revenue}) \\ -(\$50\text{ million revenue 5 years ago}) \\ -(\$27\text{ million acquired revenue}) \\ -(\$5\text{ million from revenue recognition changes}))/ \\ (\$50\text{ million revenue 5 years ago})\end{array}}{5\text{ years}} - \frac{2\%\text{ average annual}}{\text{price increase}} = 0.4\%
$$

Gross Profit Percentage

The gross profit percentage reveals the profit left over from operations after all variable costs have been subtracted from revenues. In essence, it shows the efficiency of the production process in relation to the prices and unit volumes at which products are sold.

There are two way to measure the gross margin. The most common approach is to add together the costs of overhead, direct materials, and direct labor, subtract them from revenue, and then divide the result by revenue. This approach takes into account all costs that can be reasonably associated with the production process. The formula is:

$$\frac{\text{Revenue} - (\text{Overhead} + \text{Direct Materials} + \text{Direct Labor})}{\text{Revenue}}$$

The trouble with this approach is that many of the production costs are not truly variable. Under a much more strictly defined view of variable costs, only direct materials should be included in the formula, since this is the only cost that truly changes in lock-step with changes in revenue. All other production costs are shifted into other operational and administrative costs, which typically yields a very high gross margin percentage. The formula is:

$$\frac{\text{Revenue} - \text{Direct Materials}}{\text{Revenue}}$$

For example, the Spanish Tile Company bases its sales quoting system on the gross margin assigned to its products—prices quoted must have a gross margin of at least 25% in order to cover administrative costs and create a modest profit. Recently, the Iberian Tile Company has been taking business away from the Spanish Tile Company through more aggressive pricing. Investigation of its competitor's quoting practices reveals that it uses an alternative gross margin model that uses only direct material costs as a deduction from revenues. This means that Iberian Tile always is in a position to offer lower prices, as it does not incorporate direct labor and overhead costs into its pricing model. Iberian Tile is in danger of quoting excessively low prices if it continues to use its gross margin model, so it focuses on how prospective sales will impact its bottleneck operation, which is the tile kiln. If a prospective sale requires a great deal of kiln time, it is charged a much higher price than other quotes that do not use as much of this valuable resource. As a result of this survey, Spanish Tile realizes that its competitor has a more precise and aggressive quoting model that likely will result in more lost sales in the future.

Operating Profit Percentage

The operating profit percentage reveals the return from standard operations, excluding the impact of extraordinary items and other comprehensive income. Use of this percentage reveals the extent to which a company is earning a profit from standard operations as opposed to resorting to asset sales or unique transactions to post a profit.

The formula is to subtract from sales the cost of goods sold as well as all sales, general, and administrative expenses. In order to obtain a percentage that is related strictly to operational results, be sure to exclude interest income and expense from the calculation, since these items are related to a company's financing decisions rather than its operational characteristics. Expense totals used in the ratio should exclude all extraordinary transactions as well as asset dispositions, since they do not relate to continuing operations. The formula is:

$$\frac{\text{Sales} - (\text{Cost of Goods Sold} + \text{Sales, General and Administrative Expenses})}{\text{Sales}}$$

For example, the Swiss Mountain Chocolate Company has a loan with the local bank whose covenants include the stipulation that the loan will be callable immediately if the company's operating profit percentage drops below zero. In the current month, the company will incur an operating loss of $15,000, which will allow the bank to call its loan. The calculation it is using to derive the operating loss is:

Revenue	$1,428,000
Cost of goods sold	571,000
Gross margin	857,000
Operating costs	849,000
Interest expense	23,000
Operating profit/loss	$ −15,000
Operating profit percentage	−1%

Since there is no specification in the loan agreement of the operating loss calculation, the company defines it as excluding financing activities, removes the interest expense from the calculation, and achieves an operating profit of $8,000. To be ethically correct, the CEO also specifies the exact contents of the calculation in her next report to the bank.

Net Profit Percentage

Net profit percentage is used to determine the proportion of income derived from all operating, financing, and other activities that an entity has engaged in during an accounting period. It is the percentage most commonly used as a benchmark for determining a company's performance, even though it does not necessarily reflect a company's cash flows, which may be negative even when net profits are reported.

The formula is to divide net income by revenue. If this percentage is being tracked on a trend line, it may be useful to eliminate from the calculation any extraordinary income items, such as losses from disasters, since they do not yield comparable period-to-period information.

$$\frac{\text{Net Income}}{\text{Revenue}}$$

For example, the Quick Cuts Hair Salon is a franchise operation that pays for the initial fixed assets required by each franchisee. This involves an investment of about

$200,000 per hair salon. The management team is determined to grow the operation as fast as possible while still reporting healthy profits. To do so, it sets the capitalization limit very low, at just $250, so that nearly everything it purchases is capitalized. Because it uses a ten-year depreciation period for all fixed assets, this results in the recognition of costs over many future periods that normally would be recognized at once if a higher capitalization limit were used. Its operating results for a typical store are:

	Per-Store Results
Sales	$350,000
Wages	260,000
Supplies	75,000
Assets < $1,000	42,000
Net income	$ 15,000
Net income percentage	4%

The key line item in the table is the assets costing less than $1,000; if the company had set a higher capitalization limit, these costs would have been recognized as expenses at once, which would have yielded a loss on operations of $27,000 per store. As a result, the company's accounting policy is creating false profits. When combined with the high initial setup cost of each store, it is apparent that this seemingly healthy franchise operation is actually burning through its cash reserves at a prodigious rate.

Cash Flow Measurements

The measurements noted in this section focus on a company's cash sufficiency in order to sustain operations. If you do not pay attention to these measures, an organization may quite suddenly find itself in need of outside funding. Consequently, cash flow measures should be parked near the top of your list of must-have measurements.

Cash Flow from Operations

Under generally accepted accounting principles, a company can report a large income figure quite easily, even while its cash reserves are draining away. The cash flow from operations ratio can be used to determine the extent to which cash flow differs from the reported level of either operating income or net income. Any difference in the ratio that varies significantly from 1 is indicative of substantial noncash expenses or sales in the reported income figures. Cash flow problems are likely if the ratio is substantially less than 1.

The formula can be generated in two formats. One is to divide operational cash flow by income from operations while the second format is to divide cash flow from all transactions (including extraordinary items) by net income. The first format yields a more accurate view of the proportion of cash being spun off from ongoing operations; the second version shows the impact of any unrelated transactions that are unrelated to operations. Both formulas are shown next.

$$\frac{\text{Income from Operations} + \text{Noncash Expenses} - \text{Noncash Sales}}{\text{Income from Operations}}$$

$$\frac{\text{Net Income} + \text{Noncash Expenses} - \text{Noncash Sales}}{\text{Net Income}}$$

For example, the Bargain Basement Insurance Company (BBIC) is opening new stores at a rapid clip, trying to gain premium locations before its key competitor, Super Low Premiums, Inc., grabs the same spots. BBIC is reporting net income of 20% from its operations, which is considered reasonable in the insurance business. However, it cannot understand why its bank continues to refuse additional loans to fund ongoing operational needs. The bank is concerned about BBIC's cash flow from operations ratio. The company's relevant projections are shown next.

	Current Year	Next Year	Following Year
Sales	$5,000,000	$10,000,000	$15,000,000
Net income	1,000,000	2,000,000	3,000,000
Revenue recognition of future insurance payments	800,000	1,600,000	2,400,000
Annual cash flow	200,000	400,000	600,000
Cash flow from operations ratio	20%	20%	20%

The table reveals the key problem for BBIC, which is that it is recognizing insurance as revenue prior to the receipt of cash from policy holders in some cases. Consequently, its rapid growth is resulting in only modest positive cash flow, which translates into a poor cash flow from an operations ratio of 20%. The bank correctly finds this ratio to be probably indicative of BBIC's future inability to pay back a loan and so refuses to extend one.

Cash Flow Return on Assets

The cash flow return on assets calculation is used to determine the amount of cash that a company is generating in proportion to its asset level. It can be used as a substitute for the popular return on assets measure, since the net income figure used in the return on assets calculation is subject to greater manipulation through the use of noncash accounting entries.

The formula is to add together net income and any noncash expenses, such as depreciation and amortization. Then subtract from this amount any noncash sales, such as revenue that has been recognized but is unbilled. Then divide the result by the *net* value of all assets; this should include accounts receivable net of a bad debt reserve, inventory net of an obsolescence reserve, and fixed assets net of depreciation. The formula is:

$$\frac{\text{Net Income} + \text{Noncash Expenses} - \text{Noncash Sales}}{\text{Total Assets}}$$

For example, the CEO of the Glowering Tail Light Company, resellers of 1950s-era taillights, has been told by his controller for several years that the company has a sterling return on assets. He would like to verify this by comparing the measure to the cash flow return on assets. He collects the information shown in the next table.

	Return on Assets	Cash Flow Return on Assets
Net income	$1,000,000	$1,000,000
Depreciation		$+105,000
Pension fund gains		$ −45,000
Bill and hold revenue		$−132,000
Percentage of completion revenue		$−154,000
Total assets	$3,250,000	$3,250,000
Measurement	30.8%	23.8%

The return on assets figure listed at the bottom of the table is derived by dividing net income of $1,000,000 by total assets of $3,250,000. To arrive at the cash flow return on assets, the CEO must add back the noncash depreciation expense and subtract a series of noncash accounting entries that have increased the revenue level artificially. The result is:

$$\frac{\text{Net Income} + \text{Noncash Expenses} - \text{Noncash Sales}}{\text{Total Assets}}$$

$$= \frac{\$1,000,000 \text{ Net Income} + \$105,000 \text{ Noncash Expenses} - \$331,000 \text{ Noncash Sales}}{\$3,250,000 \text{ Total Assets}}$$

$$= \frac{\$774,000 \text{ Cash Flow}}{\$3,250,000 \text{ Total Assets}} = \underline{23.8\%} \text{ Cash Flow Return on Assets}$$

Although the cash flow return on assets percentage is quite acceptable, it is also considerably less than the reported return on assets.

Cash/Working Capital Ratio

The cash/working capital ratio is useful for determining the proportion of working capital that is made up of either cash or investments that can be converted readily into cash. If this ratio is low, this can be an indication that a company may have trouble meeting its short-term commitments due to a potential lack of cash.

The formula is to add together the current cash balance as well as any marketable securities that can be liquidated in the short term, and divide it by current assets, less current liabilities. The key issue is which investments to include in the measurement—since this is intended to be a measure of short-term cash availability, any investments that cannot be liquidated in one month or less should be excluded from the calculation. The formula is:

$$\frac{\text{Cash} + \text{Short-Term Marketable Securities}}{\text{Current Assets} - \text{Current Liabilities}}$$

For example, the Arbor Valley Tree Company has a large inventory of potted plants and trees on hand, which comprises a large proportion of its inventory and is recorded as part of current assets. However, they turn over only three times per year, which does not make them very liquid for the purposes of generating short-term cash. The CEO wants to know what proportion of the current ratio really is comprised of cash or cash equivalents, since it appears that a large part of working capital is skewed in the direction of this slow-moving inventory. She has this information:

Fund Type	Amount	Liquidity
Cash	$ 55,000	Immediately available
Money market funds	180,000	Available in 1 day
Officer loan	200,000	Due in 90 days
Accounts receivable	450,000	Due in 45 days
Inventory	850,000	Turnover every 4 months
Current liabilities	450,000	Due in 30 days

Based on this information, she calculates the cash/working capital ratio as:

$$\frac{\text{Cash} + \text{Short-Term Marketable Securities}}{\text{Current Assets} - \text{Current Liabilities}}$$

$$= \frac{\$55,000 + \$180,000}{(\$55,000 + \$180,000 + \$200,000 + \$450,000 + \$850,000) - (\$450,000)}$$

$$= \frac{\$235,000}{\$1,285,000}$$

$$= \underline{18\%}$$

She did not include the note receivable from the company officer, since it would be available for 90 days. This nearly halved the amount of the ratio to 18%, which reveals that the company should be extremely careful in its use of cash until more of the accounts receivable or inventory balances can be liquidated.

Liquidity Measurements

The measurements noted in this section are critical to your knowledge of the short-term liquidity of assets. The days of accounts receivable measure should be reviewed no less than once a week to verify that the credit and collections function is working properly. Inventory turnover is worthy of a monthly review, preferably on a trend line basis, to ensure that a company is not investing too much in its on-hand inventories. Similarly, a weekly review of accounts payable days will inform you if bills are being paid either too early or too late. The quick ratio is more useful as a summary-level review of the other liquidity measures.

Average Receivable Collection Period

The speed with which a company can obtain payment from customers for outstanding receivable balances is crucial for the reduction of cash requirements. A very long accounts receivable collection period indicates that a company's credit and collections function is very good at avoiding potentially delinquent customers as well as collecting overdue funds. This format is particularly useful when it is compared to the standard number of days of credit granted to customers. For example, if the average collection period is 60 days and the standard days of credit is 30, customers are taking much too long to pay their invoices. A sign of good performance is when the average receivable collection period is only a few days longer than the standard days of credit.

The formula is to divide annual credit sales by 365 days, and divide the result into average accounts receivable. The formula is:

$$\text{Average Accounts Receivable} = \text{Annual Sales}/365$$

For example, the new CEO of the Flexo Paneling Company, makers of modularized office equipment, wants to determine the company's accounts receivable collection period. In the June accounting period, the beginning accounts receivable balance was \$318,000 and the ending balance was \$383,000. Sales for May and June totaled \$625,000. Based on this information, he calculates the average receivable collection period as:

$$
\begin{aligned}
&\text{Average Accounts Receivable} \\
&= \text{Annual Sales}/365 \\
&= \frac{(\$318,\!000 \text{ Beginning Receivables} + \$383,\!000 \text{ Ending Receivables})/2}{(\$625,\!000 \times 6)/365} \\
&= \frac{\$350,\!500 \text{ Average Accounts Receivable}}{\$10,\!273 \text{ Sales per Day}} \\
&= \underline{\underline{34.1}} \text{ Days}
\end{aligned}
$$

Note that the CEO derived the annual sales figure used in the denominator by multiplying the two-month sales period in May and June by 6. Since the company has a stated due date of 30 days after the billing date, the 34.1-day collection period appears reasonable.

Collection Effectiveness Index

Most liquidity measurements for receivables, such as accounts receivable turnover or the days of delinquent sales outstanding, are impacted easily by spikes or declines in sales, so they are not valid measures of collection performance. Instead, use the collection effectiveness index (CEI), which more precisely determines the effectiveness of the credit and collections staff. This measure compares what was collected in a given period to what was available to collect. A score close to 100% indicates a high degree of collection effectiveness.

The formula is to add together the beginning receivables for the measurement period plus credit sales during the period, and subtract ending total receivables. Divide this number by the sum of beginning receivables and credit sales, and subtract ending current receivables. Finally, multiply the result by 100 to obtain a percentage.

The formula is:

$$\frac{\text{Beginning receivables} + \text{Credit sales} - \text{Ending total receivables}}{\text{Beginning receivables} + \text{Credit sales} - \text{Ending current receivables}} \times 100$$

For example, the sales and receivable information for Moonlight Productions is:

Beginning receivables	$4,500,000
Credit sales	3,200,000
Ending current receivables	2,800,000
Ending total receivables	5,000,000

Based on this information, Moonlight's CEI is:

$$\frac{\$4,500,000 + \$3,200,000 - \$5,000,000}{\$4,500,000 + \$3,200,000 - \$2,800,000} \times 100 = 55\% \text{ CEI}$$

The credit sales in this calculation are assumed to be generated over a one-month period. If the calculation were to cover a longer period, divide the credit sales figure by the number of months being measured. For example, to measure the CEI for a quarter, divide the credit sales for the quarter by 3 before using it in the formula.

Inventory Turnover

Inventory frequently is the largest component of a company's working capital; in such situations, if inventory is not being used up by operations at a reasonable pace, a company has invested a large part of its cash in an asset that may be difficult to liquidate in short order. Accordingly, keeping close track of the rate of inventory turnover is a significant function of management. This section describes several variations on the inventory turnover measurement, which may be combined to yield the most complete turnover reporting for management to peruse. In all cases, these measurements should be tracked on a trend line in order to see if there are gradual reductions in the rate of turnover, which can indicate to management that corrective action is required in order to eliminate excess inventory stocks.

The simplest turnover calculation is to divide the period-end inventory into the annualized cost of sales. You also can use an *average* inventory figure in the denominator, which avoids sudden changes in the inventory level that are likely to occur on any specific period-end date. The formula is:

$$\frac{\text{Cost of Goods Sold}}{\text{Inventory}}$$

A variation on this formula is to divide it into 365 days, which yields the number of days of inventory on hand. This may be more understandable to the layperson; for example, 43 days of inventory is clearer than 8.5 inventory turns, even though they represent the same situation. The formula for the days of inventory on hand is:

$$365 \Big/ \frac{\text{Cost of Goods Sold}}{\text{Inventory}}$$

For example, the Rotary Mower Company, maker of the only lawn mower driven by a Wankel rotary engine, is going through its annual management review of inventory. Its CEO has the information shown.

Balance Sheet Line Item	Amount
Cost of goods sold	$4,075,000
Direct materials expense	$1,550,000
Raw materials inventory	$ 388,000
Total inventory	$ 815,000

To calculate total inventory turnover, the CEO creates the next calculation:

$$\frac{\text{Cost of Goods Sold}}{\text{Inventory}}$$

$$= \frac{\$4,075,000 \text{ Cost of Goods Sold}}{\$815,000 \text{ Inventory}} = \underline{5} \text{ Turns per Year}$$

To determine the number of days of inventory on hand, the CFO divides the number of turns per year into 365 days:

$$365 \Big/ \frac{\text{Cost of Goods Sold}}{\text{Inventory}}$$

$$= 365 \Big/ \frac{\$4,075,000 \text{ Cost of Goods}}{\$815,000 \text{ Inventory}} = \underline{\underline{73}} \text{ Days of Inventory}$$

Accounts Payable Days

A calculation of the days of accounts payable gives you a fair indication of a company's ability to pay its bills on time. If the accounts payable days are inordinately long, this is probably a sign that the company does not have sufficient cash flow to pay its bills and may find itself out of business in short order. Alternatively, a small amount of accounts payable days indicates that a company either is taking advantage of early payment discounts or is simply paying its bills earlier than it has to.

The formula is to divide total annualized purchases by 360 days and divide the result into the ending accounts payable balance. An alternative approach is to use the *average* accounts payable for the reporting period, since the ending figure may be disproportionately high or low. The amount of purchases should be derived from all nonpayroll expenses incurred during the year; payroll is not included, because it is not a part of the accounts payable listed in the numerator. Also, depreciation and amortization should be excluded from the purchases figure, since they do not involve cash payments. The formula is:

$$\frac{\text{Accounts Payable}}{\text{Purchases}/360}$$

For example, the Drain-Away Toilet Company has beginning accounts payable of $145,000 and ending accounts payable of $157,000. On an annualized basis, its total expenses are $2,400,000, of which $600,000 is payroll and $50,000 is depreciation. To determine its accounts payable days, we plug this information into the next formula:

$$\frac{(\text{Beginning Accounts Payable} + \text{Ending Accounts Payable})/2}{(\text{Total Expenses} - \text{Payroll} - \text{Depreciation})/360}$$

$$= \frac{(\$145,000 \text{ Beginning Payables} + \$157,000 \text{ Ending Payables})/2}{(\$2,400,000 \text{ Total Expenses} - \$600,000 \text{ Payroll} - \$50,000 \text{ Depreciation})/360}$$

$$= \frac{\$151,000 \text{ Average Accounts Payable}}{\$1,750,000 \text{ Purchases}/360} = \underline{31} \text{ Days}$$

Quick Ratio

The quick ratio excludes inventory from the current assets portion of the current ratio. By doing so, you can gain a better understanding of a company's very short-term ability to generate cash from more liquid assets, such as accounts receivable and marketable securities.

The formula is to add together cash, marketable securities, and accounts receivable, and divide the result by current liabilities. Be sure to include only those marketable securities that can be liquidated in the short term and those receivables that are not significantly overdue. The formula is:

$$\frac{\text{Cash} + \text{Marketable Securities} + \text{Accounts Receivable}}{\text{Current Liabilities}}$$

For example, the Huff-Puff Shed Company, makers of sheds that are guaranteed not to blow down in any wind under 100 miles per hour, appears to have a comfortably high current ratio of 2.5:1. The components of that ratio are broken down as:

Account	Amount
Cash	$ 120,000
Marketable securities	$ 53,000
Accounts receivable	$ 418,000
Inventory	$2,364,000
Current liabilities	$ 985,000
Current ratio	3:1
Quick ratio	.6:1

This more detailed analysis reveals that the presence of an excessive amount of inventory is making the company's liquidity look too high with the current ratio. Only by switching to the quick ratio is this problem revealed.

Solvency Measurements

The measures noted in this section address the ability of a firm to pay off its debts. This ability is applicable not only in high-debt situations but also in prospective ones, where you must model the level of corporate solvency that will result from some major financing activity, such as an acquisition that is paid for with debt.

Times Interest Earned

The times interest earned ratio reveals the amount of excess funding that a company still has available after it has paid off its interest expense. If this ratio is close to 1, the company runs a high risk of defaulting on its debt. Any higher ratio shows that the company is operating with a comfortable amount of extra cash flow that can cushion it if its business falters.

The formula is to divide the average interest expense by the average cash flow. Cash flow is a company's net income, to which all noncash expenses (such as depreciation and amortization) have been added back. This ratio should be run on a monthly basis rather than annually, since short-term changes in the amount of debt carried or cash flow realized can have a sudden and dramatic impact on it. The formula is:

$$\frac{\text{Average Cash Flow}}{\text{Average Interest Expense}}$$

As an example, the Cautious Bankers Corporation (CBC) is investigating the possibility of lending money to the Grasp & Sons Door Handle Corporation (GSR). It collects the information shown for the last few months of GSR's operations.:

	January	February	March
Interest expense	$ 45,000	$43,000	$41,000
Net income	83,500	65,000	47,000
Depreciation	17,000	17,250	17,500
Amortization	2,500	2,500	2,500
Net cash flow	103,000	84,750	67,000
Times interest earned	2.3	2.0	1.6

The table reveals that, although GSR's interest expense is dropping, its cash flow is dropping so much faster that the company soon will have difficulty meeting its interest payment obligations. The CBC examiner elects to pass on providing the company with any additional debt.

Debt Coverage Ratio

A key solvency issue is the ability of a company to pay its debts. This can be measured with the debt coverage ratio, which compares reported earnings to the amount of scheduled after-tax interest and principal payments to see if there is enough income available to cover the payments. A ratio of less than 1 indicates that a company probably will be unable to make its debt payments. The measure is of particular interest to lenders, who are concerned about a company's ability to repay them for issued loans.

The formula is to divide the scheduled amount of principal payments by the inverse of the corporate tax rate. This yields the amount of after-tax income required by a company to pay back the principal. Add the interest expense to be paid, and divide the sum into the net amount of earnings before interest and taxes. An alternative treatment of the numerator is to use earnings before interest, taxes, depreciation, and amortization, since this yields a closer approximation of available cash flow. The formula is:

$$\frac{\text{Earnings before Interest and Taxes}}{\text{Interest} + \dfrac{\text{Scheduled Principal Payments}}{(1 - \text{Tax Rate})}}$$

As an example, prior to implementing the owner's suggested round of Christmas bonuses, the Egyptian Antiques Company's CEO wants to be sure that earnings will be sufficient to pay upcoming debt requirements. The expected operating income for the year, prior to bonuses, is $135,000. The interest expense is expected to be $18,500. The tax rate is 34%. Upcoming principal payments will be $59,000. The CEO uses the next debt coverage calculation to see if Christmas bonuses can still be paid:

$$\frac{\text{Earnings before Interest and Taxes}}{\text{Interest} + \dfrac{\text{Scheduled Principal Payments}}{(1 - \text{Tax Rate})}}$$

$$= \frac{\$135,000 \text{ Operating Income}}{\$18,500 \text{ Interest} + \dfrac{\$59,000 \text{ Principal Payments}}{(1 - 34\% \text{ Tax Rate})}}$$

$$= \frac{\$135,000 \text{ Operating Income}}{\$107,894 \text{ Debt Payments}} = \underline{125\%} \text{ Debt Coverage Ratio}$$

The ratio indicates that extra funds will be available for Christmas bonuses since operating income exceeds the amount of scheduled debt payments.

Return on Investment Measurements

Investors want to know what kind of return they are getting on their investment in a company, and you must be prepared to tell them. This section contains measures that address the same issue in different ways. The return on assets employed and the return on equity are the two most commonly used measurements for return on investment (ROI); you should be thoroughly familiar with both. The economic value added (EVA) measure is a more recent attempt at defining the value added to underlying assets by a company, while the dividend payout ratio addresses the needs of those investors who are interested only in the amount of cash paid directly to them by the company.

Return on Assets Employed

Investors deem a company efficient if it can generate an adequate return while using the minimum amount of assets to do so. This also keeps investors from having to put more cash into the company and allows the entity to shift its excess cash to investments in new endeavors. Consequently, the return on assets employed measure is considered a critical one for determining a company's overall level of operating efficiency.

The formula is to divide net profits by total assets. Although the assets figure sometimes is restricted to just fixed assets, it should include accounts receivable and inventory, since both of these areas can be major users of cash. The amount of fixed assets included in the denominator is typically net of depreciation; it also can be recorded at its gross value, as long as the formula derivation is used consistently over multiple time periods, thereby ensuring consistent long-term reporting. The formula is:

$$\frac{\text{Net Profit}}{\text{Total Assets}}$$

For example, Mr. Willston is the new CEO of Southern Sheet Metal, a metal stamping company. He purchased the company for $3 million and wants to retrieve as much of these funds as possible by increasing the company's return on assets. He creates the next table of information about company income and assets.

	Year-end Results	Days on Hand
Sales	$3,070,000	
Net income	215,000	—
Accounts receivable	512,000	60
Inventory	461,000	90
Fixed assets	1,950,000	—
Total assets	$2,923,000	—

Based on the table, the calculation of net assets employed is:

$$\frac{\text{Net Profit}}{\text{Total Assets}} = \frac{\$215,000}{\$2,923,000} = \underline{7.4\%}$$

Mr. Willston is not certain which of the fixed assets can be eliminated safely while maintaining productive capacity. However, he is quite sure that the days of accounts receivable and inventory, as noted in the table, are much too high. Accordingly, he improves collection activities and early payment discounts and drops the outstanding accounts receivable balance from 60 days to 45, reducing this asset to $384,000. He also installs an improved inventory management system, reducing the on-hand inventory balance from 90 to 60 days and reducing this asset to $309,000. By taking these actions, he has eliminated $280,000 of assets, which he can take out of the business. He also has improved the net assets employed measurement to 8.1%, which is calculated as:

$$\frac{\text{Net Profit}}{\text{Total Assets}} = \frac{\$215,000}{(\$2,923,000 - \$280,000)} = \underline{8.1\%}$$

Return on Equity Percentage

The return on equity percentage is calculated to determine the amount of return investors are receiving from their investment in a company. The measure can be misleading, because a management team that is eager to increase a company's return on equity can do so easily by incurring new debt and using these funds to buy back stock. Although the amount of equity is thereby reduced, making the ratio more favorable, this also means that the company has an obligation to pay back the debt and related interest. An overly zealous pursuit of this approach can result in such a large debt load that a small downturn in sales will not allow the company to pay off the debt, possibly ending in bankruptcy.

The formula is to divide net income by total equity. To obtain a better picture of the ability of a company to generate a return from operating activities only, the measure can be modified to be net income from operations, divided by total equity. The basic formula is:

$$\frac{\text{Net Income}}{\text{Total Equity}}$$

As an example, Ms. Mo Funds, CEO of the Lounger Chairs Furniture Company, has been provided by the board of directors with a bonus plan that is largely based on her ability to increase the return on equity for the shareholders. There is $1 million of equity on the books, of which $400,000 is closely held and the other $600,000 is held by a variety of small investors. She estimates that she can buy back $300,000 of the stock from small investors by obtaining a loan, which has an after-tax interest rate of 8%. She compiles the next information to see if the stratagem makes sense:

	Before Stock Buyback	After Stock Buyback
Sales	$5,000,000	$5,000,000
Expenses	4,850,000	4,850,000
Debt interest expense	—	24,000
Profits	150,000	126,000
Equity	1,000,000	700,000
Return on equity	15%	18%

The strategy appears to be a good one. Although expenses will be driven up by the interest cost of the debt, the amount of equity will be reduced to such an extent that the return on equity will increase by three percent. However, before implementing this strategy, the CEO should investigate the company's ability to generate enough cash flow to pay off or at least maintain the debt.

Economic Value Added

Economic value added (EVA) shows the incremental rate of return in excess of a firm's total cost of capital. Stated differently, this is the surplus value created on an initial investment. It is *not* just the difference between a firm's percentage cost of capital and its actual rate of return percentage, since it is designed to yield a *dollar* surplus value. If the measurement is negative, a company is not generating a return in excess of its capital costs. It is extremely important to break down the drivers of the measurement in order to determine what parts of a company are keeping the measure from reaching its maximum potential.

EVA has become the most fashionable measurement for determining the ability of a company to generate an appropriate rate of return, thanks in part to the efforts of several consulting firms that specialize in installing the systems that roll up into this measurement. Some studies have shown that a favorable EVA measurement correlates closely with the market price achieved by a company's stock, so it can become the cornerstone of a company's efforts to increase its market value. It also can be linked to a company's compensation system, so that managers are paid (or not) based on their ability to combine efficient asset utilization with profitable operating results.

The formula is to multiply the net investment by the difference between the actual rate of return on assets and the percentage cost of capital. The three elements of the calculation are:

1. *Net investment.* The net investment figure used in the formula is subject to a great deal of variation. In its most limited form, you can use the net valuation for all fixed assets. However, some assets may be subject to accelerated depreciation calculations, which greatly reduce the amount of investment used in the calculation; a better approach is to use the straight-line depreciation methodology for all assets, with only the depreciation *period* varying by type of asset. A variation on this approach is to also add research and development as well as training costs back into the net investment, on the grounds that these expenditures are made to enhance the company's value over the long term. Also, if assets are leased rather than owned, they should be itemized as assets at their fair market value and included in the net investment figure, so that managers cannot use financing tricks to enhance their ROI.

2. *Actual ROI.* When calculating the ROI, research and development as well as training expenses should be shifted out of operating expenses and into net investment (as noted in the last point). In addition, any unusual adjustments to net income that do not involve ongoing operations should be eliminated. This results in an income figure that is related to just those costs that can be legitimately expensed within the current period.

3. *Cost of capital.* The formulation of the cost of capital is a derivation of the weighted average cost of a company's debt and equity.

The formula is:

(Net Investment) × (Actual Return on Investment − Percentage Cost of Capital)

For example, the CEO of the Miraflores Manufacturing Company wants to see if the company has a positive EVA. Based on his calculation of outstanding debt, preferred stock, and common stock, as noted in the next table, he estimates that the firm's cost of capital is 13.7%.

Type of Funding	Amount of Funding	Cost of Funding
Debt	$ 2,500,000	8.5%
Preferred stock	$ 4,250,000	12.5%
Common stock	$ 8,000,000	16.0%
Total	$14,750,000	13.7%

He then takes the balance sheet and income statement and redistributes some of the accounts in them, in accordance with the next table, so that some items that usually are expensed under generally accepted accounting principles are shifted into the investment category.

Account Description	Performance	Net Investment
Revenue	$8,250,000	
Cost of goods sold	5,950,000	
General and administrative	825,000	
Sales department	675,000	
Training department		$ 100,000
Research and development		585,000
Marketing department	380,000	
Net income	$ 420,000	
Fixed assets		2,080,000
Cost of patent protection		125,000
Cost of trademark protection		225,000
Total net investment		$ 3,115,000

The ROI, as based on the net income and investment figures in the preceding table, is 13.5% (net income divided by the total net investment). Using this information, he derives the next calculation to determine the amount of EVA:

(Net Investment) × (Actual Return on Assets − Percentage Cost of Capital)
= ($3,115,000 Net Investment) × (13.5% Actual Return − 13.7% Cost of Capital)
= $3,115,000 Net Investment × −.2% = −$6,230 EVA

In short, the company is destroying its capital base by creating actual returns that are slightly less than its cost of capital.

Dividend Payout Ratio

The dividend payout ratio tells an investor what proportion of earnings are being paid back in the form of dividends. This is particularly important when the ratio is greater than 1, since it indicates that a company is dipping into its cash reserves in order to pay dividends, which is not a sustainable trend. Alternatively, if only a small proportion of earnings is being paid back as dividends, you can assume that the remaining cash is being plowed back into operations, which should result in an increase in the stock price. If the stock price is stagnant or declining, investors have a valid concern regarding the proper use of corporate earnings.

The formula is to divide the dividend per share (DPS) by the earnings per share (EPS). It is allowable to include the cash flow from nonoperating items in the EPS figure, since they will impact the amount of cash available for distribution as dividends. However, if nonoperating items having no immediate cash flow impact, such as restructuring reserves, are included in the EPS figure, they should be removed; such items do not properly reflect a company's ability to pay dividends. Also, it may be necessary to add expected capital expenditures to the EPS figure, if this is expected to require a significant proportion of the cash provided by earnings. The formula is:

$$\frac{DPS}{EPS}$$

For example, Ms. Jones has invested a large part of her savings in the stock of Illinois Gas Distribution Company, operator of a nationwide gas pipeline. She wants to see if the company can continue to issue its semiannual dividend of $4.00 per share, based on its most recent earnings report. The report contains this information:

Net income	$15,430,000
Goodwill impairment	$ 7,000,000
Depreciation	$ 3,500,000
Capital purchases	$ 3,750,000
Restructuring reserve	$ 4,500,000
Number of shares outstanding	5,450,000

Ms. Jones adjusts the $15,430,000 by adding back $7,000,000 in goodwill impairment, depreciation of $3,500,000, and a restructuring reserve of $4,500,000, since none of these items involve cash flows (although the restructuring reserve may require a cash outflow at some point in the future). She also adds back $3,750,000 of capital expenditures. The net income after all of these adjustments is $26,680,000. She calculates the dividend payout ratio using the next formula.

$$\frac{DPS}{EPS} = \frac{\$4.00\,DPS}{\$26,680,000\,\text{Adjusted Net Income}/5,450,000\,\text{Shares}}$$

$$= \underline{82\%}\,\text{Dividend Payout Ratio}$$

The ratio reveals that the company is capable of paying out dividends from its EPS. However, nearly all of the funds acquired through earnings are being paid out, so there may be some danger of a cut-back in dividends in the future if the company's profit level drops by a small amount or if it needs to use its earnings to fund an increase in its rate of growth.

Market Performance Measurements

The CEO of a publicly held company must be aware of the organization's key market performance measurements on a daily basis in order to field calls from analysts about them. The sales/stock price ratio reveals investors' expectations about an organization's ability to increase its sales volume, while the price/earnings (P/E) ratio reveals investors' same expectations regarding corporate profits.

Sales/Stock Price Ratio

The sales/stock price ratio indicates investors' opinions regarding a company's ability to increase its sales volume. If sales increase and there is no change in the stock price, the rate of growth in sales is within investors' expectations. If there is an increase in the stock price, sales have exceeded investors' expectations; a drop in the stock price is indicative of sales levels that do not meet their expectations.

The formula is to divide annualized net sales by the average common stock price for the reporting period. The annualized net sales figure used in this calculation should be the prospective sales figure for the current reporting year, since this represents the announced sales figure that company management has release to investors and is the number on which they are basing their decisions to buy or hold the stock. The average common stock price should be used instead of the ending stock price; doing so removes some fluctuation from the price. The formula is:

$$\frac{\text{Annual Net Sales}}{\text{Average Common Stock Price}}$$

As an example, the CEO of the Gonging Clock Company has been given a stock compensation package that will reward him richly if he can double the stock price within one year. He elects to do so by focusing solely on increases in sales. The display clocks that the company produces are sold almost entirely during the Christmas selling season. To increase sales, he allows customers to pay for their clocks within 180 days, instead of the usual 30 days, and also offers discounts for bulk purchases. As a result, the company experiences a massive increase in sales, investors bid up the stock price, and the CEO retires with a large stock bonus. Unfortunately, his actions so thoroughly clog the company's distribution pipeline with product that its sales volume in the following year dives down to less than one-quarter of the sales level in the preceding year. The board of directors learns its lesson from this experience and revises its senior management incentive plan to focus on more long-term value objectives.

Price/Earnings Ratio

By comparing earnings to the current market price of the stock, you can obtain a general idea of investors' perception of the quality of corporate earnings. For example, a ratio that is substantially lower than the average rate for the industry can indicate an expectation among investors that a company's future earnings are expected to trend lower. Alternatively, a high ratio could indicate the excitement of investors over a new patent that a company has just been granted or the expected favorable results of a lawsuit—the possible explanations are legion. The key point when using the P/E ratio is that a result that varies from the industry average probably indicates a change in investor perceptions from the rest of the industry in regard to a company's ability to continue to generate income.

The formula is to divide the average common stock price by the net income per share. The net income per share figure typically is used on a fully diluted basis, accounting for the impact of options, warrants, and conversions from debt that may increase the number of shares outstanding. The formula is:

$$\frac{\text{Average Common Stock Price}}{\text{Net Income per Share}}$$

For example, an investment analyst wants to determine the price-earnings ratio for the Mile-High Dirigible Company. The industry average P/E ratio for lighter-than-air transport manufacturers is 18:1. She accumulates this information:

Most Recent Stock Price	$ 32.87
Number of Shares Outstanding	3,875,000
Net Income	$8,500,000
Extraordinary Income	$2,250,000

If she chooses to leave the extraordinary income in the total net income figure, she uses the next calculation to derive the P/E ratio:

$$\frac{\$32.87 \text{ Stock Price}}{(\$8,500,000 \text{ Net Income}/3,875,000 \text{ Shares Outstanding})} = \underline{\underline{15:1}} \text{ P/E}$$

So far, the P/E ratio appears to compare favorably to the industry average. However, if she excludes the extraordinary gain from net income, the EPS figure drops to $1.61 per share. When incorporated into the P/E formula, this change increases the ratio to 20:1, which is higher than the industry average. Accordingly, she considers the stock to be overpriced relative to the industry and forbears from recommending it to her clients.

Summary

The ratios presented in this chapter should form the core of a comprehensive set of performance measurements for a diligent CEO. Depending on the industry and the circumstances of each company, some of these measurements will be more or less useful, so pick and choose those that make the most sense to monitor. There also may be some extremely industry-specific metrics that are worth layering onto the measurements noted here. Thus, the actual set of measurements that you choose to follow should be custom-tailored to your needs and may vary substantially from what was presented.

You also may find that some metrics require only a brief review at long intervals while others are indicators of such key issues that you have to examine them every day. Accordingly, you should make your wishes known to the CFO, who is responsible for presenting this information in the format you want and at the intervals you request.

Note that the contents of a measurement report may change over time, depending on the circumstances of the company, so schedule an annual review session with the CFO to decide which measurements you still want to see and how frequently you want to see them.

CHAPTER 12

Cost Reduction Analysis

The typical corporation goes through cycles of growth and contraction. During a contraction phase, the chief executive officer (CEO) will want to know which expenses should be reduced. The worst possible approach is an across-the-board cost reduction, since it impacts both key areas and less crucial ones equally. A better approach is to undertake a carefully targeted analysis that results in the selective pruning of only those costs that a company can afford to lose most easily. This chapter describes various techniques for cost reduction analysis, including spend analysis, supplier consolidation, and workforce reduction. It also provides an overview of a number of analysis tools, including check sheets, Ishikawa diagrams, and value stream mapping.

Types of Reports Used for Cost Reduction Analysis

A cost reduction analysis project should start with a general overview of the target area that results in a graphical presentation of potential cost reductions. The format in Exhibit 12.1 shows the potential cost reduction impact of numerous projects across the bottom axis and implementation difficulty on the vertical axis. Cost reductions in the lower right corner are low-hanging fruit that generate significant returns in exchange for a modest effort. Conversely, items in the upper left corner require a great deal of effort and produce minimal returns. This format is a good guideline for deciding which projects to address first and which can be delayed safely.

In the exhibit, the commission restructuring in the upper left corner is projected to have such a low payback and high difficulty of implementation that it is not worth doing; the procurement card program, however, is highly worthwhile, since it has the reverse characteristics.

A variation on the cost reduction payoff matrix is one that itemizes a number of additional factors, such as the risk of project failure, implementation duration, and level of support. If any prospective project has a high risk score in any category, the project manager should consider alternative projects or work on risk mitigation strategies. A sample risk matrix is shown in Exhibit 12.2. In the exhibit, the riskiest project appears to be the office merger, which contains three high-risk scores, while the single MRO (maintenance, repair, and operations) distributor option is the safest, with four low-risk scores.

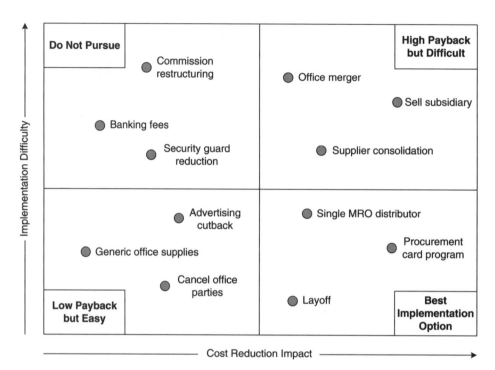

EXHIBIT 12.1 Cost Reduction Payoff Matrix

Exhibits 12.1 and 12.2 provide only an overview of potential cost reduction projects. The next step in an organized cost reduction system is to generate greater detail regarding potential reductions. The format is shown in Exhibit 12.3, which begins with the general topics already shown in the cost reduction payoff matrix and then notes and quantifies specific opportunities. The matrix is split into two parts; those projects estimated to have low levels of implementation difficulty are listed at the top, and those with more difficult implementation difficulty are listed at the bottom.

EXHIBIT 12.2 Cost Reduction Risk Matrix

	Cost Overrun	Customer Turnover	Extended Implementation	Management Support	Project Failure
Advertising cutback	1	4	3	2	1
Layoffs	2	1	2	4	1
Office merger	3	1	4	5	4
Single MRO distributor	1	1	4	1	2
Supplier consolidation	2	1	5	1	3
Scoring	1 = low risk	1 < 1 month	1 < 1 month	1 = high	1 = low risk
	5 = high risk	5 > 1 year	5 > 1 year	5 = low	5 = high risk

EXHIBIT 12.3 Cost Reduction Itemization Matrix

Topic Area	Opportunity	Action	Implementation Difficulty	Cost Reduction (000s)
Advertising cutback	All of advertising is spent on NASCAR sponsorship	Drop sponsorship and switch to mix of Internet and magazine advertising	Low	$380
Cancel office parties	Currently have Christmas and summer parties for 14 offices	Eliminate all summer office parties	Low	170
Generic office supplies	Using brand names for 140+ types of office supplies	Standardize on generic office supplies	Low	30
Layoff	10% of production staff is currently idle	Lay off 5% of the production staff, leaving the remainder on staff to maintain capacity	Low	490
Procurement card program	Purchase orders used for virtually all purchases	Implement a procurement card program, and mandate its usage for purchases under $500	Low	640
Single MRO distributor	Currently use 15 MRO distributors	Centralize orders and shift to standard generic supplies	Low	520
		Total Cost Reduction for Low Implementation Difficulty		**$2,230**
Banking fees	Currently paying account fees for a separate bank account for each office and not aggregating cash for investing purposes	Switch all accounts to a single bank, and roll all cash into an investment account, using zero-balance accounts.	High	40
Commission restructuring	Junior-level base pay is 25% higher than comparable rates in the market	Drop base pay to market rate for all new hires	High	75

(continued)

EXHIBIT 12.3 (*Continued*)

Topic Area	Opportunity	Action	Implementation Difficulty	Cost Reduction (000s)
Office merger	Denver and Boulder offices service approximately the same group of customers	Eliminate the Boulder office, sublease the space, and shift staff to the Denver office	High	390
Security guard reduction	Currently have evening on-site security guards for all 14 offices	Switch to a private contractor that patrols the area periodically	High	85
Sell subsidiary	Wynona Brewery is the only brewery still owned by the company	Sell the subsidiary	High	790
Supplier consolidation	Have over 1,000 suppliers for 5,400 stock-keeping units	Consolidate the supply base to 300 suppliers, and realize a 3% overall cost reduction	High	500
		Total Cost Reduction for High Implementation Difficulty		**$1,880**

Spend Analysis Overview

Spend analysis is the process of organizing procurement information by suppliers and commodities and then using this information to achieve volume discounts and rebates with a reduced number of suppliers. A spend analysis system requires the creation and enhancement of a spend database as the source of a spend analysis, followed by the gradual concentration of ordering volume with a select group of suppliers; this is followed by continual efforts to monitor the company's compliance with the new system. This lengthy process can result in major cost reductions.

Spend Database

The spend database is a highly organized cluster of files containing key information about *what* a company buys, *how much* it spends, and *who* it buys from. The database needs input feeds from the procurement systems of every company subsidiary, which should be updated on at least a quarterly basis. By aggregating all of this purchasing information, a company can see cost saving opportunities at the corporate level that would not have been present at the subsidiary level.

Next, the information must be *cleansed* and *enriched*. Cleansing is improving on and correcting the information already contained within a database; enrichment is adding new information to the database. As an example of cleansing, the same supplier may be recorded under a slightly different name in the feeds coming from different subsidiaries, such as International Business Machines, IBM, and I.B.M. When this happens, it is difficult to determine the amount of a company's total spend with a specific supplier. To fix the problem, the spend database should link all of the name variations for a single supplier to a single parent-level supplier name. For example, IBM could be used as the parent supplier name, and I.B.M. and International Business Machines are linked to it.

A considerable amount of cleansing may be required for item descriptions. An identical item listed in the item master records of five subsidiaries can easily have five wildly different descriptions, and it can be very difficult to match them. One way to correct the situation is to load supplier part numbers and part descriptions into the spend database, so that a part number arriving through a feed from a subsidiary automatically will pull in the correct part description.

Part of the database enrichment process includes adding commodity codes to each purchase. A commodity code assigns a general spend category to a supplier. The company can then aggregate purchase dollars for each commodity code to see where it is spending the bulk of its money, and use this information to negotiate volume purchase discounts with suppliers.

It also may be useful to enrich the spend database with a supplier credit rating. This information is updated periodically through an input feed from a third-party credit rating agency. The spend analysis system issues reports containing just those suppliers whose credit ratings indicate that they are in financial difficulty, which the company uses to re-source with different suppliers.

Another possible enrichment is to update periodically the spend database with the company's in-house supplier ratings. The supplier ratings are useful for steering more work toward those suppliers that consistently have high ratings on such issues as quality and on-time performance.

A fully loaded spend database is not usable unless it has an excellent report writing package, since the ability to drill down through the data is of paramount importance to spend management. Consequently, the database should be equipped with a report writer that can report on information at multiple levels, including by subsidiary, commodity code, and geographic region.

Supplier Consolidation Analysis

The primary spend analysis strategy is to consolidate purchases in order to increase buying volume with a smaller number of preferred suppliers. These consolidation activities should be based on the number of available suppliers and the dollar volume of goods purchased. If there are few suppliers available, single sourcing in exchange for a cooperative approach to cost reduction may be the only cost reduction strategy. However, if there are many suppliers available and the dollar volume of purchased quantities is high, a company can engage in a global search for the lowest-cost provider or reverse auctions to bid down prices. If there are many suppliers but dollar volumes are low, global sourcing is probably not cost effective, but sourcing through a single distributor may yield the lowest overall cost. These options are shown in the cost reduction strategy matrix in Exhibit 12.4.

If a company elects to follow a global sourcing strategy, this will yield the greatest cost reductions if products have a very high labor content; international suppliers typically have access to labor rates far below those in the domestic market. Global sourcing does not work as well for raw materials, since international suppliers probably have no better access to low-cost raw materials than do domestic suppliers (and must incur higher freight costs to deliver to the company).

Commodity Purchases			Strategic Partnerships
High dollar value, many substitutes and suppliers		High dollar value, few suppliers or substitutes	
Invest in global sourcing if high labor content, otherwise e-auctions for high material content		Use sole source, cooperative cost reduction	
Low dollar value, many substitutes and suppliers		Low dollar value, few suppliers or substitutes	
Nonstrategic, so use e-auctions, distributors		Use sole source, cooperative cost reduction	
Low-Value Expendables			Key Purchases

Purchase Value ↑

← Alternate Sourcing Difficulty →

EXHIBIT 12.4 Cost Reduction Strategy Matrix

As a company gradually shifts its business toward its preferred suppliers, its spend analysis will focus on the remaining nonpreferred suppliers. This will be a substantial list, but one toward which an ever-shrinking proportion of the company's spend is directed. The most cost-effective approach is to continually review the highest-dollar commodities that have not yet been addressed, pick a preferred supplier within each one, and direct the bulk of the business in that commodity to that supplier.

Parts Consolidation Analysis

Spend analysis highlights problems with parts duplication. This issue arises when different subsidiaries use slightly different versions of the same parts. If the parts description fields in the spend database have been normalized so that descriptions are comparable, the spend analysis team can spot opportunities for standardizing on a smaller number of parts. If essentially the same part is coming from different suppliers, immediate consolidation of parts with a single supplier is possible. However, this analysis also may call for a longer-term solution, which is designing parts standardization into new versions of the company's products. In the latter case, cost savings may take years to realize.

Parts duplication analysis tends to be a distant second effort behind supplier consolidation, but it can provide significant savings. For example, if a smaller firm can standardize its parts, it can order the remaining parts in greater volumes; its cost per unit therefore may decline to the point where the company can compete effectively on price against a much larger competitor that has not taken advantage of parts standardization. This effect comes from buying large quantities of a smaller number of items.

Maintenance, Repair, and Operations Item Analysis

Maintenance, repair, and operations items typically are bought in great variety and very small quantities, which makes them difficult to consolidate for volume purchases. Instead, enlist the services of a distributor in examining the company's MRO purchases. The distributor can recommend replacing stock-keeping units with less expensive ones, or ones that can be shipped at lower freight expense or that have lower support costs. The distributor deals with these MRO items every day in much greater volumes than the company does, and so has greater knowledge of cost effectiveness. Distributors will perform this service if the company consolidates its MRO purchases with them.

This is the single most important MRO cost reduction initiative, because a company essentially can shift a large part of its investigative labor to a third party.

Spend Compliance

The end result of spend analysis is a much greater concentration of a company's spend with a much smaller number of preferred suppliers. However, given the multitude of locations from which a large corporation can initiate purchases and a corporation's ever-changing needs, keeping this small and select supplier base from rapidly expanding again, thereby diluting the effort of the original spend analysis, can be quite difficult. A number of ways to improve compliance with a completed spend analysis project are listed next.

- *Contracts database.* The foundation for spend compliance is to construct a database containing all contracts that the company has entered into with its approved suppliers. This database is used to match subsequent purchasing information against what should have been purchased through these key suppliers and the terms at which items were purchased from them. As an example of how the contracts database can be used, Contractor ABC has agreed to issue Smith Company a 2% rebate once Smith purchases 30,000 widgets from ABC. Smith Company matches its purchases against the contracts database and finds that Contractor ABC did not issue it the rebate once the 30,000-unit threshold was surpassed. Smith contacts ABC and extracts not only the rebate but also interest income for the delayed payment.
- *Incumbent rebates and discounts.* The contracts database can be loaded immediately with any existing supplier contracts; by doing so, and matching the contracts database against the spend database, a company may realize an immediate benefit, which is that suppliers may not have issued rebates and discounts based on *existing* contracts and purchase volumes.
- *Maverick spenders.* Some employees do not route purchase requests through the purchasing department, and they do not purchase through the approved corporate online purchasing catalog. They prefer either to buy their favorite brand or to use their favorite supplier. By doing so, they reduce a company's purchase volumes with preferred suppliers, which results in fewer rebates and discounts. Some ways to deal with maverick spenders include bringing their activities to the attention of senior management, discussing maverick spending during employees' annual performance reviews, and charging their departments for lost savings.

Spend Analysis Reports

There is no better spend analysis report than one that clearly states exactly how much money a company can save if only it complies with directing orders to the lowest-cost supplier. The table shown in Exhibit 12.5 for a single part number illustrates the concept. The exhibit shows the lowest (and approved) price in the top row, then the various prices being paid to other suppliers (and even the same supplier by a different subsidiary (!)—see the fourth row), along with the additional costs being incurred by continuing to use the other suppliers. This report is a powerful argument for showing exactly how to reduce expenses for each subsidiary, supplier, and component through a focused purchasing effort.

Commodity codes are multilevel, and reporting only at the topmost level may not provide a sufficient level of detail regarding the volume of spend or the number of suppliers. The report shown in Exhibit 12.6 drills down through multiple levels of commodity codes to provide this additional detail.

EXHIBIT 12.5 Compliance Profit Impact

Widget, Part #123

Subsidiary	Supplier	Approved?	Unit Price	12-Month Purchase Volume (Units)	Variance from Approved Unit Price
Northridge	J.C. Hammonds	X	$1.00	25,000	—
Sonoma	Dithers & Sons		1.05	15,000	$ 750
Denver	Arbuthnot Corp.		1.08	18,000	1,440
Atlanta	J.C. Hammonds		1.10	42,000	4,200
Birmingham	Checkers Ltd.		1.15	15,000	2,250
				Total profit impact	**$8,640**

Another useful report is to show a quarterly trend of spend with the company's suppliers. Not only does the report show the ongoing concentration of spend with top suppliers, but (of more importance) it can be used in ongoing negotiations to obtain further price reductions, discounts, and rebates as the company directs more business toward its top suppliers. The report also shows the remaining spend *not* with the top suppliers, which shows the company the extent of additional spend concentration that it can achieve. An example is shown in Exhibit 12.7.

It is also possible to aggregate information at a considerably higher level to see what proportion of total spend has been shifted to approved suppliers by commodity type. The purpose of this report is to measure progress toward gradually shifting spend into a small cluster of preferred suppliers. It does not measure cost savings, focusing instead on general levels of concentration. An example is shown in Exhibit 12.8.

EXHIBIT 12.6 Multilevel Commodity Spend Report

Level 1 Commodity	Level 2 Commodity	Level 3 Commodity	Total Suppliers	Total Spend (000s)
Metal manufacturing	Steel product	Iron and steel pipe	8	$13,540
		Rolled steel	4	4,710
		Steel wire	3	3,900
	Steel product total		15	$22,150
	Aluminum product	Aluminum sheets	2	2,370
		Extruded aluminum	9	970
		Other aluminum	11	320
	Aluminum product total		22	$ 3,660
	Nonferrous metal	Extruded copper	14	1,900
		Copper wire	2	1,110
		Other nonferrous	5	880
	Nonferrous metal total		21	$ 3,890
Supplies total			50	$29,700

EXHIBIT 12.7 Supplier Spend Trend Report

Ranking	Supplier Name	Spend (000s)			
		Quarter 1	Quarter 2	Quarter 3	Quarter 4
1	Columbus Framing	$17,980	$18,020	$18,400	$18,940
2	Masonic Metalcastings	9,730	10,030	10,170	10,500
3	Jacobean Fittings	7,090	7,260	7,605	7,865
4	Bricklin Supply	5,995	6,190	6,430	6,990
5	J.C. Hammonds Corp.	5,450	5,780	6,000	6,150
	Subtotals	$46,245	$47,280	$48,605	$50,445
Remaining suppliers		90,410	89,045	86,830	84,060
	Grand totals	$136,655	$136,325	$135,435	$134,505
Remaining suppliers percent of total		**66%**	**65%**	**64%**	**62%**

EXHIBIT 12.8 Preferred Supplier Concentration by Commodity

	20×1		20×2		20×3	
Commodity	Preferred Supplier Spend (000s)	Percent of Total Spend	Preferred Supplier Spend (000s)	Percent of Total Spend	Preferred Supplier Spend (000s)	Percent of Total Spend
Facilities	$1,400	14%	$1,623	18%	$2,044	29%
Fittings	170	3%	350	8%	482	11%
Fixed assets	13,079	32%	16,080	39%	15,750	37%
Materials	2,450	10%	5,030	20%	5,850	24%
Supplies	—	0%	80	4%	130	10%

An overall result of spend analysis is to reduce the number of suppliers. At a general level, it is useful to aggregate this information to see how much concentration is occurring. The intent is not to shift *all* spend into a small number of suppliers, since it is not cost effective to spend time eliminating the smallest tier of suppliers. Instead, the aim of the report is to highlight the *proportion* of spend concentrated in the top tier of suppliers. An example is shown in Exhibit 12.9.

EXHIBIT 12.9 Spend Concentration Report

For the Year Ended December 31, 20x3

	Facilities	Fittings	Fixed Assets	Materials	Supplies
Total spend (000s)	$7,048	$4,382	$42,568	$24,375	$1,300
Total suppliers	108	240	42	289	98
Suppliers with 80% of spend	22	50	10	63	25
Suppliers with 90% of spend	51	82	18	90	31
Suppliers with 95% of spend	73	129	25	135	43

The example spend concentration report reveals that the company has a considerable amount of supplier consolidation work to do; roughly 20% of the total number of suppliers receive 80% of total spend in each commodity category, which does not depart appreciably from what a Pareto analysis would reveal. In other words, the supplier distribution does not depart significantly from what would be expected if the company had taken no action at all to concentrate its spend with preferred suppliers.

Workforce Reduction Analysis

The first step in workforce cost reduction is to determine the cost directly attributable to each employee. Exhibit 12.10 shows a good format for this calculation. From left to right, it shows base-level annual compensation, followed by all related payroll taxes and net benefit costs. It continues with several additional expenses that can be traced directly to each employee. The Social Security tax is applicable only below a certain maximum wage level, which is noted in the lower left corner of the exhibit. The 401k pension withholding for each employee is not an expense but is included in order to show the company 401k match, which *is* an expense. The exhibit is sorted in alphabetical order by employee last name.

Overhead costs should be considered if a sufficient number of positions are eliminated to trigger an immediate overhead reduction. Exhibit 12.11 uses the same format as Exhibit 12.10, but now the assumption is that by laying off entire *groups* of employees, a block of clearly identifiable overhead expenses can be eliminated. In the exhibit, employees are now sorted by store location, so that the elimination of an entire group of employees and their associated overhead costs can be clumped together. The cost reduction decision point is no longer the individual employee but rather an entire company location.

Thus far, the analysis has addressed only the cost of each employee or group of employees; it has not incorporated any revenue that employees may generate directly, such as in a service environment. Without this information, a company may lay off its most expensive employee without considering that the same person also generates a great deal of revenue for the company.

Exhibit 12.12 shows a breakdown of both revenue and cost for employees, so that now profitability now be ascertained on an individual level. The exhibit compresses the level of expense detail, thereby making room for revenue and profit information. The exhibit includes a column for a commission expense, which is subtracted from the revenues to arrive at a net revenue amount for each employee.

Workforce Reduction Issues

A workforce reduction is designed to save money, but it may do the reverse in the short term, since there are a number of expenses associated with any workforce reduction. Several expenses to consider and several ways to mitigate them are presented next.

EXHIBIT 12.10 Employee Cost Rollup

Employee Name	Annual Pay	Social Security	Medicare	401K Withhold	50% 401K Match	Medical	Medical Deducts	Annual Phone	Annual T&E	Total Cost
Andrews, Bill	$ 42,750	$ 2,651	$ 620	$ 4,000	$ 2,000	$ 14,185	$ (5,242)	$ 1,200	$ 5,000	$ 63,163
Brennan, Charles	$ 125,000	$ 6,622	$ 1,813	$16,500	$ 8,250	$ 17,265	$ (6,780)	$ —	$ —	$ 152,169
Cantor, David	$ 80,000	$ 4,960	$ 1,160	$ 7,250	$ 3,625	$ 6,175	$ (1,225)	$ 1,200	$ 8,500	$ 104,395
DiMaggio, Ernest	$ 77,500	$ 4,805	$ 1,124	$ 2,500	$ 1,250	$ 17,265	$ (6,780)	$ 1,450	$ 500	$ 97,114
Entenmann, Franklin	$ 142,500	$ 6,622	$ 2,066	$16,500	$ 8,250	$ 17,265	$ (6,780)	$ 1,200	$18,500	$ 189,623
Fairview, George	$ 37,500	$ 2,325	$ 544	$ 500	$ 250	$ —	$ —	$ 1,200	$ 1,250	$ 43,069
Gorman, Hercules	$ 225,000	$ 6,622	$ 3,263	$16,500	$ 8,250	$ —	$ —	$ 1,200	$32,750	$ 277,084
Henderson, Ian	$ 85,000	$ 5,270	$ 1,233	$ 4,000	$ 2,000	$ 17,265	$ (6,780)	$ 1,200	$ 1,750	$ 106,938
Innes, Julie	$ 73,000	$ 4,526	$ 1,059	$ —	$ —	$ —	$ —	$ —	$ —	$ 78,585
Jackson, Kari	$ 119,000	$ 6,622	$ 1,726	$14,250	$ 7,125	$ 6,175	$ (1,225)	$ —	$ —	$ 139,422
Klerk, Larry	$ 170,000	$ 6,622	$ 2,465	$16,500	$ 8,250	$ 14,185	$ (5,242)	$ 1,450	$ 800	$ 198,530
Lincoln, Mandy	$ 95,000	$ 5,890	$ 1,378	$ 9,000	$ 4,500	$ 6,175	$ (1,225)	$ 1,200	$ 4,250	$ 117,168
Masters, Nancy	$ 62,500	$ 3,875	$ 906	$ 1,000	$ 500	$ 14,185	$ (5,242)	$ 1,200	$ —	$ 77,924
	$1,334,750	$ 67,410	$19,354		$54,250	$130,140	$(46,521)	$12,500	$73,300	$1,645,182
Percent of total	81%	4%	1%		3%	8%	–3%	1%	4%	100%

Tax percentage   6.20%   1.45%
Maximum cap $106,800   None

EXHIBIT 12.11 Employee Cost Rollup with Overhead

Napa Store:	Annual Pay	Social Security	Medicare	401K Withhold	50% 401K Match	Medical	Medical Deducts	Annual Phone	Annual T&E	Total Cost
Andrews, Bill	$ 42,750	$ 2,651	$ 620	$ 4,000	$2,000	$14,185	$(5,242)	$ 1,200	$ 5,000	$ 63,163
Entenmann, Franklin	$142,500	$ 6,622	$2,066	$16,500	$8,250	$17,265	$(6,780)	$ 1,200	$18,500	$ 189,623
Jackson, Kari	$119,000	$ 6,622	$1,726	$14,250	$7,125	$ 6,175	$(1,225)	$ —	$ —	$ 139,422
Klerk, Larry	$170,000	$ 6,622	$2,465	$16,500	$8,250	$14,185	$(5,242)	$ 1,450	$ 800	$ 198,530
Lincoln, Mandy	$ 95,000	$ 5,890	$1,378	$ 9,000	$4,500	$ 6,175	$(1,225)	$ 1,200	$ 4,250	$ 117,168
Masters, Nancy	$ 62,500	$ 3,875	$ 906	$ 1,000	$ 500	$14,185	$(5,242)	$ 1,200	$ —	$ 77,924
										$ 785,830
									Annual Rent:	$ 156,000
									Annual Utilities:	$ 28,000
										$ 969,830
Santa Rosa Store:										
Brennan, Charles	$125,000	$ 6,622	$1,813	$16,500	$8,250	$17,265	$(6,780)	$ —	$ —	$ 152,169
Cantor, David	$ 80,000	$ 4,960	$1,160	$ 7,250	$3,625	$ 6,175	$(1,225)	$ 1,200	$ 8,500	$ 104,395
DiMaggio, Ernest	$ 77,500	$ 4,805	$1,124	$ 2,500	$1,250	$17,265	$(6,780)	$ 1,450	$ 500	$ 97,114
Fairview, George	$ 37,500	$ 2,325	$ 544	$ 500	$ 250	$ —	$ —	$ 1,200	$ 1,250	$ 43,069
Gorman, Hercules	$225,000	$ 6,622	$3,263	$16,500	$8,250	$ —	$ —	$ 1,200	$32,750	$ 277,084
Henderson, Ian	$ 85,000	$ 5,270	$1,233	$ 4,000	$2,000	$17,265	$(6,780)	$ 1,200	$ 1,750	$ 106,938
Innes, Julie	$ 73,000	$ 4,526	$1,059	$ —	$ —	$ —	$ —	$ —	$ —	$ 78,585
										$ 859,353
									Annual Rent:	$ 172,000
									Annual Utilities:	$ 32,500
										$1,063,853

EXHIBIT 12.12 Employee Profitability Calculation

Employee Name	Revenues			Annual Pay	Expenses			Profit	Profit %
	Annual Revenues	Commission	Net Revenues		Payroll Taxes	Benefits	Total Cost		
Andrews, Bill	$ 101,890	$ 4,076	$ 97,814	$ 42,750	$ 3,270	$ 17,143	$ 63,163	$ 34,651	35%
Brennan, Charles	$ 234,750	$ 9,390	$ 225,360	$ 125,000	$ 8,434	$ 18,735	$ 152,169	$ 73,191	32%
Cantor, David	$ 119,250	$ 4,770	$ 114,480	$ 80,000	$ 6,120	$ 18,275	$ 104,395	$ 10,085	9%
DiMaggio, Ernest	$ 142,120	$ 5,685	$ 136,435	$ 77,500	$ 5,929	$ 13,685	$ 97,114	$ 39,321	29%
Entenmann, Franklin	$ 267,040	$ 10,682	$ 256,358	$ 142,500	$ 8,688	$ 38,435	$ 189,623	$ 66,736	26%
Fairview, George	$ 71,020	$ 2,841	$ 68,179	$ 37,500	$ 2,869	$ 2,700	$ 43,069	$ 25,110	37%
Gorman, Hercules	$ 203,150	$ 8,126	$ 195,024	$ 225,000	$ 9,884	$ 42,200	$ 277,084	$ (82,060)	-42%
Henderson, Ian	$ 173,350	$ 6,934	$ 166,416	$ 85,000	$ 6,503	$ 15,435	$ 106,938	$ 59,479	36%
Innes, Julie	$ 123,950	$ 4,958	$ 118,992	$ 73,000	$ 5,585	$ —	$ 78,585	$ 40,408	34%
Jackson, Kari	$ 225,290	$ 9,012	$ 216,278	$ 119,000	$ 8,347	$ 12,075	$ 139,422	$ 76,856	36%
Klerk, Larry	$ 274,040	$ 10,962	$ 263,078	$ 170,000	$ 9,087	$ 19,443	$ 198,530	$ 64,549	25%
Lincoln, Mandy	$ 92,650	$ 3,706	$ 88,944	$ 95,000	$ 7,268	$ 14,900	$ 117,168	$ (28,224)	-32%
Masters, Nancy	$ 129,740	$ 5,190	$ 124,550	$ 62,500	$ 4,781	$ 10,643	$ 77,924	$ 46,626	37%
	$2,158,240	$86,330	$2,071,910	$1,334,750	$86,763	$223,669	$1,645,182	$426,728	21%

- *Severance package.* The most minimal severance package is simply severance pay, but a package can include a number of other costs, such as benefits continuation, the use of a company phone or computer, and outplacement services. Severance pay typically is linked to the number of years of employee service, so the payout can be severe if the workforce reduction includes personnel with high seniority.
- *Accrued vacation.* If employees have not used some portion of their earned vacations, the company must pay employees for that vacation time when the workforce reduction takes place.
- *Stock grant acceleration.* If employees are part of a stock grant program, the program likely will have an award acceleration clause, where vesting in the shares is accelerated in the event of a change in control of the company. If employees are being laid off because of the change in control, it is likely that they will receive the stock grant at termination. If so, the company must record a noncash expense at the time of vesting to reflect the recognition of all remaining expense associated with the stock grant.
- *Unemployment insurance.* If a company frequently lays off its employees, they in turn will draw down the state's unemployment fund, which the state government must replenish by increasing the company's unemployment contribution rate in the following year.
- *Potential lawsuits.* There is always a risk that some employees will sue the company for wrongful termination. Even if there is no likelihood of a payout, the company still must pay legal fees to defend its position. To avoid this issue, make any severance payment conditional upon employee agreement not to file a claim against the company.

The severance and vacation expenses just noted can be mitigated to some extent by paying them out based on an average of an employee's pay for the past few years rather than on the final pay level (which is presumably higher). This pay calculation should be fully documented in the employee manual.

Workforce Reduction Alternatives

Many companies try to avoid a workforce reduction. However, there are still prospects for reducing payroll costs. The next techniques are available.

- *Review overtime pay.* There should be a formal supervisory review of all overtime hours claimed, which can be triggered by an automated timekeeping system. Better yet, an analyst should review the reasons why the bulk of the overtime hours were incurred and see if there are any alternatives that can avoid the future incurrence of this cost.
- *Use vacation time.* By encouraging its staff to take unused vacation time, a company still incurs a cash outflow to pay for the vacations. However, this may soak up a considerable amount of unused vacation time, so employees will be more available later, when they may be needed for revenue-generating activities.

- *Delay new hires.* If there is a reasonable expectation that business will improve soon, hold off on making offers to new hire candidates. If offers already have been extended, consider delaying their start dates while paying them a stipend and moving expenses.
- *Attrition.* The most noninvasive form of workforce reduction is simply to not replace employees when they retire or leave the company for other reasons. This is a long-term solution, since employee departures may occur over quite a few years before a company has reduced its headcount to its targeted level.
- *Delay or reduce scheduled pay raises.* If a medium-term business downturn is expected, management can authorize a significant delay in scheduled pay raises or reduce the amount of raises that will be granted. This approach should be shared by all, to gain acceptance.
- *Require unpaid days off.* There may be cases where occasional unpaid days off for the entire workforce will resolve financial difficulties. If so, reduce the sting for employees by allowing them to pick which days to take off. For example, the days off may coincide with school vacations or be adjacent to federal holidays.
- *Shorten the workweek.* If there is not enough work for a large part of the company, the company can elect to shorten the workweek for some period of time, with reduced pay to match the shorter work period. This alternative works best for a single-day reduction from a five-day to a four-day workweek, since the result is a 20% pay cut for everyone in the company.
- *Shorten working hours.* In a retail environment, it may make sense to determine when the bulk of customers are shopping and contract store hours to match.
- *Use unpaid leaves of absence.* An unpaid leave of absence only encourages employees to look for new jobs and so likely will result in a very high turnover level in the near term. However, if the company offers to continue paying benefits during leaves of absence, employees may be more inclined to stay out of work longer and still return to the company at the end of their leaves.
- *Offer paid sabbaticals.* If the business downturn is expected to be extensive, management can offer a sabbatical with a moderate rate of pay to those employees judged to have sufficient seniority. The amount paid can be viewed as a retainer for consulting services, which the company can exercise by occasionally calling in employees on sabbatical to assist during high-volume periods.
- *Freeze pay.* Employees may accept a complete pay freeze for a limited period of time, if they understand that the situation is caused by economic conditions that put the company at risk. This approach works best if everyone is included in the pay freeze.
- *Implement a pay cut.* A more drastic alternative is to mandate a pay cut. If implemented, this cut should be universal, so that no charges of favoritism can be levied. Further, the pay cut should be even greater for the management team, which creates a solid reason for the management group to work the company back into profitability.

Enacting either a shorter workweek or fewer working hours during the business day also will reduce the amount of vacation and sick hours employees accrue, so there is a cumulative cost reduction effect.

5S Analysis

The 5S system is about organizing the workplace in order to eliminate waste. From a cost reduction perspective, it promotes workplace efficiency. As the name of this tool implies, there are five steps, and their names all begin with "s."

1. *Sort.* Review all of the items within a work area, retain those needed for daily operations, and dispose of all other items.
2. *Straighten.* Reposition furniture and equipment to best serve the process flow, and move all other items out of the way.
3. *Scrub.* Clean the area completely.
4. *Systematize.* Establish schedules for cleaning the area repetitively.
5. *Standardize.* Incorporate the 5S system into standard company operations, so that it is performed on an ongoing basis.

A company should not embark on a 5S clean sweep of the entire organization at the same time, since that would create a great deal of disruption. Instead, this is a methodical process that is used gradually to address all locations, after which it starts over again in a continual cycle.

Error Quantification

Any error that results in a scrapped or reworked product or document piles up costs. A company can create an information tracking system to aggregate error information, which is summarized into a report such as the one shown in Exhibit 12.13. The report notes the number of incidences of an error event during the measurement period. It also notes the lost throughput of each item. If an item is scrapped, the associated throughput (revenue minus totally variable costs) is lost forever. If an item is

EXHIBIT 12.13 Error Quantification Report

Error Type	Number of Incidents	Lost Throughput per Incident	Total Lost Throughput	Total Rework Time	Total Rework Cost
Rework—Adjust paint gaps	14	$11.14	$155.96	3:30	$70.00
Rework—Cut off excess trim	29	8.23	238.67	5:00	100.00
Rework—Redrill unaligned hole	8	4.88	39.04	2:00	40.00
Rework—Smooth rough edges	11	7.35	80.85	1:00	20.00
Scrap—Broken base unit	10	19.20	192.00	—	—
Scrap—Crushed packaging	4	6.10	24.40	—	—
Scrap—Dented electronics	17	12.05	204.85	—	—

reworked, the cost of the rework labor is offset against the lost throughput to yield a reduced level of throughput. Further, the report indicates the time and labor cost required for rework.

The error quantification report example reveals that the worst scrap issue to investigate is dented electronics, since the company loses the most throughput dollars from this problem. Among the rework issues, the cost of additional labor must be offset against the potential lost throughput to see if rework is worthwhile. The redrilling work is costing more to fix than the throughput that otherwise would be lost; these items should be scrapped instead. The other rework efforts all yield a higher throughput than would be the case if no rework were done.

Fixed Cost Analysis

A common decision point is whether to incur a large fixed cost (such as a high-capacity machine) in order to achieve higher margins through greater production efficiency. The answer, in many cases, is no. The reason is that a large fixed cost increases a company's breakeven point, so that it must make more sales before it can begin to earn a profit. This can be a risky scenario in a volatile market. The issue can even be reversed: Should existing fixed costs be eliminated in exchange for variable costs that result in somewhat lower margins? In many cases, yes. It is worthwhile to be somewhat less profitable in exchange for having a more flexible company that can earn a profit over a broader range of revenues and margins. This issue can extend to a variety of nonproduction issues, such as leasing office space rather than buying a building.

Ishikawa Diagrams

An Ishikawa diagram reveals the causes of a specified event. The diagram, as shown in Exhibit 12.14, has the general appearance of the bones of a fish. The problem to be solved lies at the head. Major bones represent groups of major causes, and minor bones represent subcauses. An Ishikawa diagram is an excellent starting point for a cost reduction analysis, since solving the issues listed along the various branches of the diagram will likely solve the initial problem, which may have been a source of considerable expense.

The exhibit shows the categories of issues causing late product deliveries to customers. The issues are clustered under general categories, such as Policy, Products, and Machine. For example, under the Machine category, incorrect machine setups are delaying the production of goods and inadequate preventive maintenance is increasing machine downtime. Each of the items on the diagram can be addressed in order to ultimately reduce the incidence of late product deliveries to customers.

There are a large number of major causes under which subcauses can be clustered. Possible headings include environment, equipment, inspection, manpower, materials, maintenance, management, policies, prices, procedures, processing, products, promotions, and suppliers.

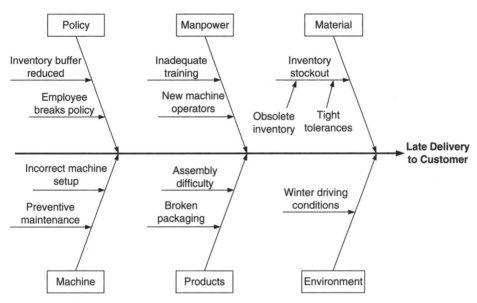

EXHIBIT 12.14 Ishikawa Diagram

Value Stream Mapping

Value stream mapping (VSM) focuses on the identification of waste across an entire process. A VSM chart identifies all of the actions required to complete a process while also identifying key information about each action item. Key information will vary by the process under review but can include total hours worked, overtime hours, cycle time to complete a transaction, error rates, and absenteeism.

The VSM chart shown in Exhibit 12.15 addresses the entire procurement cycle, from the initial placement of a requisition through processing of the resulting supplier invoice. Under each processing step, the VSM chart itemizes the amount of overtime, staffing, work shifts, process uptime, and transaction error rate. The chart then shows the total time required for each processing step as well as the time required between steps. It also identifies the types of time spent *between* steps (e.g., outbound batching, transit time, and inbound queue time).

The chart reveals that most of the procurement cycle time is used between processing steps, especially in the transit time of orders from suppliers to the company. If total cycle time is an issue, a reasonable conclusion would be to either source locally or expend more for faster delivery services. However, if the emphasis is on speedier in-house processing, the chart shows that the purchase order processing stage is the most time-consuming; it is also probably a bottleneck operation, given the amount of overtime incurred. Likely conclusions would be to reduce the error rate in the purchasing area by working on a reduction of errors in the upstream requisitioning area, offloading purchasing work with procurement cards, or bolstering capacity by adding purchasing staff.

Another option for shrinking the long cycle time is to have the receiving staff send receiving documents to the payables department more frequently than once

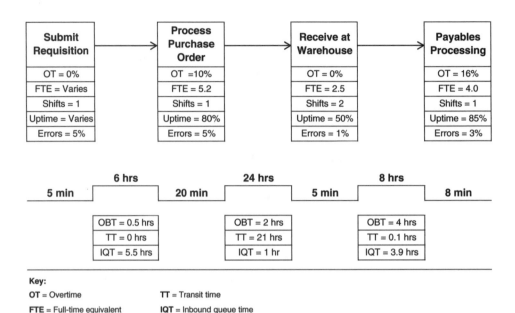

Key:

OT = Overtime   TT = Transit time

FTE = Full-time equivalent   IQT = Inbound queue time

OBT = Outbound batch time

EXHIBIT 12.15 Value Stream Map

every four hours; cutting the outbound batch time in half would eliminate two hours from the total cycle time.

VSM works best in highly focused, high-volume processes where it makes sense to spend time wringing a few seconds out of repetitive processes.

Waste Analysis

Cost reduction can be performed simply by identifying the various types of waste and then working to reduce them. Here are seven types of waste to be aware of.

1. *Additional processing.* This is any production process that does not directly add value to a product, such as a quality control review.
2. *Defects.* Any processing that destroys or harms production that already has passed through the bottleneck operation is a form of waste, because it eliminates valuable throughput and may require additional expenditures for rework.
3. *Inventory.* Inventory of all types requires a working capital investment, incurs storage costs, and is at risk of obsolescence. It also hides other cost issues, such as production imbalances and poor work practices.
4. *Motion.* Any motion by employees that does not add value is a waste. This includes any equipment setup time.
5. *Overproduction.* Any production exceeding specific customer orders is a waste, because it uses materials and other resources, which incur storage costs and are subject to obsolescence.

6. *Transportation*. This is the movement of materials between any operations that transform the materials, such as between workstations in a production process. The more something moves, the more opportunity there is to damage materials. Spending on materials handling equipment or conveyor belts is also a form of waste.

7. *Waiting*. Any time when a machine or its operator is waiting is considered a waste of that resource. Waiting can be caused by unbalanced workloads, over-staffing, materials shortages, and so forth.

Summary

Cost reduction is a perilous activity. You may find it necessary to make expense reductions in the short term, but you cannot afford to cut the wrong expenses, which might imperil the company's ability to compete over the long term. In this chapter, we have provided a number of tools for pruning expenses in a highly targeted manner. You can use spend analysis, parts concentration, and MRO analysis to concentrate spending with a smaller number of suppliers while using workforce analysis to eliminate entire functions or locations that are least necessary rather than plucking out a few employees here and there. There are also several other tools that assist in finding the root causes of problems that may be causing unnecessary expenses throughout the company. You should use all of these tools to create a company that is focused on minimizing costs while still being able to compete effectively.

CHAPTER 13

Mergers and Acquisitions

O ne of the signature areas in which a chief executive officer (CEO) leaves her
mark on a company is mergers and acquisitions, since a successful one can
catapult the company into great prominence. Unfortunately, a poor acquisition can
lead to bankruptcy and ruin the CEO's reputation, so you need to know how to
determine which potential acquirees make a good fit and how much to pay for
them. In this chapter, we address the types of acquisition analyses that your acquisition team should engage in as well as how to calculate an appropriate price to pay.
We also cover a variety of legal structures to use for an acquisition, which can be
critical from a tax perspective.

When reading this text, keep in mind that the terms "merger" and "acquisition"
are not the same thing. An *acquisition* is when both the acquiring and acquired
company are still left standing as separate entities at the end of the transaction. A
merger results in the legal dissolution of one of the companies, and a *consolidation*
dissolves both of the parties and creates a new one, into which the previous entities
are merged.

Evaluating Acquisition Targets

The analysis of an acquisition is like no other type of financial analysis—not because
the analysis itself is different, but because of the logistics of the situation. Typically, a
potential acquisition situation arises suddenly, requires the fullest attention of the
staff for a short time, and then subsides, either because the acquisition is judged not
to be a good one or because the deal is completed and a separate integration team
takes over the activities of melding the organizations together.

You should be aware of the main areas in which an analysis team conducts
reviews of potential acquirees, if only to ensure that they are addressing all possible
areas of concern. The key areas are listed next.

- *Personnel.* If a company has need of employees with great experience or skill, it
  can fill the need by buying a company that employs them. This is a rare circumstance when only a few people are involved, since it is easier to hire them away
  with employment offers. However, if a potential acquiree has one or more
  departments that are justly famous for their work, buying the company may be

worthwhile in order to obtain those specific departments. This situation arises most frequently with engineering or research firms. The main analysis needed here is to determine the current compensation levels of the people being acquired and how these pay levels compare to both internal and industry pay standards. Additional considerations include the presence of any long-term compensation agreements and their net present value (NPV).

- *Patents.* A target company may possess one or more valuable patents, especially ones that can be used to enhance the value of the acquiring company's products. This approach is most common with research and drug firms. In this case, the primary analysis focuses on the cost of maintaining those patents, the number of years remaining prior to expiration, and (especially) the expected cash flows to be obtained from them prior to their expiration.
- *Brands.* A brand name is immensely valuable if it has been maintained carefully for many years, has been strongly supported with proper marketing, and represents excellent products. This is a good reason to acquire a target company, and is most common in the consumer goods field. The analysis for this type of acquisition focuses on the incremental profits to be gained by use of the brand name in relation to the cost of maintaining the brand.
- *Capacity.* If a company is faced with a long lead time or technological challenges to acquire greater production capacity, it may be worthwhile to purchase a production facility from another company. The analysis for this type of acquisition focuses on the age and usefulness of the machinery and facility purchased.
- *Assets and liabilities.* When an entire company is purchased, the acquiring organization is taking over virtually all assets as well as all associated risks. In this instance, a comprehensive review of all balance sheet line items is mandatory.
- *Profitability.* A company may be bought because it has a greater percentage of profitability than the acquiring company, which increases the acquiring company's combined profitability. For this acquisition, a close review of the income statement and balance sheet is necessary.
- *Cash flow.* If a company has a large store of cash or continuing cash flows, it is a prime target for purchase by companies that need the cash, possibly to fund further acquisitions. For this type of acquisition, an intensive review of the balance sheet, income statement, and funds flow statement is necessary.
- *Legal.* A company may have obligations that require it to make expenditures of such size that they seriously reduce the value of the entity. There also may be restrictions contained in various legal agreements that potentially can cause problems with the company's ability to do business. It takes a great deal of investigative effort to unearth these issues.

Personnel Analysis

If the main reason for acquiring a target company is to hire away a specific person or group of people who are deemed to have valuable skills, you have one of two analysis options to pursue. If the company has chosen to purchase the entire target company, a full-blown analysis of all assets, liabilities, controls, and legal issues must be conducted. The analysis for those categories is noted under the subsequent sections of this chapter. However, if the company has persuaded the target company to accept payment in exchange for the transfer of some smaller portion of the company that includes the targeted employees, the analysis work becomes much more specific.

An example of a partial purchase to obtain employees is when a target company decides to eliminate one of its lines of business and sells the related customer list and assets to the acquiring company. As part of the transaction, the target company lays off employees who were associated with the line of business that is being transferred to the new company. The acquiring company obtains a list of these employees from the selling company and contacts them to offer them jobs. Because of the nature of this transaction, it is essentially nothing more than a transfer of assets, which greatly reduces the amount of required analysis. Only the next analyses, which are targeted specifically at the employees to be hired, with an emphasis on their quality, cost, and turnover, should be conducted:

- *Investigate employee names listed on patents.* If individual employees are named on patents or patent applications filed by the target company, it is a good bet that those employees may be in a revenue-sharing agreement with the company employing them. If so, research further to determine the amounts paid to the employees for use of the patents, such as a fee per unit sold or an annual payment. These patent payments must be added to employee salaries to determine the true cost of bringing in the new personnel.
- *Interview customers and suppliers about employees.* If there are problems with the desired employees, the target company is almost certainly not going to reveal this information, since it is trying to obtain payment for "selling" them to the acquiring company. Accordingly, it may be necessary to call the target company's suppliers or customers to see if they have had dealings with the people under consideration and what their opinions may be.
- *Compare employee pay levels to industry and internal averages.* Obtain the pay rates for the entire department to be acquired, and determine the distribution of pay through the group to see if there are any inordinately highly paid people. Then compare these rates not only to the industry average but also to the acquiring company's average, to determine the difference between the pay levels about to be brought in and the existing rates. If there is a major difference between the two pay rates, an additional cost of the acquisition may be to bring the pay levels of the in-house staff up to match those of the incoming personnel in order to avoid turmoil caused by the pay differential.
- *Determine the current turnover rate in the targeted department.* If there is a high turnover rate in the department being acquired, a high risk of losing the entire group may make the cost of acquisition not worthwhile.
- *Review long-term compensation agreements.* If a target company has obtained the services of a number of exceptional employees, it is quite possible that it has done so by offering them expensive, long-term employment contracts. You therefore should review contracts not only for the projected payment amounts, increases, and NPV but also for golden parachute clauses that pay these employees exorbitant amounts if the target company is purchased.

The upshot of what you are looking for when reviewing the acquisition of personnel is the actual cost of those employees and the potential impact on their

EXHIBIT 13.1 Analysis Report for Acquisition of Personnel

Description	Additional Information	Summary Costs
Total cost of incoming staff (15 staff)		$1,237,500
Average cost of incoming staff	$82,500	
Average cost of in-house staff	73,000	
Prior year employee turnover level	10%	
Additional cost to match in-house salaries to incoming salaries (13 staff)		123,500
Net present value of projected patent payments to employees		420,000
Cost of employment contract buyouts		250,000
Total cost of employee acquisition		$2,031,000
Total cost per employee acquired (15 staff)		$ 135,400
Industry average pay rate per person		**$ 80,000**
Percentage premium over market rate		**69%**

counterparts. The first item is purely financial in nature, while the second is a matter for conjecture regarding the impact of a group of higher-paid employees on the existing, in-house group that is paid less. An example of the analysis report for an acquisition based on personnel is shown in Exhibit 13.1.

Note that the cost of acquisition has been converted at the bottom of the example into a cost per employee, which then is compared to the average market rate. The premium to be paid over the market rate gives management its best idea of the true cost of the staff it is acquiring, and whether it is a good idea to proceed with the acquisition.

Patent Analysis

If a company wants to acquire a patent from another company, it usually does not go to the extreme of buying the whole company. Instead, it negotiates for the patent itself, which makes the analysis work substantially easier. There are few measures to investigate, with an emphasis on the existing costs and revenues currently experienced by the holder of the patent. Management may require additional analysis to include the estimated additional revenues and costs that subsequently will be incurred by its use of the patent, which may vary from the use to which it has been put by the current patent owner. The primary analyses are listed next.

- *Determine annual patent renewal costs.* Annual patent costs are quite minimal but should be included in any patent analysis, such as the one shown in Exhibit 13.2, in order to present a comprehensive set of cost information.
- *Determine current patent-related revenue stream.* This information is needed to determine the amount of money that the company is willing to pay for a patent; however, if the company wants to shift the focus of the patent to a different application, this number has less use. Without cooperation from the target

EXHIBIT 13.2 Analysis Report for Patent Acquisition

Description	Additional Information	Summary Revenues and Costs
Years left prior to patent expiration	10 years	
Net present value of cash inflows		$1,200,000
Discounted cost of remaining filing costs		– 42,000
Discounted cost of expected annual legal fees		– 375,000
Net present value of patent		**$ 783,000**

company, this number can be very difficult to determine; the only alternative is to contact companies that are licensed to use the patent and see if they will reveal the per-unit payment they are required to make to the target company for use of their patent. If the target company is willing to reveal this information, obtain it for the last few years to see if there is an upward or downward trend line for the revenues; if the trend is downward, the revenue stream for which the company is paying is worth less.

■ *Ascertain extent of current litigation to support patent.* A major issue for any patent holder is the amount of money it must spend to keep other entities from encroaching on the patent with parallel patents or just by issuing products that illegally use technology based on the patent. These legal costs can be enormous. If a company wants to take over a patent, it must be aware of the extent of encroachment and the cost of legally pursuing the encroachers.

An example of the analysis report for a patent purchase is shown in Exhibit 13.2. The bottom line of the patent acquisition analysis report is the NPV of all cash flows, which you can use as the highest recommended amount to pay for the patent. However, given alternative uses for the patent that they may be contemplating, you may anticipate a higher cash inflow that will allow for a higher price for the patent.

Brand Analysis

The analyses needed to review a brand name are relatively simple from the financial perspective, although somewhat more involved from the legal side, since the analysis team must conduct research to ensure that there is a clear title to the trademark and to ascertain the extent of possible infringements on the brand name and the extent and recent history of litigation needed to support the brand. The primary analyses are listed next.

■ *Determine the amount of annual trademark fees.* This is a very minor item but can grow to considerable proportions if the trademark is being maintained worldwide, which requires filings and maintenance fees in a multitude of jurisdictions.

■ *Determine clear title to the brand name.* This is not just a matter of paying for a small amount of research by a legal firm to determine the existence of any countervailing trademarks; it also requires a search in multiple jurisdictions if the buying company wants to expand the brand to other countries.

- *Ascertain the amount and trend of any current cash inflows from the brand name.* The two best analysis options are to measure just that portion of sales that is due specifically to licensing agreements (and therefore easily traceable) or to measure the incremental difference in cash flows from all products under the brand name in comparison to those of the industry average or specific competitors.
- *Note the amount and trend of any legal fees needed to stop encroachment.* A quality brand frequently attracts a number of companies that build inexpensive knockoffs and sell them illegally for vastly reduced prices. Given the reduced quality and prices, the net impact of these fake goods is to cheapen the brand's image. Consequently, constant legal pursuit of these companies is the only way to keep imitating products off the market. The analysis team should roughly estimate the cost of current lawsuits either by reviewing all current lawsuits that are public record or by asking the target company. If the acquiring company wants to maintain the brand image, it must be willing to continue to use legal alternatives; for this reason, the current legal cost can be used as a reasonable benchmark of future costs as well.
- *Note any challenges to use of the brand name.* Yet another legal issue is that there may be lawsuits pending that claim the trademark of another person or corporation supersedes the one about to be purchased. If so, a search of all open lawsuits should reveal this information. Once again, if the company contemplates worldwide usage of the brand name, a much more extensive search for competing trademarks in other locations is necessary. If there are cases where someone else has filed for the right to use the brand name in another country, calculate the estimated cost of acquiring the rights to that name.

In Exhibit 13.3, we itemize the financial analysis associated with a brand name acquisition.

Capacity Analysis

When a company purchases a specific manufacturing facility from another company, it usually is doing so to increase its capacity. With this end in mind, the key analyses revolve around the condition and cost of the facility so that you can determine the amount of replacement machinery to install as well as the actual production capacity

EXHIBIT 13.3 Analysis Report for a Brand Acquisition

Description	Additional Information	Summary Revenues and Costs
Net present value of current cash inflows		$ 500,000
Discounted cost of annual trademark fees		−65,000
Cost of trademark search (for clear title)		−175,000
Discounted cost of annual legal fees		−780,000
Cost to purchase competing brand names	See note	−2,250,000
Total net cost of brand name		**$−2,770,000**

Note: A competing trademark already has been filed by Company XYZ in all countries of the European Community and Japan. The cost required to purchase this trademark is included in the analysis.

EXHIBIT 13.4 Analysis Report for Capacity Acquisition

	Costs at Minimum Capacity Usage	Costs at Normal Capacity Usage	Costs at Maximum Capacity Usage
Facility overhead cost	$ 1,000,000	$ 3,500,000	$ 5,000,000
Capital replacement cost*	0	0	400,000
Equipment maintenance cost	0	450,000	600,000
Cost of environmental damage insurance	50,000	50,000	50,000
Cost to investigate possible environmental damage	100,000	100,000	100,000
Facility modification costs	0	0	700,000
Total costs	**$1,150,000**	**$4,100,000**	**$6,850,000**
Percent capacity level	0%	50%	85%
Cost per percent of capacity	**N/A**	**$ 82,000**	**$ 81,000**

*Represents depreciation on capital replacement items.

percentage, the cost per percent of capacity, and the facility's overhead cost. For many of the analyses, the information assembled must be for three activity levels: minimum, normal, and maximum capacity levels. The reason for the threefold format (as shown in Exhibit 13.4) is that management may not use the facility as much as it anticipates, in which case it must be aware of the minimum costs that still will be incurred as well as the extra costs that must be covered if the facility runs at the highest possible rate of production. The primary analyses are listed next.

- *Determine the facility overhead cost required for minimum, standard, and maximum capacity.* Any facility requires a minimum cost to maintain, even if it is not running. Such costs include taxes, security, insurance, and building maintenance. You must know this minimum cost level in case the company does not use the facility but still must pay for the upkeep. Also, current accounting records will reveal the overhead needed to run the facility at a normal level, and the industrial engineering or production personnel can estimate the additional costs needed to run the plant at full capacity.
- *Ascertain the amount of capital replacements needed.* Some machinery will be so worn out or outdated that it must be replaced. An industrial engineer or production manager can walk through the facility and determine the condition of the equipment. If the condition is not readily apparent, perusing the maintenance records will reveal which machines require so much continuing work that a complete replacement is a more efficient alternative.
- *Find out the periodic maintenance cost of existing equipment.* Even if equipment does not require replacement, it still must be maintained, which can be a considerable cost. This information should be obtained for the normal run rate and estimated for the maximum capacity level.
- *Determine the maximum production capacity.* The industrial engineering staff must estimate the maximum capacity level at which the facility can run, subject to expenditures for equipment replacements and facility modifications.

- *Investigate any environmental liabilities.* Sometimes the target company is more than willing to get rid of a facility if it suspects there is environmental damage that must be fixed. This can be an extraordinarily expensive item and sometimes can exceed the cost of the entire facility. To guard against this problem, determine the cost of conducting an environmental investigation as well as the cost of insurance to provide coverage in case such damage is discovered after the purchase date.
- *Determine the cost of modifications needed to increase the capacity of the facility.* Unless a facility has been laid out very carefully in the beginning for the highest possible maximization of throughput, it is likely that it can use a significant overhaul of its layout. To do this, the industrial engineering staff must review the current situation and recommend the shifting of equipment and installation of additional materials movement capabilities.

The preceding analyses are summarized in the sample capacity analysis report shown in Exhibit 13.4, which includes low-medium-high categories for costs based on projected capacity utilization levels. At the bottom of the example, all costs are converted into a dollar amount for each percent of capacity used. Note that there is no utilization listed for the minimum level, since the facility is shuttered under this assumption.

Assets Analysis

A company sometimes will acquire just the assets of another organization. This is most common when there is some risk associated with the liabilities of the target company, such as lawsuits or environmental problems, or an excessive amount of debt. When assets are purchased, the buyer can be quite selective in buying only those assets that are of the most value, such as patents, brands, or personnel, which have been covered in previous sections. At this point, we note only these additional analyses needed to ensure that all other assets are reviewed properly prior to an acquisition:

- *Conduct a fixed asset audit.* Before paying for an asset, make sure that the asset is there. The fixed asset records of some companies are in such poor condition that assets still on the books may have been disposed of years before. An appraiser or an internal audit team can conduct this review.
- *Appraise the value of fixed assets.* Even if an asset exists, it may have far less value than the amount listed in the fixed asset database. To be sure of the current value of all assets, have an appraiser review them and determine their value. The final appraisal report should contain two values for each asset—the rush liquidation value and a higher value based on a more careful liquidation approach. These two values can be the focus of a great deal of negotiating between the buyer and the target company, since the buyer will want to pay based on the rush liquidation value and the target company will prefer to sell at the price indicated by the slower liquidation approach.
- *Ascertain the existence of liens against assets.* A company should not purchase an asset if there is a lien against it. Liens usually occur when the target company has used the asset as collateral for loans or used leases to finance the purchase of specific assets. The standard procedure in an acquisition is to have lenders remove liens prior to the completion of an acquisition, which frequently requires

paying off those lenders with a new "bridge" loan that covers the period of a few weeks or days between the removal of liens and the transfer of payment from the buyer to the target company, which is used to pay off the bridge loan.

- *Determine the collectibility of accounts receivable.* If the purchase includes all current accounts receivable, trace the largest invoices back to specific shipments and confirm them with the customers to whom the invoices were sent. Also, be sure to trace the history of bad debt write-offs to determine an appropriate average amount that will reflect the amount of the current accounts receivable that will become bad debt.
- *Verify the bank reconciliation for all bank accounts.* For any checking or investment account, verify the amount of cash at the bank and reconcile it to the amount listed in the corporate accounting records. Also, investigate any reconciling items to ensure that they are appropriate.
- *Audit the existence and valuation of remaining assets.* There are usually a number of smaller-dollar assets on the books, such as the payoff value of life insurance, deposits on rentals and leases, and loans to employees or officers. All of these items must be audited, both through investigation of the original contracts on which they are based and through confirmations from those entities that owe the target company money.
- *Determine the value of any tax loss carryforward.* If the buyer is acquiring a tax loss carryforward from the target company, it can use this to reduce its own tax burden. Use either the corporate tax staff or outside auditors to review not only the validity of the target company's tax returns to ensure that the reported loss on which the carryforward is based is valid but also the tax laws to ensure that the company is qualified to use the loss carryforward (which, under current laws, can be recognized only over a very long time period).

A sample of an analysis report for assets is noted in Exhibit 13.5.

In Exhibit 13.5, only the appraised rapid liquidation value of the assets to be purchased is listed in the "Valuation Summary" column; two other forms of asset valuation are noted in the "Additional Information" column. The reason for this treatment of asset values is that the report is designed to present the lowest possible asset

EXHIBIT 13.5 Analysis Report for Assets

	Additional Information	Valuation Summary
Appraised value of assets (rapid liquidation)		$ 16,000,000
Appraised value of assets (slow liquidation)	$18,500,000	
Book value of assets	19,000,000	
Book value of assets with outstanding liens	19,000,000	
Book value of accounts receivable		5,500,000
Recommended bad debt reserve		−150,000
Value of cash and investments		750,000
Net present value of remaining assets	Discount rate is 13%	629,500
Net present value of tax loss carryforwards	Discount rate is 13%	2,575,000
Total asset valuation		**$25,304,500**

value, which is used to determine the lowest offering price for the purchase of the target company's assets. The other higher asset values are included as notations, in case you want to bid a higher dollar amount and need to determine its upper boundaries for a reasonable offer price. In addition, the value of remaining assets and the tax loss carryforward are both listed at their NPVs. The reason for using discounting for these two items is that they may not be liquidated readily in the short term. For example, other assets may include loans to employees or officers that will take several years to collect, while usually only a small portion of a tax loss carryforward can be used in each year. Accordingly, the discount rate for the NPV calculation for each of these line items is noted in the "Additional Information" column in the example. Also, the bad debt deduction from the accounts receivable is not the one used by the target company but is the one compiled by the analysis team, following its review of the history of bad debt write-offs and the risk of bad debt occurrences for the current group of accounts receivable.

Liabilities Analysis

If a company decides to purchase a target company as a complete entity rather than buying pieces of it, the liabilities side of the balance sheet also will be part of the purchase and will require analysis. The main liability analyses are presented next.

- *Reconcile unpaid debt to lender balances.* There may be a difference between the amount recorded on the company's books as the debt liability and the lender's version of the amount still payable. If there is some doubt regarding whose version is correct, always use the amount noted by the lender, since this entity will not release its lien on company assets until it believes itself to be fully paid.
- *Look for unrecorded debt.* A target company may have incorrectly reported a capital lease as an operating lease or may be recording some other form of debt payment as an expense without recording the underlying debt liability. Review the target company's stream of payments to see if there are any continuing payments—most likely in the same amount from period to period—that indicate the presence of a debt paydown.
- *Audit accounts payable.* Verify that all accounts payable listed on the target company's books are actual expenses and not duplications of earlier payments. Also, investigate the unvouchered accounts payable to see if these are all approved and binding expenses, and if there are additional receipts for which there are no existing accounts payable listed in the accounting records.
- *Audit accrued liabilities.* A target company that wants to obtain the highest possible selling price will downplay these expenses, so be careful to verify the existence of all possible accrued expenses and then recalculate how the accruals were derived to ensure that the underlying expenses that these accruals eventually will offset are accurate. These are among the more common accruals:
  - Income taxes
  - Payroll taxes
  - Personal property taxes
  - Warranty costs
  - Product recalls

EXHIBIT 13.6 Analysis Report for Liabilities

Description	Additional Information	Summary Revenues and Costs
Book balance of debt		$ 3,750,000
Add: Additional lender balance due	See Note 1	15,000
Add: Unrecorded capital leases	See Note 2	175,000
Book balance of accounts payable		2,200,000
Add: Unrecorded accounts payable	See Note 3	28,000
Subtract: Duplicate accounts payable	See Note 4	–2,000
Book balance of accrued liabilities		450,000
Add: Additional accrual for property taxes	See Note 5	80,000
Add: Accrual for workers' compensation insurance	See Note 6	15,000
Total liabilities valuation		**$6,711,000**

Note 1. Company recorded $15,000 in late interest payments as a debt reduction.
Note 2. Capital leases for six forklifts recorded as expenses.
Note 3. No supplier invoice recorded for maintenance supplies received on last day of the month.
Note 4. Supplier invoices for in-house construction work recorded under both vouchered and unvouchered accounts payable.
Note 5. Original accrual did not reflect an increase of 2.3% in the tax rate.
Note 6. Original accrual based on a payroll level that is 15% lower than the actual payroll amount.

All of the preceding analyses are summarized into the sample analysis report for liabilities shown in Exhibit 13.6. Of particular interest are the line items for reconciliation problems, such as extra debt and accounts payable, as well as corrections to the accrued expenses. All of these adjustments are used to negotiate a lower price for the target company, since the higher liabilities reduce its net value.

Profitability Analysis

There are several methods you can use when reviewing the profitability of a target company. One is to track the trends in several key variables, since these will indicate worsening profit situations. Also, it is important to segment costs and profits by customer, to see if certain customers soak up an inordinate proportion of the expenses. Further, it may be possible to determine the headcount associated with each major transaction, to determine the possibility of reducing expenses by imposing transaction-related efficiencies that have worked for the acquiring company. The intent of these analyses is to determine quickly the current state and trend of a target company's profits as well as to pinpoint those customers and costs that are associated with the majority of profits and losses. The main analyses are presented next.

- *Review a trend line of revenues.* If there has been a decline in the rate of growth or an overall decline in revenues, review the company's percentage of the total market to see if the cause might be a shrinkage in the overall market. If not, review sales by product and customer to determine the exact cause of the problem.

- *Review a trend line of bad debt expense.* As a market matures and additional sales are harder to come by, a company's management may loosen its credit terms, allowing it to increase sales at the cost of a higher level of bad debt, which may exceed the additional gross margin earned from the incremental sales that were added. To see if a target company has resorted to this approach to increasing sales, review the trend line of bad debt expense to see if there has been a significant increase. Also, review the current accounts receivable for old invoices that have not yet been written off as bad debt, and also see if there are sales credits that are actually bad debts. The sum of these items constitutes the true bad debt expense.

- *Review a trend line of sales discounts.* As a follow-up to the last item, management may offer discounts to customers in advance for additional sales or add customers who are in the habit of taking discounts, whether approved or not. These issues are most common when a company's sales are no longer trending upward and management is looking for a new approach to spur sales, even at the cost of reduced margins due to the discounts. These discounts may be stored in a separate account for sales discounts or mixed in with sales credits of other kinds.

- *Review a trend line of material costs.* For most organizations outside of the service sector, material costs are the largest cost, and so require a reasonable degree of attention. The analysis team cannot hope to delve into all possible aspects of material costs during a due diligence review, such as variances for scrap, purchase prices, or cycle counting adjustments. However, it is easy to run a trend line of material costs for the last few years, just to see if these costs are changing as a proportion of sales. Due to the large overall cost of materials, a small increase in costs here can relate to the entire cost of a department in other areas of the company, so a change of as little as 1% in this expense category is a cause for concern.

- *Review a trend line of direct labor costs.* Review the trend line of direct labor costs in much the same manner as for material costs. Although this is usually a much smaller cost than for materials, it is still sufficiently large to be a cause for concern if there is a significant trend line of increasing expenses.

- *Review a trend line of gross margins.* This measure is worthy of comparison to industry averages or to the gross margins of specific competitors so the acquiring company can gain some idea of the production efficiencies of the company it is attempting to purchase.

- *Review a trend line of net margins.* If the gross margin looks reasonable, proceed to a trend-line analysis of net margins. If there is a declining trend here that was not apparent in the preceding gross margin analysis, focus on the sales, general, and administrative expense areas to see where the cost increase has occurred.

- *Ascertain the gross profit by product.* Review the gross profit for each product at the direct cost level to determine which ones have excessively low profit levels and are targets for either withdrawal from the market or a price increase. If possible, also determine the cost of fixed assets that are associated with each product (i.e., product-specific production equipment), so that the buyer can budget for an asset reduction alongside any product terminations.

- *Review a trend line of overhead personnel per major customer.* Determine the overhead needed to support a profitable base of customers with a ratio of overhead personnel to the number of major customers. This review can extend much more deeply to determine which customers require inordinate amounts of time by the support staff, although this information is rarely available.

■ *Review a trend line of overhead personnel per transaction.* Determine the number of personnel involved in all major transactions, such as accounts payable, accounts receivable, receiving, and purchasing, and divide this number into the annual total of all these transactions. If there appears to be an excessive number of employees per transaction, the acquirer may be able to reduce personnel costs in these areas.

As part of a due diligence analysis, these measures and trend lines will tell where to focus the bulk of the analysis team's attention in determining the extent of problem areas and their impact on profitability. In the example analysis report shown in Exhibit 13.7, a qualitative review of each analysis area is noted, since this review is intended to find further problems, not to devise a valuation for the target company

EXHIBIT 13.7 Analysis Report for Profitability

Type of Analysis Conducted	Notes
Review a trend line of revenues	Percentage rate of growth has declined in last two years.
Review a trend line of bad debt expense	Bad debt expense has increased, due to relaxation of credit standards.
Review a trend line of sales discounts	80% of the newest customers have all been given sales discounts of 10 % to 15%.
Review a trend line of material costs	No significant change.
Review a trend line of direct labor costs	No significant change.
Review a trend line of gross margins	The gross margin has dropped 13% in the last two years, entirely due to increased bad debts and sales discounts.
Review a trend line of net margins	Slightly worse reduction than indicated by the gross margin trend-line analysis.
Ascertain the gross profit by product	All products experienced a reduction in gross profit in the last two years.
Ascertain the gross profit by customer	Sales to older customers have retained their gross margin levels, but newer customers have substantially lower margins.
Review a trend line of overhead personnel per major customer	There has been a slight increase in the collections staffing level in the last two years due to the difficulty of collecting from newer customers.
Review a trend line of overhead personnel per transaction	No significant change.

Conclusion and recommendations: The target company has experienced flattening sales and so has shifted new sales efforts to low-end customers who cannot pay on time and will accept only lower-priced products, which also increases the overhead needed to service these accounts. Recommend dropping all low-margin, low-credit customers as well as all associated overhead costs to increase profits.

Cash Flow Analysis

The analysis of a target company's cash flows is a critical item if the entire organization is to be purchased. If you were to miss this item, the company could find itself paying for an organization that must be supported with a massive additional infusion of cash. The key cash flow analyses to focus on are presented next.

- *Review trend line of net cash flow before debt and interest payments.* Begin with the cash flows shown on the statement of cash flows. Ignore the impact of debt and interest payments, since inordinately high cash flows to pay for these two items may mask a perfectly good underlying business. If there is a pronounced additional requirement for more cash to fund either the acquisition of fixed assets or working capital, identify the culprit and proceed with the next cash flow analyses. This first trend line, then, was to determine the existence of a problem and to define it more precisely.
- *Review trend line of working capital.* Poor customer credit review policies or inadequate collection efforts will lead to an increased investment in accounts receivable, while excessive production or product obsolescence will increase the inventory investment. Also, a reduction in the days of credit before payments are made to suppliers will reduce the free credit that a company receives from them. To see if there is a problem in this area, add the total accounts receivable to inventory and subtract the accounts payable balance to arrive at the total working capital amount. Plot this information on a trend line that extends back for at least a year. If there is a steady increase in total working capital, determine which of the three components has caused the problem.
- *Segment working capital investment by customer and product.* Focus on the accounts receivable and finished goods inventory investments to see if there a specific customer is responsible for a working capital increase, or review just the inventory investment to see if a specific product is the cause. Cross-reference this information against analyses for profitability by customer and product to see if there are any combinations of low-profit, high-investment customers or products that are obvious targets for termination.
- *Review trend line of capital purchases.* This is a simple matter to investigate by general fixed asset category, since this information is reported on the balance sheet. However, there may be good reasons for large increases in fixed asset investments, such as automation, the addition of new facilities, or a general level of competitiveness in the industry that requires constant capital improvements. Only by understanding the underlying reasons for cash usage in this area can you be certain that cash can be saved here by reducing the volume of asset purchases.

The analysis report for cash flows is composed primarily of judgments regarding the need for historical cash flows, estimates of future cash flows, and how the acquiring company can alter these flows through specific management actions. A sample of such a report is shown in Exhibit 13.8.

Legal Analysis

Besides purely financial issues, the legal staff must peruse a wide array of legal issues. In most cases, the analysis issues noted here are related to various kinds of

EXHIBIT 13.8 Analysis Report for Cash Flow

Type of Analysis Conducted	Notes
Review trend line of net cash flow before debt and interest payments	The target company is experiencing a massive cash outflow in both the working capital and fixed assets areas.
Review trend line of working capital	There is a severe cash outflow due to $2 million in accounts receivable invested in the Gidget Company, as well as a large investment in five distribution warehouses for its Auto-Klean product, each of which requires $1.5 million in inventory.
Segment working capital investment by customer and product	The main cash outflows are due to the Gidget Company customer and the Auto-Klean product.
Review trend line of capital purchases	Has purchased $10 million of automation equipment to improve margins on its sales to the Gidget Company.

Conclusions and recommendations: There is a major investment in sales to the Gidget Company, which is not justified by the 5% return on sales to that customer. The receivable investment of $2 million can be eliminated by stopping sales to this customer, while $5 million can be realized from the sale of automation equipment used for the production of items for sale to it. Also, the number of distribution warehouses for the Auto-Klean product can be reduced by two, which will decrease the inventory investment by $3 million. The amount of cash investment that can be eliminated as a result of these actions is $10 million.

contracts. When these issues arise, a key analysis point is to see if they can be dissolved in the event of a corporate change of control. Many contracts contain this feature, so that onerous agreements will not cause a potentially high-priced purchase to fall apart. Key legal reviews are presented next.

- *Bylaws.* This document will include any "poison pill" provisions that are intended to make a change of control very expensive.
- *Certificate of incorporation, including name changes.* This document is used to find the list of all names under which the target company operates, which is needed for real estate title searches.
- *Employment contracts.* Key employees may be guaranteed high pay levels for a number of years or a golden parachute clause that guarantees them a large payment if the company is sold.
- *Engineering reports.* These documents will note any structural weaknesses in corporate buildings that may require expensive repairs.
- *Environmental exposure.* Review all literature received from the Environmental Protection Agency (EPA) and from the Occupational Safety and Health Administration (OSHA), and conduct environmental hazard testing around all company premises to ascertain the extent of potential environmental litigation.
- *Insurance policies.* Verify that the existing insurance policies cover all significant risks that are not otherwise covered by internal safety policies. Also, compare these policies to those held by the buyer to see if consolidating the policies for both companies can lead to savings.
- *Labor union agreements.* If the target company is a union shop, the union contract may contain unfavorable provisions related to work rules, guaranteed pay

increases, payouts, or guaranteed retraining funds in the event of a plant closure, or onerous benefit payments.

- *Leases.* Creating a schedule of all current leases tells a buyer the extent of commitments to pay for leased assets as well as interest rates and any fees for early lease terminations.

- *Licenses.* A license for a target company to do business, usually granted by a local government but also by another company for whom it is the distributor or franchisee, may not be transferable if there is a change of ownership. This can be quite a surprise to a buyer that now finds it cannot use the company it has just bought.

- *Litigation.* Litigation is a broad area that requires a considerable amount of review before legal counsel can be reasonably satisfied as to the extent and potential liability associated with current and potential litigation. This review should encompass an investigation of all civil suits and criminal actions that may include contract disputes, fraud, discrimination, breach of employment contract, wrongful termination, inadequate disclosure issues, deceptive trade practices, antitrust suits, or other issues. It also should include tax claims and notices of potential litigation received from any of these government agencies:
  - Department of Justice
  - Department of Labor
  - Equal Employment Opportunity Commission
  - Federal Trade Commission
  - Internal Revenue Service
  - Securities and Exchange Commission (applies only to a publicly held entity)

- *Marketing materials.* The target company's advertising of its product capabilities can be a source of potential litigation if the publicized product claims are overstated.

- *Pension plans.* Determine the size of the employer-funded portion of the pension plan. Doing this will require the services of an actuary to verify the current cost of required future funding.

- *Product warranty agreements.* Review the published warranty that is issued for each product to verify its term as well as what specific features it will replace in the event of product failure.

- *Sponsorship agreements.* A target company may have a long-term commitment to sponsor an event that will require a significant expenditure to maintain or terminate.

- *Supplier or customer contracts.* A target company may be locked into a long-term agreement with one or more of its suppliers or customers, possibly guaranteeing unfavorable terms that will noticeably impact profits if the buyer purchases the company.

Although these nonfinancial issues are related primarily to the legal liabilities of a corporate entity, in a few cases the analysis team may need to estimate possible attendant costs. For example, the team may have to quantify the extra cost required to fulfill any poison pill provisions. You also can determine the NPV of all employment, labor union, and lease provisions that require a specified minimum set of payments for a designated time period. An example of the format used to summarize these expenses is shown in Exhibit 13.9.

EXHIBIT 13.9 Analysis Report for Legal Issues

Description	Additional Information	Summary of Costs
Poison pill payout provision	Bylaws section 2, clause 14	$ 12,500,000
Golden parachute provision	For all officers	3,250,000
Discounted cost of all lease provisions	Copiers, forklifts	320,000
Discounted pension plan funding requirements		4,750,000
Discounted cost of sponsorship agreement		220,000
Termination payment for long-term supplier contracts		540,000
Total cost of contractual and legal issues		**$21,580,000**

Complexity Analysis

The primary objective of complexity analysis is to determine if it will be too difficult to integrate an acquiree; a secondary objective is to determine the level of risk posed by the acquiree's general level of complexity.

One area to consider is the sources of the acquiree's revenue. The level of complexity and risk is increased when revenue is derived from multiple businesses, since the acquirer must devote additional levels of management resources to each of those businesses. Complexity and risk also increase when a significant percentage of revenue is derived from a small number of large transactions that are custom-tailored to individual customers. These transactions tend to be highly volatile in their amount and frequency, making it difficult to estimate future revenue levels and attendant cash flows.

The tax rate also can contribute to complexity and risk. This is especially true if the acquiree has located its headquarters in a tax haven, which indicates a strong interest in tax avoidance that likely has led to the use of a variety of complicated tax avoidance schemes. A further indicator of tax complexity is a substantial difference between the reported level of book and tax income. Finally, a volatile effective tax rate indicates that the acquiree is engaged in a variety of one-time tax dodges. Although all of these issues may be caused by completely legal transactions, they clearly indicate that the company has altered its operations in a variety of ways to take maximum advantage of the tax laws, and this may require considerable ongoing effort to maintain.

Another indicator of complexity is the presence of off-balance-sheet assets and liabilities, such as variable-interest entities, research and development partnerships, and operating leases. The intent of these transactions may have little to do with dressing up the balance sheet and may be based on solid operational reasons, but they still are more likely to cause sudden changes in the reported condition of the company if underlying accounting rules are altered to require their full presentation.

Finally, a key area that many acquiring companies completely neglect is the consideration of cultural differences. Although these issues are difficult to analyze quantitatively, they can be the primary issue that results in a failed merger, and so are worth considerable review time. Some of the key factors to consider are listed next.

- What is the company's intent in forcing the acquired company to use its business practices?
- What are the key differences in the decision-making processes of the companies?
- What are the differences in the performance monitoring and bonus payment systems of the companies?
- How do the companies resolve conflicts?
- What types of formal and informal communication systems are used by the companies?
- What is the command structure of the companies?

If there are significant differences between the companies in more than one of the listed areas, the success of the acquisition will be at risk. If so, consider in detail what changes will be needed in order to make the two company cultures work together, or scrap the acquisition entirely.

Valuing an Acquisition Target

Once a buyer has identified a prospective target, it needs to establish an initial valuation for it. In this section, we describe a variety of valuation methods, the concept of the control premium, the discounted cash flow model, a variety of qualitative factors that can influence the valuation, and reasons for using different forms of payment.

Alternative Valuation Methods

There are a number of ways to value a target company. The most common is discounted cash flow, but it is best to evaluate a number of alternative methods and compare their results to see if several approaches arrive at approximately the same general valuation. Doing this gives the buyer solid grounds for making its offer.

Using a variety of methods is especially important for valuing newer target companies with minimal historical results, and especially for those growing quickly—all of their cash is being used for growth, so cash flow is an inadequate basis for valuation.

If the target company is publicly held, the buyer simply can base its valuation on the *current market price per share*, multiplied by the number of shares outstanding. The current trading price of a company's stock is not a good valuation tool if the stock is thinly traded. In this case, a small number of trades can alter the market price to a substantial extent, so that the buyer's estimate is far off from the value it normally would assign to the target. Most target companies do not issue publicly traded stock, so other methods must be used to derive their valuation.

When a private company wants to be valued using a market price, it can adopt the unusual ploy of filing for an initial public offering while also being courted by the buyer. By doing so, the buyer is forced to make an offer that is near the market valuation at which the target expects its stock to be traded. If the buyer declines to bid that high, the target still has the option of going public and realizing value by selling shares to the general public. However, given the expensive control measures mandated by the Sarbanes-Oxley Act and the stock lockup periods required for many new public companies, a target's shareholders are usually more than willing to accept a buyout offer if the price is reasonably close to the target's expected market value.

Another option is to use a *revenue multiple* or *EBITDA (earnings before interest, taxes, depreciation, and amortization) multiple*. It is easy to look up the market capitalizations and financial information for thousands of publicly held companies. The buyer converts this information into a multiples table, such as the one shown in Exhibit 13.10, which itemizes a selection of valuations within the consulting industry. The table should be restricted to comparable companies in the same industry as that of the seller and of

EXHIBIT 13.10 Comparable Valuations Table

| | ($ Millions) | | | | | |
	Market Capitalization	Revenue	EBITDA*	EBITDA* Percentage	Revenue Multiple	EBITDA* Multiple
Large Caps (> $5 billion)						
General Dynamics	$36,220	$27,240	$3,113	11%	1.3	11.6
Lockheed Martin	$43,020	$41,862	$4,527	11%	1.0	9.5
Northrop Grumman	$25,350	$32,018	$3,006	9%	0.8	8.4
Medium Caps (< $5 billion)						
ManTech International	$ 1,630	$ 1,448	$ 114	8%	1.1	14.3
Perot Systems	$ 1,850	$ 2,612	$ 184	7%	0.7	10.1
SAIC, Inc.	$ 3,640	$ 8,935	$ 666	7%	0.4	5.5
SRA International	$ 1,540	$ 1,269	$ 93	7%	1.2	16.6
Small Caps (< $1.5 billion)						
CACI, Inc.	$ 1,470	$ 1,938	$ 146	8%	0.8	10.1
ICF International	$ 258	$ 727	$ 71	10%	0.4	3.6
SI International	$ 299	$ 511	$ 39	8%	0.6	7.7
Stanley, Inc.	$ 570	$ 409	$ 25	6%	1.4	22.8
Micro Caps (< $250 million)						
Dynamics Research Corp.	$ 92	$ 230	$ 13	6%	0.4	7.1
Keynote Systems	$ 210	$ 68	$ (5)	−7%	3.1	(42.0)
NCI, Inc.	$ 249	$ 304	$ 22	7%	0.8	11.3
Tier Technologies	$ 152	$ 111	$ (22)	−20%	1.4	(6.9)
Averages by Capitalization						
Large caps	$34,863	$33,707	$3,549	11%	1.0	9.8
Medium caps	$ 2,165	$ 3,566	$ 264	7%	0.6	8.2
Small caps	$ 649	$ 896	$ 70	8%	0.7	9.2
Micro caps	$ 176	$ 178	$ 2	1%	1.0	87.9

*Earnings before interest, taxes, depreciation, and amortization.

roughly the same market capitalization. If some of the information for other companies is unusually high or low, eliminate these outlying values in order to obtain a median value for the company's size range. Also, it is better to use a multiday average of market prices, since these figures are subject to significant daily fluctuation.

The buyer can use this table to derive an approximation of the price to be paid for a target company. For example, if a target has sales of $100 million and the market capitalization for several public companies in the same revenue range is 1.4 times revenue, the buyer could value the target at $140 million. This method is most useful for a turn-around situation or a fast-growth company, where there are few profits (if any). However, the revenue multiple method pays attention to only the first line of the income statement and completely ignores profitability. To avoid the risk of paying too much based on a revenue multiple, it is possible to compile an EBITDA multiple for the same group of comparable public companies, and use that information to value the target.

Better yet, use both the revenue multiple and the EBITDA multiple in concert. If the revenue multiple reveals a high valuation and the EBITDA multiple a low one, it is possible that the target is essentially buying revenues with low-margin products or services or extending credit to financially weak customers. Conversely, if the revenue multiple yields a lower valuation than the EBITDA multiple, this is more indicative of a late-stage company that is essentially a cash cow or one where management is cutting costs to increase profits, but possibly at the expense of harming revenue growth.

The revenue and EBITDA multiples just noted are not the only ones available. The table can be expanded to include the *price/earnings ratio* for a public company's traded stock. Also, if the comparable company provides one-year projections, the revenue multiple can be renamed a *trailing multiple* (for historical 12-month revenue), and the forecast can be used as the basis for a *forward multiple* (for projected 12-month revenue). The forward multiple gives a better estimate of value, because it incorporates expectations about the future. The forward multiple should be used only if the forecast comes from guidance that is issued by a public company. The company knows that its stock price will drop if it does not achieve its forecast, so the forecast is unlikely to be aggressive.

Revenue multiples are the best technique for valuing high-growth companies, since these entities usually are pouring resources into their growth and have minimal profits to report. Such companies clearly have a great deal of value, but it is not revealed through their profitability numbers.

However, multiples can be misleading. When acquisitions occur within an industry, the best financial performers with the fewest underlying problems are the choicest acquisition targets and therefore will be acquired first. When other companies in the same area later put themselves up for sale, they will use the earlier multiples to justify similarly high prices. However, because they may have lower market shares, higher cost structures, older products, and so on, the multiples may not be valid. Thus, it is useful to know some of the underlying characteristics of the companies that were sold previously, to see if the comparable multiple should be applied to the current target company.

Another possibility is to replace the market capitalization figure in the table with *enterprise value*. The enterprise value is a company's market capitalization, plus its total debt outstanding, minus any cash on hand. In essence, it is a company's theoretical takeover price, because the buyer would have to buy all of the stock and pay off existing debt while pocketing any remaining cash.

Another way to value an acquisition is to use a *database of comparable transactions* to determine what was paid for other recent acquisitions. Investment bankers have access to this information through a variety of private databases, and a great deal of information can be collected online through public filings or press releases.

The buyer also can derive a valuation based on a target's *underlying real estate values*. This method works only in those isolated cases where the target has a substantial real estate portfolio. For example, in the retailing industry, where some chains own the property on which their stores are situated, the value of the real estate is greater than the cash flow generated by the stores themselves. In cases where the business is financially troubled, it is entirely possible that the purchase price is based entirely on the underlying real estate, with the operations of the business itself being valued at essentially zero. The buyer uses the value of the real estate as the primary reason for completing the deal. In some situations, the prospective buyer has no real estate experience and so is more likely to heavily discount the potential value of any real estate when making an offer. If the seller wishes to increase its price, it could consider selling the real estate prior to the sale transaction. By doing so, it converts a *potential* real estate sale price (which might otherwise be discounted by the buyer) into an achieved sale with cash in the bank and also may record a one-time gain on its books based on the asset sale, which may have a positive impact on its sale price.

An acquiree's real estate may even be the means for an acquirer to finance the deal. For example, if the acquiree owns property, it may be possible to enter into a sale-and-leaseback transaction that generates enough cash to pay for the acquisition. Another possibility is to look for property leases held by the acquiree that are below current market rates and sublease them for a profit. Finally, it may be possible to consolidate acquiree locations and sell any remaining properties that are no longer needed.

If a target has products that the buyer could develop in-house, an alternative valuation method is to compare the *cost of in-house development* to the cost of acquiring the completed product through the target. This type of valuation is especially important if the market is expanding rapidly right now, and the buyer otherwise will forgo sales if it takes the time to pursue an in-house development path. In this case, the proper valuation technique is to combine the cost of an in-house development effort with the present value of profits forgone by waiting to complete the in-house project. Interestingly, this is the only valuation technique where most of the source material comes from the buyer's financial statements rather than those of the seller.

The most conservative valuation method of all is the *liquidation value* method. This is an analysis of what the selling entity would be worth if all of its assets were to be sold off. This method assumes that the ongoing value of the company as a business entity is eliminated, leaving the individual auction prices at which its fixed assets, properties, and other assets can be sold off, less any outstanding liabilities. It is useful for the buyer to at least estimate this number, so that it can determine its downside risk in case it completes the acquisition but the acquired business then fails utterly.

The *replacement value* method yields a somewhat higher valuation than the liquidation value method. Under this approach, the buyer calculates what it would cost to duplicate the target company. The analysis addresses the replacement of the seller's key infrastructure. This can yield surprising results if the seller owns infrastructure that originally required lengthy regulatory approval. For example, if the seller owns a chain of mountain huts that are located on government property, it is essentially impossible to replace them at all, or only at vast expense. An additional factor in this analysis is the time required to replace the target. If the time period for replacement is considerable, the buyer may be forced to pay a premium in order to gain quick access to a key market.

It also is possible to create a *hybrid valuation model* that mixes several of these methods. For example, the buyer could calculate the liquidation value of a target and add to that number the next two or three years of free cash flow. This method yields a conservative valuation that the buyer would be hard put *not* to realize and which might form the basis for a minimum bid.

Although all of these methods can be used for valuation, they usually supplement the primary method: the discounted cash flow (DCF) method, which is addressed shortly.

Control Premium

Why does a buyer offer to pay more for a target than the price at which the target's shares currently trade? One reason is certainly to keep other potential bidders from entering the fray with their own bids. However, the real reason is that shares trade based on their value to individual shareholders, who have no control over the business; thus, a share price is based only on the prospective financial return that a shareholder expects to achieve. However, if a buyer wishes to obtain control over the target, it should expect to pay a control premium over the current stock price. By doing so, it has complete control over the potential size and timing of cash flows. Historically, this has made the control premium worth somewhere in the range of 35% to 50% of a target's freely traded stock value. Recent control premiums for the purchase of publicly traded companies can be found in the annual *Control Premium Study* published by Mergerstat (located at www.mergerstat.com).

Synergy Gains

If the buyer pays the full share value of a target as well as a control premium, how does it expect to earn a return? The target's existing shareholders appear to be receiving all of the value inherent in the business. There are certainly cases where the target's stock price may be unusually low, such as when industry is at the low point of a business cycle, where profits are minimized. In such cases, the buyer snaps up deals based on timing. However, these are isolated instances. In most cases, the buyer is depending on the realization of synergies between its own company and the target, which may be considerable.

A buyer with expert knowledge of potential synergy gains can earn substantial amounts that comfortably exceed the purchase price. However, a buyer may run into an experienced seller who wants a share of those synergy gains. If the seller wants payment for an excessive portion of the expected gains, the buyer must walk away from the deal—there is simply no way to earn a profit from the transaction.

Synergies are realized only by strategic buyers, not financial buyers. A financial buyer simply buys a business in order to hold it and gain appreciation value from its internal growth over time. A strategic buyer, however, is willing to pay a higher price in the knowledge that it can squeeze out extra value. Thus, the strategic buyer may be willing to pay a higher price than a financial buyer, perhaps in the range of a 5% to 20% premium over what a financial buyer would pay.

Thus, a canny seller will court strategic buyers in order to maximize the price paid. In so doing, the seller must be aware that it has to leave a generous amount of the potential synergies to the buyer, in order to make the acquisition sufficiently tempting.

Discounted Cash Flow Model

The best possible reason to buy a company is for the cash that it can generate. The DCF model is designed to reveal the *free cash flow* that is available for distribution to investors at the end of each year shown in the model. This means that the model not only must reveal the cash generated by ongoing operations but also must subtract out all planned capital expenditures and tax payments, so that completely un-restricted cash surpluses or shortfalls are revealed for each year in the model.

The typical DCF model includes a projection of the target's cash flows for the next five years, plus a terminal value for what the target theoretically will be sold for at the end of that time period (which is based on prices currently being obtained for comparable companies). An example of a DCF is shown in Exhibit 13.11.

EXHIBIT 13.11 Discounted Cash Flow Model

	Year 1	Year 2	Year 3	Year 4	Year 5	Terminal Value
+ Revenues	$438	$473	$511	$552	$596	
−Cost of goods sold	$175	$189	$204	$221	$238	
= Gross margin	$263	$284	$307	$331	$358	
−General and administrative	$171	$184	$199	$215	$232	
= Earnings before interest and taxes	$92	$99	$107	$116	$125	
−Interest	$5	$5	$5	$5	$5	
−Taxes	$33	$35	$38	$41	$44	
−Incremental working capital change	$22	$24	$26	$30	$33	
−Incremental fixed asset change	$15	$16	$18	$19	$20	
+ Depreciation	$14	$15	$17	$18	$19	
= Cash flow	$31	$34	$37	$39	$42	$120
Discount rate	10%	10%	10%	10%	10%	
Annual discount rate	0.90909	0.82645	0.75131	0.68301	0.62092	0.56447
Discounted cash flows	$28	$28	$28	$26	$26	$68
Net present value	$204					

EXHIBIT 13.12 Weighted Average Cost of Capital Calculation

Capital Type	Amount Outstanding	Interest Rate	Cost
Debt	$25,000,000	7%	$1,750,000
Preferred stock	10,000,000	10%	1,000,000
Equity	30,000,000	14%	4,200,000
Totals	$65,000,000	**10.7%**	$6,950,000

The buyer should beware of models where the terminal value is by far the largest component of the model; the terminal value is the least predictable part of the valuation, because it is the farthest into the future and assumes a specific sale price that is very difficult to justify. If the terminal value comprises the bulk of the DCF, the buyer will need to supplement the DCF analysis with other forms of valuation analysis.

A major part of the DCF analysis is the interest rate that is used for discounting the value of future cash flows to the current period. This interest rate is equivalent to the buyer's incremental cost of capital. The cost of capital is the weighted average cost of the buyer's debt, preferred stock, and equity. The cost of equity is the most difficult to determine but usually involves the capital asset pricing model. On an extremely simplified basis, the cost of equity is at least 5% to 7% higher than the current interest rate on U.S. government treasury notes, and it can be substantially higher. As an example, Exhibit 13.12 shows the dollar amount of the three components of a company's cost of capital, yielding a weighted average cost of capital of 10.7%.

It is preferable to use the *incremental* cost of capital, which incorporates the buyer's most recent cost of debt. The incremental rate is better than the overall corporate rate, because that is the rate at which the buyer will need to obtain funding to pay for the target.

It also is possible to adjust the cost of capital for the perceived risk of the target company. For example, if the target is a well-established one with predictable cash flows, the buyer simply can use its cost of capital as the discount rate. However, if the target's cash flows are more uncertain, the buyer can add a risk percentage to its discount rate. By doing so, cash flows that are farther in the future will be worth less in the DCF, resulting in a lower valuation for the target.

The buyer also may adjust the discount rate downward for any especially valuable characteristics that the seller may have, such as subject-matter experts or patents on key technology. However, this is an entirely subjective reduction. The buyer would do better to attempt to quantify these characteristics of the seller elsewhere in the model, such as an increase in revenues from company-wide use of the seller's patented products.

The interest rate used in the debt portion of the cost of capital can vary considerably, resulting in significant changes in the value of the target company. For example, if interest rates increase, the buyer's cost of capital also increases. When the buyer uses this increased cost of capital as its discount factor in the DCF model, target company valuations will decline. Conversely, if interest rates drop, target values increase. Thus, external economic factors driving interest rates are related directly to acquisition prices.

Also, the size of the target can alter the buyer's cost of capital. For example, if the prospective deal would require a large amount of financing by the buyer, it is likely that its incremental debt cost will increase, which in turn impacts its cost of capital. If this is the case, use the projected increase in the cost of capital as the most appropriate discount rate in the DCF model; this will make the acquisition look less attractive.

The DCF is the most reliable method for valuing a mature, slow-growth company with established cash flows. It is not used so frequently for high-growth entities that are using all available cash to support their increasing working capital needs. Instead, buyers tend to use comparable valuations for these targets. However, it is always of some value to run a DCF, too, because it reveals a reliable minimum valuation for the target. The buyer also can create a variety of cash flow projections for the target that are farther out in the future than the usual five years used for the model, in order to get some idea of what the target's cash flows will be like once its high growth period is over.

Constructing Cash Flow Scenarios

Where does the buyer obtain the information needed to construct a cash flow analysis? The seller will prefer to show estimates of future sales, which inevitably reveal an optimistic *hockey stick* of sudden growth in "just a few more months." If the buyer were to use just these projected numbers, it would likely arrive at a valuation that is too high and would overpay for the seller. A better method is to create multiple scenarios, where the seller's estimates are reserved for the most optimistic version. Another most likely estimate should be based on the seller's most recent historical results; a conservative version assumes that the seller's historical results worsen significantly.

Although the use of three cash flow scenarios certainly shows some valuation prudence, it can hide unsupported assumptions within the scenarios. For example, an analyst might assume a simplistic revenue decline of 10% in the conservative version, which is not based on any concrete risk analysis. Instead, use documented changes in specific variables in the three versions. For example, if there appears to be a risk of soft pricing in the market, use the conservative scenario to model price declines of various sizes specifically. Similarly, if there is a risk of supplier bottlenecks, model the impact of price increases for key materials. Also, if the target must match research expenditures elsewhere in the industry, review percentage changes in these expenditures. By taking the time to document these more detailed analyses, a buyer can determine the price points, volume levels, and cost structures at which a target breaks even and when the target potentially can earn a great deal of money.

Another factor to consider in one or more of the valuation scenarios is the presence or absence of seller risk guarantees. For example, if the seller is guaranteeing to pay for any undocumented lawsuits or payouts related to documented lawsuits, the buyer can eliminate this factor from its conservative scenario. In essence, the more risks the seller guarantees, the lower the expenses shown in the model, and the higher the valuation that the buyer can offer to the seller.

Once these cash flow versions are constructed, the buyer should multiply each one by a weighting factor, and not simply average them. The most likely scenario should receive the bulk of the weighting, such as 60% or 70%, with the outlying conservative and optimistic versions receiving the remainder. Thus, a 20-60-20 or 15-70-15 weighting essentially assumes that the seller's most recent historical results are most likely to continue into the future.

A more conservative method of cash flow analysis is to construct an estimate based entirely on historical results, with a weighting system that favors the most recent year. For example, if the buyer wants to model the target's past five years of results, it can multiply the target's cash flows by 5 for the most recent year, by 4 for the immediately preceding year, and so on. Once all five years have been added together, divide by 15 to arrive at the weighted cash flow for the five-year period. The resulting 5, 4, 3, 2, 1 weighting system gives some credence to relatively old cash flows and great merit to recent results. This method is not recommended, since it is based entirely on prior results and gives no weighting at all to a target's future prospects.

Cash Flow Adjusting Factors

The buyer cannot simply run a DCF of a target's existing operations and consider itself done. This would imply that the buyer intends to make virtually no changes to the target once it has completed the acquisition. In reality, there are multiple changes to be considered, many of which should be included in the projected cash flow.

In many acquisitions, the buyer assumes that the combined entities will be able to increase revenues beyond what the companies were achieving separately. However, revenue synergies are notoriously difficult to achieve, because they require the cooperation of a third party: customers. An experienced buyer usually reduces or even eliminates any revenue synergies in the cash flow model. Instead, it focuses on cost reductions, which are entirely within its control.

Not only should the buyer *not* budget for revenue gains, but it should strongly consider modeling for a modest revenue *decline* at the target that is caused by some degradation in its customer base. This is caused by any changes in service levels, salespeople, or products that customers may experience as a result of the acquisition. Also, competitors likely will be circling the target's customers like sharks, hoping to pick off a few. Further, if the buyer is planning to acquire just a single division of a larger company, the target may lose some customers simply because the associated services or products of its parent company will no longer be sold, or not as a package. Thus, a reasonable modeling technique is to incorporate a modest decline in the target's customer base, especially during the initial year of the acquisition. A common reduction in the customer base is in the range of 2% to 5%.

The buyer also must assume a variety of acquisition expenses, including legal fees, valuation services, appraisals, environmental audits, and financial audits. If the buyer has engaged in a number of acquisitions, it can easily compile a database of what these costs have been in the past and use it to estimate such costs in a prospective valuation. If the buyer anticipates diverting a substantial amount of management time toward the integration of the target's operations into those of the buyer, it also can estimate the impact of this "soft" cost on the entire business.

One likely cost control scenario is that some employees will be let go. If so, there will be some cost savings by eliminating their positions, but there also will be a short-term additional cost associated with severance pay. If the buyer is taking on this obligation, it must factor severance pay into its cash flow assumptions.

A special case is adjustments to the cash flows associated with a target's defined benefit pension plan. These costs can vary substantially over time, so an analyst should review the actuarial assumptions underlying any such plans intensively. For example, if the buyer believes that the plan is underfunded, it has reasonable grounds for demanding a reduction in the purchase price, so that it can offset the imminent funding liability. Conversely, if the plan is overfunded, the seller can bargain for a purchase price increase, which effectively pays it back for the amount of the overfunding. The funding status is by no means obvious, since it is driven by the future interest rate assumption used by the plan actuary; the higher the rate, the fewer existing assets are needed to offset projected plan liabilities. Consequently, arguments over the correct interest rate assumption will alter the purchase price and will result in changes to the DCF.

Another issue is the cyclicality of the industry in which the target is located. If there are strong historical cycles, the buyer should assume that there will be a recurrence. Industry cyclicality requires that the cash flow model assume the presence of both the upside and downside of that cycle, using historical information for both the duration and size of the cycle. This more refined cash flow model gives the buyer a reasonable idea of how cash flows will change over time. In many instances, highly variable cyclical results will force the buyer to abandon a deal, because the downside of the cycle eliminates or reverses the profits generated during other years.

An area missed by many cash flow models is the immediate sale of some assets following the acquisition. Either party may have duplicative or obsolete assets that can be dispositioned for immediate cash. If the buyer can presell some assets before a purchase agreement even closes, this is a "hard" cash inflow to include in the cash flow model.

The buyer also should be aware of the seller's fixed asset replacement cycle. It is entirely possible that the buyer has delayed key asset purchases in order to give the appearance of having excellent cash flow. However, its equipment and facilities may be so run down now that the buyer must expend significant amounts over multiple years to replace the assets. The dollar value of the replacement amounts should be gleaned during the due diligence stage and entered into the DCF.

The buyer also should include in the DCF the impact of any cost escalation clauses in the seller's contracts with its suppliers. For example, there may be a series of scheduled annual increases in a building lease or a price increase in a raw materials contract. As was the case with fixed asset replacements, these costs are not readily apparent and must be found during the due diligence process.

Finally, the buyer may have some concern about the accuracy of the financial statements it is using to compile a cash forecast, if the target cannot provide audited financial statements. If there has never been an audit, and especially if the buyer's due diligence indicates some issues with the presented financial information, it may have to adjust cash projections downward or base a valuation only on the most conservative scenario. To avoid this, the target should have its books audited for the past year (and preferably two years), in order to qualify for high cash flow assumptions in the buyer's valuation model.

Earnout

There are times when the buyer and the seller have entirely different concepts of the valuation to be used for the acquisition, usually because the buyer is basing its valuation on the seller's historical performance while the seller is using a much higher forward-looking view of its prospective performance. The *earnout* frequently is used to bridge the valuation perception gap between the two parties. Under an earnout, the seller's shareholders will be paid an additional amount by the buyer if it can achieve specific performance targets (usually the same ones it has already claimed it will achieve during the acquisition negotiations).

The earnout is also a useful tool for the buyer, because the seller's management team has a strong incentive to grow the business for the next few years. In addition, the buyer can shift a portion of its purchase price into a future liability that likely can be paid from cash earned in the future by the seller. It is also useful for the seller's shareholders, since it defers income taxes on the payment.

However, many earnouts also result in lawsuits, because the buyer merges the acquiree into another business unit, charges corporate overhead to it, or shifts key staff elsewhere in the company—all factors making it extremely difficult for the acquiree's management team still to earn the additional payment or even to determine what its performance has become. Even if there are no lawsuits, the acquiree's management team may be so focused on achieving their earnout that they do not assist the rest of the buying entity with other matters, so that corporate-level goals are not reached. Also, if the earnout award is based strictly on the achievement of revenue rather than profit, the acquiree's management team may pursue unprofitable sales in order to meet the earnout goals.

The problems with earnouts can be mitigated by continuing to track the acquiree's performance separately in the financial statements, carefully defining the earnout calculation in the original acquisition document, requiring earnouts to be based solely on net income achieved, and adding an additional layer of compensation that is based on working more closely with the rest of the buying company, such as commissions for cross-selling. Also, to keep the acquiree happy, do not institute a "cliff" goal, where no bonus is paid unless the entire target is reached. Instead, use a sliding scale, so that some bonus is paid even if only a portion of the performance target is achieved.

Qualitative Factors

Thus far, the valuation discussion has centered entirely on a quantitative analysis of how much to pay for the selling entity. Although quantitative analysis certainly forms the core of a valuation, the buyer also must consider a broad array of qualitative factors. A sampling of the more common ones are listed next.

- *Difficulty of duplication.* If a buyer perceives that the barriers to entering a seller's field of operations are high, or if the cost of duplicating the seller's operations is excessive, the buyer may be more inclined to pay a premium for the business. For example, a proprietary database may take so long to duplicate that a buyer will value the seller just based on the cost it otherwise would incur to create the database from scratch.
- *Risk of expiring contracts.* A seller whose revenues are tied to short-term sales, without immediate prospects for renewing the backlog, will be perceived to have a lower valuation than an entity possessing a strong backlog and clear evidence of long-term sales agreements with its customers.

- *Management.* A seller's cost structure, perception in the marketplace, and customer relations are driven in large part by the quality of its management team. If this group is perceived to be first class, it can increase the corporate valuation, since these people typically have exceptional skill in growing businesses and in anticipating and overcoming operational problems.
- *Client base.* A significant factor in determining valuation is the size, type, and distribution of clients. For example, a seller with a single client will be perceived to be at great risk of losing all of its sales if the client is dissatisfied. Alternatively, a broad mix of clients, particularly those large enough to support multiple sales, will reduce the perceived risk of sales loss.
- *Inherent risk.* A seller whose financial performance can be impacted dramatically by adverse situations will have a comparatively lower valuation. For example, farm businesses can be severely impacted by drought conditions.
- *Disaster analysis.* Even beyond the inherent risk just noted, the buyer should closely review the characteristics of the seller's business to see if there is any risk of a truly catastrophic failure, such as a facility being destroyed because it is situated on an earthquake fault line. Even if the probability of a disaster is low, the consequences may be so large that the buyer must either walk away from the deal or find a mitigating action to offset the risk.
- *Lawsuits.* Nothing will drive a buyer away faster than an unresolved lawsuit, especially one with a demand for a large settlement. Even if there is no lawsuit, the prospect of one, as evidenced by lawsuits targeted at others in the same industry, can have a negative impact on valuation.
- *Patents.* If a seller has established key patents or processes that give it a clear competitive advantage, this can increase its valuation level.
- *Branding.* If a seller has invested a great deal of time and effort in creating brands for its products or services, this can give it a significant boost in valuation. However, if the seller has not continued to invest in its brand, there is a risk of brand degradation that will require years to rebuild.

It is best to wait until the quantitative analysis has been completed and adjust the baseline quantitative results with estimates of the additional impact of the items just noted.

Which Valuation Method Is Best?

The buyer should use a number of different valuation models. By doing so, it can obtain a high-low range of estimates that gives it the general boundaries for a valuation. The best valuation estimate usually begins with a DCF analysis, adjusted for comparable transaction multiples. For example, a standard DCF analysis may reveal that a target is worth $15 million, which is approximately 8 times its most recently reported EBITDA. However, because the target is located in a "hot" industry, with unusually high multiples of 12 times EBITDA, the buyer should consider increasing the size of its offer to match the going rate. Its alternative is to wait until such time as the industry valuation gradually declines, at which point the DCF results and comparables are in closer alignment.

An example of what a range of values could look like is shown in Exhibit 13.13, which uses several methods that were discussed earlier in the "Alternative Valuation

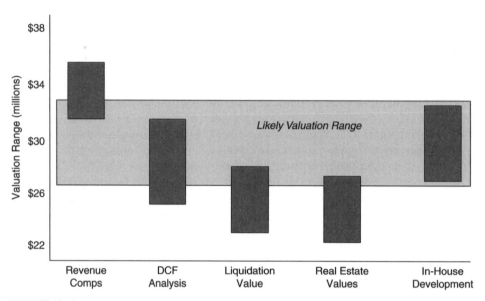

EXHIBIT 13.13 Valuation Range Analysis

Methods" section earlier in this chapter. In the example, note that the revenue multiple method yields a clearly outsized valuation while the real estate values method results in an excessively low one. Since these valuations are clearly beyond what the other methods are indicating, the high-low valuation extremes are excluded from the likely valuation range.

The buyer also should create a hard cap on the valuation, beyond which it will not go under any circumstances. To derive it, the CEO should review all of the valuation models and use them to set a price ceiling. This executive should not be directly involved in the prospective acquisition, and so has no personal interest in whether the buyer acquires the target. The resulting price cap is the absolute maximum that the buyer will pay. By establishing such a cap, the buyer can avoid overbidding in the heat of negotiations.

Also, although initially it may seem odd to do so, the buyer should consider establishing a floor price. By establishing a price that is reasonably fair to the seller, there is less risk that the seller will back out at the last moment and court other bidders. Also, the seller is more cooperative with subsequent integration efforts if it believes it was paid a fair amount. Of course, if the seller is in desperate straits and wants to sell at any price, the buyer should hardly balk at paying too little!

Method of Payment

The buyer can pay the seller in cash, debt, or stock. If the seller accepts *cash*, it must pay income taxes on its gain immediately. However, the seller also obtains an entirely liquid asset and is no longer tied to the future results of its business. Generally speaking, the buyer is willing to pay less if the payment is in cash, since the buyer will have to dip into its capital resources to obtain the funds, rendering it less able to deal with other issues that may require cash funding. If the buyer goes on to achieve significant synergy gains, its shareholders will receive the entire benefit of the gains while the seller's shareholders will receive no gain. Finally, the buyer may want to pay cash simply because it can and other bidders cannot. If the buyer is cash-rich and interest rates are so high that the cost of debt is prohibitive for other bidders, it can make an offer that the seller literally cannot refuse.

If the buyer pays in *stock*, the seller gains tax-deferred status on the payment. If the seller is in no immediate need of cash, this might make a stock payment a reasonable form of compensation. The other consideration in a stock payment is the buyer's expectation that it will create sufficient synergies to improve the value of its stock. By paying the seller in stock, the buyer's shareholders are forgoing some of the synergy gains to be achieved and giving them to the seller. Conversely, if the seller suspects that it cannot achieve sufficient synergies, it can offload some of the risk to the seller by issuing stock. Finally, if the buyer is a private company, the seller has no clear path to eventually liquidating any shares paid to it, which makes this an extremely unpalatable option.

The buyer's payment behavior also is driven by its perception of how fairly the market currently is valuing its stock. If the buyer feels that its stock price currently is trading at a maximum level, it will be more inclined to use its stock for acquisitions, and it will act in the reverse manner if its stock is trading at a low price. If the buyer consistently uses its stock to acquire multiple companies in succession, the market may feel that this is a sign that the buyer's management is believes that the stock has reached a maximum valuation and so will tend to trade down its price.

If the buyer pays with *debt*, the seller is in the worst position of all three payment scenarios. The seller's shareholders do not obtain any liquid assets in the short term, they do not share in any upside potential caused by synergy gains that would have been realized by stock ownership, and they are totally dependent on the buyer's management team to create enough cash flow to pay them. If the seller has collateralized the assets of the sold business, the collateralization is still not adequate, since the buyer may have stripped the entity of assets by the time the seller obtains possession of it.

In short, the seller prefers cash for its liquidity value but forgoes the opportunity to share in any synergy gains that stock ownership would have provided. The buyer prefers a cash payment if it is sure of its ability to achieve significant synergies, which it wants to retain through stock ownership. A debt payment is the worst-case scenario for the seller, which obtains neither liquidity nor appreciation value. Although these choices frequently are driven solely by the financing available to the buyer, this is not always the case. If the buyer has the option of paying in stock or cash, but pays in cash, this is a significant indicator that it believes it can reserve significant synergy gains for its shareholders. If the buyer has the same option but pays in stock, it may be more concerned with its ability to achieve synergy gains, and so is offloading some of the risk onto the seller.

The buyer can model its payment options with a pro forma spreadsheet, such as the one shown in Exhibit 13.14. The exhibit contains an example of a 100% stock payment, followed by a 100% cash payment. The key financial information for the buyer and seller are identical in both scenarios. In the stock payment scenario, the buyer plans to achieve $535,000 in savings through various cost reductions. However, because it plans to pay in stock, it is passing some of the gains over to the

EXHIBIT 13.14 Payment Scenarios

Stock Payment Scenario	Buyer	Seller	Adjustment	Adjustment Notes	Combined Results
Revenues	$24,000	$3,000			$27,000
Cost of sales	$16,000	$2,000	−$ 360	(1)	$17,640
Administrative	$ 6,000	$ 500	−$ 175	(2)	$ 6,325
Interest	$ 100	$ 50			$ 150
Income before tax	$ 1,900	$ 450			$ 2,885
Income tax at 34%	$ 646	$ 153			$ 981
Net income	$ 1,254	$ 297			$ 1,904
Outstanding shares	400	100			
Seller shares retired			−100		
Buyer shares issued			150	(3)	550
Earnings per share	$ 3.14	$ 2.97			**$ 3.46**

Cash Payment Scenario	Buyer	Seller	Adjustment	Adjustment Notes	Combined Results
Revenues	$24,000	$3,000			$27,000
Cost of sales	$16,000	$2,000	−$ 360	(1)	$17,640
Administrative	$ 6,000	$ 500	−$ 175	(2)	$ 6,325
Interest	$ 100	$ 50	$ 180	(4)	$ 330
Income before tax	$ 1,900	$ 450			$ 2,705
Income tax at 34%	$ 646	$ 153			$ 920
Net income	$ 1,254	$ 297			$ 1,785
Outstanding shares	400	100			
Seller shares retired			−100		
Buyer shares issued					400
Earnings per share	$ 3.14	$ 2.97			**$ 4.46**

(1) 2% reduction in purchasing costs for the combined entities.
(2) Overlapping administrative costs eliminated.
(3) Share exchange is 1.5 buyer shares for each seller share.
(4) Sale price is 1 × revenues, financed with 6% loan.

selling shareholders, as reflected in the earnings per share figure. In the cash pay-ment scenario, the buyer plans to achieve the same savings but also must incur the interest cost of a loan that it uses to pay cash to the seller's shareholders. Although the added interest burden drags down the net earnings of the combined entities, the existing buyer shareholders receive the entire synergy gains, resulting in an impres-sive earnings per share boost.

Types of Acquisitions

In an acquisition, the overriding issue for the seller is to avoid paying income taxes. In order to do so, the form of reorganization must comply with several key sections of the Internal Revenue Code (IRC), specifically sections 354 to 358 and 367 to 368.

These sections define the various types of permissible tax-free acquisitions and the conditions under which they apply. These sections of the chapter address the various types of acquisitions and their tax (and other) implications for the participants.

Tax Implications of an Acquisition

When determining the proper structure of an acquisition, the taxability of the transaction to the seller plays a key role. It is possible that the seller may want to pay income taxes immediately rather than delaying the recognition of a gain. This scenario arises when the seller's tax basis in the acquiree is more than the price being paid for it, resulting in the complete avoidance of taxes. However, it is far more likely that the seller will have a minimal tax basis in the acquiree and so wishes to avoid the immediate recognition of a gain. To avoid gain recognition, the Internal Revenue Service (IRS) has stipulated that these requirements be met:

- The transaction must have a bona fide business purpose other than tax avoidance.
- There must be a *continuity of interest*, where the ownership interests of the selling stockholders continue into the acquiring entity. This is achieved by having the buyer pay a substantial portion of the purchase price in its own stock. The IRS considers a "substantial portion" of the purchase price to be at least 50%. Some transactions are structured to pay sellers preferred stock rather than common stock so that they still meet the requirements of the continuity-of-interest rule but also give the sellers rights to additional payments, as would be the case with debt.
- There must be a *continuity of business enterprise*, where the buyer must either continue the seller's historic business or use a significant proportion of the acquired assets in a business.

The IRS has incorporated these requirements into four types of legal reorganization, which are commonly described as Type A, B, C, or D reorganizations. The letter designations come from the paragraph letters in the IRC under which they are described. All four types of reorganizations, as well as several variations, are described in greater detail later in this chapter.

In an acquisition, the buyer generally recognizes no gain or loss. Instead, its primary tax concern is the tax basis and holding period of the assets it acquires. Ideally, it wants to restate the assets to their fair market values (FMV), on the assumption that the FMV is higher than the tax basis of the seller. If the FMV is indeed higher, the buyer can record a larger amount of asset depreciation, which reduces its future tax liability. The buyer can restate assets to their FMV only if it acquires them through an asset acquisition (see next section). Otherwise, it will retain the assets' tax basis and holding period. However, retaining the original tax basis and holding period may be acceptable if the purchase price of the assets is less than their carryforward basis, since the buyer can recognize more depreciation expense than if it were to restate the assets to their FMV.

There is one scenario where the buyer can complete a nontaxable reorganization and still record the acquired assets at their FMVs. This is possible under Section 338 of the IRC, which allows this treatment if the buyer acquires at least 80% of the total voting power and 80% of the total value of the seller's stock within a

12-month period. However, Section 338 is laced with restrictions that reduce its applicability.

In short, the primary driver of the type of acquisition used is the seller's need to defer taxes. Because the buyer's interests involve a far smaller tax impact than that experienced by the seller, the seller's wishes generally determine the method used.

Asset Acquisition

The only type of acquisition that is *not* addressed by the IRC is the asset acquisition, because this is a taxable transaction.

In an asset acquisition, the buyer acquires either all or a selection of the seller's assets and liabilities. This transaction is most favorable to the buyer, which can record the acquired assets at their FMV (which is usually an increase from the seller's tax basis), thereby yielding more depreciation to use as a tax shield. This also results in a smaller gain if the buyer subsequently sells the assets. However, the buyer also must obtain legal title to each asset it acquires, which can require a considerable amount of paperwork. Also, depending on the circumstances, the seller may have to notify its creditors of the impending transaction. For example, if the buyer intends to acquire a seller's below-market asset lease agreement, the lessor may agree to the sale only if it can increase its lease rate.

An asset sale is not tax efficient for the seller. Of primary importance is that the seller must pay income taxes on the difference between the consideration received and the seller's basis in the entity. The situation is more dire if the selling entity is a C corporation, due to a dual taxation scenario. First, the C corporation must pay taxes to the extent that the total consideration received exceeds its adjusted basis in the assets sold. In addition, assuming that the C corporation intends to distribute its remaining assets to stockholders and dissolve, the stockholders must pay taxes to the extent that the distributions received exceed their cost basis in the stock.

Also, if the seller previously had claimed an investment tax credit on an asset that it is now selling, the credit may be recaptured, thereby increasing its income taxes.

An asset acquisition can be used to avoid acquiring unknown or contingent liabilities. For example, if the selling entity is the subject of a lawsuit and the buyer wishes to avoid any liability related to the lawsuit, it can selectively purchase assets, leaving the selling entity with responsibility for any legal settlement. However, some environmental laws stipulate that the liability for future hazardous waste cleanups can attach to assets. Consequently, the buyer of real estate assets should go to considerable lengths to verify the extent of any environmental contamination prior to purchase.

An asset acquisition also is useful for the partial sale of a business that has multiple products or product lines. For example, a buyer may want to purchase only a single product in order to fill out its product line, leaving the seller with most of its original business intact. Although it also is possible to spin off such assets into a separate legal entity, often it is easier simply to conduct an asset sale.

The form of the purchase agreement varies from that used for an entity purchase. Instead, the parties use a general assignment and bill of sale, with an attached schedule that itemizes each asset or liability being transferred.

Depending on the proportion of assets sold to the buyer, this transaction can require the direct approval of at least a majority of the seller's stockholders.

The selling entity remains in existence and continues to be owned by the same stockholders. However, if most or all of its assets are sold, the seller's stockholders normally liquidate the entity.

Type A Reorganization

A Type A reorganization is governed by paragraph A of Section 368(a)(1) of the IRC, which simply states that a reorganization is "a statutory merger or consolidation." To expand on this limited definition, a statutory merger involves the transfer of all seller assets and liabilities to the buyer in exchange for the buyer's stock; a statutory consolidation involves the transfers of the assets of two companies into a new entity in exchange for the stock of the new entity. In both cases, the selling entities are then liquidated.

An additional requirement of a Type A reorganization is to have a continuity of interest. In order to meet this rule, the buyer should issue at least 50% of its stock as part of the purchase price. The transaction also must meet the continuity-of-business-enterprise rule.

This transaction allows for tax deferral by the seller of that portion of the purchase price paid with the buyer's stock. The buyer must assume all of the seller's assets and liabilities.

The boards of both entities must approve the transaction, as must at least a majority of the stockholders of the selling entity. Since the selling entity's board of directors must approve the transaction, this is not a suitable vehicle for a hostile takeover.

The principal difference between Types A and B reorganizations is that other consideration besides stock can be paid under a Type A, whereas the price paid under a Type B must be solely for stock. Also, the selling entity is dissolved in a Type A but can be retained in a Type B reorganization.

The Type A reorganization is not commonly used when valuable contracts are associated with the selling entity, because they may be terminated at the option of the business partners when the selling entity is liquidated at the end of the reorganization.

In summary, the Type A reorganization is primarily of benefit to the seller, which can obtain some cash, debt, or preferred stock as part of the purchase price while still retaining tax deferred status on the purchase price that is paid with the buyer's stock. It is less useful for the buyer, which runs the risk of losing contracts associated with the selling entity.

Type B Reorganization

A Type B reorganization is governed by paragraph B of Section 368(a)(1) of the IRC. The paragraph reads:

> *The acquisition by one corporation, in exchange solely for all or a part of its voting stock (or in exchange solely for all or a part of the voting stock of a corporation which is in control of the acquiring corporation), of stock of another corporation if, immediately after the acquisition, the acquiring corporation has control of such other corporation (whether or not such acquiring corporation had control immediately before the acquisition).*

In essence, the buyer exchanges nothing but its stock for the stock of the seller, resulting in the selling entity becoming a subsidiary of the buyer. The IRS has clarified the basic definition to state that only *voting* stock can be used in the transaction. For example, if the buyer issues any preferred or nonvoting stock as part of the deal, it no longer qualifies as a Type B reorganization. Also, the seller cannot give the selling entity's stockholders the option of being paid with cash instead of stock.

In addition, the buyer must gain immediate control over the seller, which the IRS defines as the buyer receiving at least 80% of the stock of the selling entity. However, it is allowable to gain *creeping control* over the seller, where the buyer gains control over a period of no more than 12 months. Creeping control is allowable only if the buyer has a plan for gaining control during this time period.

Finally, this transaction is subject to the IRS's continuity-of-interest and continuity-of-business-enterprise requirements.

In summary, the Type B reorganization is most useful when the selling entity must be retained, usually because it has valuable contracts that otherwise would be terminated if the entity were to be liquidated.

Type C Reorganization

A Type C reorganization is governed by paragraph C of Section 368(a)(1) of the IRC. The paragraph states:

> *The acquisition by one corporation, in exchange solely for all or a part of its voting stock (or in exchange solely for all or a part of the voting stock of a corporation which is in control of the acquiring corporation), of substantially all of the properties of another corporation, but in determining whether the exchange is solely for stock the assumption by the acquiring corporation of a liability of the other shall be disregarded.*

In order to be a nontaxable transaction, paragraph C requires that the seller transfer essentially all of its assets in exchange for the buyer's voting stock. Further, those assets transferred must be critical to the continuation of the business, which is an element of the continuity-of-interest requirement discussed earlier. Also, the continuity-of-business-enterprise requirement must be fulfilled. Finally, the stock paid for the transaction must be entirely the seller's *voting* stock, and the selling entity must liquidate itself.

To qualify under the asset transfer requirement of the Type C reorganization, the seller must transfer to the buyer at least 90% of its net assets, including all of those assets considered critical to the ongoing operations of the business.

It is possible for the buyer to pay some cash as part of this transaction. However, at least 80% of the FMV of the assets purchased must be solely for stock, so only the remaining asset value can be paid for with cash. The seller must pay income taxes on any portion of the purchase that is not paid for with the buyer's stock.

Any dissenting shareholders may have the right to have their ownership positions appraised and then paid in cash. The extent of these cash payments will increase the total proportion of nonstock payment made, which can affect the nontaxable nature of the entire transaction. Thus, a significant proportion of dissenting shareholders can prevent the Type C reorganization from being used.

In summary, the Type C reorganization is most useful when the seller is willing to accept mostly stock in payment and the buyer does not need the selling entity, which is liquidated. The buyer also can record the acquired assets at their FMV, which is generally higher than the tax basis that otherwise would be inherited from the seller.

Type D Reorganization

A Type D reorganization is governed by paragraph D of Section 368(a)(1) of the IRC. The paragraph reads:

> *A transfer by a corporation of all or a part of its assets to another corporation if immediately after the transfer the transferor, or one or more of its shareholders (including persons who were shareholders immediately before the transfer), or any combination thereof, is in control of the corporation to which the assets are transferred; but only if, in pursuance of the plan, stock or securities of the corporation to which the assets are transferred are distributed in a [qualifying transaction].*

Type D reorganizations can be either *acquisitive* or *divisive*. An *acquisitive* reorganization is when the seller transfers substantially all of its assets to the buyer in exchange for at least 80% of the buyer's voting and nonvoting stock. This is also known as a *reverse merger*.

A divisive Type D reorganization is when a single entity separates into two or more separate entities. The division occurs in two steps. First, a company transfers some of its assets to a corporation in exchange for voting control of that entity. It transfers the acquired control to its own stockholders. There are three types of divisive reorganizations, all of which are tax-free.

1. *Spin-off.* Stockholders end up with shares of both the original and new entities.
2. *Split-off.* Some stockholders retain their shares in the original entity while others swap their stock in the original entity for shares of the new entity. This approach is most useful if there is a difference of opinion among the stockholders regarding the future direction of the original entity, since they now have a choice regarding which entity to own.
3. *Split-up.* The original entity creates two new entities, transfers its assets to them, and liquidates. Stockholders end up with shares in the surviving entities. As was the case with a split-off, this approach also is useful for separating internal factions that disagree about how the company is being managed.

All of the variations noted here are also subject to these four requirements.

1. The original entity must distribute the stock of the new entity to its stockholders, resulting in their control of it.
2. The original entity can distribute only the stock of the new entity to its stockholders.
3. Subsequent to the transaction, both entities must be actively engaged in business.
4. The transaction cannot be intended to avoid tax payments.

A Type D reorganization is intended primarily to govern the tax-free division of a company into smaller entities rather than to acquire another entity.

Triangular Merger

A triangular merger is a reorganization in which a subsidiary owned by the buyer merges with the seller, with the selling entity liquidating. As it is a merger rather than an acquisition, the transaction will eliminate all minority stockholders, since they are legally required to accept the buyer's purchase price. Also, the approval of only the selling entity's board of directors is needed, not the selling stockholders.

For a triangular transaction to be nontaxable, the buyer must have at least 80% control over its subsidiary and must acquire at least 90% of the FMV of the buyer's net assets. Also, the transaction between the subsidiary and the selling entity must satisfy the requirements noted earlier for a Type A reorganization, which include the presence of a continuity of interest and a continuity of business enterprise.

Reverse Triangular Merger

A reverse triangular merger is a reorganization in which a subsidiary owned by the buyer merges into the seller, with the subsidiary liquidating. The voting stock of the buying parent company is transferred to the selling stockholders in exchange for their stock in the selling entity. As it is a merger rather than an acquisition, the transaction will eliminate all minority shareholders, since they are legally required to accept the buyer's purchase price. Also, the approval of only the selling entity's board of directors is needed, not the selling stockholders.

For a reverse triangular merger to be nontaxable, the selling entity must acquire substantially all of the assets of the buyer's subsidiary, and the buyer must obtain at least 80% control of the selling entity. Also, the buyer must acquire at least 90% of the FMV of the buyer's net assets.

The reverse triangular merger is used most commonly when the selling entity has valuable contracts that otherwise would be canceled if the selling entity were not to survive the acquisition transaction. It also is used when the selling entity's stock is too widely held to make a direct stock purchase practicable or where there may be a significant proportion of dissenting stockholders.

Sellers tend to be less enthralled with a reverse triangular merger, because this type of reorganization severely limits the amount of cash they can receive. Because the selling entity must give up at least 80% of its stock for the stock of the buyer's subsidiary, no more than 20% of the total purchase price is available for payment in cash. Nonetheless, the reverse triangular merger is one of the most common types of reorganization in use.

Summary

The CEO ultimately is responsible for every acquisition in which her company engages, since these acquisitions can have a massive impact on the long-term fortunes of the business and its shareholders. Because the CEO must have a deep understanding of the issues surrounding acquisitions, we paid particular attention in this chapter to the key aspects of reviewing a prospective acquisition and of deriving the most appropriate price for it. It is hoped that this will help you to avoid acquisitions that do not make sense and to avoid from overpaying.

The most essential issue to take away from this chapter is that you should be looking for reasons why an acquisition does *not* make sense rather than finding any way possible to make a deal work; the potential for an acquisition disaster is so great that you must exercise great caution in this area.

The Public Company

Initial Public Offering

The initial public offering (IPO) is considered by many chief executive officers (CEOs) to be the true sign of success—they have grown a business to the point where its revenue volume and profitability are large enough to warrant public ownership. However, the road to an IPO is both expensive and time consuming, and requires significant changes to a company. This chapter describes the pluses and minuses of being public as well as the steps required and costs to be incurred in order to achieve that goal.

Reasons to Go Public

Although a management team may not say it, a major reason for going public is to create a market for the shares they already own. These shares may not be available for sale for some time after the IPO), but eventually they will eventually be able to cash in their shares and options, potentially generating considerable profits from doing so. This reason is not publicized to the public, which would be less likely to invest if it though the management team is simply cashing in and leaving the business.

A slight variation on the wealth creation theme is that, by having a broad public market for their shares, original shareholders are likely to see a rise in the value of their shares, even if they have no intention of selling them. The reason is that there is no longer a penalty for not having a ready market for the shares, which adds a premium to what the shares would have been worth if the company had remained privately held.

The same logic can be used as a tool for employee retention. A private company can issue options to its employees, but they are worth little to the employees unless there is a market in which they can sell the shares. By going public, a company may experience increased employee retention, due to employees' wish to wait until their options vest so they can cash in the resulting shares for a profit.

Going public also is useful from the estate planning perspective. If the owner of a private company dies, his or her heirs often are forced to sell the entire business in order to pay estate taxes (although with proper planning, life insurance payouts can be used instead). By taking the company public, the heirs are forced to sell only a portion of the company to pay estate taxes, which leaves them some portion of the business as a residual.

From an operating perspective, going public gives a company a large pot of cash, which it can use to increase its competitiveness by increasing its asset base, improving marketing, hiring qualified staff, funding more product research, and so on. This can be such a competitive advantage that other companies in the same market segment may be forced to go public as well, just to raise enough funds to survive against their newly funded competitor.

Along the same lines, having publicly held shares allows a company to more readily include its shares in the purchase price of an acquisition. The acquiree is much more willing to accept this form of compensation, since it can sell the shares for cash to other investors. This is a powerful tool for some companies, which use it as the primary method for consolidating a group of smaller, privately held organizations within an industry.

From a financing perspective, going public lowers a company's cost of capital. The main reason is that investors are willing to pay a higher price for a company's stock than if the shares had been privately issued, since they can sell the shares easily. This premium can reduce the cost of capital by several percent. In addition, issuing shares to the public reduces the power that private investors previously may have had over the business, which could have included restrictions on operations, guaranteed dividend payments, or prior approval of a potential sale of the business. Also, by being publicly held, it is much less time consuming and less expensive to raise funds through subsequent rounds of financing.

Another financing reason to go public is that new equity drastically lowers the proportion of debt to equity that is recorded on the corporate balance sheet, which lenders look on with great favor. With the new equity in hand, a company can ask lenders for a larger amount of debt, which they will be likely to lend until the amount handed over results in a significantly higher debt/equity ratio.

Thus, there are excellent wealth-creating, operating, and financing reasons to pursue an IPO. However, there are just as many reasons for *not* doing so, which are itemized in the next section.

Reasons Not to Go Public

One of the best reasons for not going public is its cost. These costs are detailed in the next section, while the fees for trading on an exchange are listed later in this chapter in the "Trading on an Exchange" section. In brief, a small company will be fortunate indeed to incur less than $0.5 million in up-front fees as part of an IPO. A large company can expect to pay many times these base-level expenses. Also, a company conducting a small offering will find that the proportional cost of obtaining equity funding is extremely high, since the underwriter will charge a higher fee as a percentage of the amount raised in order to cover its costs and still earn a profit on the transaction.

Besides the initial cost of going public, there will be incremental increases in ongoing expenses. Most obviously, additional staff must be hired into the accounting department, whose job will be to keep up with all reports required by the Securities and Exchange Commission (SEC). In addition, the cost of directors' and officers' (D&O) insurance will skyrocket from what would have been paid when a company was privately held, assuming that the insurance can be obtained at all. The reason for this increase is the vastly increased pool of investors who may be tempted to sue the company on the grounds of material misstatements in its public comments (such as its registration statement for the IPO) in the event that the stock price drops. You can reasonably expect the cost of this insurance to increase by a factor of at least 10.

Another problem is that a smaller company with a modest market capitalization will have difficulty establishing a market for its stock. If it is too small, institutional investors (which like to buy and sell in large blocks of stock) will have minimal interest in making an investment. Because of this small market, a company's stock will be more likely to be subject to manipulation by a small number of investors, who can short sell it to drive the stock down and purchase large blocks of stock at a reduced price in order to gain some measure of control over the company.

Loss of control is quite possible, unless the owner has retained a large proportion of corporate stock or unless a separate class of super-voting stock has been established that gives the owners additional votes at shareholder meetings. Otherwise, outside investors either can buy up shares to create large voting blocks or can band together to create the same result.

Information disclosure is yet another problem. In addition to the expense of having additional accounting staff to organize and report this information, there is the problem of disclosing information to a company's competitors, which need only to access the SEC's Web site to access all required reports filed by the company. Although many pundits claim that the types of information disclosed will not harm the competitive posture of a public company, competitors can tell from its financial statements when it has put itself out on a financial limb by obtaining too much debt and can easily start a price war at this point that could cause the company to miss debt payments and possibly go into bankruptcy.

A serious concern is the risk of shareholder class action lawsuits. These arise when there is a drop in the stock price that shareholders claim was the result of material misstatements in the registration statement or in any other information releases thereafter. These lawsuits are the reason for much more expensive D&O insurance. They will be targeted at the company as a whole, the corporate directors, whoever signed the registration statement, any experts who have given statements on behalf of the company, and its underwriters. The threat of lawsuits is one of the main reasons why IPO prices frequently are set somewhat low—there is less chance that the price will drop further, giving investors no reason to sue.

Another issue is the constant pressure from investors and analysts to show improved results every quarter. If a company had been private, it could easily stand lower profits for a year or so while it ramps up new products and markets; being public makes this completely practical approach to growing a business more difficult to implement. Investors can attempt to unseat the management team by approving a different board of directors if they feel that growth rates are below their expectations. This issue can be dealt with only by continually informing the investing public of management's intentions for corporate growth, so that investors will adopt a longer-term perspective.

Finally, the management team must understand that it now exists not to serve itself but to serve the investing public. This major shift in focus calls for the elimination of unusually high compensation packages to the managers as well as a commitment to increasing shareholder value over other objectives that may have been in vogue at the company prior to going public. Management may be uncomfortable with this paradigm shift, resulting in investor unhappiness with a perceived lack of management attention to their needs.

There are so many negative reasons for going public that the managements of many perfectly good private companies have elected to stay away from the public markets. In addition, a great many companies that have gone public find these issues to be so burdensome that they have elected to take themselves private once again.

Cost of an IPO

Even a small company should expect to pay a minimum of $0.5 million to complete an IPO. This expense is comprised of a number of fees. Accounting and legal fees will consume the largest proportion of the total. Expect to pay at least $250,000 in legal fees. Audit fees will vary, depending on the size and complexity of the company, but certainly expect to pay at least three times the cost of a normal audit. This figure will increase if there are weak internal control systems that require the auditors to conduct more extensive audit tests. Further, printing costs for the prospectus will exceed $100,000 for all but the most "plain Jane" documents, a figure that will increase if a large number of revisions to the registration statement are required prior to printing. Also, initial filing fees with a number of government and regulatory bodies likely will consume a minimum of another $25,000.

In addition to these professional fees, the underwriter requires a significant payment that is based on the percentage of capital raised. The usual fee is in the range of 6% to 7% if an offering exceeds $20 million, with the percentage gradually increasing to as much as 15% of the total offering if it is quite small (in the $1 million to $3 million range). This cost can be reduced if a company accepts "best efforts" marketing by the underwriter, whereby it does not guarantee a full sale of the entire stock offering. In this case, the percentage fee will drop by 2% to 3%.

To make the situation worse, with the exception of the underwriter fee, most of these costs are incurred prior to the sale of any stock, so a company will be charged with the full expense of an IPO even if it is never completed. If the company withdraws from the IPO process, it must pay the fees incurred to that point by its underwriter, although this obligation usually is not required when the underwriter withdraws. Furthermore, if the IPO is merely delayed, many of the costs must be incurred again, since the underlying operational and financial information on which the original offering was contemplated will have changed and must be reexamined by the lawyers and accountants.

Preparing for the IPO

Preparing for an IPO begins years before the actual event, because the company must "clean up" prior to being presented to the investing public as a quality investment. This housecleaning involves 12 steps.

Step 1. *Increase the competence of the management team.* The single greatest driver of corporate value is the quality of the management team. The owners must evaluate each management position and replace anyone who is not a team player, who does not drive efficiency and effectiveness throughout his or her department, and who does not have a tight strategic vision. Obtaining a manager who is well known at a national level can have a startling positive impact on the perceived value of the company as a whole. A key point is that a management team is not a one-man show. Investors need to see a competent supporting team that can readily take over the business in the event that one key manager dies or leaves the company.

Step 2. *Create a reward system that is tied to strategy.* With the assistance of a compensation expert, design a reward system not only for the management team but for the entire company that incents them to focus their activities on those areas of the business that must be improved prior to the IPO (as described in all the points in this section). A key area is in the use of stock options, which can be issued several years prior to the IPO, when the company's value is substantially lower, resulting in significant gains for the recipients after the company goes public. To do this, you should set aside a large pool of stock for option conversions, and do so well in advance of the IPO, in order to avoid having the new shareholders vote to create it.

Step 3. *Obtain audited financials.* A reputable audit firm, and preferably one with a national presence, should audit the financial statements for the three years prior to the IPO. The audit firm *must* be registered with the Public Company Accounting Oversight Board (PCAOB). A review or compilation is not acceptable—these less expensive and less thorough forms of an audit will be rejected by the underwriter and the SEC when the registration statement is filed.

Step 4. *Obtain a top securities law firm.* Although there may be little perceived need for a law firm well in advance of an IPO, it is useful to have such a firm examine the legal structure of the business and recommend changes that will position the company properly for the IPO. The need for this firm will rise dramatically during the IPO filing period, when its lawyers review the company's prospectus and registration statement to ensure their completeness in accordance with SEC regulations. The lawyers also will channel all communications to and from the SEC in regard to both the initial registration and filings subsequent to the IPO.

Step 5. *Strip out personal transactions.* The owners of a private business typically mesh their personal affairs with those of the company to a considerable extent. This can include keeping personal servants on the company payroll, having the company guarantee personal loans, lending company money to their other businesses, and giving themselves inordinate levels of compensation. Stopping these practices can be quite difficult for an owner, whose overall level of compensation may drop substantially as a result.

Step 6. *Show 25% annual growth.* Potential investors want to invest in companies with a record of strong growth, preferably at least 25% for each of the last few years. To create a business in line with these expectations, the business owner must close down or sell off those portions of the business that have no reasonable near-term prospect for growth, or (worse) those areas that not only are *not* growing but that also require substantial cash infusions that could be better applied to higher-growth business segments.

Step 7. *At least show breakeven profitability.* Investors understand that extra expenses must be incurred in order to ramp up sales, so they are not looking for inordinate profit levels in addition to high sales growth rates. However, there should be no losses appearing on the income statement for the past few years; losses would imply an inability by management to control costs, which brings into question the viability of the entire business model. The intent to go public also may require a business to switch away from some tax reduction strategies that it may have pursued as a private company in order to reduce its tax liability in favor of ensuring that some degree of profitability appears in the financial statements. Another alternative for ensuring some profitability is a tighter focus on cost controls, perhaps through the use of benchmarking or best practices implementations that are recommended by consultants.

Step 8. *Fill the product pipeline.* Investors want to see a company that has established a clear competitive differentiation in the market place. This can be done through the advance funding of research and development projects that lead to the creation of a stream of new products. Since it takes a long time to create new products, investment in this activity should begin far in advance of the IPO. It is particularly important not to appear like a one-hit wonder, with only a single winning product; be sure to create a process that reliably generates a continuing stream of products.

Step 9. *Achieve critical mass.* In order to attract the attention of institutional investors, a company must have a market capitalization of at least $100 million. At this point, their participation will yield an active market for the stock, which can help to drive up the stock price. To reach this capitalization level, a company requires substantial revenue volume. Although roughly one-quarter of all public companies have revenues of less than $10 million, a much higher level is required to reach the crucial $100 million capitalization level. In order to do this, company management may need to concentrate on making acquisitions in the years leading up to the IPO, with the objective of building enough critical mass for the IPO.

Step 10. *Expand high-growth segments.* Investors want to see a high rate of growth in areas where other public companies have been rewarded with high price/earnings multiples. To do this, the management team should be aware of P/E multiples for all companies in its market segment and allocate funding to those areas of the business that will reward the company with a high P/E multiple when it goes public. This capital allocation process is a difficult one, for the market can increase or decrease P/E multiples in a very short time period, depending on its perception of how hot a market segment may be.

Step 11. *Pick an independent board.* Investors want a majority of the board of directors to be independent from the management team, in order to place investor interests ahead of those of the management team. Although this group can be selected just prior to the IPO, it is better to do so at least a year in advance, in order to give members time to settle into their roles and learn about company operations.

Step 12. *Protect owner wealth.* The owner of a company that has just gone public and who has sold some proportion of his or her shares to the public should expect to be paying a large amount of taxes. To reduce this tax burden, the owner can spend the previous few years gifting company stock to heirs, which can be given tax-free in blocks of $10,000 per year to each recipient (or $20,000 if the owner is married). In addition, if there are potential capital losses on any investments, this is the year in which they should be recognized in order to offset the gains from the IPO.

The main point of this section is to impress on the CEO the need for advance planning for an IPO, preferably beginning a minimum of three years prior to it. Only by taking this long view to going public can a company position itself properly to achieve the maximum value for its shareholders while minimizing the tax impact for its original owners.

Finding an Underwriter

The process of becoming a public company begins with the search for a qualified underwriter that can lead the company through the maze of steps needed to go public. An underwriter is a an entity that sells company shares either directly to individual investors or to institutional buyers, such as mutual fund managers. The largest underwriters operate on an international scale; others have a regional focus or concentrate their attention on specific market niches in which they have built up a considerable degree of expertise. A major underwriter may have built up a large retail brokerage operation and have significant institutional sales capacity, although some of these underwriters have elected to focus more on one of the two sales channels over the other.

It is better to use underwriters with an established reputation, despite their higher cost; investors tend to trust them more, which can result in a higher stock price. Conversely, using an underwriter with a poor reputation (i.e., for drumming up the price of stocks that later crash) is much more likely to result in unhappy investors, potential investor lawsuits, and a thinly traded stock. It is also important to use an underwriter with a strong research capability and a commitment to use this resource to distribute information about the company and its industry to investors. A good way to determine who has the best analyst coverage of an industry is to ask investors and other brokerage houses whose reports they feel are the most complete and accurate.

Underwriters have a tendency to sell shares to institutional investors, because these are sophisticated investors that buy in large volumes, thereby reducing the sales efforts of the underwriters. This can be a problem if a large percentage of the company's shares are being sold to the public, because institutional investors are much more likely to either gain control over the company or at least gain a formidable block of voting stock that can be used to influence the company's direction.

If an IPO is a small one, an underwriter may handle the entire issuance by itself. However, it more commonly leads a team of underwriters as the managing underwriter if there is a substantial amount of stock to be sold to the public. It creates this syndication not only to spread its own risk in the transaction but also to ensure that shares are sold to a wide cross-section of the investing public, which is critical for creating a strong market for the company's stock.

A larger company with a strong track record will attract the attention of a number of underwriters that are eager to take it public. When selecting from among this group, look for a business with a strong reputation for successfully bringing new offerings to market; this fact can be discerned easily by reviewing the business press for the last few years. Another key factor should be its distribution capacity, since the company will want a broad range of investors rather than a small number of powerful institutional investors. The underwriter also should be able to commit to the creation of a strong aftermarket in the company's stock, which can be verified by making reference calls to the other companies that it has already taken public as the managing underwriter. These reference calls should include queries about the level of service provided, the level of underwriter expertise, and the breadth of share placement among investors. If the underwriter already employs an analyst for the company's industry, this is a strong indicator of the underwriter's commitment to an aftermarket. Of particular concern should be the underwriter's history of bringing companies public as the *managing* underwriter rather than as one of a large syndicate. If the underwriter has been primarily a syndicate member, this is a strong indication that it lacks experience in managing the IPO process.

Unfortunately, most companies are too small to attract a flurry of underwriter interest. Instead, they must work hard to attract the attention of just one or two. To do so, the CEO should have already accomplished all of the long-range targets noted in the last section. In addition, the management team should construct a detailed business plan that dovetails with prior company results while also showing exactly how it plans to use the cash received from the stock offering to achieve future growth and profitability. The plan should most certainly *not* describe any intent by management to sell off its shares; this tells underwriters that managers want to cash out of the company, potentially leaving investors to shift for themselves. This document should include a detailed description of all key members of the management team, since underwriters are well aware of the importance of a strong team. Further, the plan should itemize all risk areas and how the company plans to hedge those risks while pursuing its growth plans. Above all, the plan must present a compelling story that will attract a quality underwriter.

If an underwriter is sufficiently interested in the company, it will conduct an exhaustive due diligence process to verify that what the company says about itself is true. This is likely to include interviews throughout the company, a detailed analysis of all operations, company tours, and reference calls to company suppliers and customers. In particular, the underwriter will investigate the background of each key executive in detail, so be sure that their published resumes are accurate. The underwriter must conduct this level of detailed review in order to protect itself in case problems arise after the IPO that it should have seen prior to the stock offering. If there is even a hint of the company trying to mislead the underwriter about material issues, the underwriter will walk away; be certain to verify all information in the business plan prior to releasing it to the underwriter.

If the underwriter remains interested in the company after the due diligence phase, it will sign a letter of intent with the company. This letter outlines these issues:

- *Type of agreement.* The letter will state if the arrangement with the underwriter will be a *firm commitment* deal or a *best efforts* deal. The firm commitment approach is used by most large underwriters and requires them to purchase a fixed number of shares from the company at a fixed price, which is discounted from the price at which they will sell the shares to investors. This is the preferred approach, since a company will be guaranteed a fixed amount of cash. The alternative is a best efforts deal, under which the underwriter merely tries to sell as many shares as it can and takes a commission on those shares it sells. This alternative does not guarantee a company any cash and still requires it to meet with the various requirements of being a publicly held entity, so it is much less preferable. A best efforts deal is most common when a company's prospects are considered sufficiently risky that the underwriter is uncomfortable purchasing the entire stock offering, thereby putting itself at risk of being unable to resell them.

- *Expenses.* The underwriter will outline the expenses it expects to charge the company. The largest portion of these costs will be a percentage of the stock offering. More information about this is listed in the "Cost of an IPO" section, earlier in this chapter. This is a good time to consider swapping an issuance of warrants to the underwriter in exchange for a lower commission rate. Another significant cost listed in the agreement will be the legal expenses incurred by the underwriter for its legal counsel to review state "blue sky" laws to see how they apply to the offering. You should insist on a cap to these expenses, which can be substantial. The underwriter also may require the company to pay for any out-of-pocket expenses that incurs if the company withdraws from the IPO—if so, be sure to insert a maximum expense cap in the agreement. There should be no expense reimbursement requirement if the underwriter is the party that withdraws from the offering.

- *Overallotment option.* This option is another manner in which the underwriter can profit from a potentially lucrative stock offering. It allows the underwriter to purchase additional shares from the company, up to a specified maximum amount, within a short time period following the IPO date. If the underwriter feels that it can sell additional shares at a high price, it will buy the extra shares from the company, sell them to investors, and pocket the difference. The overallotment option is usually acceptable to company management, unless the additional shares sold potentially might interfere with their control of the company.

- *Expected stock price.* The agreement will list a price at which the underwriter expects to sell the company's shares. This is strictly a preliminary number that can vary considerably, depending on market fluctuations and the receptiveness of institutional investors to the proposed price during the subsequent road show.

During the period between when the company engages the services of an underwriter and 25 days after its securities begin trading, the company is in a so-called *quiet period*, when it should not issue any marketing statements or materials that could be construed as an attempt to promote the stock. For example, no projections about expected company performance should be issued. To avoid any chance of breaking the SEC's quiet period regulations, any company communications during this period should be cleared by legal counsel prior to release.

Once the letter of intent is signed by both parties, they jointly move forward into the IPO registration process, which is described in the next section.

Registering for and Completing the IPO

Registering for and completing the IPO process usually takes three to four months. The basic steps in the process are due diligence investigations of a company's operations and finances, followed by the creation of a registration statement, whose contents are updated based on SEC comments. This is followed by a road show, final pricing of the stock, filing of the final prospectus with the SEC, and closing the deal with the underwriter. The next discussion is based on a firm commitment deal with an underwriter. A best efforts deal differs from this discussion primarily in the length of time required to obtain payment from the underwriter; it may require two to three extra months following the registration effective date.

The due diligence process is conducted by the underwriter and is a vastly expanded version of the due diligence it went through when it was initially investigating the company. In this case, it will require outside auditors to comb the company's financial records at a level of detail significantly greater than a standard audit and issue a *comfort letter* to the underwriter, stating the additional procedures it completed at the request of the underwriter. These procedures usually relate to unaudited financial information that is included in the registration statement. The auditors send the comfort letter to the underwriter once the initial registration statement has been filed.

The registration statement is comprised of a prospectus and additional information required by the SEC. The statement is the SEC's Form S-1. The prospectus portion of the statement is an overview of the company's operations and finances and is carefully designed to be a balance of marketing language intended to bolster the stock and a tedious itemization of every conceivable risk to which the company is or may be subject, with the intent of avoiding liability in case the company's prospects sour after it goes public. It also includes all standard financial reports, such as the balance sheet, income statement, statement of cash flows, and shareholders' equity. It also will include interim financial statements if the registration statement is declared effective (more on that shortly) more than 134 days subsequent to the company's fiscal year end. The registration statement is a complex document, so expect 30 to 60 days to pass before the initial version is ready for review by the SEC.

The registration statement is forwarded to the SEC, which usually takes one month to review it. Then the SEC issues a letter of comment, which contains required changes that must be added to the statement in order to bring it into compliance with SEC regulations. Their comments can include such issues as an expansion of risk disclosures, cross-referencing information within the prospectus, questions about the use of certain accounting policies, and adding information to support claims made. Once these changes are made in an amended filing, the SEC has the right to continue reviewing the document until it declares the statement to be effective.

The company also must submit the registration statement to the Financial Industry Regulatory Authority, which wants to ensure that the underwriter's compensation is not excessive. In addition, the statement must be sent to each state in which the company plans to offer its shares for sale, so they can verify that the offering meets individual state reporting requirements.

The prospectus portion of the registration statement is sent to prospective investors. This *red herring* version of the statement may not yet have been approved by the SEC and will not include a final stock price but will list a range within which the final price will fall. This version is used to educate investors in advance about the offering but not to solicit the sale of stock. It is also sent to the syndicate of other underwriters that the primary, or "managing," underwriter will assemble to help sell the stock.

After filing the registration statement and prior to its effective date, the CEO and chief financial officer (sometimes accompanied by other members of management) go on a road show to visit a number of key institutional investors and analysts, where they make a sales pitch about the company but do not attempt to sell any shares. This is a physically exhausting process that typically lasts about two weeks. Preparing for the road show also requires long hours, frequently including training by speech coaches and even etiquette consultants.

While the management team is conducting the road show, its legal counsel will file an application with the stock exchange on which it wishes to be listed and select a registrar (who tracks all stock, pays out dividends of various types, and mails reports to shareholders) and a stock transfer agent (who handles the transfer of shares between parties) to handle subsequent stock-related issues. Legal counsel also will submit filings in accordance with the securities laws of all states in which the company expects to sell shares.

Once the SEC is satisfied with all changes made to the registration statement, company management meets with the underwriter to set the final price of the stock. Price setting is part science and part art form. Ostensibly, the price should be based on a quantitative measure, such as the existing P/E multiple or price/revenue multiple for similar companies. Other operational issues many be considered that will modify the price to some extent, such as backorder volume, sales trends, the proportion of expenses to sales, the quality of management, outlook for the entire industry, severity of current or potential competition, pending pollution issues, or presence of valuable patents. However, the comments of institutional investors that were contacted during the road show will have a strong bearing on the final price. They usually are relied on to purchase a significant proportion of the company's stock, and if they show resistance to purchasing stock at a specific price, the underwriter will recommend a price reduction. In addition, the underwriter will underprice the issuance slightly in order to ensure a complete sale of all shares offered to the public; this also gives the underwriter some grounds for avoiding a lawsuit in case the stock price later declines, and investors claim that the initial price was too high. The extent of the underpricing tends to be greater during the IPO in comparison to secondary offerings, so management may want to consider selling slightly fewer shares at this time in order to avoid dilution.

Underwriters like to price IPO shares in the range of $10 to $20, on the grounds that this avoids penny stock status (which is $5 or less) and the perception that investors will be less likely to buy shares priced above $25. To achieve this range, the company may have to conduct either a *stock split* or a *reverse stock split*. For example, if the underwriter decides that a company's total valuation is $50 million and that the stock price will be $20, there should be 2.5 million shares outstanding in order to achieve the designated price per share. If the company actually has 10 million shares outstanding, it must conduct a four-for-one reverse stock split in order to bring the number of outstanding shares down to the required 2.5 million level.

The underwriter also will want to sell in excess of 1 million shares during the IPO, not only to create an active trading market for the stock but also to meeting the minimum outstanding shares rules of the stock exchanges (as noted further in the "Trading on an Exchange" section later in this chapter).

Once all parties agree to the stock price, the price is included in the registration statement as an amendment, along with the net proceeds by the company resulting from the offering and the underwriter's commission. The company asks the SEC to declare the registration statement "effective." This request typically is accompanied by a request to accelerate the SEC's standard 20-day waiting period between the filing date of the last amendment and the date when the registration is declared effective, which the SEC generally agrees to as long as the prospectus already has been sufficiently widely circulated to prospective investors in its red herring format. After the registration is declared effective, the company issues the prospectus to the investors that previously received the red herring as well as any others who wish to review it.

The underwriter and the company then sign a *lockup agreement*, under which management restricts itself from selling any company shares it owns for a minimum period, usually of at least a half year.

Finally, at a closing meeting that usually takes place about one week after the registration effective date, the underwriter hands over payment for all shares proffered under the IPO offering in exchange for the share certificates. This delay of a few days is needed for the underwriter to collect cash from its investors, which then receive the stock from the underwriter. The company is now officially a public entity.

Alternatives for Selling Securities

A traditional IPO may not be available to a company for a variety of reasons. Potential underwriters may feel that a company's underlying technological prowess is too unproven to make a convincing case to potential shareholders. The same reasoning may apply to its rate of growth or the perceived quality of its management team. Or the market may be saturated with other IPOs, so there is no room for another one without accepting an unreasonably low price. If any of these circumstances apply, a company may consider using the options listed in this section—an *open IPO* offering, the purchase of a shell corporation, or a small corporate offering registration (SCOR) offering.

Open IPO

One alternative to the traditional sale of stock through an underwriter is to use an open IPO auction. Under this approach, potential investors download a prospectus over the Internet from an underwriter that specializes in this type of offering. If they wish to bid on the shares, they open an account with the underwriter, select a bid price and the number of shares desired, and send the underwriter a check for that amount. This bid can be withdrawn at any time prior to the offering date. Based on the range of bids received, the underwriter then creates a public offering price at which share purchases will be accepted (which matches the price of the lowest bid received, below which all other bids exceed the number of shares to be offered). All investors bidding above this price will be issued their full share allocations while those whose bids were below the price will be refunded their money. Those investors bidding the exact amount of the public offering price will receive some portion of their requested number of shares, depending on how many other investors requested shares at that price and how many shares are still available for sale. This approach tends to result in higher share prices, resulting in either more proceeds flowing to the company or fewer shares being sold (resulting in more control by the original shareholders).

Example

A company wishes to sell 1 million shares to the public. Investors bid for 500,000 shares at $14 each while bids are also received for 300,000 shares at $13.50 and 600,000 at $12.00. Since the entire offering can be sold at a price of $12, this becomes the public offering price. All investors bidding at prices of $14 and $13.50 per share will receive their full allocations of shares and will pay $12 per share. Of the 600,000 shares bid at $12, investors will receive only one-third of their requested amounts, since this will result in 1 million shares being sold, which was the original target.

Reverse Merger

An IPO is extremely expensive and requires a great deal of management time to initiate. An alternative that uses less of both resources is the reverse merger. Under this approach, a company buys the shell of a company that has already gone public and merges itself into the shell. A corporate shell is an entity that has suspended ongoing operations and that generally has few assets.

The cost of a reverse merger ranges from $100,000 to $300,000, plus the cost to obtain the shell corporation (which will vary widely, depending on the value of its assets and the presence of any liabilities or other legal issues). A reverse merger can be completed in as little as 45 to 90 days, which allows management to return quickly to a focus on operational issues.

Another advantage of the reverse merger is that the shell company usually has sustained losses in the past, resulting in a sometimes sizable net operating loss (NOL) that can be used to offset the earnings of the acquiring company. However, the use of these NOLs likely will be restricted if there is a change in control of the shell, which is the usual scenario.

A disadvantage is that a shell may have unsettled legal claims that could be brought against the acquiring company. A considerable amount of due diligence is needed to locate potential or existing claims, which also increases the cost of the reverse merger.

Another problem is that the shell may not have kept up its required filings with the SEC; they must be brought up to date before the reverse merger can be completed.

Further, the acquiring company must issue some stock to the shareholders of the shell corporation to pay for the acquisition, possibly as much as 20% of all shares, resulting in dilution of the ownership interests of shareholders in the acquiring company and possibly of the value of their stock.

A very likely additional problem is that the shell's original shareholders may sell their shares as soon as possible following the reverse merger, resulting in a sudden decline in the traded stock price. This issue can be mitigated by incorporating timing restrictions on stock sales into the acquisition agreement.

Finally, companies that go public through reverse mergers tend to have only modest revenues and growth prospects and so are ignored by stock analysts and brokers who might otherwise increase investor interest in the stock.

To summarize the key issues, the reverse merger is an attractive alternative to the IPO, but the potential for hidden liabilities requires in-depth due diligence to ensure that the acquiring company does not become mired in lawsuits and the settlement of other liabilities.

SCOR

Another alternative is to file for a SCOR. This is a simplified registration used by companies that want to raise up to $1 million within a 12-month period. You must complete the 50-question Form U-7 and file it with the state securities commission for the state in which the company operates. The form requires no review by the SEC, but it must be reviewed by the state securities commission. This form can be used as a prospectus by the company in its search for investors (since this approach does not normally involve an underwriter). This approach can be taken by any entity incorporated in either the United States or Canada, except for investment or public companies.

The SCOR approach falls under the restrictions of Rule 504 of the SEC's Regulation D, which governs private and limited stock offerings. Rule 504 allows a company to sell shares to an unlimited number of investors, who do not have to meet any accreditation standards. It also allows the company to advertise the stock offering and does not restrict the resale of stock in any way. In short, the SEC is unusually liberal in its regulation of small stock offerings in the size range of a SCOR.

Although the SCOR approach is far less expensive than an IPO, it carries other risks and uncertainties. First, a company using this approach may try to avoid expenses by not using legal counsel. This approach may lay it open to potential shareholder lawsuits due to some unexpected oversight in the registration and solicitation process. The obvious mitigation approach to this risk is to bring the best legal counsel into the SCOR filing process as soon as possible and to solicit its advice at every step of the offering. Also, the management team must sell the shares to investors, an activity that may not fall within its range of expertise. Finally, due to the lack of an underwriter, there will not be a ready market for subsequent sales of the stock, making investment liquidations a chancy affair for investors.

Trading on an Exchange

After a company has completed an IPO, its stock is not yet traded on a stock exchange. If a company is not listed on an exchange, its securities will be designated as over-the-counter (OTC) stocks and most likely will appear in the Pink Sheets. The "pink sheet" name is derived from the color of stock price sheets that were distributed by the National Quotation Bureau starting in 1904 and that served as a pricing reference for stock trades through local stock dealers. This market is a dangerous one for investors, who must conduct their own research into prospective investments and who are at considerable risk of losing their entire investments in companies that may be in distressed circumstances or whose stocks are so thinly traded that they are subject to large price swings. Consequently, avoiding OTC status by enrolling in a stock exchange is considered highly advantageous.

Gaining entry to a stock exchange requires an application to it, in which the company states that it meets or exceeds all entry requirements of the exchange. These requirements are not just financial—for example, the major stock exchanges all require a listed company to have an audit committee, usually with at least a majority of the directors being independent of the company. If the exchange accepts an application, the company's shares are listed on the exchange, and an exchange representative is assigned to the company in order to advise it on exchange rules and how to market itself most effectively to investors through the exchange. This service comes at a cost—both an initial listing fee and an ongoing annual charge.

The highest-volume stock exchanges in the United States are the American Stock Exchange (Amex), Nasdaq Stock Market (Nasdaq), and New York Stock Exchange (NYSE). Each of the three major exchanges have differing requirements for entry, with the AMEX and Nasdaq SmallCap being the easiest to enter and the NYSE being the most difficult. An increasingly popular alternative is the Alternative Investment Market (AIM) of the London Stock Exchange, which allows companies to avoid many of the onerous rules required by U.S. exchanges.

American Stock Exchange

The Amex targets smaller companies with modest market capitalizations. It is easily the most aggressive of the three exchanges in attracting new listings. Its staff regularly scans new stock registrations that are filed with the SEC and contacts registrants about listing with the exchange. Staff also is sent out to prospects to discuss the advantages of listing. Thus, a micro-cap company is far more likely to be petitioned by the Amex than any other exchange.

The Amex provides a number of services to each listing company, as shown next.

- *Specialist.* The key Amex benefit is an assigned trading specialist. The specialist is obliged, to the extent reasonably practical, to purchase and sell a listed company's securities for his or her own account in order to help maintain an orderly market, with minimal price changes between transactions. Listed companies have direct access to their specialist, who can tell them about the market activity in their shares.
- *Liaison.* The Amex assigns a liaison, called an Amex Issuer Services Director (ISD), to every listed company. The ISD assists each company in obtaining services provided by the Amex.
- *Amex Online Web site.* This Web site allows listed companies to conduct peer analysis comparisons and historical charting, locate analyst ratings, research

contact information for analysts and investment management firms, and view a complete calendar of earnings releases and conference calls.

- *Strategy seminars.* The Amex makes available a pair of strategy seminars each year to listed companies. These seminars focus on topics in investor relations, investment banking, corporate governance, equity trading, and regulatory issues.
- *CEO dinners.* The Amex coordinates a series of CEO dinners throughout the country that allow CEOs to network with their counterparts in other Amex-listed companies.
- *Investor relations audit.* The Amex conducts a review of a listed company's communication materials, develops an investor fact sheet, and provides buy-side and sell-side contacts.

The Amex's listing requirements are designed to attract smaller companies with relatively small floats. In order to be accepted for listing on the Amex, a company can qualify under any one of the four standards shown in Exhibit 14.1.

In addition, there are stock distribution guidelines, which are intended to ensure that a sufficiently broad array of investors own a company's stock. They are shown in Exhibit 14.2.

A close reading of these listing guidelines reveals that the Amex is extremely amenable to listing almost any company, and it has created many variations on its acceptance criteria in order to attract the largest possible number of companies. For example, only Standard 1 even requires reported income; in all other cases, the Amex does not require evidence of profitability. Also, three of the standards do not require an operating history, so short-lived entities can become listed very quickly. Standard 4 was specially designed for telecommunications companies, which rarely report profits but which have considerable revenue and assets. The only area in which the Amex has significant requirements across all standards is the market value of a company's public float. Thus, as long as a company has a sufficient volume of tradable stock, the Amex is interested in listing it.

Of some interest, the official Amex guidelines are literally "guidelines." The Amex has been known to waive some listing requirements, so it is best to make inquiries rather than simply assume that certain initial listing standards are unattainable.

On an ongoing basis, a listed company must maintain a $1 million market value of public float. In addition, it must maintain $2 million in stockholders' equity if it has

EXHIBIT 14.1 American Stock Exchange Initial Listing Guidelines

Requirements	Standard 1	Standard 2	Standard 3	Standard 4
Pretax income	$750,000			
Market capitalization			$50 million	$75 million or
Total assets				$75 million and
Total revenue				$75 million
Market value of public float	$3 million	$15 million	$15 million	$20 million
Minimum price	$3	$3	$2	$3
Operating history		2 years		
Stockholders' equity	$4 million	$4 million	$4 million	

EXHIBIT 14.2 American Stock Exchange Stock Distribution Guidelines

Public stockholders	Option A: 800
	Option B: 400
	Option C: 400
Public float (shares)*	Option A: 500,000
	Option B: 1,000,000
	Option C: 500,000
Average daily volume	Option C: 2,000

*Public float is all shares not held directly or indirectly by any officer or director of a listed company, or by any other person who is the beneficial owner of more than 10% of the total shares outstanding.

had losses in two of the most recent three years, or $4 million if it has had losses in three of the most recent four years, or $6 million if it has had losses in the five most recent fiscal years. If a company cannot satisfy these equity requirements, it still can remain on the Amex if it has a market capitalization of at least $50 million or total assets and revenue of $50 million each. The Amex does not have an ongoing minimum stock price requirement.

In short, the Amex is ideal for listing by smaller companies. Its main competition is the Nasdaq's Capital Market, which similarly caters to smaller entities.

Overview of the Nasdaq

"Nasdaq" stands for the National Association of Securities Dealers Automated Quotation. In brief, it is the largest electronic stock market in the United States. Being entirely electronic, it executes orders faster and at lower cost than most other stock exchanges. However, there is no assigned specialist who makes a market in a company's stock. This can result in somewhat greater stock volatility as well as a larger relative spread (see the "Comparing the Stock Exchanges" section later in this chapter).

The Nasdaq operates the Market Intelligence Desk (MID), which monitors the activity of a listed company's stock. The investor relations officer can contact the MID for updates about recent stock activity. This contact is through a MID director, who is a predetermined point of contact for each company. In isolated instances, the MID may contact the IRO by phone or e-mail if there is unusual market activity.

The MID director arranges for additional services to its listing companies. These include a full-service corporate insurance broker, a research report service, and investor relations services. However, in most cases, a listed company will incur extra fees for these services.

Nasdaq Capital Market

The Nasdaq operates a stock exchange for smaller companies, called the Nasdaq Capital Market. This exchange competes with the American Stock Exchange.

A company can qualify under any one of the three standards shown in Exhibit 14.3 in order to be accepted for listing on the Nasdaq Capital Market.

EXHIBIT 14.3 Nasdaq Capital Market Initial Listing Standards

Requirements	Standard 1	Standard 2	Standard 3
Stockholders' equity	$5 million	$4 million	$4 million
Market value of publicly held shares	$15 million	$15 million	$5 million
Operating history	2 years		
Market value of listed securities		$50 million	
Net income from continuing operations (in latest fiscal year or in two of last three fiscal years)			$750,000
Publicly held shares	1 million	1 million	1 million
Bid price	$4	$4	$4
Round lot shareholders	300	300	300
Market makers	3	3	3

On an ongoing basis, a company must exceed one of the three standards shown in Exhibit 14.4 to continue to be listed on the exchange.

As was the case with the Amex, the Nasdaq Capital Market substantially reduces its continued listing requirements from the initial listing requirements, so that it is relatively easy to continue to be listed on the exchange.

Nasdaq Global Market

The Nasdaq operates a stock exchange for larger companies, called the Nasdaq Global Market. This exchange competes with the New York Stock Exchange.

A company can qualify under any one of the three standards shown in Exhibit 14.5 in order to be accepted for listing on the Nasdaq Global Market.

In addition, an applicant must have either 450 round-lot stockholders, or a total of 2,200 stockholders, and 1,250,000 publicly held shares.

On an ongoing basis, a company must exceed one of the two standards shown in Exhibit 14.6 to continue to be listed on the exchange.

EXHIBIT 14.4 Nasdaq Capital Market Continued Listing Standards

Requirements	Standard 1	Standard 2	Standard 3
Stockholders' equity	$2.5 million		
Market value of listed securities		$35 million	
Net income from continuing operations (in latest fiscal year or in two of last three fiscal years)			$500,000
Publicly held shares	500,000	500,000	500,000
Market value of publicly held securities	$1 million	$1 million	$1 million
Bid price	$1	$1	$1
Round lot shareholders	300	300	300
Market makers	2	2	2

EXHIBIT 14.5 Nasdaq Global Market Initial Listing Standards

Requirements	Standard 1	Standard 2	Standard 3
Pretax earnings	Aggregate $11 million in past three years, and $2.2 million in each of past two fiscal years, and $0+ in past three years		
Cash flows		Aggregate $27.5 million in past three years, and $0+ in each of prior three fiscal years	
Market capitalization (average over prior 12 months		$550 million	$850 million
Revenue (previous fiscal year)		$110 million	$90 million
Bid price	$5	$5	$5
Market makers	3	3	3

EXHIBIT 14.6 Nasdaq Global Market Continued Listing Standards

Requirements	Standard 1	Standard 2
Stockholders' equity	$10 million	
Market value		$50 million
or		or
Total assets/total revenue		$50 million/$50 million
Publicly held shares	750,000	1.1 million
Market value of publicly held shares	$5 million	$15 million
Bid price	$1	$1
Round lot stockholders	400	400
Market makers	2	4

New York Stock Exchange

The New York Stock Exchange specifically caters to the largest and wealthiest public companies in the world. It is considered prestigious to be listed on the NYSE. To keep this club exclusive, the NYSE has the toughest initial and continued listing standards of any exchange. Besides prestige, the main advantage of a NYSE listing is that some fund managers are allowed to invest only in NYSE-listed companies, so the pool of potential investors is quite large.

The NYSE hosts a number of virtual investor forums, which are web conferences designed to provide investors with direct access to executives from companies listed on the NYSE. It also hosts industry-specific conferences, which the executives of NYSE-listed companies can attend.

The NYSE also assigns a client service team to each listed company, which fulfills the same role as the Amex's ISD and the Nasdaq's MID director. Also, as with the Amex, a newly listed company selects a specialist who is responsible for making a market in the company's stock.

The NYSE's listing requirements are designed to attract larger companies with significant market capitalizations and operating results. It requires minimum standards in two areas, which are stock distribution and financial results. Its stock distribution requirements are:

- 400 round-lot stockholders, or
- 2,200 total stockholders and average monthly trading volume for the last six months of 100,000 shares, or
- 500 total stockholders and average monthly trading volume for the last 12 months of 1 million shares

An additional stock distribution requirement is to have 1.1 million public shares outstanding, with a market value of $100 million.

The NYSE also has multiple variations on its initial listing requirements relating to financial results. They include:

- Aggregate pretax earnings over the past three years of $10 million, and a minimum of $2 million in each of the two most recent years, or
- Aggregate operating cash flow of $25 million over the last three years (applicable only for companies with at least a $500 million market cap and $100 million revenues during the most recent 12 months), or
- Revenues for the most recent fiscal year of at least $75 million, and a market capitalization of at least $750 million

On an ongoing basis, a listed company must maintain performance under one of three standards, which are outlined in Exhibit 14.7. This is a simplified version of the

EXHIBIT 14.7 New York Stock Exchange Continued Listing Standards

Requirements	Earnings Standard	Cash Flow Standard	Pure Valuation Standard
Average closing price over 30-day trading period	$1	$1	$1
Average market capitalization over 30-day trading period	$75 million and	$250 million and	$375 million and
Total stockholders' equity	$75 million or		
Average market capitalization over 30-day trading period	$25 million		
Total revenues for most recent 12 months		$20 million	
Total revenues for most recent fiscal year			$15 million

complex NYSE standards; see the www.nyse.com site for a complete set of continued listing standards.

Comparing the Stock Exchanges

There are significant differences in the fees charged by the various stock exchanges. Exhibit 14.8 lists the initial listing fees for the exchanges, showing the lowest and highest possible prices. For companies having in excess of 50 million shares, the maximum fees will apply.

The Amex has positioned itself to be slightly less expensive than the Nasdaq Capital Market, although the pricing difference is minor. Similarly, the Nasdaq Global Market has positioned its prices to be clearly below those of the NYSE. However, for companies with the resources to list on the NYSE, its higher fees are probably not a significant factor.

In addition, each exchange charges an annual listing fee, which is shown in Exhibit 14.9. Again, rather than showing the full range of prices, the table reveals the lowest and highest possible prices. The maximum annual listing fee for the NYSE is misleading, since it only applies to a very high share volume. Accordingly, an additional row is included for 50 million shares, to give some indication of pricing for a midrange share volume.

The differences between the annual fees charged by the Amex and the Nasdaq Capital Market are insignificant. If a very large company lists on the NYSE, its annual fees can substantially exceed those it would incur if it listed on the Nasdaq Global Market.

The number of required *round-lot* stockholders (those owning at least 100 shares) does not vary significantly among the exchanges, with the usual requirement

EXHIBIT 14.8 Comparison of Stock Exchange Initial Listing Fees

Shares	Amex	Nasdaq Capital Market	Nasdaq Global Market	NYSE
Up to 5 million	$45,000	$50,000	$100,000	$150,000
50+ million	70,000	75,000	150,000	250,000

EXHIBIT 14.9 Comparison of Stock Exchange Annual Listing Fees

Shares	Amex	Nasdaq Capital Market	Nasdaq Global Market	NYSE
Up to 5 million	$16,500	$27,500	$30,000	$38,000
50 million	32,500	27,500	45,000	46,500
Maximum	34,000	27,500	95,000	500,000

varying between 300 and 500 round-lot stockholders. Once a company has been trading on an exchange for a few months, it usually exceeds these figures by a substantial amount.

All of the exchanges allow a company to be listed even if it does not report pretax income, by alternatively requiring a higher float, cash flow, or market capitalization. These alternative requirements are easier to meet on the Amex and Nasdaq Capital Market and more difficult on the Nasdaq Global Market and NYSE.

The continued listing requirements are much lower than the initial listing requirements for all of the exchanges. For example, the Amex has no minimum stock bid price for a continued listing, while the Nasdaq Capital Market's bid price requirement drops from an initial listing requirement of $4 to $1, and the Nasdaq Global Market's requirement drops from $5 to $1.

Amex directors do not sell products or services to their assigned companies, whereas a Nasdaq director's compensation is based partially on his or her ability to sell products and services to assigned companies. A company may not experience any real change in costs because of these differences, but there is certainly more selling pressure in the Nasdaq environment.

All of the exchanges require compliance with a variety of governance standards, such as a majority of independent directors, audit committees, and codes of conduct. There are no significant differences between the governance standards required by the various exchanges.

Over-the-Counter Stocks

If a publicly traded company cannot meet the listing requirements of a stock exchange, it can choose to have its shares traded OTC. The best two vehicles for such trading are Pink Sheets LLC and the OTC Bulletin Board, which is operated by Nasdaq.

The OTC Bulletin Board operates an electronic exchange that handles bid and price information on about 3,300 securities of various kinds. For a company to have its securities quoted in the OTC Bulletin Board exchange, it first must find at least one market maker who is willing to quote the stock; this person must be an SEC-registered broker-dealer. Listing also requires that a company be registered with the SEC, which lends considerable credence to securities quoted on this exchange. The exchange charges no fees for a security to be quoted in its system.

Pink Sheets LLC (www.otcmarkets.com) operates an Internet-based, real-time quotation service for OTC equities and bonds, of which about 5,000 are currently traded. It is not a registered stock exchange. For a company to have its securities quoted in the Pink Sheets exchange, it must find at least one market maker who is willing to quote the stock; this person must be an SEC-registered broker-dealer. Pink Sheets LLC does not require that a company register with the SEC before being listed in its exchange service. Because of this lack of registration requirements, being listed by Pink Sheets LLC tends to give a company the reputation for having questionable financial results.

Summary

The objective of many successful business owners is to take their companies public, so they eventually can sell off some portion of their shares in the business and retire. However, this reasoning does not always work out in practice, because of the considerable expense of the IPO, the ongoing cost of reporting to the public and of ongoing exchange listing fees, potential investor lawsuits, and the risk of loss of control of the business. Consequently, an increasing number of business owners have concluded that they would rather take their companies private. Doing so requires special reporting requirements, which are discussed in Chapter 17, Taking a Company Private.

CHAPTER 15

Investment Community

The investment market is divided into two halves: the sell side and the buy side. The sell side is the middlemen who assist companies in locating funding or in selling company shares to investors. Sell-side entities include investment bankers and brokerage firms, and they employ analysts, stock traders, investment bankers, and institutional salespeople. The buy side is any entity managing capital funds, such as pension funds, mutual funds, or individual investors. A company can work through the sell side to reach the buy side or work with the buy side directly. In this chapter, we cover how to deal with both sides of the market.

Analyst's Perspective

A key player on the sell side is the analyst. This person sometimes is perceived as a partly mythical creature who can instantly accelerate or crash a company's stock price, who is constantly demanding more information than the management team is prepared to give, and who becomes decidedly cantankerous when the company's actual results do not attain expected levels. It is useful to understand the pressures faced by analysts and the environment in which they operate, so that the company can better support their needs.

The first factor to consider is that sell-side firms now budget for fewer analysts than in the boom years of the 1990s. Since the number of public companies has not declined, this means that analysts have withdrawn their coverage from some companies, usually those with smaller capitalizations. Small-cap companies suffer the most from the decline in analysts, because an analyst's recommendation must maximize commissions for the employing sell-side firm, and companies with small capitalizations have an insufficient float to generate much commission volume.

The second point to consider is the types of companies that an analyst is willing to cover. A large sell-side firm with a massive sales staff is likely to authorize coverage only for larger public firms, since they need to sell massive volumes of stock in order to earn sufficient commission volume. Conversely, an analyst employed by a smaller firm will be more willing to look at smaller companies that are not being provided coverage by larger firms. Thus, a company initially trying to attract analysts should ignore the larger sell-side firms and instead concentrate its efforts on smaller firms that are more likely to be receptive.

A third key factor to consider is the method by which analysts are paid. An analyst is paid to correctly predict the direction in which a company's stock price will move. If the prediction is correct, the analyst's firm will earn trading commissions on the purchase of the company's stock. Conversely, analysts suffer reduced compensation or are fired if they incorrectly predict stock price movements. This explains why analysts are nonplussed when management reports unexpected earnings levels— they can lose their jobs over the resulting stock price decline. Thus, it is critically important to be conservative in providing guidance as well as open and responsive in issuing changes to guidance. Analysts appreciate the notice, so they can change their estimates in a timely manner.

Sell-side firms also try to pull in acquisition work or stock placement assistance by dangling the prospect of analyst coverage in front of a company. Since most companies occasionally engage in either or both of these activities, it makes sense to obtain assistance from a firm that also can provide analyst coverage. Better yet, parcel out this business to multiple firms, so that coverage will be given by several analysts. However, because such coverage can be short-lived if a company does not continue to dole out business to the same sell-side firms, this is not a reliable source of coverage. Also, Section 501 of the Sarbanes-Oxley Act of 2002 states that employees of a broker-dealer who are:

> *involved with investment banking activities may not, directly or indirectly, retaliate against or threaten to retaliate against any securities analyst employed by that broker or dealer or its affiliates as a result of an adverse, negative, or otherwise unfavorable research report that may adversely affect the present or prospective investment banking relationship of the broker or dealer with the issuer that is the subject of the research report.*

Thus, obtaining analyst coverage as part of a broader services deal may be a two-edged sword, since there is no guarantee that the coverage will be favorable.

Finally, analysts are unwilling to anger a company's management with negative ratings, as doing so could lead to their being excluded from access to the company. Accordingly, they use a broad range of recommendation types that keep them from having to label a company clearly with a buy, hold, or sell rating. Instead, the "buy" category is divided into (in increasing order of fervor) moderate buy, long-term buy, outperform, and strong buy. Many analysts will assign a rating of moderate buy, or some similar term, to a company's stock in order to pacify a management team when their company's earnings performance is mediocre, without taking the more drastic steps of assigning a hold or sell rating. In reality, a company whose stock is assigned a moderate buy rating may never be brought to the attention of the analyst firm's sales staff.

These observations lead to some conclusions regarding how to work with an analyst. First, do not repeatedly make outrageously high earnings claims, because this will result in wildly gyrating stock prices when earnings estimates are not met and when management makes stratospheric claims yet again. Under these circumstances, analysts will be at risk of not estimating earnings properly and likely will drop their coverage of the company. Second, protect every analyst's job by issuing consistently conservative guidance based on clearly understandable assumptions.

In addition, adopt and publicize a business plan that results in a quarterly earnings pattern consistent with the plan. Then analysts will feel that the company is providing them with sufficient information to anticipate and understand the reasons for changes in actual earnings. This approach may even result in coverage by additional analysts, because they know that any earnings estimates and recommendations they issue will very likely be correct. Thus, conservative guidance, consistently applied, is the key to the long-term analyst happiness.

Finding the Right Analyst

Analysts usually specialize in a single industry and then on only a few companies within that industry. It takes a considerable amount of effort to understand an industry thoroughly, so analysts rarely depart from their chosen industries to provide coverage of companies in other areas. Also, they generally provide coverage to companies whose market capitalizations fall within a predetermined range. Thus, the pool of analysts who might be interested in providing coverage for a specific company is relatively limited. However, if they already cover a company's industry, they may be willing to provide coverage, since doing so represents a minimal amount of additional work. Consider using these approaches to find these analysts:

- Determine who provides coverage for comparable companies. Some public companies list on their Web sites the names and contact information of the analysts who cover them. This is especially common for smaller companies that only have limited coverage. Larger firms being covered by dozens of analysts rarely list analyst contact information.
- Hire an investor relations firm that has established contacts with the analyst community and that can provide a short list of the most likely analyst candidates.

Once you have developed a pool of likely analysts, the next step is to contact them. The best approach is to provide them with a stream of useful information, such as industry data that they may not already have. If you do so, analysts are more likely at least include your company in their industry-wide research reports. Also, providing this service creates a sense of obligation; analysts are at least more likely to agree to an initial meeting in which the company can present an overview of its operations. This initial meeting is covered in the next section.

Sell Side: Analysts

This discussion assumes that a company is large enough to attract analyst attention. It is extremely difficult to obtain analyst coverage if a company's market cap is less than $100 million to $200 million. If your company's market cap is too small, do not waste time trying to attract analysts who are unlikely to be interested; instead, shift your attention to specific types of brokers who are amenable to micro-cap situations, as discussed later in this chapter.

When planning for a meeting with an analyst, always send an advance packet of preparatory information. This packet should include a fact book about the company's strategy, performance, and products. Analysts must perform a considerable amount of analysis before issuing a recommendation, so providing the fact book will allow them to create an initial set of questions, which they will pose during the meeting. Thus, sending advance information enables analysts to get the most out of meetings.

When preparing for an analyst meeting, it is extremely important to anticipate all questions that might be asked. If a manager were to appear befuddled by a question, the querying analyst might be concerned about the manager's ability to run the business and would decline to provide coverage of the stock. To avoid this problem, retain a list of questions that have been asked during meetings with other analysts, and supplement the list with questions asked during investor conference calls or other investor meetings. In addition, brainstorm the types of questions that might be asked in response to current or prospective changes in the business. If other comparable companies are hosting conference calls prior to the analyst meeting, listen to those calls to see if analysts are asking any new questions that you have not heard before. With these questions in hand, construct a standard set of answers, and have a dress rehearsal with the managers who will attend the analyst meeting.

An analyst expects to be provided with a considerable amount of information about the company. During the meeting, you should address the types of products and services that the company sells, which ones provide the bulk of the company's revenues, and the geographic areas and markets in which the products and services are sold. This sales discussion should include the overall size of the company's markets, the future of those markets, the company's share of those markets, the market growth rate, and management's expectation for its eventual market share. Analysts are very interested in competitors, so be prepared to discuss primary competitors, their sales volume and market share, and their strengths and weaknesses. If there have been acquisitions in the past or are likely to be in the near future, be prepared to discuss the criteria the company uses to select acquirees and how it integrates acquirees into the rest of the organization. In addition, be prepared to talk about growth goals, how the company plans to meet them, and the company's recent track record for meeting those goals. Finally, analysts concentrate heavily on how various risks will impact a company's prospects, so cover the key risks the company faces and how the company is prepared to protect itself from them.

In addition, analysts are very interested in intangible issues, such as the ability of the management team to run the company. For this reason, they likely will probe management's commitment to long-term planning, profit planning, and control systems, all of which are cornerstones of long-term management success. In addition, they probably will want to meet with the managers of the product development and marketing departments, to ascertain their skills in these two key areas. Given the likelihood of this level of questioning, you should ensure that anyone who comes in contact with an analyst is coached in the legalities of disclosing information.

The discussion of comparable companies (comps) is a key element of an analyst meeting that has a major bearing on the analyst's target price for the company's stock. Unless persuaded otherwise, most analysts will base their target stock prices on the stock prices of comparable companies in the same industry. For example, if the stock prices of comparable companies result in market capitalizations that are two times revenues, analysts will assume the same ratio for all companies in the industry. Analysts may not even bring up this issue, assuming that the usual industry comparisons will be used. If you feel that the company is more comparable to other companies, perhaps outside of the industry, this meeting is a good time to discuss which companies are better comps and why the analyst should use them as such. In short, if you do not define a group of comps for the company, analysts will do so independently, which likely will result in analysts assigning lower target prices to the company.

If an analyst decides to provide coverage of the company, part of her research will include in-depth discussions with the company's customers, suppliers, and employees to verify that the information presented to her by the company is correct. These discussions also will include a search for undisclosed issues that may impact the company's financial performance. Although this may appear to be an undue degree of prying, the management team must become used to this detailed level of review on an ongoing basis. Indeed, you can assist analysts with this review work by providing them with contact information.

Once the analyst has completed a detailed review of the company, she creates a research report that includes an earnings estimate, a recommendation, and a price target for the stock. She will update the report periodically as new information about the company or its industry appears, if that information will result in a material change in the earnings estimate and price target.

After an analyst issues a recommendation, you should review it in detail. Analysts are among the most knowledgeable independent observers of a company and its industry, so their commentaries are worthy of considerable review and discussion within the management team. In particular, note any commentary regarding how an analyst has arrived at a particular estimate of revenue or profit, especially the assumptions used to arrive at those numbers. By understanding analyst assumptions, it is possible to predict their behavior when the company's metrics change in the future. Also, if an analyst points out in a report a perceived flaw in the company's strategy or operating assumptions, the flaw may be indicative of a general market perception that is keeping the company's stock from achieving its full valuation. Treat these perceived flaws as opportunities for strategic changes or perhaps as grounds for additional education of the marketplace to mitigate the perceived impact of the flaws.

Negative Analyst Report

The reason for attracting the attention of analysts is to obtain favorable research reports, which presumably will result in an increase in the price of a company's stock. However, favorable reports do not last forever. At some point, the stock price will reach an analyst's target level, after which the analyst likely will change from a buy recommendation to a hold or sell recommendation. Also, some analysts occasionally act on incorrect information or incorrectly interpret information, resulting in a negative report. Further, junior analysts with little industry experience are more likely to issue earnings estimates that vary significantly from what a company expects to achieve. Management should expect these negative reports from time to time and should not be flustered or react angrily to them. Instead, the best approach is not to comment on the reports at all, and instead to provide a steady flow of information to the investing public. This method will help analysts arrive at high-quality earnings estimates that eventually will result in renewed buy recommendations. The most aggressive action a chief executive officer (CEO) should ever consider is contacting an analyst's research director to discuss perceived factual errors in a research report that might have negatively impacted the recommendation. A key point is that analysts will publish earnings estimates no matter what information they have available, so it is always in the company's best interests to give them more information rather than less.

The worst reaction to a negative analyst report is a public rant (which usually seems to occur during a quarterly conference call). Such behavior merely gives analysts an unflattering view of the management team. Also, it is not wise to cut off an analyst from access to company information or mailing lists, just because she issued a negative report. If you do so, the analyst will have even less information to use for future reports, which may result in increasingly inaccurate recommendations.

Sell Side: Brokers

More than 600,000 brokers are registered with the Financial Industry Regulatory Authority (FINRA). Maintaining contact with each of these brokers over a long period of time is not always cost effective, given the relatively small volume of share purchases that each one may generate. Given this problem, the best way to maintain broker relations is to determine which ones are considered opinion leaders by their peers and to ply these key individuals with a continuing stream of information about the company. If the opinion leaders are convinced, they will pass along their opinions to their broker networks, which can create a significant amount of share purchase volume.

An excellent approach for meeting brokers is to sponsor a gathering at a public venue shortly after the markets close. Alternatively, consider sponsoring a luncheon at a brokerage firm (where participation rates are usually very high) or at a popular local restaurant. In either case, the company pays for all food and drinks provided. The presentation should be short, certainly no more than 30 minutes, and should give brokers an overview of the company's operations and prospects. The emphasis in this type of presentation is much less on numerical performance and more on a company's story. Have written materials available for any brokers interested in additional information. Unlike analyst meetings, which are one on one, broker meetings usually include many participants, who are free to arrive or leave at any time during a presentation. The better brokers who will be of the most assistance in creating new stock sales may be difficult to identify or chat with, since they are so busy that they are likely to arrive late and leave early.

If a company has a low level of market capitalization (i.e., is a *micro-cap*), it will have a difficult time attracting brokers, because most of them are told which stocks to pitch to their clients, and those stocks almost always involve companies with larger capitalizations. To avoid this problem, do not waste time contacting brokers with conservative clients (usually those approaching retirement age), since these clients are unlikely to put their money into higher-risk investments. Also, only deal with brokers having at least 10 years of experience with the same firm, since they are more likely to have been given some leeway in making stock recommendations. These more senior brokers are also more likely to have as clients high-net-worth individuals, who are more likely to make investments in micro-cap companies if there is a significant level of perceived reward.

Another method for locating brokers willing to recommend micro-cap stocks is to call local brokerage firms after trading hours and ask the branch manager if any of the brokers specialize in companies with lower market caps. Another option is to hire an investor relations firm that already knows these brokers and that can arrange introductions with the CEO.

A broker does not need as detailed a set of information as an analyst requires. Instead, brokers require information about only a few key issues, which they will pass along to their clients. They are looking for stock that is actively traded, so their clients can buy and sell easily without any liquidity problems. Also, a company should have a solid performance record, demonstrated by multiple quarters of gradually increasing profitability. Finally, a company should have excellent visibility in the marketplace in the form of active public relations and investor relations programs. If these three factors are in place, a company has the capability to attract the attention of a large number of brokers.

Brokers are especially appreciative if the company itself creates a prepackaged set of sales pitches and supporting information that they can use to pitch the company to their clients. The company can create several variations on the sales pitch, based on conversations with key brokers. In addition to sales pitches, consider issuing reprints of articles about the company, which brokers can pass along to their clients.

Sell Side: Investment Bankers

An investment banker locates money on behalf of a company. The usual process is that the company and investment banker mutually create a multiyear forecasting model of the company's likely growth rate, cash flow, and valuation (based on the valuations of comparable public companies). The investment banker then sends a summary of the model and the company's operations and strategy to a select group of fund managers to obtain an initial expression of interest. If some interest is expressed, the investment banker helps the company's management team create a presentation, which ranges in length from 30 to 45 minutes, and coaches them through several iterations of the presentation. Once ready, the management team goes on a road show to pitch their case to the fund managers who expressed initial interest. Usually this means making multiple presentations per day in New York, Chicago, San Francisco, and Dallas, where many of the funds are located. The investment banker contacts the fund managers to see who is interested in making an investment and under what terms, and then closes the deal. The investment banker usually is paid based on a sliding scale of the amount of funds raised.

When picking an investment banker, base the decision on the person's experience with the company's industry. Only certain fund managers will invest in that industry, and the investment banker must have relationships with those managers. Also, a company very likely will require additional funding at some point in the future, so it makes sense to select an investment banker who can be a trusted advisor and confidant.

Sell Side: Investor Relations Specialists

Investor relations specialists represent a public company to brokers and analysts. They have extensive contacts with the sell side and will make many contacts on behalf of a company. They do not engage in analyst or broker meetings, nor do they fulfill any public relations functions. Their stock-in-trade is strictly their sell-side contacts. These specialists are retained most frequently by smaller over-the-counter companies with small floats and low stock prices, in hopes of achieving rapid stock price increases. Although the desired price increase may very well occur, the increase likely will be short term if it exceeds the company's underlying fundamentals.

Many sell-side specialists agree to be paid in stock, since smaller public firms are not always able to pay in cash. This gives the specialists a strong incentive to increase the price of the stock, since it increases their own compensation. However, given the thin trading volumes of the companies they represent, specialists can have difficulty liquidating their stock holdings.

If a company chooses to deal with sell-side specialists, they should supplement their investment in this activity with other public and investor relations activities and operational improvements, so that the resulting stock price increases are not short-lived but can form the foundation for long-term value for investors.

Buy Side: Types of Investors

There are several types of investors, each one with different reasons for buying, holding, and selling stock. The first type focuses on high *growth rates*; if a company can maintain a high rate of revenue or earnings growth, they continue to buy its stock, but they also dump the stock at the first report of a slowdown in growth. Another investor type focuses on the *value play*. They buy only when a stock is at a very low price, and they sell when they think the stock is fully valued. This investor tends to retain stock longer than a growth investor, because it may take a considerable amount of time for the stock to reach the predetermined price point. These investors may snap up a large amount of stock if the stock price has cratered and can be very effective in keeping the price from heading even lower. A third investor type focuses on *assured returns*. They buy stock when the company offers dividends and disappear if dividends are cut. Yet another type of investor, variously known as a technical analyst or chartist, focuses on *stock momentum*. These investors forecast stock prices based on their historical behavior rather than on a company's future prospects.

Within these categories, investors frequently restrict their activities to specific industries that they expect will achieve outsized returns. They also may focus on companies within a specific range of market capitalizations, which they feel will perform better under certain economic circumstances.

Although you may try to pigeonhole all investors into these categories, a significant proportion of investors may not hold the company's stock for any particular reason at all. In many cases, they have inherited the stock and have no plans or expectations for it. These stock holders are unlikely to sell their existing holdings or to acquire new stock. Instead, they passively retain their stock positions no matter what actions you take.

There are points in a company's life cycle when all of these types of investors will buy and sell its stock, resulting in a continually varying mix of investors. You may consider many of these investors to be transient and therefore undesirable, as they continually shift in and out of company stock holdings. Nonetheless, a public company is likely to experience all of these types of investors at some point during its life.

Buy Side: Institutional Investors

A professional investor is usually the manager of a fund, such as a pension fund or mutual fund, and commonly is described as an institutional investor. An analyst working for or serving the needs of a fund is considered a buy-side analyst.

Before contacting institutional investors about buying company stock, first determine their investment strategies to see if the company meets their criteria. For example, about 30% of all institutional stock portfolios invest in stock indexes, where the amount and mix of shares held are determined automatically by the index. If a company is listed on an index, institutional investors will buy it. If not, they have no interest.

Also, institutional investors do not usually invest in micro-cap companies, because their stock is so thinly traded. When there is minimal trading, a fund manager will have great difficulty acquiring a large volume of shares and will have difficulty later in selling those shares without initiating a stock price decline. Also, if a company's stock is not listed on an exchange, a fund manager will not consider it to be a viable investment. In these situations, do not expend any effort to contact institutional investors; they will not purchase company stock under any circumstances.

There is also a type of investor that a company does *not* want as an investor in its stock: the shareholder activist. These investors may attempt to have their nominees elected to the board of directors, push unwanted measures onto the annual shareholder ballot, or publicly demand other changes to the company's operations or governance. To some extent, there is little you can do to prevent such investors from acquiring its stock. However, you should certainly investigate the level of shareholder activism of any institution before arranging a meeting to pitch the company's prospects—it would hardly do to encourage these institutions to invest in the company.

The discussion thus far has been on those institutions *not* to pursue for an investment. Conversely, there are several ways to locate those funds that would be acceptable investors. First, contact an investor relations consultant who has contacts among the fund managers and who knows their preferred investment types. Also, review the Web sites maintained by the various funds; often their investment strategies are outlined. In addition, continually review the industry news to see who is quoted in feature articles. In many cases, a company manager will discuss how the company grew following an investment by a specific institution.

Another option is to look for institutions that invest in peer companies having similar investment characteristics, such as being in the same industry or having a similar growth rate in revenue, profits, or cash flow. These peer companies may not be in the same industry. Once you determine this peer group, the institutional Web sites to determine which ones are investing in the peer groups. Then contact their investment managers to point out the similarities between the company and the companies in which they currently invest and to ask for a familiarization meeting.

Whichever search method is used, the key point is to target fund managers, investment advisors, or buy-side analysts who either invest or recommend investments based on general guidelines within which they can choose the stocks of individual companies. If these people are locked into very specific investments by their fund investment policies, there is no point in contacting them.

If institutional investors are interested in investing in a company, one of their first actions is to delve into what is said in an analyst's report about that company without paying much attention to the actual rating given. They understand that the rating is, to some extent, assigned based on the analyst's unwillingness to offend management, and so it may not exactly reflect the contents of the report. Consequently, be thoroughly familiar with the contents of analyst reports, and be prepared to answer questions from institutional investors who are equally familiar with them.

You need to understand how institutional investors expect to be treated. First, they expect a tailored one-on-one meeting, where management makes a private presentation to them and sets aside sufficient time to answer all of their questions. Second, they will expect management to conduct a quarterly conference call, so that they can receive the latest information about the company's operational and financial results and have an opportunity to pose questions to management. Third, do not inundate them with annual reports and promotional materials; they already are wading through enormous amounts of material sent to them by other companies. Instead, prepare a summarized version of key information from public filings, and send it to them in the format they prefer. This may seem like a great deal of work, but retaining an institutional investor is important, and they appreciate it if you pay special attention to their needs.

Most CEOs would love to have a few prominent funds invest in their company's stock, but there are repercussions to having such investors. The main problem is that these funds accumulate so many shares that the trading environment becomes illiquid, with few remaining shares available for trading. Also, when institutions sell their stock holdings, the volumes sold are so large that there is a significant chance of a stock price decline.

Buy Side: Individual Investors

In an ideal world, individual investors are the best kind of investor, because they tend to be more loyal than institutional investors, holding their stock for much longer periods of time. These "sticky" investors are prized because their steadfast refusal to sell stock keeps the stock price and volume of sales from gyrating excessively.

The best possible kind of individual investor is the high-net-worth investor, since a few contacts by the CEO may result in significant stock purchases. To locate these individuals, consider retaining an investor relations consultant who has a contact list. Alternatively, use the network of existing high-net-worth investors to determine who they use as advisors, and reach out to these advisors to spread information about the company through their other contacts. Once high-net-worth investors become interested in the company, be prepared to assist them in obtaining additional information, because they are unlikely to have much research support.

Another source of new investors is the owners of the company's products. If a company is in the consumer products business and has a reputation for high quality, it is a good bet that consumers will be sufficiently enamored of the company to buy and hold its stock. To attract these investors, put information about the company's public status on product packaging. Conversely, consider turning current investors into product consumers by offering them discounts on company products. The main risk with this approach is ensuring that products continue to have a high level of quality. If the company begins to have product problems, investors originally attracted by the product line may leave in droves.

It also may be possible to target investors in competing firms. If so, you must prove to these investors why purchasing the company's stock represents a superior investment over that of the competitor. This can be a difficult sales proposition if the competitor is the dominant player in the market, since these firms tend to generate the best investor returns. Another difficulty with this approach is that the targeted investors may feel that their current portfolio mix represents a sufficient weighting in the company's market, so they will invest in the company only if they also sell their holdings in the competing firm.

Another way to attract investors is through the brokers of existing investors. If the current group of investors bought the company's shares based on a broker recommendation, building a direct relationship with that broker may very well result in the acquisition of new investors through the same broker. This method requires a long-term commitment to excellent broker relations, including the retention of key brokers on all mailing lists and invitations to them to participate in periodic investor conference calls. If a company drops its efforts in this key area, expect those investors brought in by brokers eventually to sell their shares.

If a company has a low capitalization, you will have an especially difficult time locating investors. Usually, only high-net-worth individuals are willing to invest in micro-cap stocks. These people typically are looking for outsize growth rates in excess of 20% for revenue, income, or cash flow. They need high returns, because the transaction costs of buying and selling micro-cap shares are higher than for larger-cap stocks, and they must be reimbursed for the added risk. For example, a key transaction cost for a micro-cap stock is the impact that a large buy or sell order has on the market price, which can shift significantly as a result of the order. There is also a time delay in obtaining or selling stock (since there may be few shares available for trading), during which time the stock price may shift unfavorably for the investor. These costs can make it several times more expensive to deal in micro-cap stocks than in stocks having a large float.

Another option for locating investors is the *nondeal road show.* This is a presentation to investors with the objective of spreading information about the company.

Nondeal road shows generally are scheduled four times per year, immediately after each quarterly conference call. By using this timing, you can speak on most topics without violating fair disclosure rules, since all key topics were fully disclosed during the conference call. When scheduling nondeal road shows, consider setting them up in a broad range of geographic areas. Many CEOs focus their attention on the region near company headquarters, which eventually results in saturation of the local market. By shifting presentations away from this home market, the company can tap a much larger pool of investors.

When arranging a nondeal road show, it is best not to present directly to buy-side investors without the involvement of a sell-side firm. The reason is that the sell side can earn commissions from the eventual purchase of company stock that may result from the road show. The potential earnings may result in additional sell-side analyst coverage, which in turn yields more positive press and therefore an even higher stock price. To maximize this effect, have a different sell-side firm arrange investor presentations in each city, so that more sell-side firms are beholden to the company, resulting in more analyst coverage. If there currently is no interest from sell-side firms, consider hiring an investor relations firm with contacts in the targeted geographic regions to arrange for investor presentations.

Clearly, there are many ways to locate prospective investors. The real problem is doing so in a cost-effective manner. You should try all of the options noted here at least once, and then narrow down the search methodology over time, based on which methods return the largest number of stock sales for the least effort.

Buy Side: Presentations to Investors

It is customary to give presentations to groups of individual investors. Given the millions of potential investors available, this means that a company should have a perpetual schedule of investor meetings; some large public companies schedule as many as 200 investor meetings per year. Only institutional investors warrant one-on-one meetings, because they have the potential to invest in a large proportion of a company's stock.

The aim of the investor presentation is to be short and to the point. Ideally, such a presentation should last no more than 15 minutes and use a maximum of 30 slides, which the presenter should adhere to strictly in most situations. First, make a brief statement about the company's primary strengths and competitive factors as well as the core concept that makes it a good investment. Second, describe its strategy as succinctly as possible. Third, describe the company itself: what it makes, how it distributes to customers, the size of its markets, and why the company chooses to be in those markets. If significant to the business, it also may be worthwhile to mention the barriers to entering the company's business and how the company maintains those barriers. Finish with a description of the company's financial structure, and then open the meeting for questions. The presentation should focus on giving investors a taste of the company, so that they learn enough in a short period of time to decide whether to request additional information that could lead to an investment. The intent is *not* to bury attendees with an overwhelming amount of information.

And a final thought: Never, ever cancel a scheduled presentation, even if there is an excellent reason for doing so. If you cancel a presentation, investors will think that something has happened at the company that management wants to hide, and they will have a predilection to abandon the stock or perhaps even sell stock short.

Summary

The sell side of the investment market is of great use to the CEO; not only can it attract capital for the company, but it also can contribute greatly to increases in its stock price. Several studies have shown that the greater the number of analysts following a company (which implies greater publicity for the company), the higher the stock's price/earnings ratio. Because of its importance, you must deal with the sell side in an appropriate manner, which involves consistently providing to the marketplace conservative guidance that is supported by easily understandable assumptions.

A great deal of planning is required before you make any buy-side contacts. You should conduct an evaluation of potential investors to determine how investor relations activities are to be prioritized for each one and what types of communications are to be used. A crucial part of this analysis is determining which types of investors are underserved and which ones are the most likely to retain company stock over the long term. The ideal plan is one that results in a shift from a small number of owners with massive holdings to a larger shareholder base with each shareholder retaining proportionally fewer shares.

CHAPTER 16

Public Company Activities

I n a publicly held company, the investor relations officer (IRO) handles a large part of the activities related to the investment community. However, there are still several areas in which the chief executive officer (CEO) must participate directly or make decisions regarding how the IRO is to handle certain situations. The two activities in which the CEO directly participates are investor conference calls and road shows. The CEO also should make decisions about what kind of guidance (if any) to issue about the company's performance and how to deal with short sellers. All four topics are addressed in this chapter.

Investor Conference Call

The conference call gives the investment community an opportunity to interact with the management team to learn about the latest quarterly results and hear any guidance updates for future projections. It is best to schedule conference calls to be held immediately after the latest 10-K or 10-Q filing, so there should be at least four conference calls per year.

The IRO should prepare an extensive set of written remarks for every conference call. If the management team delivers off-the-cuff remarks from a short outline of topics, listeners will not think that the team is taking the conference call seriously. Also, using a script gives the management team plenty of time to develop a clear, thorough presentation, so that no information is missed that might be open to interpretation by analysts. A prepared script also allows you to develop a central theme to the call that participants can state clearly and repeatedly.

When constructing the formal remarks for a conference call, pay particular attention to the informal rule of keeping such calls under 30 minutes. If the formal remarks extend even longer, listeners will have less time to ask questions, since most companies prefer to limit the total length of a conference call to one hour. The trend for the duration of formal remarks is dropping below the 30-minute mark; remarks lasting as few as 20 minutes are increasingly common. If the call runs too long, expect to have participants drop out or to shift the task over to an associate.

If a company faces a difficult issue, such as a decline in sales or the departure of a key employee, always address that issue within the conference call script. By doing so, you can formulate a considered answer to the issue and present it in the best possible light. Otherwise, someone may ask about it during the question and answer (Q&A) section of the call, and then the management team will have to answer it without a script.

The IRO is responsible for compiling an extensive set of answers to every question that possibly can be asked during the Q&A portion of the conference call; this process reduces the risk that the management team will seem unprepared to listeners. An excellent source of questions is the conference calls conducted by peer companies; listen to them to determine what questions are being asked of those companies, and be prepared to respond to the same questions. Also, review analyst reports to determine the areas in which they have concerns about the company. Another possibility is to scan the chat rooms on financial Web sites to see what questions investors are asking or what issues appear to be of most concern at the moment. Finally, organize a list of the most troublesome questions that may be asked, and spend extra time preparing answers to them.

An excellent way to organize the questions and answers is to post them around the meeting room on whiteboards or sheets of paper; this makes it easier to find and read off an answer quickly without any shuffling of paperwork that would be apparent to anyone listening over the phone. The team needs to show a very high level of operational knowledge during conference calls, because this gives investors a higher level of confidence in their ability to run the company; prewritten answers are a good way to give this impression.

Be prepared for speculative questions, such as "What would you do if the price of oil doubled next week?" The correct response is to state initially that the company does not engage in speculation and then answer the underlying question. For example, in response to the last question, the CEO might say, "We purchase key supplies for 180 days in advance in order to stabilize our raw material costs." If the underlying question is difficult to discern, ask the questioner to restate the question.

The conference call is not a good place to extol the virtues of the company. This is a forum in which listeners want to hear about a company's immediately preceding results, how it interprets those results, and any changes to its guidance for future results. Thus, this is a mostly factual discussion and is not the place to make general claims about future performance.

The IRO schedules conference calls at least three days in advance (preferably a week), and sends out notifications by press release, e-mail, and fax, specifying the time when the call will be conducted and the phone number to call in order to participate. If sent by fax, the notifications should be on corporate letterhead. No matter what form of distribution is used, the notice should come from the CEO and state the purpose of the call, which company managers will be on the call, and whether a Q&A session will be conducted. Some companies include in this notification a summary of the information to be covered during the conference call; doing this allows participants extra time to think of questions to ask during the Q&A part of the call.

When scheduling the conference call, it helps to place it immediately *after* those of peer companies (based on their historical or scheduled release dates and times); in this way, you can listen to their conference calls and hear what questions are being asked and learn the peers' results. However, if the company will impart bad news during its conference call, it may be better to schedule the call *before* the calls of peer companies, so that analysts will badger them during their calls about the issue that impacted your company. Also, it is better to schedule both the earnings press release and conference calls for after the markets have closed. Otherwise, the market might react to the earnings release before hearing what the company has to say during its conference call.

Company employees attending the conference call should be the CEO, chief financial officer (CFO), and IRO. Occasionally it may be necessary to bring in an expert, such as the manufacturing manager, to answer any anticipated questions that call for a deep level of expertise. However, do not use additional people often; otherwise listeners may think it is acceptable to call the new person directly for more information. Also, have a staff person on hand to write down listener questions on a whiteboard. With this extra staff assistance, the main meeting participants can concentrate on answering questions.

When the conference call begins, the IRO should introduce everyone from the company who will be participating in the call and then read a safe harbor statement. She introduces the CEO, who is the main speaker and who should speak exclusively from the scripted remarks. The CEO may hand off to the CFO to discuss numerical results or present the entire scripted comments by himself. After 20 to 30 minutes of prepared remarks, the CEO turns the meeting back over to the IRO, who accepts questions from callers and moderates the discussion until the conference call concludes after about one hour. The IRO sometimes may call back some of the call participants for feedback on how the call was conducted.

Once a conference call is complete, have a postmeeting review to determine which elements of the call can be improved. The IRO should chair this meeting, since she is not presenting during the bulk of the call and so is in the best position to evaluate it. This meeting should result in an improvement memo that is carried forward to the next conference call and forms the foundation of an advance meeting to improve that call. In addition, each member of the presentation team should listen to a recording of the call to see how to improve their individual presentation skills.

Other variations on the conference call are to have a separate call that focuses on a specific topic or to add a theme to each conference call where there is special emphasis on one topic. The intent is to increase the knowledge of the investment community about some special aspect of the company, such as a new product release or an expansion into a new country, a postacquisition update, or a patent that was just granted. If the call focuses entirely on the special topic rather than earnings, consider having the operational managers in charge of the subject area participate in the call.

Consider recording the call and posting it on the company Web site, for people who were unable to attend the call to listen to, There is no need to retain conference call recordings for very long; the information presented in the calls will become stale once the next conference call occurs.

Road Show

The road show is a repetitive series of meetings with the intent of raising money, in which a team of company presenters give essentially the same presentation multiple times over several days, often in multiple cities. The road show is the most versatile event tool at a company's disposal, because its subject can be altered to match the audience. For example, it can be an informational meeting with current shareholders living in a specific area, a sales pitch to a group of local brokers, or one-on-one meetings with institutional investors or large stockholders. Each of these audiences requires a different presentation based on their specific needs, so the management team will impart a different set of information to each one.

Given the repetitive nature of the presentation and the heavy travel schedule involved in a road show, there are several best practices to be aware of that can lighten the overall level of participant stress. These best practices are listed next.

- *Preparation.* The presentation should be thoroughly prepared in advance. By being prepared, the speakers can relax between meetings and spend more time mingling with attendees. This level of preparation usually calls for a practice session prior to each road trip, to ensure that presenters are thoroughly familiar with their materials.

- *Starting point.* Begin the road show in a regional market, not with major prospects. By doing so, the management team can become comfortable with the presentation and learn the most likely questions investors may pose. The team should be well prepared by the time it presents to key investors.

- *Duplication.* Given the intense travel schedule of a road show, there is a high probability that something will be lost or fail at some point. To mitigate this risk, keep a separate set of backup speaker notes and copies of the presentation. Also, bring chargers for cell phones and laptop computers, and consider bringing spare batteries and projector bulbs, too.

- *Arrive early.* If the first meeting of the day starts late, this problem probably will roll forward into all of the meetings that day. The solution is to do whatever it takes to be early for the first meeting of the day.

- *Buffer time.* Always leave enough time between meetings for travel between locations and on-site setup. If this means that there will be time for fewer meetings during the day, then fine—schedule a longer road trip.

- *Building passes.* Getting through building security can delay the presentation team substantially. This is a particular problem in New York City, where security is especially tight. To reduce the security wait, send one team member ahead with the driver to obtain building passes for the next meeting.

- *Shipping.* The presentation package for each attendee may add up to a considerable amount of shipping weight. If so, preship the presentation materials in advance to each meeting location. If this is not workable, store the materials in the group's carry-on luggage, which minimizes the risk of it being lost in transit.

- *Audio-visual equipment.* Bring presentation equipment only if it is not available at the various meeting locations. Bringing a laptop computer and projector is not only a hassle, but there is a risk of breakage. Thus, always call in advance to verify what equipment will be on hand.

- *On-site branding.* Assign a subordinate the task of branding the company name at each location. Doing this can involve using the company logo on attendee name tags, presentation materials, and signage. This person does not have to go on the trip but must have overall control over the design of the materials brought on the trip.

- *Trip logistics.* The speakers need plenty of time to decompress between meetings, so have someone else handle all luggage for the group as well as travel connections. If possible, hire a van and driver during the group's entire stay in each city. A van is particularly useful if the management team might need to assemble between meetings in order to refine the presentation. A van equipped with a small conference table, adequate lighting, and presentation monitors is ideal for this purpose. Further, obtain the name and cell-phone numbers of chauffeurs at least one day in advance, in order to coordinate pickups properly.
- *Phone list.* A road show may involve dozens of meetings as well as multiple hotels, drivers, and other people involved in logistics. Put the contact information for everyone on a single document, and keep spare copies of this document somewhere easily accessible. The chances are good that the team will have an emergency at some point during the road show and will need this information.
- *Specialists.* If a road show involves an unusually large number of meetings, participants, and/or cities, consider hiring a road show specialist. This person reviews the itinerary for trouble spots and advises on how to optimize the schedule.
- *Backup planning.* Anything can go wrong during a road show, and frequently does. To guard against these problems, have a backup team that can assist with such issues as sending additional equipment on a rush basis and rerouting information in the event of traffic delays.

During a road show presentation, the CEO is the primary speaker and is responsible for telling attendees about the investment opportunity presented by the company. The CFO presents the financial aspects of the business and may repeat any guidance that has already been issued elsewhere. The IRO is responsible for the logistics of each road show and may bracket presentations with introductory and concluding comments.

This group should be absolutely consistent in making the same presentation in every meeting. This creates a rhythm to the meetings, which allows the team to operate almost on autopilot, except for those times when an attendee interjects a question. By doing so, the group will experience much less stress through the day and can avoid looking tired or discouraged toward the end of the day.

The CEO, CFO, and IRO may not feel comfortable presenting to a large number of people. If so, a PowerPoint presentation projected onto a screen shifts the audience's attention away from the speakers and to the screen, which may alleviate some speaker nervousness. However, if a presenter is comfortable with the audience and especially if he can speak off the cuff from limited notes, by all means eliminate the projection equipment and let the audience focus directly on the speaker. A team of skilled speakers is a powerful tool, and the group should work hard to polish its speaking skills to reach this level of expertise.

Irrespective of the speaking ability of the presentation team, it still should use a PowerPoint presentation, if only to control the sequence of topics covered. It is critical to reduce the *number* of these slides to the bare minimum while also keeping the *contents* of each slide as minimal as possible. Presenters may be so eager to tell the company's story that they bury attendees with too much information.

The contents of every presentation are different, depending on what type of message a company wants to impart. However, the presentation should contain this information:

- *Overview.* States what the company does in as few bullet points on one slide as possible.
- *Investment highlights.* Investors will pay attention to this slide, so spend time constructing four or five points, and be prepared to discuss them at length, if asked.
- *Market size.* State the size of the market, any subcategories, and the source of the information.
- *Customers.* Either name the general type and characteristics of the target customer or (better yet) list the names of better-known customers and their proportion of total company sales.
- *Growth strategy.* State how the company plans to grow, such as through an industry roll-up, new store roll-outs, new geographic markets, and so forth.
- *Competitive positioning.* Show the company's positioning in relation to its main competitors. This may be best presented in chart form. In addition, and on a separate slide, state the company's competitive advantages, such as its technology, intellectual property, regulatory approvals, or low-cost structure.
- *Financial statements.* Show financial results for at least the past three years, with projections for the next year. Attendees will be particularly interested in the trend of gross margins and net profits, so provide this information. The balance can be in summary format, and for just the most recent year-end.
- *Management team.* Note the name, title, responsibility, and experience of each member of the senior management team.
- *Summary.* In four or five bullet points, state the key points that a prospective investor should remember.

A CEO who can restrict the number of PowerPoint slides to 10 is to be lauded; 30 slides should be considered the upper end of the acceptable range. When there are too many slides and the presentation is limited to an hour or less, the management team becomes driven by the need to ram through the presentation as fast as possible, which leaves little time for a Q&A session.

If a road show presentation is to brokers, the presentation is simplified and employs a considerable amount of repetition. Brokers want to know how they can make money from the stock, so present the investment message at the beginning of the presentation, reinforce it several times as the talk progresses, and finish with a reiteration of the same message.

Of all the various types of investor relations events, the road show presents the greatest risk of overcommunication. The problem is that the management team may fall into the habit of visiting the same people repetitively, which is roughly comparable to preaching to the choir. Realistically, there is no justification for meeting with the same people even once a year; they already know the company's story and do not need to hear it again. If you persist in meeting with the same people too frequently, everyone who has heard about the company will have bought its stock already, resulting in no new demand. Instead, shift the road show to new cities on a regular basis, or at least use different sell-side contacts to arrange meetings with new people who have not heard of the company before.

A final note about road shows: How effective are they? The CEO, CFO, and IRO may be spending a considerable proportion of their time on the road, meeting with the investment community. This is a considerable investment in executive time, so there must be a discernible trade-off between the labor and out-of-pocket cost of road shows and the number of shares placed that are directly related to them. A reasonable goal over the long term is to stay below a road show cost of $0.05 per share placed. If the cost increases beyond this benchmark, work on targeting a smaller group of road show attendees whose investment interests are more closely aligned with those of the company.

Concept of Guidance

Most larger public companies provide some form of earnings guidance to the investment community. It is an important part of how the sell side and buy side determine valuation, and so is a key issue. But before getting into a discussion about the form and frequency of guidance to provide, we first must consider whether a company should provide any guidance at all.

Without guidance, analysts and investors have no idea how a company will perform in the future; therefore, they must make their own estimates of the situation. These estimates may vary considerably from person to person. The result is a heightened amount of stock price volatility, since everyone is assuming a different future earnings level.

Stock price volatility is not a desirable state of affairs for a company. It tends to attract short sellers, who make money from rapid changes in the stock price. It also drives away institutional investors, who prefer stocks whose prices move within a narrow range. Since institutional investors are driven away, there is less demand for a company's stock, and its price will decline. This results in a higher cost of capital for the company, since it must issue more shares in order to obtain a specific amount of cash. Thus, there are serious consequences to not providing guidance.

Also, a company may have no analyst following, which is the norm for micro-cap entities. If so, there is no one who can independently provide earnings predictions to the buy side, which leaves the marketplace completely devoid of information if a company refuses to provide guidance. This situation is most likely to result in excessive stock price volatility. Thus, in order to avoid volatility in the absence of analysts, it is even more necessary to provide guidance.

Although these issues are compelling, there is a situation in which it still makes sense to avoid issuing guidance: That is when management does not have a clear picture of future results. This situation is most likely to occur when a company is generating a large part of its operating results from a series of acquisitions, is experiencing large swings in its material costs, or is entering new markets. In all of these cases, operating results may vary so significantly that it would be doing the investment marketplace a disservice to issue guidance that could be proved erroneous very quickly. Under this scenario, it is better to state the situation and promise that guidance will be provided at some point in the future, once results become more predictable.

An alternative to a promise to provide guidance in the future is to provide it now, but within a very wide guidance range. This scenario is particularly appropriate for a company that is already providing guidance and does not want to send an excessively negative message to the market by terminating guidance entirely due to various uncertainties. Instead, explain the situation, prepare scenarios, and describe the assumptions used in the most recent guidance. This method gives analysts some information to work with, as opposed to a sudden absence of guidance.

It is also possible that a company's forecasting systems are so inadequate that it routinely exceeds or falls short of its guidance by significant amounts. In this case, the investment community will assume that the management team is incapable of forecasting its own business. In such cases, it may be better to forgo guidance until the company can install better forecasting systems that result in predictable guidance.

A downside of guidance is that a management team may have a propensity to focus too much attention on making the numbers that it has projected. Such behavior is not useful, since it diverts management's attention from the detailed operational conduct of the business. It also increases the risk of financial statement reporting fraud when operational results have fallen short; management may be tempted to adjust the numbers to attain the forecast. This is a particular concern when the financial goals stated in guidance are so aggressive that they are difficult to attain.

In summary, guidance is useful for most companies to smooth stock price volatility. However, it can be misleading and counterproductive when a company is uncertain of its own results or if it persists in issuing aggressive guidance.

Form of Guidance Issued

If your decision is to provide guidance, the next issue to resolve is the form of guidance to be issued. This section notes a variety of alternatives.

The most common type of guidance issued is for either a range or specific point, and it usually includes all key factors that would be of interest to an investor, such as revenue, margins, net income, and earnings per share. The range of expected results issued should be relatively narrow for the near future and should expand as projections go farther into the future, thereby allowing for greater uncertainty.

Example

We are raising our guidance for the fiscal year ended December 31, 2012. We now expect 2012 sales to range between $120 and $135 million, resulting in net profits of between $14 and $17 million, and diluted earnings per share ranging from $1.43 to $1.49. For the year 2013, we are expecting sales to range between $130 and $160 million, resulting in net profits of between $16 and $21 million and diluted earnings per share ranging from $1.48 to $1.60.

An alternative is to provide guidance using percentages. By doing so, analysts can construct their own models of a company's performance and plug in the latest guidance to reach their own conclusions about the company's likely performance. This type of guidance should include some sensitivity analysis, where the guidance states how a given percentage change in revenue will impact the gross margin and net profit. Some companies even itemize the business assumptions underlying their models.

Example

Our projected revenue growth is 7% to 10%. Based on our estimated increase of 5% in cost of goods sold, we are projecting gross margins in the range of 50% to 55%, with the low end of the range based on 7% revenue growth and the high end based on 10% revenue growth.

If a company is not willing to provide this level of guidance, a lesser alternative is to discuss anywhere from a one- to five-year projection, the long-term strategy, or the business cycle within which the company operates and how that cycle impacts its results. Analysts, however, deem these alternative choices insufficient; such broad categorizations of results are of little use to them when they are trying to construct an earnings forecast.

Examples

- We expect continued revenue growth of 60% to 80% for the next three years, as we continue a rapid expansion through our franchising model. Due to expansion costs, we expect net profits and earnings per share to grow during that period at a reduced rate of 15% to 25%.

- Our long-term strategy is to expand our successful franchising model throughout the North American region, with a target store opening rate of 150 per year.

- The airline industry's fortunes are closely tied to the price of oil, since we must pass through the majority of oil price increases to our customers. During the past year, the price of oil increased 20%, resulting in an 18% increase in ticket prices and a decline in our passenger volume of 11%.

An alternative to the various types of formal guidance just shown is to release a broad range of nonmaterial information to analysts. They can use this information to create their own models of a company's operations and likely operating results. This is called the *mosaic* approach, because analysts must assemble disparate information into a composite picture of the company. This is a useful approach for a company, because it can avoid any specific guidance, but it is painful for analysts, who must work much harder to create their earnings models.

Finally, once the decision is made to release a certain type of information to the marketplace, be prepared to continue issuing it on a long-term basis. Otherwise, the market may react quite negatively when information is discontinued, on the suspicion that the company is hiding information that no longer casts it in the best light. For example, a medical products company changed its guidance from a discussion of growth rates that included acquisitions to a discussion that focused solely on organic growth. When the altered (and substantially reduced) guidance was released, the company's stock price declined by 25% in a single day and did not recover. Thus, if you feel that information formerly included in guidance is now irrelevant, be sure to explain the reason for the discontinuance in detail, in order to avoid a significant price decline.

In short, guidance can range from a narrow range of prospective results to broad discussions of company and industry prospects. The most common form of guidance by far is the inclusion of ranges of specific dollar values, as shown in the first example in this section.

Frequency and Timing of Guidance

If you give guidance, update it in a timely manner. Doing this usually involves the consistent use of a forecast updating schedule, with quarterly guidance being the most common, usually right after the quarterly Form 10-Q is released. Analysts depend on quarterly guidance so they can revise their own estimates of company performance. If a company elects to forgo quarterly guidance in favor of some longer period, some analysts may find it too difficult to provide estimates regarding company performance and may drop their coverage. If this happens, stock price volatility may increase, due to uncertainty about how the company is performing. Thus, frequent guidance updates are needed to avoid excessive stock price movement.

Those companies that provide only annual guidance claim that the practice tends to provide longer-term valuations that are less susceptible to short-term variation. If a company intends to follow this path, it should at least consider providing updates whenever it expects a material change in results.

There are situations in which you would be justified in issuing guidance even more frequently than on a quarterly basis. For example, if a company has an analyst following and a large proportion of those analysts are projecting excessively high or low short-term results, it may be necessary to give unscheduled and immediate guidance. By doing so, analysts can alter their projections at once, thereby keeping the company's stock price from tracking the incorrect estimates.

Another scenario is when a company is in hypergrowth mode, which can happen when it is conducting an industry roll-up through a string of acquisitions or when it first issues a fabulously successful new product. In either case, investors may bid up its stock price to extremely high levels. When the price/earnings ratio becomes too high, the stock price is likely to fluctuate continually, as the market reacts to any news it can scrounge up about the company. In this case, the market requires a constant flow of information. The company can provide this information by issuing guidance more frequently than normal.

Some companies routinely issue small amounts of additional information in advance of their regular quarterly guidance, in what is called a *preannouncement*. This extra level of communication states the date of the regular earnings call and points out that guidance will be updated during that call. Stating in advance that new guidance will be issued shortly tends to forestall analysts from making their own estimates prior to the call.

The preannouncement is not just a notification of an earnings call; it also can be used to disseminate new, material information to the market. Using the preannouncement to issue new information results in shorter periods during which a company runs the risk of inadvertently issuing material, nonpublic information. Thus, many companies use a quarterly preannouncement, timed to be well before the earnings call, to create a constant flow of new information to the market.

If a preannouncement is used to issue material information that the market might react strongly to, it is helpful to set up a special conference call immediately after the preannouncement to explain the new information. This is especially important if the preannouncement reveals a material decline in the operating results that were projected in the last guidance.

Finally, if a company does not revise its guidance, the investment community will assume that the information contained in the last guidance is still current. If management becomes aware that changed circumstances have made the current guidance misleading, it should consider issuing new guidance in advance of the normal guidance release schedule. This scenario normally applies only if the level of change is substantial. Also, when formulating the new replacement guidance to be issued, it is better to wait somewhat longer to verify the latest operational results, in order to have a higher confidence level in the new guidance—it would not do to issue replacement guidance that itself must be replaced in short order. You must exercise judgment in determining whether to issue unscheduled guidance and how long to wait before doing so.

Aggressiveness of Guidance

Under no circumstances should a company issue aggressive guidance, where the targeted results will be extremely difficult for a company to achieve. Doing this may result in a short-term ramp-up in the stock price but will inevitably yield a price crash when the company eventually cannot achieve its own guidance. If you persist in issuing aggressive guidance that the company cannot sustain, the result will be persistent price gyrations, unusually high price volatility, and the arrival of short sellers.

A much better alternative is always to provide guidance that is solidly within the management team's comfort zone. If everyone in a company knows they can attain the guidance levels, they will be less fixated on reaching the target, which reduces the risk of fraudulent reporting. Also, analysts find companies that provide reasonably conservative guidance to be more trustworthy and reliable, and they will be more likely to provide coverage.

However, this does not mean that the company always should issue excessively low guidance. If a company routinely exceeds its guidance by a substantial margin, analysts will come to expect it in the future. Thus, if it were just to meet its own guidance, analysts might treat this as poor performance and issue negative projections. Accordingly, the best level of guidance is to issue *slightly* conservative numbers.

Finally, there will inevitably be cases when you find it necessary to revise guidance downward. When this happens, assume that there is an underlying problem causing the downgrade and that this problem will take a considerable amount of time to resolve. By incorporating the long-term resolution assumption into the revised guidance, a company will give itself an extraconservative cushion of downgraded performance. This will yield extra time for the company to fix its problem and enable it to avoid another guidance shortfall in the near term.

In short, it is far better to adopt a slightly conservative stance when issuing guidance, so that a company can comfortably achieve its numbers without giving the appearance of drastically underreporting guidance.

How Short Sellers Operate

A short seller is someone who expects a company's stock price to decline in the near term and who acts on this presentiment by selling borrowed stock with the expectation of earning a profit by buying back the stock at a lower price on a later date.

The basic short-selling process involves a three-step trading strategy:

1. The short seller borrows the targeted company's stock, usually from a broker.
2. The short seller sells the shares on the open market.
3. The short seller waits for the stock price to (it hopes) decline and then repurchases the shares (known as short covering) and returns them to the lender.

A variation is *naked short selling*, where the short seller sells shares without first borrowing them. This method may lead to an excessive amount of downward pricing pressure on a stock. Naked short selling is generally illegal, with a few exceptions. The Securities and Exchange Commission (SEC) regulations governing naked short selling are not closely enforced, so it likely still occurs. Naked short selling occurs most often when there is some difficulty in borrowing shares.

Short covering can increase the stock price, especially when many short sellers are repurchasing stock at the same time. Assuming that the share repurchase price was less than the initial sale price, the short seller pockets the difference as a profit.

Short selling is an extremely risky activity, since there is a potential for unlimited losses if the stock price goes up instead of down. For example, if an investor sells stock when the price is $10, the maximum possible profit on a short sell is $10 (and only if the price craters to $0); however, if the stock price jumps to $50, the investor must buy back at the higher price, resulting in a loss of $40. Given this high level of risk, investors rarely sell short unless they feel strongly that a stock's price has topped out.

Because of the high level of risk, short sellers like to slam a company's prospects as publicly as possible, thereby influencing other investors to sell their shares, which in turn lowers the stock price. A favorite forum for short sellers is the Internet investment boards, where they can post anonymous messages that anyone can read. They also may post messages using multiple aliases, so innocent visitors may think that a large number of investors are all selling their holdings in a targeted stock. When a major short-selling attack is going on, short sellers can effectively take over message boards with an extremely high volume of message traffic. Major investment message boards are located on the Motley Fool, Yahoo!, and Raging Bull Web sites.

If an investor finds that a negative publicity campaign does not work, and the stock rises instead, the customary reaction is to reduce losses by quickly buying shares to cover the short positions. If there are many short sellers, this sudden buying frenzy will drive up the stock price even more, forcing any remaining holdout short sellers to buy even more shares to cover their positions. This *short squeeze* phenomenon is especially common with stocks whose prices are highly volatile.

One special scenario is the monitoring of the restricted stock holdings of company investors by short sellers. Restricted stock can be sold after one year under SEC Rule 144. Since the timing of restriction cancellations and the amounts of restricted stock holdings are public knowledge, it is an easy matter for short sellers to anticipate the sale of large stock holdings, which should reduce the price of the stock when it is dumped on the market. The classic short-selling strategy in this situation is to sell shares at a higher price just prior to the restricted stock becoming available for sale and then to buy offsetting shares after the now-unrestricted stock has been sold, when prices are presumably lower.

How to Handle Short Sellers

A common reaction by a CEO who sees short-selling activity is to attempt to force sellers out of their short positions by publicly issuing guidance of better-than-expected results. This type of publicity may increase the stock price in the very short term, creating a short squeeze that drives away short sellers. However, the more aggressive guidance also makes it more difficult to meet investor expectations, which thereby attracts even more short sellers as the CEO gradually paints the company into a performance corner. Eventually it becomes impossible to meet the company's own increased guidance, so the reported earnings are bound to fall below the enhanced expectations of investors. The result is a stock price decline, allowing short sellers to reap profits that were very nearly guaranteed by the CEO's own actions to drive them away.

There are several effective methods for dealing with short sellers. First and most important, do not issue aggressive earnings guidance . . . ever. Aggressive guidance raises investor expectations to heights that are difficult to sustain, resulting in increased stock price volatility and the arrival of short sellers. Instead, issue only conservative guidance that the company can meet comfortably on a long-term basis. This approach flattens stock price volatility, which keeps short sellers away.

It also pays to be proactive in dealing with short sellers by monitoring the larger message boards for sudden increases in activity concerning the company. These activity surges usually coincide with actual short sales, which are reported by the stock exchanges and which are conveniently posted on www.shortsqueeze.com. Thus, an efficient approach to monitoring short sales is to review the shortsqueeze.com site each day to track short-selling volume and start reviewing the message boards as soon as there is a jump in reported that volume. Another source of information is well-connected investors, who may hear rumors before anyone in the company. If you maintain good relations with these investors, they will be more likely to forward any information they hear. In either case, the company may elect to counteract the rumors by issuing statements that address the allegations.

At the first sign of trouble at a company, short sellers tend to circle like sharks, assuming that more bad news will follow. To avoid this problem, it is better to fully disclose every aspect of a bad news item at once rather than dribbling it out over a long period of time. By doing so, the stock probably will suffer a single, sharp price drop to a new level that is not attractive to short sellers. Otherwise, short sellers will feast on each successive negative piece of news to reach the market, which allows them to reap profits from continuing declines in the stock price.

Short sellers may pose questions during conference calls, in partly to probe for information that strengthens their case and in part to lead management into an argument that will cast the company in a negative light. If such questions arise, state the counterargument in a simple and straightforward manner, and move on to the next question as quickly as possible. It rarely makes sense to give a short seller credence by making a lengthy response that seems to give weight to the question. Under no circumstances should the Q&A exchange grow heated.

Although it is unusual, it may be possible to open a line of communication with short sellers to hear why they are selling short. This is not usually necessary, since short sellers are likely to sprinkle their opinions all over the investment message boards, where you can access them easily. When this information is available, consider including a statement in the next press release or conference call that offers a counterargument. This statement should be based heavily on facts rather than opinions. Under no circumstances should the statement mention any short-selling activity. Instead, take the position that the company is merely presenting additional information to the marketplace, which it can interpret in any way it chooses.

Finally, create a list of preset responses to a variety of worst-case scenarios that can be rolled out quickly through press releases. For example, there may be boilerplate responses to a product recall, patent litigation, loss of a customer, or the departure of a key executive. By having canned responses available, the management team will spend far less time mulling over the appropriate response and will appear to respond quickly and well to a crisis. This obviously competent response to crises tends to result in less stock volatility and so keeps short sellers at bay.

Measuring Short-Seller Activity

It is not especially difficult to monitor short-selling activity on an ongoing basis. As noted earlier, go to the shortsqueeze.com site to determine the number of shares currently being sold short. Divide this number by the average daily volume of shares traded to arrive at the *short interest ratio*. This ratio shows the proportion of short selling to total trading activity. When tracked on a trend line, any spikes will reveal sudden increases in short-selling activity. The ratio also can be used to determine the number of days of average trading that it will take before short sellers can cover their positions. For example, if the ratio is 3.5, it will take short sellers $3\frac{1}{2}$ days to cover their positions. As this ratio rises, it becomes increasingly difficult for short sellers to cover their positions in a timely manner through stock purchases; eventually this situation will result in their scaling back from aggressive short positions in order to contain their risk.

Summary

Of all the public company activities that the CEO is most likely to be involved in on a continuing basis, the investor conference call is the most common. You are the centerpiece of the conference call and so should practice enough to be comfortable, not only in reading a prepared statement but also in answering investor questions during the call. The road show is somewhat less frequent, but periodically you will be called on to make presentations to the investment community. This calls for good presentation skills, so be willing to undergo multiple practice sessions, and consider hiring a coach to polish your presentation skills.

You also must make the decision to issue guidance or not, and how frequently to do so. The IRO can handle the actual issuance of guidance, so this is more of a one-time decision than ongoing participation. In general, larger public firms issue guidance; there are an increasing number of reasons for smaller firms not to do so. Similarly, you need to decide how to handle short sellers. Once you make this decision, the IRO will carry through with its execution.

Thus, conference calls and road shows require your active participation while guidance and short selling only involve a management decision with periodic follow-up to decide whether the company's course is the correct one.

CHAPTER 17

Taking a Company Private

M any companies find that the cost and liability of operating a publicly owned business is not worth the hassle and elect to remove themselves from public trading. Doing this involves the filing of a schedule with the Securities and Exchange Commission (SEC) and management of the number of shareholders, topics that are described in this chapter.

Going-Private Transaction

If a publicly held company wishes to go private, it must disclose information that is itemized under the SEC's Rule 13e-3, which is located in the Securities Exchange Act of 1934. This rule applies to situations where a company plans to buy back its securities, as described in the next section.

The information required under these circumstances must be filed on Schedule 13E-3, to which amendments must be added if there are material changes to the information presented on it. The primary information listed on the schedule includes complete company financial statements and various financial information on a per-share basis. The company also must include information regarding the identity of the persons filing the schedule, terms of the arrangement, future plans, the reason for going private, and the source and financing terms for the funding required to complete the transaction. A key goal of this filing (from the perspective of the SEC) is to force the company to describe the impact of the going private event on unaffiliated security holders.

Rule 13e-3

The SEC's Rule 13e-3 applies to any transaction where equity securities are being purchased by the issuing company or when a tender offer for those securities is being made by the issuing company or an affiliate. Such a transaction must result in having fewer than 300 people hold the equity security or the removal of that class of equity securities from being listed on a national exchange.

When an equity security is withdrawn from circulation by the issuing company, the rule also states that information about the withdrawal shall not be misleading or attempt to defraud a security holder.

The rule requires the issuing company to file Schedule 13E-3 prior to withdrawing a class of securities and to file amendments to it to reflect any material changes in the information itemized in the original filing. These amendments will be concluded with an amendment reporting the final results of the withdrawal transaction.

The rule further requires that the issuing company disclose to security holders this information:

- A summary term sheet.
- The purposes, alternatives, reasons for, and effects of the transaction.
- Fairness of the transaction to the security holder.
- Reports, opinions, appraisals, and negotiations related to the transaction.
- Information concerning the rights of the security holders to conduct appraisals.
- All other information listed in Schedule 13E-3, except for exhibits. A "fair and adequate summary" can be substituted for this information.

If there are changes to the information offered to security holders, the rule requires that these changes be reported to them promptly. In any event, the original set of disclosures must be issued to the security holders no later than ten business days prior to any withdrawal transaction. If securities are held in trust for securities holders by a broker/dealer, the issuer must forward these information materials to the broker/dealer, with instructions to forward it to the security holders.

These reporting requirements are not required if the issuer offers security holders another equity security in exchange for the one being retired if the replacement security has essentially the same rights as the old security, including voting, dividends, redemption, and liquidation rights, or if common stock is offered. The reporting also is not required if the security withdrawal is already allowed under the specific provisions itemized in the instrument creating or governing that class of securities.

300-Shareholder Limit

In order to go private, a company must have fewer than 300 shareholders *of record*. This means that the company's stock transfer agent must have 299 or fewer shareholders listed in its database. However, some of those shareholders of record can be the brokers with whom shareholders have placed their stock certificates. Thus, a single broker in the stock transfer agent's database may represent the shares of a multitude of shareholders.

Because brokers can represent shareholders in the calculation of shareholders of record, a company actually can have far more than 300 shareholders and still qualify to go private. Thus, you would think that the most common strategy for going private is simply to encourage shareholders to shift their stock certificates to brokers. However, the possibility of a *broker kick-out* makes this a less tenable alternative. In a kick-out, a broker returns stock certificates to their owners once a company goes private. Since a kick-out is at the option of the broker, you can never tell when the number of shareholders of record suddenly may jump above the 300-shareholder limit. Consequently, because of the danger of a broker kick-out, it is usually better to reduce the number of shareholders by other means.

Form 15

The going-private transaction is much easier if a company already has fewer than 300 shareholders. In this case, you simply can file the one-page Form 15, declaring that the company no longer plans to fulfill any ongoing reporting requirements to the SEC. If the company has used the Schedule 13E-3 previously to reduce its shareholder base to a level below 300, it also files the Form 15.

Thus, the going-private transaction is essentially a two-step process. If a company needs to reduce its shareholder base to a level below 300, it begins with a Schedule 13E-3 and then files a Form 15 once it has attained the sub-300 goal. If the company is already below 300 shareholders, it simply files the Form 15.

Summary

Filling out the 13E-3 schedule is a time-consuming process. The Internal Revenue Service estimates that it takes 150 hours to do so, so plan to use a project team to work through this lengthy document. Also, be sure to have legal counsel review the schedule, and also subject it to accuracy reviews, so that security holders cannot later claim there are any inaccuracies in the schedule that give them a reason to sue for damages of any kind. If completed properly, the schedule is the foundation document for a successful withdrawal of securities from public ownership so that a company can go private.

If your company already has fewer than 300 shareholders of record, going private is incredibly easy: Simply file the one-page Form 15 with the SEC, and you are done.

New CEO Checklist

A person who has been newly hired into the chief executive officer (CEO) position may feel overwhelmed by the vast number of tasks to be completed and may wonder where to begin. The list here gives some guidance about the priority of tasks.

The first few priorities are heavily stacked in favor of spotting short-term crises, such as cash flow, tax, or legal problems. If you cannot fix these items, there is no reason to waste time on longer-term value creation activities, since the company will not be in existence much longer. Immediate priorities are listed next.

Immediate Priorities

Priority	Action	Description
1	Forecast cash	Any other action is useless if the company runs out of money, so review the cash forecast with the chief financial officer (CFO). If cash flow is questionable, set up a schedule of weekly reviews.
2	Review tax liabilities	If the company owes money to any government authority, there can be a serious risk of shutdown by the government. Review these liabilities with the CFO or any tax consultant that the company uses.
3	Review lawsuits	If there is an existing lawsuit or a possible one of which the company has been notified, you need to determine the potential size and probability of any settlements. Review any lawsuits with the company's legal counsel.
4	Review regulatory issues	Government regulators can shut down a company, so review with the company's legal counsel any notices received from regulatory agencies.
5	Review debt agreements	If a debt agreement requires repayment in the near future, you need to know about it and about the CFO's plans for refinancing such debt. Also be aware of any past or impending covenant defaults.
6	Review audit opinion	If the company's auditors believe there is a risk of corporate failure, they may include a "going concern" statement in their opinion of the

(continued)

(*continued*)

> company's financial statements, which can trigger
> adverse debt covenants. To see if this is the case,
> interview the audit partner regarding the status of
> any audits currently in progress.

If any of the preceding steps indicate that the company is in serious danger, likely you will likely have to avoid many of the short-term issues discussed next and focus instead on crisis remediation. If, however, the company appears to be on a stable footing, proceed to the next block of steps, which center on measuring the company's current performance and estimating its near-term results. Short-term issues are described next.

Measure the Business: Short-Term Issues

Priority	Action	Description
1	Establish basic metrics	Have the CFO create a set of performance measurements targeted at basic items, such as days of inventory on hand, days of accounts receivable outstanding, and gross margins. Track this information by month for the past year to establish a trend line. The objective is to see if the company has issues in its basic operations.
2	Track metrics required in loan covenants	If there are metrics included in the company's loan covenants, receive these metrics on a regular basis, along with a comparison to the minimum covenant thresholds and an estimation of whether the company may not meet the covenants.
3	Create a sales forecast	The sales manager should send you a weekly update of anticipated sales for at least the current month as well as changes in the backlog, so that you are aware of any projected variations in the near term.
4	Create a flash report	Have the CFO incorporate the total periodic sales listed on the sales report in a flash report that itemizes the latest expectation for total financial results for the reporting period. As with the sales report, you should receive this every week. This gives you a solid picture of near-term results.

You should spend no more than one or two days on the preceding items. You are delegating essentially everything to other people—the CFO, sales manager, and corporate counsel in particular—so no single task should require much of your time. The objective thus far has been to obtain a quick understanding of the immediate, short-term risks. Once you have reviewed these items, it is time for a much more in-depth review of the company. The next items explain how to get to know the company.

Get to Know the Company

Priority	Action	Description
1	Meet with administrative assistant	You should have an administrative assistant, and you should meet with this person regularly in order to delegate as many routine tasks as possible. Some CEOs would place this task first of *all* priorities, since a competent administrative assistant who can organize the CEO's time and filter out unwanted distractions is nearly priceless.
2	Meet with managers	Meet one-on-one with all direct reports and possibly with the managers who report to your direct reports. The immediate goal is to begin building relationships with this group.
3	Meet with staff	If there are not too many employees, create a plan to gradually cycle through the company, meeting informally with all employees. If the company is large, have your administrative assistant create a schedule where you meet with key employees, or representatives of employee groups, on a regular basis.
4	Meet with subject matter experts	Find out who the key people are whose knowledge is at the core of the company's business. Meet with them, and encourage an ongoing dialog. They likely will know more about the company's prospects than you do.
5	Meet with key customers	Meet with a selection of the company's most important customers, and have your administrative assistant set up an ongoing series of these meetings. If the company has problems, customers are the first to know, so these contacts are crucial.
6	Meet with key suppliers	If the company is dependent on good relations with a few key suppliers, establish relations with them early on, and encourage an ongoing dialog.

The next step is to create a corporate strategy. You should not manage any corporate strategy planning sessions; hire a consultant to organize and run the meetings. You need to be listening to the opinions of others and putting forward your own thoughts during these meetings. The corporate strategy likely will evolve over a period of time, as the team considers a variety of external and internal factors that eventually lead it to settle on a particular competitive posture. The way to develop a strategy is described next.

Develop a Strategy

Priority	Action	Description
1	Learn the business	You cannot develop a strategy until you learn how the business operates. Accordingly, create a plan to meet with anyone who knows more than you do about all aspects of the business and question them for as long as it takes to gain a solid understanding of how the company works.
2	Have planning sessions	Meet with the senior management team to determine the general type of strategy that the company should follow (i.e., product differentiation, low cost, or niche strategy) as well as the general characteristics of that strategy. Expect this process to consume multiple meetings over several weeks.
3	Match processes to strategy	Meet with both senior and middle management to determine which processes should be changed to support the company's strategy properly.
4	Examine bottlenecks	Every company has a bottleneck that prevents it from growing. Find out what is it, how it can impact the company's strategy, and what the options are for circumventing it.
5	Determine required resources	Work with the management team to decide what additional resources are required to implement the strategy and which resources will no longer be needed. Determine if the company has the financial wherewithal to obtain the required resources.
6	Examine risks	Review the key risks to which the company has been subjected in the past and any possible new ones arising from the strategy, and incorporate risk mitigation into the overall corporate strategy.
7	Add iterations as necessary	Conduct as many iterations of the planning process as necessary, until the management team has accounted for any issues with processes, bottlenecks, resources, and risks.

Once your management team has formulated a strategy, you need to tie it to a cohesive system of budgets, compensation plans, and controls, and spread the message throughout the company. The steps to create a budget and related systems are presented next.

Create a Budget and Related Systems

Priority	Action	Description
1	Oversee creation of the budget model	The CFO is responsible for creating the budget; you should ensure that the budgeting process is tied to achieving the corporate strategy and monitor its various iterations to see how the management team believes it can accomplish the strategy.
2	Review the capital budget	You should spend a significant amount of time reviewing proposed expenditures for fixed assets, because they may involve a large cash commitment and also may affect the company's production capacity.
3	Match the compensation system to the budget	People behave in accordance with how they are paid, so work with the human resources manager to adjust the compensation system to match the type of behavior that will support the corporate strategy.
4	Review controls that support the budget	Controls are primarily the responsibility of the CFO, but you should review them to see if there are any glaring control issues that may interfere with or support the corporate strategy.
5	Announce the complete plan	Work with the management team to create a complete package of a summary-level strategy, detailed budget, compensation plans, and controls, and have them present it to their staffs. You are available in a supporting role for these meetings. You also should continue to present the message to the entire company many times on an ongoing basis to reinforce it.

Once the budget model is complete and the company is acting on it, you have a good opportunity to review how well your management team is operating in achieving the model. Prior to this point, it would have been difficult to determine the abilities of your managers, but now you can judge their performance against a concrete set of criteria. This review is critical, since you succeed through their efforts; managers must be capable of supporting the strategic plan effectively; if not, you should replace them with other managers who are more capable. Next we describe how to review the management team.

Review the Management Team

Priority	Action	Description
1	Create a review system	Meet with the human resources manager and develop a process for reviewing all managers on an ongoing basis.

(*continued*)

(continued)

2	Review managers	Meet with and review the performance of senior managers regularly, providing feedback and advice as necessary.
3	Identify prospective managers	Have the human resources manager develop a system for locating and grooming potential managers within the company. Meet regularly with the human resources manager to be updated on changes in this information, and develop an action plan for each person.
4	Replace managers as necessary	Have the human resources manager develop an internal and external recruiting process to bring in replacements for those managers who are not performing in accordance with your expectations.

With the company now heading down the path dictated by the strategic plan and supporting budget, and with the correct management team in place, you can spend more time reviewing risks. We have dealt with risks already at a cursory level in earlier steps, primarily based on the opinions of others. Now you need to invest more time to gain a thorough understanding of risk, as described next.

Review Risks

Priority	Action	Description
1	Conduct industry risk analysis	Have the risk manager conduct a review of the risks incurred by the industry as a whole and experienced by other companies in particular, and decide whether these risks pertain to the company.
2	Conduct historical risk analysis	Meet with the risk manager to review risks encountered by the company in the past, what they cost the company, and how the company dealt with them.
3	Review contracts	Have corporate counsel review all major contracts that have not expired and summarize any contractual risks that are outstanding.
4	Plan to mitigate risks	Work with the risk manager and corporate counsel to mitigate all identified risks. They should create a formal plan for risk mitigation, which you should discuss with the board of directors and senior management team.
5	Review insurance	Once the risk mitigation plan is in place, you will know which risks require additional mitigation through insurance coverage. Have the risk manager compile a summary of all insurance and recommend which coverage should be modified to match the company's risk profile. Alter the insurance coverage to match this plan.

Strategy and risk mitigation are certainly key responsibilities of every CEO, but one would be remiss not to pay close attention to costs. If a company loses control over its costs, it will not earn a profit, no matter how excellent its strategy may be. Cost review steps are presented next.

Review Costs

Priority	Action	Description
1	Create department metrics	Have a financial analyst develop operating metrics for all departments and determine where efficiencies are in most need of improvement.
2	Assign cost responsibilities	Ensure that every cost is assigned to someone within the company and that the CFO has installed a reporting system that informs these people of how their assigned costs are performing in comparison to expectations.
3	Schedule periodic cost reviews	Have regular meetings with the senior management team to explore all costs incurred in the most recent accounting period and create specific action plans to reduce costs.

This priority list should not lead you to believe that once an item is completed, it does not have to be addressed again. On the contrary, further problem areas likely will be revealed during the completion of each priority item that will require additional work to address. In addition, any system is likely to degrade over time, requiring repeated reviews to ensure that the system is operating properly. In short, you should cycle through this list repeatedly.

About the Author

Steven Bragg, CPA, has been the chief financial officer or controller of four companies as well as a consulting manager at Ernst & Young. He received a master's degree in finance from Bentley College, an MBA from Babson College, and a bachelor's degree in economics from the University of Maine. He has been the two-time president of the Colorado Mountain Club and is an avid alpine skier, mountain biker, and certified master diver. Mr. Bragg resides in Centennial, Colorado. He has written these books:

Accounting and Finance for Your Small Business
Accounting Best Practices
Accounting Control Best Practices
Accounting Policies and Procedures Manual
Advanced Accounting Systems
Bookkeeping Essentials
Billing and Collections Best Practices
Business Ratios and Formulas
Controller's Guide to Costing
Controller's Guide to Planning and Controlling Operations
Controller's Guide: Roles and Responsibilities for the New Controller
Controllership
Cost Accounting
Cost Reduction Analysis
Essentials of Payroll
Fast Close
Financial Analysis
GAAP Guide
GAAP Policies and Procedures Manual
GAAS Guide
IFRS Made Easy
Inventory Accounting
Inventory Best Practices
Investor Relations
Just-in-Time Accounting
Management Accounting Best Practices
Managing Explosive Corporate Growth

Mergers and Acquisitions
Outsourcing
Payroll Accounting
Payroll Best Practices
Revenue Recognition
Run the Rockies
Running a Public Company
Sales and Operations for Your Small Business
The Controller's Function
The New CFO Financial Leadership Manual
The Ultimate Accountants' Reference
The Vest Pocket Controller's Guide
The Vest Pocket GAAP Guide
The Vest Pocket IFRS Guide
Throughput Accounting
Treasury Management

Free Online Resources by Steven Bragg

Mr. Bragg maintains the www.accountingtools.com Web site, which contains the accounting best practices podcast, an accounting blog, and a comprehensive index of articles on all possible accounting subjects.

Index